Music and Levels of Narration in Film

Music and Levels of Narration in Film
Steps Across the Border

Guido Heldt

intellect Bristol, UK / Chicago, USA

First published in the UK in 2013 by
Intellect, The Mill, Parnall Road, Fishponds, Bristol, BS16 3JG, UK

First published in the USA in 2013 by
Intellect, The University of Chicago Press, 1427 E. 60th Street,
Chicago, IL 60637, USA

A catalogue record for this book is available from the
British Library.

Cover designer: Holly Rose
Copy-editor: Michael Eckhardt
Production manager: Jelena Stanovnik
Typesetting: Contentra Technologies

Print ISBN: 978-1-84150-625-8
ePDF ISBN: 978-1-78320-209-6
ePub ISBN: 978-1-78320-210-2

Printed and bound by Gomer Press, UK

Contents

Preface

A monograph may promise a solid summing-up of a topic, but this book finds itself in an uncertain place. It has grown in a time of vertiginous development in film musicology, and as satisfying as it has been to watch that development, it means that the shelf-life of whatever insights the book may offer is likely to be limited. But perhaps one should welcome that, not deplore it.

Time is an aspect of the uncertainty in yet another sense. In some ways, it is an old-fashioned book, harking back to discussions in narratology and film scholarship of the 1970s, 1980s and 1990s. It tries to put that scholarship to use to address questions that are still bothering film musicology, and I can only hope that its (tentative) conclusions will remain of interest for a little while.

Uncertainty also describes its academic place. Film musicology is by definition interdisciplinary, but that means that it is done not by film musicologists, but by musicologists who do film studies or by film scholars interested in music (or by scholars who have come to film from yet other disciplines). On one side that means that everyone has different things to contribute, on the other side everyone has gaps and disciplinary blind spots. My background is in musicology, but this book is not specifically aimed at a musicological audience; I hope that it is of interest for a wider range of scholars and students interested in film music. Musicological terminology has been used sparsely, though I hope not to the detriment of the book.

The book was helped along a lot by the University of Bristol and the Arts and Humanities Research Council, which allowed me to take time off teaching. Beyond that, I owe thanks to many people who have influenced this project in one way or another. Albrecht Riethmüller at the Free University Berlin provided an academic setting that re-kindled an interest in film music that had lain dormant during the years of my PhD (in a very different field). A bit later, that interest found a home in the *Kieler Gesellschaft für Filmmusikforschung* (Kiel Society for Film Music Research) and its journal and conferences, the most enjoyable an academic can hope to attend. I thank all of my colleagues and friends in the *Gesellschaft,* but especially Hans Jürgen Wulff, who once upon a time saw my first, stumbling steps into film musicology in my student days in Münster. Here in Britain, I want to thank my fellow film musicologists Annette Davison, Miguel Mera, Nicholas Rayland and Ben Winters for ideas and discussions (and across the Atlantic James Buhler for a late exchange about focalization). More than anyone else, I thank my students at the University of Bristol Department of Music: my PhD students Timothy Summers, Jonathan Godsall and Hans Anselmo Hess, the students on the MA in Composition for Film and TV, and my undergraduate students, on whom I have tried out ideas and who have contributed numerous observations, ideas and questions. They have been a crucial part of the nicest university department I know. Finally, my thanks go to the staff at Intellect (especially to my editor Jelena Stanovnik and my copy-editor Michael Eckhardt), who have supported this project with patience and professionalism.

Chapter I

Introduction: Film Music Narratology

i. Laughing with film theory

A book written and published in Bristol might do worse than to start with a scene from a film by Bristol's second-best claim to cinematic fame, animation studio Aardman.[1] The film is *Wallace & Gromit in 'The Curse of the Were-Rabbit'* (2005), and the scene shows the villagers gathered in the church, anxious because of mysterious goings-on in their vegetable gardens. The old parish priest is wheeled in and, accompanied by ominous orchestral chords, gives a fire-and-brimstone speech, surmising that the culprit is 'no man', but something more terrible, and that in their reckless quest for ever larger vegetables the villagers have brought a terrible curse upon themselves – a curse promptly underlined by a fortissimo organ repeating the chords. But then the village policeman barks at someone to be quiet, the image cuts away from the nave, and we see the organist in her corner, fingers still on the keys, and everyone in the cinema is laughing.

Why do we laugh? Because the organist is not supposed to play this music in this situation, and to pull the rug from under our expectation works like the punchline of a joke. The organist is supposed to be stuck in the storyworld of the film, while the organ chords are at first assumed to belong to a different order of filmic elements: to the machinery that presents the storyworld to us, selects, frames, structures, highlights, comments upon it, but is not part of it. We may just about accept that the village organist is familiar with the topoi of horror film music. But she takes her cue from the preceding orchestral underscore – plasticine life imitating art – and usurps the task of a different kind of filmic agency, crossing a conceptual borderline we usually accept without thinking about it, because it is part and parcel of our understanding of cinema.

When the music is shown to thunder from the organist's instrument, its ostensible source is a surprise. The question at the heart of that surprise – where the music comes from – is the basis of this study. Not, of course, in real-world terms: in one sense, the music comes from a musician in a recording studio; in an equally relevant sense, it comes from a loudspeaker in the cinema or on our television set. But that tends not to be in our mind when we are immersed in a film. For our experience of a film, the real-world circumstances of its production recede into the background, as do the circumstances of its projection (e.g. that sounds actually issue from locations in the cinema or living

---

1 The city's foremost claim to film fame is Archibald Alexander Leach, better known as Cary Grant and born in Horfield/Bristol in 1904.

room, not from their putative sources on the screen[2]). Instead, other frameworks for comprehension take over (though the question 'How did they do this?' may be close to the surface of our consciousness, the willing suspension of disbelief rarely more than a temporary arrangement). One such framework is narrative: how does storytelling work in the interplay between the world unfolded in a film and the ways the medium uses to unfold (or rather suggest) it?

In the church scene from *Wallace & Gromit in 'The Curse of the Were-Rabbit'*, that interplay can be approached from different angles. The transition or transgression of the borderline between storyworld and storytelling does not so much tell us what the music 'really' is (i.e. a storyworld event), but lands us in an uncertain space. The reveal of the origin of the organ chords in the film's plasticine world tells us that our initial understanding of them as part of the machinery of horror storytelling was wrong. But elderly village organists do not normally play horror chords to underscore the vicar's sermons, and the music much better fits its interpretation as clichéd horror scoring. To locate this kind of music inside the storyworld seems also wrong, or at least not quite right – we are stuck in an amusingly deceptive space where neither our general knowledge of the world (telling us what music to expect in a village church) nor our knowledge of films (telling us what music normally goes with which kinds of scenes) suffice to make complete sense of the scene. The psychological effect – surprise and uncertainty because of the double 'wrongness' of the music – is arguably more relevant to our experience of the film than the eventual anchoring of the music in the storyworld. We not only learn about the storyworld, but also how the film (mis)leads us to construct our idea of that world, including the sources of knowledge we need to make sense of the film: knowledge about the 'real world', but also knowledge about film – about the way images are framed and camera movements dispense information, and knowledge about musical idioms and how they are employed in films. Given most people's reaction to the scene, it is not hard to argue that the trick the film plays on us is as crucial for our enjoyment of it as our immersion in the story it tells.

But the matter does not end there. If we apply our knowledge of film genres with only slightly more sophistication, the fact that *Wallace & Gromit in 'The Curse of the Were-Rabbit'* is not a horror film but a horror spoof might have made us suspicious. Such reveals are a common feature of spoofs; famous examples occur in Woody Allen's *Bananas* (1971) or Mel Brooks' *Blazing Saddles* (1974) and *High Anxiety* (1977). This is so obviously the case that the scene in *Wallace & Gromit in 'The Curse of the Were-Rabbit'* takes on overtones of a meta-spoof, or at least of an affectionate homage to a spoof tradition, the nostalgic use of a cliché-as-cliché (see also R. Brown 1994: 67–68; Bordwell

---

2 Michel Chion points out that in cinema 'the sounds truly *take place*' only once they have reached the viewer's brain, where they are processed together with the images to which – a plausible connection between them provided – they attach themselves in what Chion calls 'spatial magnetization'. We mentally locate sounds at their putative source in the image (Chion 2009: 248–49).

and Thompson 2010: 291, and chiefly Biancorosso 2009[3]). In this intertextual respect, the film also positions itself historically and tells us which films to use as framework for understanding it.

The village church joke relies on the interaction of two different domains of narrative control, further differentiating the picture:

- The first is the control over what we see and hear (or, rather, how the film cues us to construct an agency that controls what we see and hear). First we hear the organ chords, but do not see a plausible source in the storyworld, nor have any clues that would suggest one. The music matches the preceding orchestral music and the semiotics of horror scoring so well that this seems the most likely explanation. Then we see the policeman admonish the organist, and finally see the organist herself at her instrument, which leads us to reconstrue that this is where the music came from all along, but that whatever agency controls the framing of images and the sequence of shots chose to *withhold* that information until the opportune moment – the moment for the punchline of the audio-visual joke. We extrapolate the information provided by the sequence of shots and the soundtrack into an idea of a fully-formed spatio-temporal world, and reconstrue shot sequence and soundtrack as a *restriction* of the information we might have had access to, had the narrating agency allowed us to see into the corner sooner than it did.

  This is the equivalent of narrative situations in real life: a friend telling us over a pint in the pub what happened to her that day, using the selection, restriction and ordering of information, but also rhetoric, gestures and facial expressions to make the story suspenseful, funny, harrowing, or whatever else she may want it to be. But we assume that the *facts* of the story are out there; telling them means to present them so as to achieve a certain effect. This aspect narrative concerns the means to present a story effectively, wherever that story comes from.

- The second domain is the control over the 'facts' of the fiction (or rather, what the film cues us to understand as the facts of the fiction): in this case, the decision to include in the storyworld an elderly village organist who underlines the vicar's mighty warning with a film-score cliché. At issue from this perspective is not *how* the film presents information it cues us to understand as part of its story, but *what* information it presents. At issue is the fictional nature of the story, the fact that it is made up, and more specifically, that sometimes stories show us that they are made up, and turn their fictionality into an aspect of their appeal (while other, equally fictional, stories allow us to understand them as if they had been found out there).

---

3 Giorgio Biancorosso (2009) has analyzed such moments (which he calls 'reversals') not just in comedies, but in other films as well, e.g. *The Rules of the Game/La Règle du jeu* (1939), *Fanny and Alexander/Fanny och Alexander* (1982), *Slow Motion/Sauve qui peu (La vie)* (1980) or *Eyes Wide Shut* (1999). Examples of such diegetic 'reveals' are discussed in ch. II.iv.e, and specifically in *Eyes Wide Shut* in ch. II.ii.

With this distinction between story*telling* and story*making*, we are bang in the middle of the debate over narratological concepts such as 'narrator' and 'implied author' in film, a debate that has been going on for decades (though rarely with regard to music). From a simple sight-and-sound gag everyone gets straight away, we have stumbled into thickets of film scholarship. This book does not promise to know the way out, but it can look at some of the brambles and flowers and see what place(s) music may have among them.

ii. Film/music/narratology

Narratological concepts are firmly ensconced in film studies, and narratological questions have concerned the theory and poetics of film since its early days, and were integral already to Lev Kuleshov's and Sergei Eisenstein's ideas about montage as a genuinely cinematic language. Not least the discussions about cinematic representation and reality important to André Bazin or Siegfried Kracauer touch on narratological problems. As a distinct field, however, film narratology came into its own in the 1970s, 1980s and 1990s, with authors such as Christian Metz, Seymour Chatman, David Bordwell, Kristin Thompson, Michel Chion, Edward Branigan etc., building on the work of literary theorists and narratologists from the Russian formalists via Wayne Booth, Gérard Genette, Tzvetan Todorov to Shlomith Rimmon-Kenan, Mieke Bal, David Herman, Ansgar Nünning, Manfred Jahn, Monika Fludernik etc.

In its heyday in the 1980s, film narratology also spilled over into the study of film music. Kathryn Kalinak illustrated the key question when she retold what may be the most famous anecdote of film music history. It concerns Alfred Hitchcock's *Lifeboat* (1944) and its motley crew of shipwrecked people drifting in a boat on the open ocean. The composer meant to write the music was David Raksin, and this is how he used to explain why, in the end, he did not:

> One of [Hitchcock's] people said to me, 'There's not going to be any music in our picture' and I said, 'Why?' 'Well… Hitchcock says they're out on the open ocean. Where would the music come from?' So I said, 'Go back and ask him where the camera comes from and I'll tell him where the music comes from.' (Kalinak 1992: xiii)[4]

Of course, Raksin uses a trick: without the camera, there would be no film; without music, it would just be a (perhaps quite) different one.[5] But in the defence of his profession, Raksin not only points out that film, like any work of art, is a made-up thing that cannot reasonably

4   There are different versions of this story; see Stilwell (2007: 188 & 201, note 11).
5   This argument was used by Ben Winters in his critique of the concept of nondiegetic music (Winters 2010). Winters quotes Steven Spielberg: 'Indiana Jones cannot exist without his [musical] theme. And, of course, that theme would be nothing without Indiana Jones' (Winters 2010: 224). For Winters, this 'is a statement that few would disagree with', but I am not sure. The impact of the film would be changed without the music, but it would still tell a broadly plausible story. And while in our consciousness the music may be charged with the Indiana Jones stories, it is still music one can like without knowing the films.

be measured by the yardstick of 'realism', but also that music has, far beyond its realistic representation, long become second nature to film.

'Where the music comes from' was also the question that led Claudia Gorbman to adopt, from Gérard Genette, the concepts of nondiegetic, diegetic and metadiegetic levels of narration (Gorbman 1987). Since then, the terms 'diegetic' and 'nondiegetic' (or 'extradiegetic') have become common terms to describe the relation of music to the narrative structure of a film. Much literature uses them without further ado; some authors have problematized them as too blunt to do justice to the intricacies of individual films, but the theoretical impetus as such seemed to have spent itself for a while.

But in recent years, the discussion has picked up again. Already in the 1990s, Royal S. Brown discussed music playing with the diegetic/nondiegetic divide, without (perhaps wisely) developing this into a more coherent theory (R. Brown 1994: 67–91), while Michel Chion suggested his own, related conceptual system for film sound (Chion 1994 & 2009). Since then, a raft of publications has interrogated the concepts popularized by Gorbman and suggested revisions and refinements (e.g. Levinson 1996; Neumeyer 1997, 2000 & 2009; Buhler 2001; Kassabian 2001; Biancorosso 2001 & 2009; Donnelly 2001 & 2005; Holbrook 2005a & 2005b; Stilwell 2007; Norden 2007; Binns 2008; Smith 2009; Cecchi 2010; Winters 2010; Merlin 2010; Davis, 2012; Winters 2012; Yacavone 2012).

It may be time to take stock, but also to go beyond the methodological discussion of narratological concepts to the exploration of their usefulness for shedding light on individual films and types of films – to ask how film audiences construe the sources and spaces of music, how the ambiguities of such construals and the transitions and fuzzy in-between states might be grouped and understood as instances of particular narrative techniques and of strategies typical for particular genres, situations and filmmakers. Both aspects, the methodological discussion and its application, are concerns of this book.

It does not, however, attempt a grand theory of the *functions* of film music as an element of a (predominantly) narrative art, which would be a much bigger project: 'narrative theory facilitates description only of the narrative aspects of a text and not all the characteristics, even of a clearly narrative text' (Bal 2009: 11). Functions of film music are naturally a recurrent interest of the literature, be it Aaron Copland's oft-quoted article (Copland 1949; the basis of Prendergast 1992: 213–26), Zofia Lissa's fine-grained account (Lissa 1965: 98–256), Gorbman's and Kalinak's discussion of the 'rules' of classical Hollywood scoring (Gorbman 1987: 73; Kalinak 1992: 66–110), Claudia Bullerjahn's discussion of functions in the context of the apperception of film music (Bullerjahn 2007: 53–74), or the wide-ranging survey of James Buhler, David Neumeyer and Rob Deemer (Buhler, Neumeyer and Deemer 2010, especially chs. 3–9). The analysis of music's place(s) in the narrative structure of film and that of its functions intersect in complex ways, but should be kept apart as different projects.

Narratology itself is a wide field, and with regard to that, another qualification needs to be made. My study is interested in the machinery of narrative rather than the patterns and trajectories of the stories it is used to tell. The questions about the sequence of events that make a (typical) story that interested Tzvetan Todorov, for example, or the morphological approach to story patterns developed by Vladimir Propp in his analyses of Russian folk tales, or the semiotically-orientated analysis of 'codes' in Roland Barthes' *S/Z*, do not fall not into the purview of this study. It would be interesting to see how film music might be brought into such explorations: how it can articulate story patterns or codes, or how formal propensities of different kinds of music may mesh with such patterns. But that would be a different study.

The remit of this one is much narrower. It asks not what music does in a film, but only where it comes from with regard to the film's narrative structure; or more precisely, how its place in the narrative structure can be understood and what music can do in a film by dint of this understanding.

In the wider disciplinary landscape, this is a somewhat old-fashioned project. While the narratological discussions referred to in this book go right up to the present day, their roots lie (see above) in the last third of the twentieth century. The reason for what I believe to be the timeliness of this study has to do with the relationship between (film) narratology and film musicology – a discipline that itself has developed its current state to a substantial extent over the same period.

For a long time, it was a favourite pastime of film musicologists to lament the neglect their field suffered at the hand of a discipline centred on high art music. Such lamentation has become obsolete. Film music studies is a burgeoning sub-discipline, with a fast-expanding literature with journals and conferences and much student interest, and with increasing diversification into fields such as television music, music in computer games, music on the Web, etc. Though there are still many gaps on the scholarly map (especially with regard to source documentation and studies), the features of the landscape are becoming clearer. And not only is there much literature, but that literature is diversifying in its range, covering projects from bibliographical surveys via genre studies down to monographic studies of individual film composers and scores.

This study occupies a point on the scale between the comprehensive, be it in the shape of surveys of material or of all-encompassing theories, and the minute, in the shape of studies of individual films and their music: what David Bordwell in the 1990s called 'middle-level research' in film studies (instead of the all-encompassing Theory he was criticizing) (Bordwell 1996: 27). It may also be a good candidate for what Noël Carroll called 'piecemeal' film theorizing (Carroll 1996: 40): to look in detail at a limited aspect of the field, and to use insights from other fields as required to come to terms (sometimes literally) with a particular problem, but without a theoretical framework that spans the entire discipline. When he was writing *Langage et cinéma* in 1971, Christian Metz envisaged 'a third phase [of film theory] one can hope for one day', in which the 'diverse methods may be reconciled at a deep level [...] and film theory would be a real synthesis' (Metz 1971: 13–14; my translation). At that point, however, he saw a 'provisional but necessary methodological pluralism' in which 'all film study needs to choose clearly its principle of pertinence' (1971: 13–14; my translation). Perhaps the epoch of methodological pluralism is just not over yet, but perhaps

Metz's 'real synthesis' was a bit of a pipe dream anyway, and film studies and film musicology should be happy with their different areas of expertise.

In this context, narratology as one approach to understanding the structure (and sometimes the power) of film may be well-established in film studies, but while some of its concepts are used as a matter of fact in film musicology, many of their features and problems have been explored only insufficiently or not at all. To engage with film studies, film musicology needs to work through these problems, even if it means to go back to discussions the wider discipline has, if not left behind, then at least long since integrated into its theoretical arsenal.

The plan of the book

In the following section (ch. I.iii), the introduction concludes with a sketch of basic assumptions and conditions of this study. Chapter II takes stock of key concepts of film music narratology and places them in a wider framework by tracing music through levels of narration: from title sequences and other instances of music linked to extrafictionality (ch. II.ii and II.iii) via the nondiegetic/diegetic distinction (ch. II.iv) to the narratological discussion of music and subjectivity and the concept of focalization (ch. II.v).

Chapters III, IV and V apply tools inspected in Chapter II to case studies at different levels of detail. Chapters III and IV look at narratological aspects of the ways particular film genres use music. The Hollywood musical (Chapter III) is an obvious choice because music is at its core, but also because it has developed particular ways of using and staging music, ways later films refer to in a variety of ways. Horror films (Chapter IV) may be a less obvious choice, but they show that music need not be at the centre of a genre to be used in genre-specific ways – ways in the case of horror films conditioned by the idea of category transgression and by the audience orientation of the films (which by definition have to aim for a particular effect).

Chapter V homes in on narratological aspects of music in individual films or particular narrative techniques, but in all cases with regard to musical strategies that extend across an entire film: Chapter V.i tests what a narratological analysis of music can contribute to a (medium to) close reading of a film, in this case *Once Upon a Time in America* (1984). The ground is prepared by observations on music, memory and diegetic objects in other films by Sergio Leone scored by Ennio Morricone. *Once Upon a Time in America* is further away from Leone's westerns than these are from each other, but as another exploration of American myth and men it is close enough, and it shares the fetishistic attachment of music to diegetic objects with several of the earlier films. Chapter V.ii focuses on the *The Truman Show* (1998), another obvious candidate for such an analysis because of its layered yet interacting levels of fictionality and narration, but even more interestingly because music is involved in breaking up that layering, and thereby contributes to the film's discourse on media manipulation. Chapter V.iii looks primarily at *Far from Heaven* (2002) and *Breakfast at Tiffany's* (1961), and a narrative figure I call a 'retrospective prolepsis', with regard to music in leitmotivic scores. It occurs less ostentatiously in many films, and is also discussed with regard to two of the models for *Far from Heaven*, Douglas Sirk's *All That Heaven Allows* (1955) and *Imitation of Life* (1959), and is shown in a different realization in *The Adventures of Robin Hood* (1938).

A note on the choice of films

The study is not based on a systematically structured sample of films, but sources its examples from what I hope is a reasonably wide selection. The viewpoint is that of an early twenty-first century cinema-goer in a western country (which is not accidentally my own position), probably the perspective most relevant for the likely readership of this book. At the core is the Hollywood tradition of live-action fiction (sound) films, but examples are also taken from films made in other countries, and other options (e.g. documentaries and cartoons) are represented by a few sideway glances.

The reason for the selection is not just that live-action fiction sound film is at the heart of most people's understanding of cinema in western countries (though it is), but also because other types of films or other audio-visual forms pose particular narratological problems: the truth claims of documentaries, for example, or the highly permeable distinction between diegesis and narration in cartoons, or the integration of narrative elements into other structuring frameworks in music videos. In 'silent' cinema, the relation between film and music was configured differently; in most silent films, music was not part of the work in the way it is in sound film. To do justice to such features and problems would require dedicated studies.

The same applies to the analysis of music in particular stylistic traditions of film-making (e.g. after the model of part three of Bordwell's *Narration in the Fiction Film* [1985: 147–334]), which would be one way to develop film music narratology. It applies especially to experimental forms of narrative film (discussed by Bordwell in chapters on what he calls 'art-cinema narration' and 'parametric narration', and on Godard), because such films can perhaps be better understood once the conventions against which they stand out have been established (though often it may be less a question of 'against' but one of 'further', of making tricks and techniques and structures one can also find in other films overt enough to define a film).

Film examples used in the book illustrate concepts and arguments, but also test them. It is rarely difficult to find *typical* examples of a particular theoretical category or point. How analytically useful such categories are, however, may emerge more clearly by applying them to examples that do not quite fit the mould, but raise questions, and in this way balance illustration and interrogation.

A note on 'the viewer'

The 'viewer' or 'spectator' is a common protagonist of film literature, but makes the musicologist slightly uncomfortable because ears do not seem to enter into the cinematic equation. 'Audience' is musicologically more plausible. Even though in its literal meaning it errs on the other side and privileges ears over eyes, that meaning has been sufficiently drowned out by its generalized use for many different reception situations. But 'audience' is a plural word and grammatically awkward. Some film sound literature takes its cue from Michel Chion and uses the term 'audio-viewer' (Chion 1994: 56 & 216; see also Chion 2009: 468), but while that is more accurate, it is also slightly pedantic. We know that sound cinema assumes as its standard recipient a viewer who is also a listener. For that reason, in most cases this book talks of the 'viewer', but takes it as understood that that viewer has ears as well to attend to the sound (of music) in film.

iii. Principles of pertinence

This study is framed by the considerations sketched below. They are not my catechism of film music narratology, but they may help to clarify the 'principle[s] of pertinence' of this book (in a slightly different sense from that of Christian Metz, see p. 8): foundations, conditions of and constraints for what it has to say.

1. While many of the examples in this book illustrate typical uses of music in film, many others – to put ideas to the test – show more intricate ways of building music into film narrative. For all their ingenuity, such intricacies are strictly options; they are not marks of aesthetic quality. Films do not need to use music in narratologically interesting ways; even films that restrict themselves to naturalistic diegetic music – a Dogme film, say, or *The Blair Witch Project* (1999), or a film by the Dardenne brothers – do not strike us as lacking anything (though the link between musical austerity and the aspiration to 'realism' in many such films is conspicuous; Hitchcock's *The Birds* [1963], on the other hand, shows that that need not be the case). Many other films preserve basic distinctions between extrafictional, diegetic and nondiegetic music, and never do anything remarkable with their music in relation to levels of narration without being the worse for it. If this book sometimes pursues the exceptions rather than the rules, it does so the better to understand the range of those rules (and the power of the exceptions).

2. If, however, the capacity of music to smoothly or spectacularly cross conceptual borderlines is exploited, it can weave music into the fabric of a film, and make it more than just an atmospheric or emotive halo. Film musicologists are well advised not to make exaggerated claims about the importance of their object of study. In most films, music is strictly subservient. But the reluctance of film scholars to consider it with the same rigour (or interest) as other elements of film justifies the attempt to show that, and how, music can be integral not just to the effects films have, but to the basic structure many of these effects are built on.

3. The aim of film music narratology cannot be a comprehensive system of concepts covering all imaginable angles, but only to understand a bit better the *dynamic* role of music in film narrative. The distinction between diegetic and nondiegetic music is an example. Robynn Stilwell has pointed out that its crudeness gives rise to attitudes that match its simple polarity: either 'a taxonomic approach, breaking down various stages or states between diegetic and nondiegetic', or 'dismissal – if this border is being crossed so often, then the distinction doesn't mean anything' (Stilwell 2007: 184). Naturally, this study is on the side of the refiners, not of the abolitionists. If I did not think that mapping music onto the narrative structure of films helps to understand what music contributes to them, this book would not have been written. But such mapping needs to proceed with caution. Music's movements across the map make it hard to pin down, and therein lies its charm: 'the border crossing is […] a trajectory, a vector, a gesture' (Stilwell 2007: 184–85). To trace the dynamics of such musico-narrative gestures is as important as it is to increase the scale of the map. Recent film narratology has described the diegesis as a construct the spectator uses to make sense of a film, and prefers to speak of 'diegetization': the tentative understanding of the way filmic cues suggest, undermine or modify the idea of a storyworld, a fictionally 'real' space behind the screen (more in ch. II.iv.a). The conceptual system must not become and end in itself, but remain flexible enough to allow for such dynamism.

4. Like a physician who finds a cause for a symptom just in the field of medicine she specializes in, every theoretically focused study risks to read its material only in the light of its own approach and to overlook alternative explanations. That most films, and by extension their music, *can* be understood in relation to ideas about narrative structure does not mean that they can always be *most fruitfully* explained with regard to these ideas, nor that a cinema audience would understand them in this way.

The partial autonomy of music in film is an example. Composers have their own ideas of what makes good music, and these are not always fully in tune with the filmic structures music is slotted into. (Historically, that may be particularly relevant for scores from a time when film composition was not a craft one could formally learn, but one that composers came to full of ideas and experiences from other musical contexts.) Music can be at odds with, or function on a different plane than, other structures of a film; it can establish connections across narrative boundaries without intending to make the crossing narratively relevant; it can at least occasionally and partially be understood by an audience in 'purely' musical terms. How much of a film score can be explained by such musicality in its own right can only be assessed individually for each film.

5. One motivation of cognitivist film narratology has been to theoretically 'activate' the audience: to describe film viewing as cognitive activity, and to free spectators from the mercy of ideologically suspicious strategies of subject positioning much 1970s film theory had – in a crude summary – consigned them to (see Bordwell 1996: 6–18). But it only activates the audience up to a point. For Bordwell, narration is 'the organization of a set of cues for the construction of a story' (Bordwell 1985: 62). The aim is the (re)construction of the story, which produces the enjoyment that makes the exercise worthwhile. Narrative strategies do not enter into the enjoyment equation:

For the viewer, constructing the story takes precedence; the effects of the text are registered, but its causes go unremarked. […] The spectator simply has no concepts or terms for the textual elements and systems that shape responses. It is the job of theory to construct them, the job of analysis to show them at work. (Bordwell 1985: 48)

Out of the frying pan and into the fire of another round of academic self-empowerment. But its applicability is limited. It is obvious that Bordwell's stance does not work for what he calls 'art-cinema', 'historical-materialist' and 'parametric' narration (Bordwell 1985: 205–310), and even for classical Hollywood narration it may only go so far. To focus on a subservient element of film such as music may help to see the limitation of Bordwell's view. The playfulness so many films show in their use of music makes one suspect that the fun in audio-viewing films lies not just in story (re)construction, aided and abetted by narrative techniques, but at least partly in the to and fro of attention between story and narration, between what is shown and told and how it is shown and told. Otherwise, too much of the artifice of film narration would seem gratuitous.

Looking at the way we look at art, Roger Scruton points out the 'double intentionality' of our perception of it. When we see a face in a portrait, we are 'presented with two simultaneous objects of perception: the *real* picture, and the *imaginary* face' (Scruton 1997: 87; discussed in Biancorosso 2001: § 15–23). Scruton uses the term in the context of his aesthetics of music. Music, too, we can understand as physical sound, but also as a way of making patterns and sense (see Scruton 1997: 96). We can add a further differentiation. The 'real picture' itself can be understood on two levels: as a physical object of wood and canvas and paint, and as a piece of artistry that uses colour, brushstrokes, etc., to create what in some respects resembles a human face. Strictly speaking, we see three things at once: a physical object; a painting imitating aspects of a human face; and the person that painting is meant to represent (or invent). With regard to film, these three levels would be the projection of patterns of light on a screen and sound in space; the film as a set of narrative cues; and the story we (re)construct on their basis.[6] The first level is narratologically not very interesting, but the other two are. When we watch a narrative film, what we experience (or, rather, construct) is a story presented to us through the artifice of cinematic storytelling. But we also see a piece of filmic artifice that takes a story as it subject, and the 'work' we must expend to construct the story out of what the film offers us may not just be a condition for our getting the story, but part of the fun – the journey is the reward.

Much used to be made in film scholarship of the idea that classic Hollywood storytelling was (or is) geared towards foregrounding the story and keeping the artifice of its telling in the background. But to look at the often highly self-conscious way music is used in many classic Hollywood films makes one wonder if this does not deserve to be taken with a pinch of salt. Cognitivist narratology ought to be able to entertain a broader view of audience activity, since it is concerned with understanding how the 'elements and systems that shape

---

6 Non-representative art has only two levels: a Mondrian grid painting is both a physical object of wood, canvas and paint, and a graphic pattern (though it may trigger associations of other objects).

responses' work. That should allow for the possibility that spectators understand them intuitively, even if they may not be able to put them into words.

A second lesson to be learned from a subservient element such as music is that there may be – as Kristin Thompson warned in her analysis of *Ivan the Terrible/Ivan Grozny* (1944) – 'significant structures in the work that do not contribute to the narrative', which is 'not always the most important structure in a given film, scene or segment' (Thompson 1981: 267; see also Yacavone 2012). For *Ivan the Terrible*, she describes two such non-narrative aspects: (1) its 'disjunctions and discontinuities' (Thompson 1981: 261–86), especially in comparison to contemporary Hollywood practices – disjunctions that form a coherent stylistic layer of their own and in that way dialectically contribute to the unity of the film; and (2) what she calls 'excess' (Thompson 1981: 287–303) – individual elements of a film that are enjoyable not as contribution to narrative structure or a stylistic system, but for their own sake.

Bordwell is sceptical: 'The *trouvailles* will never add up' (Bordwell 1985: 53). But they do not have to add up, do not have to offer an alternative to the story-constructing audience activity he is interested in; they only have to add allure. Here, a musically integrated soundtrack (see point 4 above) might come into its own, even if musical integration adds not much to story understanding. The composite art of film usually relies on the smooth cooperation of its elements, but also on the attractiveness of each element, sometimes even at the expense of the whole.[7]

6. Narratology is methodologically precarious. Its name proclaims that it is concerned with storytelling per se, in whatever medium it may happen. But most of its concepts were developed for the analysis of literary texts, novels in particular. Comparisons with literature *can* be enlightening for the understanding of narrative in film, and I have used them where they seemed helpful. But one must not overlook what is specific to film, and interrogate the usefulness of concepts for the medium.

A major difference is that most literary narratives (novels, short stories, narrative poems) most of the time consist of a single stream of data, while film has multiple channels, visual and auditory, each of which can simultaneously present different strands of data (through split screens or layered images or sounds), strands we may assign to different narrating agencies, levels of narration or focalizations. While it would be pointless to argue which medium allows the more complex narrative structures, it is important to recognize that they allow different kinds of complexity.

A more minor difference concerns access to information. While the idea that film is an inherently 'realist' medium has produced a lot of problematic discussion and aesthetics, and while one must not downplay the artifice of film, one should not overlook the fact that literature finds it easier to peer into characters' minds than film, which tends to be better with the outside of things. That has consequences for the representation of subjectivity in different media (discussed in ch. II.v with regard to focalization).

---

7 Peter Verstraten has argued, however, that in some cases, elements of stylistic excess are meta-functional as 'built-in guides for "reading" or watching' (Verstraten 2009: 190).

7. Narratology is methodologically precarious in yet another sense. Its objects are texts, but they make sense only in a complex configuration. If we return to the narrative ur-situation of a friend telling us over a pint in the pub what happened to her that day (see p. 5), the techniques she employs in her 'text' – her tale – are shaped by her narrational intentions, which in turn are informed by her assumptions concerning our reaction to those techniques. But narratology normally only has access to the text, not to intentions or reactions, which have to be extrapolated from the text. We can, of course, try to find out about the intentions of authors and film-makers, and can try to establish how readers and viewers actually understand narratives (discussed e.g. in Wuss 1999; Bortolussi and Dixon 2002; for the perception of music in film, see Bullerjahn 2007). But in the collaborative art of film, authorial intentions may be even more elusive than in other arts, and artists are often less than forthcoming with reliable information about their intentions. On the other side, methodologically sound empirical psychology tends to operate with too wide a mesh to capture finer theoretical distinctions, and especially with regard to the time-bound art of film there is not much hope that psychonarratology will anytime soon catch up with theory.

But even if we could find out more, historical authorship and reception are not the same as the analysis of what texts show us of intentions and the perceiver reactions they presuppose. The concepts of the 'implied author' (see ch. II.iv.d) and 'implied reader' capture the fact that narrative texts *embody* intentions and assumed reactions and can be analyzed independently of actual intentions, expectations and reactions.

And yet, empirical reality is difficult to cancel out, particularly on the reception side. The narratologist is, after all, just another audience member, and his understanding inevitably shapes the analysis of textual features that betray the narrative game of (re)presentation, implication and interpretation. For David Bordwell, (cognitive) audience activity is the core of film narratology. But he does not distinguish strictly between an 'implied viewer' as a placeholder for features of films that assume mental audience activities on the one hand, and historical audiences and their contingent understanding of films on the other. That has been criticized (e.g. by Markus Kuhn), especially with regard to Bordwell's concepts of a 'classical style' of Hollywood narration and a 'classical spectator' (Bordwell 1985: 156–204), which inform each other:

> Because Bordwell draws on a range of historical norms and rules of production for his description of the 'classical narration' that moulds the 'classical spectator', he mixes processes of reception and production and thereby creates a methodological feedback loop [...] a tautological circular argument that does not leave much space for the analysis of an individual film. (Kuhn 2011: 34–35)

But a methodological feedback loop makes sense if it describes a historical feedback loop (the 'hermeneutic circle' is a variant of this idea). It would not make much sense to claim that assumptions about audience reactions do *not* influence the way films are made, and that in turn films do *not* condition audiences to approach them with certain expectations. Textual traces of intentions, expectations and reactions are the sediment of historical processes of production and reception. Even text-immanent approaches to narrative (as advocated by Kuhn) tend to rely on (often unacknowledged) assumptions about audience perspectives; the borderline between implied and real recipients can be thin. Methodological purity becomes problematic if it fails to sufficiently capture reality.

It may make more sense – and may be unavoidable anyway – to bring that into the open: to use my own understanding of, and reactions to, films and their music to analyze textual strategies, analyses which in turn inform my understanding. I can only hope that that understanding is sufficiently representative to make sense to others; if the book says 'we', it does so in this hope. If a particular technique or example can be understood in different ways, I have tried to spell those out, but it is also unavoidable that this is not exhaustive – alternative takes are welcome.

Chapter II

The Conceptual Toolkit: Music and Levels of Narration

i. Fictional worlds and the filmic universe

Film music narratology has so far revolved around the idea of the diegesis: the world 'behind the screen' of a fiction film (and not dissimilarly a documentary), or rather, the world constructed by viewers on the basis of cues provided by the film. Etienne Souriau borrowed the term in 1950 from his daughter Anne (Souriau 1990: 581), who had borrowed it from the Greek 'diegesis' (meaning narration) – a term for the telling of a story became a term for the world the story is set in. But Souriau did not understand it as a narratological term, part of a theory of storytelling; he used it as a filmological term, part of a map of film studies (see Kessler 1997 & 2007; Fuxjäger 2007; Taylor 2007; Neumeyer 2009).

On this map, Souriau understood it as one of eight levels of *l'univers filmique*: the *afilmique* (the reality outside of cinema); the *profilmique* (the reality informing a film); the *filmographique* (film as an artefact); the *filmophanique* (the film projection); the *créatorial* (the making of a film); the *écranique* (what happens on the screen during projection); and the *spectatoriel* (what happens in viewers' minds) (Souriau 1951; see also Kessler 2007: 9–10; and Neumeyer 2009). In this system, *diégètique* was 'all that concerns the film insofar it represents something. Diegetic is everything we take into account as being represented by the film, and as part of the reality *presupposed* by the signification of the film' (Souriau 1951: 237; my translation). (The relationship of Souriau's definition to a narratological one is discussed in ch. II.iv.a.)

In this wider context, Souriau was not interested in the distinction between diegesis and narration. His system does not have a term for the nondiegetic as something not represented by the film, but doing the representing; the distinction is beyond its frame of reference. Nondiegetic music, in this system, would be part of the *filmophanique*, but only one element among others, and not conceptually linked to the diegesis.

But the career of the diegesis has happened in narratology: in film narratology, but also in narratology in general. From Genette it found its way into film musicology, mainly through Claudia Gorbman, who used Genette's terms 'diegetic' and 'extradiegetic' (the latter she calls 'nondiegetic') to replace older terms such as 'source music', 'incidental music', 'score', 'underscoring', 'background music', etc. (see Gorbman 1987: 11–30).[8]

---

8 Yet another distinction was that between 'visual vocal', 'visual instrumental' and 'background vocal' and 'background instrumental' music, which was used in Hollywood in the 1930s and 1940s in the context of fees for musicians (defined as those who played or sang in the 'background', i.e. off-screen) and actors, defined by their on-screen presence (see Neumeyer 2000: 18–19).

But therein lay the rub. Film music already had its own terms, and even if they were not much of a system and did not really link up with anything else, they belonged to a (fairly) venerable praxis, and new ones did not necessarily seem an improvement. For film composers, 'source music' and 'score' are still more common than 'diegetic' or 'nondiegetic' music, and frustrated with the crudeness of the diegetic/nondiegetic distinction, some film scholars have argued for retaining the older terms.[9]

But it is too late. The terminology film musicology has inherited from Souriau, Genette and Gorbman has become the small change of talking about music in narrative film. Yet it is not just acceptance of the inevitable that recommends that we grapple with these concepts. This book has been written by a musicologist, and musicology has always been shaped by conflicting impulses, generated by its odd position in the ivory palace of the arts and humanities: not in the central tower, where linguists, classicists, philosophers, historians and sundry others are engaged in lively conversation, but in a garden hut on the fringes of the grounds, behind high hedges of notation and music theory and their arcane signs and symbols. Everyone likes music, but almost everyone finds it hard to talk about it to musicologists, and vice versa. One impulse has been the adoption of ideas invented elsewhere to claim the relevance of music to wider intellectual concerns: music as an embodiment of the harmony of a world defined by numbers; music as rhetoric, or as mimesis; or the New Musicologies of recent decades and their attempts to learn the lessons of New Historicism, gender, racial or (post)colonial studies or the performative turn of the arts. This can turn into a breathless race to catch up, and a bit of distance may sometimes be a good thing. The other impulse has been defiant self-enclosure in the paradise garden of music's own body of theory, which give academics enough to play with for a while, but lets the hedges grow ever higher, and behind them musicology may eventually be forgotten altogether.

It is not difficult to detect traces of this problem in, for example, Anahid Kassabian's preference for the language of film music praxis rather than the theorizing of film scholars and narratologists, who have no great track record in writing about film music (see Kassabian 2001: 42–49). But there are two problems with this impulse:

- No one really doubts that music is an integral part of its film, but it is not always easy to translate that idea into scholarly practice. If film musicology wants film scholars to listen, it has to participate in film scholarship understood as an umbrella discipline encompassing many specialisms in need of a common language.
- If that sounds like too much academic opportunism, the argument can also be turned around. If the narratology lesson were already over after the adoption of the diegetic/

---

9 Anahid Kassabian, for example, who prefers 'source music', 'scoring' and 'source scoring', borrowed from Earle Hagen's *Scoring for Films* (cf. Kassabian 2001: 42–49, referring to Hagen 1971: 190-206), not least because 'source scoring' provides a fuzzy zone that helps to avoid the dichotomy suggested by the diegetic/nondiegetic distinction (see also footnotes 38 and 41 for critiques of her position.)

nondiegetic distinction, it would not be worth the fee. The problem with that distinction is not that it is simplistic, but (a) that it has sometimes been used simplistically, and (b) that it is but one element in a bigger toolbox, one which film musicology may be advised to make useful for its purposes (in pursuit of which project it may become more useful to film scholarship).

This chapter is an attempt to do that, in different ways:

- One is the attempt to expand the range of narratological concepts applied to film music. Hierarchically nested levels of narration are a standard of narratological models, and so far film musicology has failed to look at most of them in a systematic manner. Music in extrafictional contexts – e.g. in company logos, or its contribution to title sequences – have rarely been discussed. The same applies to the other end of the scale: while the role of music in establishing subjectivity in film is acknowledged, and is discussed in studies of individual films, it has not been systematically explored beyond Gorbman's concept of 'metadiegetic music' (Gorbman 1987: 22–23).
- Another one is the attempt to think about common concepts as more than boxes to file film-musical moments away in: to explore what goes on inside the boxes, e.g. what different options basic terms such as 'diegetic' and 'nondiegetic' cover.
- A third is a more sustained look at the fuzzy spaces between the categories, the zones of ambiguity in (re)constructing the place of music in the narrative structure, music's apparent 'movements' from one 'space' into another. This includes the exploration of concepts that have occasionally been mentioned, but rarely used in film musicology, such as 'displaced diegetic music', 'supradiegetic music' or the 'implied author'. This includes ambiguities produced by the application of such concepts: all those film-musical equations that cannot be solved without a conceptual remainder.

This chapter explores concepts and tests them against examples, while Chapters III, IV and V are an acknowledgement of the need to do something with the concepts. Theory has to earn its keep by showing that it allows us to see and hear more in what we study. So far, film music narratology has been focused on discussing its conceptual instruments. In the process, much of interest has been found out about music's contribution to individual films, but rather as a side effect of the methodological discussion. While that discussion is not over (in some respects it has hardly begun), we should not put off the application of the instruments for too long, even for methodological purposes, because only in their application can their usefulness be tested.

*

Hierarchies of levels of narration are a core feature of narratological systems (see, for example, Genette 1980: 227–37; Chatman 1978: 146–95; Abbott 2008: 67–82; Bal 2009: 48–74; Kuhn 2011: 81–118). This chapter uses as its framework Edward Branigan's hierarchy, which

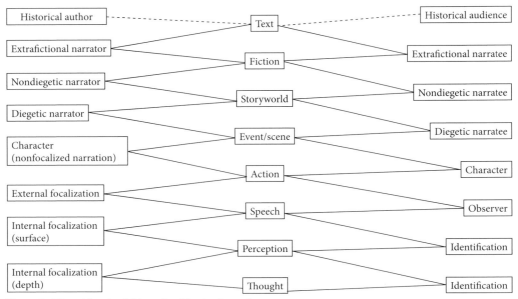

Figure 1: Edward Branigan's hierarchy of levels of narration.

distinguishes between eight levels of narrative agency or sources of narrative information and corresponding levels of reception/addressees (Branigan 1992: 87) (Figure 1).

However, my reasons for referring to Branigan's model are pragmatic rather than indicative of theoretical affiliation. Some of its features are problematic:

- A problem not of the model itself, but of its theoretical foundation is Branigan's subscription to a perceiver-centred model of narrative and his critique of communication models. (This is discussed in ch. II.iv.d with regard to the 'implied author', a level represented in the model by the 'extrafictional narrator'.)
- A second problem lies in the relationship between left- and right-hand columns. Most (film) narratology has been more interested in the sources of narrative agency, and Branigan is no exception; the addressees have been rather neglected. Some are more obvious than others: the 'historical audience' sitting in the cinema, or diegetic characters listening to a tale told within the storyworld. The roles of extrafictional and nondiegetic narratees depends on one's understanding of the conceptual role of narration and the implied author in film, but their analytical usefulness is limited, and in any case closely linked to the left-hand categories (see Kuhn 2011: 110–12), while the lower half of the categories needs to be considered in in the context of the place of focalization in the model (see below).
- The same applies to the middle column. While text, fiction and storyworld are clear, the places of event, action and speech are not; and while perception and thought make

sense as different aspects of internal focalization (see ch. II.v), the place of focalization in the model itself is problematic.

- For Genette, who coined the term, focalization is categorically different from narration (see Genette 1980: 25–32). Narration organizes the narratees' access to story information, while fozalization describes the access the narration itself has to information (see Genette 1980: 29–32). From a Genettean perspective, below the diegetic narrator is the metadiegetic level – the level of embedded narratives – while focalization specifies the restriction of access to information (see p. 121 for a model integrating both aspects).

The advantage of Branigan's model as a chapter framework is its comprehensiveness. He is pragmatic enough to include concepts that fit the theoretical foundations of his own position only uncomfortably, and also concepts other narratologists would position differently. The differentiation between two levels of internal focalization is also helpful for the particular requirements of film (more in ch. II.v). The structure that results from my skeptical adaptation of Branigan is this:

- Ch. II.ii looks at the textualization of 'historical' authorship in title sequences, and at musical mediation between extrafictionality, fiction and diegesis in such sequences. End credits also address the extrafictional aspect of film, but the chapter focuses on the title sequence as the 'prototypical paratext of film' (Böhnke 2007a: 32).
- Ch. II.iii deals with overt extrafictional narration, primarily in audience addresses. The implied author, the other aspect of this level, is discussed in ch. II.iv.d, because it is most relevant for certain uses of diegetic music.
- Ch. II.iv integrates the discussion of the nondiegetic and diegetic levels, because their relationship has been such a major concern of film musicology.
- Ch. II.v interrogates the usefulness of the concept of focalization for film music narratology.

ii. The 'historical author': extrafictionality and the title sequence

Narratology grew out of literary studies, and for most literature the 'historical author' is a relatively straightforward concept: most literature – a novel, say, or a play – is written by one person, probably sitting at a desk. It is not quite as simple, of course: there is an editing process, and the public persona of an author (created not least by the works) may differ from the person (whatever that may be). Things are obviously different in films, which are collaborative and have no single author in a meaningful sense – a lack felt so acutely in comparison with other arts that it gave rise to auteurism to fill the gap of an identifiable individual creator, by assigning that role to (usually) the director of a film.

But while different in the practicalities of text generation, narratologically a film is not dissimilar to a novel: there is an empirical level on which a film is made, by however many people in whichever way; most films suggest a story(world) with its own set of rules and fictional facts, which may invite us to mentally construct an agency responsible for inventing them (i.e. an implied author; more in ch. II.iv.d); and there is narration, the presentation of the story with the means of the medium. Even the representation of authorship is not dissimilar: books contain pages providing the names of author and publisher, a publication date, etc., and most films are bookended by credits presenting the people and organizations involved in their making. The fiction begins with an acknowledgement of its fictionality, and, strangely enough, that acknowledgement seems not to detract from viewers' subsequent story immersion, but to be almost a condition for it: the credits delimit a space within which the fiction may legitimately take place (what Roger Odin has called the 'title-sequence effect' [2000: 75–80]).

Most art delimits its space and separates itself from what is not art, at different levels: art usually takes place in specific spaces (galleries, museums, theatres, cinemas, concert halls, etc.). Inside or outside those spaces, works have their own boundaries: paintings have frames, sculptures stand on plinths, plays (and films) open and close with curtains. Cinema as a commercial institution also surrounds its core texts with other framing devices: muzak before the curtain opens, ads, trailers. On one level, such boundaries are part of the physical reality of an artwork: even an unframed painting has an edge that separates it from its surroundings; a book has to have a first and a last page; a play has to show us the first set (or an empty stage), the first entry of an actor and a first line of dialogue (if there is any); a film has a first and last frame. But an actual frame around a painting or a stage curtain does more: it points out the boundary, and says 'Here is art (and there isn't)'; it focuses attention on the work, but also contains it in a 'safe' space to which particular rules of mental disposition, behaviour, etc., apply – here be dragons, but they are only make-believe.

But the framing of books and films does yet more. In crediting author, publisher, film-makers, it attests to their made-ness, to the fact that they have been put together by real people (as does a signature on a painting). In one sense, books and films do that in a similar way. The fictional text is at the centre, while parts attesting to its production are arranged around it: a book has a dust jacket, front and rear covers, endpapers, flyleaves, front matter (frontispiece, title page, copyright page, table of contents, acknowledgements, etc.), and possibly back matter (notes, appendices, etc.). A film may have an exhibition classification and a title at the start, perhaps a title card at 'The End', and company, cast and crew credits at the beginning, or end, or both. The difference is that readers of a book can decide what of the information surrounding the core text they want to take notice of and when. In temporal arts such as theatre, music or film, audiences are bound by the progression of the work (though the display apparatus may change conditions: films shown on TV often have their end credits cut off; on a DVD player we can skip, fast forward, rewind, etc.). Yet film differs from plays or music, which rarely acknowledge their made-ness in their performance itself.

This combination of features means two things for films: they have to overcome the challenge of leading their audience from the acknowledgement of their extrafictional aspect into a storyworld in limited time; but they also have the chance to do this in a very precise way, because their temporal progression is fixed, and the audience is bound to this progression – 'the relationship of cinema to the spectator is authoritarian', at least in this respect, as Saul Bass once said (Bass 1993: 412; my translation).

That temporal structure is crucial for film title sequences. In film scholarship, they have been discussed as 'paratexts', a term introduced by Genette, albeit for books. Genette differentiates paratexts into 'peritexts' and 'epitexts' (1997: 1–15). The former are physically linked to the main text – title, author and publisher information, dedication, epigraph, annotations, etc. – while the latter reference the text, but are located elsewhere – author interviews, reviews, advertising, etc. The distinction can easily be extrapolated to film, with company logos, film title, credits, etc., falling under the former and trailers, makings-of, reviews, etc. under the latter heading.

More problematic is the distinction between text and peritext. What is realized in books as a spatial distinction can be more complex in the multichannel medium of film. While title sequences *can* be self-enclosed, more often they layer peritextual elements (e.g. lettering of title and credits) and textual elements (theme music, images, sounds or dialogue introducing the diegesis), in Hollywood films especially since the 1950s. There is still a separation: we do not assume the letters of a title superimposed on an establishing shot to float somewhere in diegetic space (though some films play with locating title or credit typography in the diegesis; see Allison 2006). The spatial separation on different pages of a book is realized here as the conceptual separation of levels of narration. But, more importantly, such layering tends to be part of a process that leads into the fiction, and it is this process and the often unanswerable question where the peritext ends and the text begins that makes 'paratext' a label applicable to film only cautiously.[10]

The transitional nature of title sequences is not just an induction into a narrative, but also into a frame of mind: 'a film's beginning must lure the audience, i.e. it must prompt the necessary attention and suspense, it must plant important information, but also set the tone and atmosphere that prepares for the film to come' (Elsaesser and Hagener 2010: 42).[11] In that sense, a title sequence can be understood as an illocutionary act, an 'invitation, persuasion, permission, or even command [...] to engage in imagining' (Biancorosso 2001: § 5), to be attuned to the fiction and the way it requires its audience to work mentally if the fiction is to

---

10 André Gardies, on the other hand, stresses the difference between the title/credit sequence and its acknowledgement of 'the film as a product' and the actual film text: 'the title sequence is fully part of the film, but not of the text' (Gardies 2006: 21; my translation).

11 Deborah Allison describes theme songs in Hollywood westerns whose lyrics pre-empt the stories, modelled on the traditions of ballads or 'story songs' (see Allison 2001: 160–87). Beyond induction, title sequences 'serve a whole array of functions: copyright law, economics, certification of employment in the context of careers, movie title, entertainment, commercials, fashion, and art' (Stanitzek 2009: 46).

work.[12] Giorgio Biancorosso has described the ritualistic aspect of this, and the role of music for the ritual (Biancorosso 2001: § 3–7).

For many decades, the market dominance and oligopolistic structure of Hollywood have intensified the ritualistic effect by repetition. The first part of title sequences are usually the logos of production amd distribution companies, many of them accompanied by music that returns in film after film. The best-known examples – Alfred Newman's 20th Century Fox fanfare, or, with a twist on sonic branding, MGM's roaring lion – eventually become more than a sonic calling card, become part of the ritual of cinema, preparing us for the willing suspension of our disbelief. With regard to this function of delimiting a space for the fiction by pointing out its made-ness, company logos are the clearest case of film music that is not just nondiegetic, but extrafictional.[13]

The other main contender for extrafictional music is that for end credits, especially if it is particular to them and not just an overspill from music previously used in the film (which we might hear less as referring to the credits, but as a sonic after-image of the story it was involved in narrating). But even a song played over the end credits that had not been used before in the film we may perceive less strongly as extrafictional than a musical company logo. The end-credit song is film-specific, while the logo is generic, repeated, and thereby indicates that this film is just one in a string of similar products.[14]

While the ritualistic aspect of company logos may be part of the remit of a title sequence as an 'invitation […] to engage in imagining', their invocation of extrafictional entities could distract from the task of guiding the viewer into the fiction.[15] The often peculiar formal solutions films have found for their opening credits can be seen as the result of a multiplicity

---

12 Georg Stanitzek describes the role of title sequences more pragmatically as a mediator between distracted and focused states of the viewer's mind: 'The curtain closes, the curtain opens again – finally, the title sequence; or, if you like, *initially,* the title sequence. "The movie has begun." "Oh come on, it's only the titles ..." – who hasn't heard this little argument among seat neighbors? It isn't worth being dogmatic, insisting on coming to a decision. Like popcorn containers and just-continuing-the-conversation-for-a-moment, it is simply part of the situation. And it is important here insofar as the title sequence presupposes and accommodates exactly this intermediary zone, accepts it and at the same time tries to give the movie a chance. The title sequence does not necessarily compel you to pay attention. However, it focuses on the situation of distractedness and diverging expectations, namely, in providing a focus that allows for a transition into the movie' (Stanitzek 2009: 44).

13 Company logos seem to point so strongly to something external to the film that scholarship can be tempted to ignore them. In his study of film title sequences, Florian Hausberger defines logos and pre-title sequences as not belonging to the title sequence (Hausberger 2006: 4). What makes sense for pre-title sequences is problematic for logos, which are often integrated with other elements of the title sequence (examples discussed below are *None But the Lonely Heart, The Holiday* and *The Blair Witch Project*).

14 Beyond brief examples in Buhler, Neumeyer and Deemer (2010: 177–80), end-credit music has so far escaped the attention of film musicology.

15 One way of dealing with the fact that credits acknowledge the made-ness of a film is to turn that acknowledgement into an attraction; see, for example, pp. 40–41 on *The Court Jester.*

of functions such sequences have to fulfil, functions that often clash, but in their clash open up space for formal experimentation:

> In its dysfunctionality, the economic/legal title sequence function assures the maintenance of a functional *space,* which the other functions [...] can slip into and, especially, which opens up room for aesthetic variations, play room, in which title sequences can develop a culture of their own. Title sequences attempt inventive solutions: to forge coherence among obstinate conglomerations of functions and requirements. The reconciliation of these heterogeneous functions poses an ever-to-be-repeated artistic challenge. (Stanitzek 2009: 49–50)

The space of relative formal freedom also allows different ways to effect the transition into the fictional world. Many films simply layer extra- and intrafictional visual elements: credit typography over images that begin to establish the storyworld. The layering of different musical elements is more problematic because it is more confusing – we are better at spatially differentiating visual than auditive information. So the musical side of things usually proceeds more orderly: discrete musical units which can be classed as extrafictional (i.e. company logo) or intrafictional (i.e. theme music). A combination of the two is the layering of theme music and purely visual company logos.

The simultaneity of extrafictional credits, nondiegetic theme music and diegetic images in a typical title sequence is in itself an indication of its liminality and transitional function. But other solutions are possible, and even title sequences broadly conforming to this model can play with the form. The following pages discuss a few options. Because so many films smoothly link extrafictional, extradiegetic and diegetic levels in their title sequences, the discussion is not restricted to music and extrafictionality, but encompasses the whole journey – theoretically impure, but reflective of the medium.

The variety of solutions to the transitional task is almost limitless, and the following selection is in not meant as a systematic survey (which might be an interesting project for a separate study), nor one of aesthetically outstanding examples, but to point out some of the subtleties involved in luring the audience into a fiction. To view them in purely functional terms, though, would fail to do justice to the fact that the title sequence perhaps more than any other part of a film is the locus to display filmic 'showmanship' (Allison 2006) or 'epideixis' (Stanitzek 2009: 50); an inventiveness not as yet shackled by the requirements of a coherent unfolding of story and narration that take over later.[16]

---

16 Deborah Allison points out that songs were common in title sequences very early in sound film history, whereas they really only enter the main body of films in the 1960s (musicals excepted), and speculates that songs may have a disruptive effect because they can be read as the mark of 'overt narration': 'The title sequence, on the other hand, cannot but be read as an instance of marked narration, of direct address to the audience. Thus a song at this point simply contributes one more layer of direct discourse to those that exist already' (Allison 2001: 100).

Example 1: *Star Wars – Episode IV: A New Hope*

Liminality is inherent in title sequences, and transitionality is normally inscribed in their structure. But sometimes the transitional quality can be brought out in telling ways. An example is the opening of the original *Star Wars* film (1977). Even more characteristic for contemporary film consumption is the opening as realized on the DVD of the amended version of the film as *Star Wars – Episode IV: A New Hope* (2004). The path from starting the DVD to the film begins with a visually and sonically (though not musically) updated version of the 20th Century Fox company logo and Alfred Newman's fanfare. The DVD sets a secondary extrafictional level above that of the film, and the 'iconic' fanfare proclaims both the idea of watching a DVD as a 'home cinema' experience and the vertical integration of the film industry, which now derives a substantial part of its income from DVDs and merchandising. The film itself begins with the same fanfare, though in the version used for its release in 1977. In the difference between the versions, the DVD also proclaims that time has passed and that the film is a classic worthy of rerelease (and could be understood to allude to the fact that the DVD version contains updated special effects). And then the fiction starts, invoking the golden age of Hollywood adventure movies with its scrolling text and John Williams' *Star Wars* theme – yet another fanfare in the style of Newman's musical logo (and in the same key, emphasizing the similarity). The extrafictional frame(s) around the film and its narration use the same musical language; the entertainment industry projects its image in the heroic terms of its product. The transition from extrafictional space into the fiction is paradoxically realized as a parallelism that washes over the boundary between them:

> Today, the roar of MGM's lion reveals the secret of all motion-picture music: a feeling of triumph that the motion picture and motion-picture music have become a reality. The music sets the tone of the enthusiasm the picture is supposed to whip up in the audience. Its basic form is the fanfare, and the ritual of musical 'titles' shows this unmistakably. Its action is advertising, and nothing else. (Adorno and Eisler 1994: 60)

But the embarrassment of fanfares leading into *Star Wars – Episode IV: A New Hope* also attests to the enduring popularity of the hope the film was made to fulfil: that it would be possible, well after the end of the studio system and the emergence of New Hollywood, to make a 1930s Errol Flynn pirate movie pastiche not in the spirit of parody, but of homage, and to lead a modern audience back to the pleasures of the golden age.

Example 2: RKO during World War II

A case of a more conscious, both playful and historically charged musical link between extrafictional and fictional space occurred in the title sequences of RKO films in World

War II. The visual logo had been used since 1929: a spinning globe with a radio transmitter on top, with letters spelling out 'A Radio Picture' (until 1936) or 'An RKO Radio Picture' (1936–56) (Figure 2), and Morse code on the soundtrack.

The Morse code spelled out 'vvvv An RKO Radio Picture vvvv', the v's being a radiotelegraphy sign for a test transmission to which no reply is expected. But during World War II, the v's could be understood to stand for 'Victory', and the Morse code for a 'v' is three dots and a dash: short-short-short-long, the rhythm of the opening of Beethoven's Fifth Symphony, used during the war by the BBC to open its news broadcasts precisely because it could be understood to Morse-spell the victory-V. So RKO introduced the Beethoven motif into its title sequences, and composers segued from Beethoven into their theme music.

What emerged was a transition in three stages: from the non-musical (or not-quite-musical) Morse code via Beethoven (through the BBC association to some extent de-musicalized) to theme music leading into the film. On another level, though, the structure strongly pointed to the extrafictional sphere, which was represented not just by the RKO logo, but also by the Beethovenian reference to the BBC and the war – the films pointed out, even if only for a second, that they were part of the war effort.

Individual variants of the pattern could have their own (conscious or accidental) subtexts. In *None But the Lonely Heart* (1944) the lettering still spells out the full 'An RKO Radio Picture', but the Morse code is reduced to 'vvvv', which conventionally leads into the Beethoven quote, which in turn is taken up by the opening motif of Hanns Eisler's theme music. Beyond the standard BBC/victory link, the idea of Beethoven as a revolutionary

Figure 2: RKO Company logo (here from *None But the Lonely Heart* [1944]).

composer in revolutionary times was fitting for the social critique of *None But the Lonely Heart*, but it was an allusion ironically derived from the musical signet of a company that was part of the culture industry Eisler and Adorno were dissecting at the same time in their work for *Composing for the Films* (1994). In the light of this, it may make sense that the Morse code spelling out the company name is omitted and only the call to attention is left, which in conjunction with the Beethoven quotation and the film's story becomes a call to arms on behalf of the downtrodden.

Example 3: *The Holiday (& Love Actually)*

A more complex example of a title sequence playing with our expectations of orderliness occurs in *The Holiday* (2006). The film is a standard-issue romantic comedy involving mis- and rematched couples, and the culture clash between England and the USA. Typical for recent romcoms, it is very self-conscious, and the title sequence shows that off as if it wanted to establish the rules of the genre game right from the start.[17]

The film opens with the Universal and Columbia logos, accompanied by an appropriately romantic theme in strings and *colla parte* piano, after a few seconds overlaid by the sound of chirping birds – seemingly a classic case of layering extrafictional acknowledgment and music we assume to be a nondiegetic layer of the fiction (Figure 3). Seventeen seconds into the film, the image changes to blurred foliage, visually justifying the bird sounds, with the company names superimposed, which are replaced by a kissing couple, soon overlaid by the name of production company Waverly (Figure 4).

Up to this point, there is nothing unusual in the title sequence: companies involved in the film are presented, layered first with music we assume to be part of the narration of the film, and then with images introducing its diegesis. Also typical is that the music serves as glue for the more heterogeneous visual elements. But our assumptions fall apart when the camera zooms out and a line of numbers and text appears below the image, before the zoom shows us the entire set-up (Figure 5).

We are in the home studio of film composer Miles (Jack Black), who is scoring the film involving the kissing couple, and the nondiegetic music of that film turns out to be also diegetic music of the film we see, played by Miles on his keyboard. What we took to be the diegesis of *The Holiday* (i.e. the kissing couple) turns out to be an embedded diegesis, and what we took to be nondiegetic music on the level of *The Holiday* turns out to be diegetic on that embedded level. But it is not simply a case of embedding a narrative layer; there is fuzziness too. The company logos appear separately, before the first images of the couple, then the company names reappear superimposed onto the pastoral scene. Universal and Columbia were distribution/production companies of *The Holiday*, but

---

17 My focus is on the first 40 seconds of the roughly three-and-a-half minutes of the title sequence, but the playing with our expectations continues. For a closer look, see Fletcher 2008: 135–41.

Figure 3: Company logos at the start of *The Holiday* (2006).

Figure 4: Company names and the kissing couple in *The Holiday*.

Figure 5: The embedded diegesis revealed at the start of *The Holiday*.

their double presentation leaves open whether we are meant to relate them to *The Holiday*, or to the embedded film, or to both. Waverly Films, too, was involved in the making of *The Holiday*, but is presented in a way that suggests it is part of the title sequence of the film about the kissing couple. We seem to see and hear the title sequence of *The Holiday* and the title sequence of the film scored by Miles within the diegesis of *The Holiday* at the same time; the extrafictional origin of *The Holiday* and the fiction it contains seem to have collapsed into one. The same applies to the music: *The Holiday* reveals it as part of its diegesis, but when that happens we have already taken it to be nondiegetic theme music, and the continuation of the title sequence reinforces its double role (more in Fletcher 2008).[18] Music in title sequences often knits together disparate elements, but here it has the additional task of binding together multiplying levels of narration.

The film about the kissing couple plays no further role in *The Holiday*; it is just an opening flourish in the relatively 'safe' space of the title sequence, as yet unencumbered by narrative necessity. But the flourish proclaims the genre affiliation of the film. It is typical for the self-conscious use of music in some newer romantic comedies (and typical for the often self-conscious title sequences of comedies more generally[19]), revealing the musical tricks of the film trade right at the start of a film that will use them itself. In this, it foregrounds the 'double intentionality' of our understanding of film (see ch. I.iii, point 5). That happens more readily in genre cinema, because it is about unwritten rules and what films can do within, but also with them.

The title sequence of *Love Actually* (2003) shows a variant of that self-consciousness (see Heldt 2012). The film begins with the cheesy voice-over of the film's nameless British Prime Minister (Hugh Grant), giving out the message that 'love, actually, is all around us'. Quickly, the film lets the air out of the pathos. We see and hear ageing rock star Billy Mack (Bill Nighy) record the vocals for his latest song, the supremely silly 'Christmas Is All Around'. Embarrassed, he asks 'This is shit, isn't it?', and his manager (Gregor Fisher) answers, 'Yep, solid-gold shit, maestro', admitting that the recording is about money, not art. But the music continues unperturbed and develops into the instrumental underscore for the seven-minute opening sequence of *Love Actually*, which introduces all of its major characters. The shameless commercialism of the fictitious Christmas hit underscores the

---

18 A much more transparent musical plunge into the diegesis is used in *The Conversation* (1974) to introduce the film's theme of auditory surveillance. The establishing shots of a city square are accompanied by a rendition of 'Bill Bailey Won't You Please Come Home' that is eventually shown to be performed in the square. But the low volume and added reverb have told us from the start that this is very unlikely to be nondiegetic theme music. The film toys with positioning the music where we would expect theme music, but also lets us know about the substitution.

19 Deborah Allison uses unstable boundaries between levels of narration in such title sequences to qualify the idea of a classical Hollywood style following the rule that 'diegetic space should be internally coherent and that filmic technique should not conspicuously impinge upon it': 'These sequences raise questions about such ways of understanding the construction and pleasures of Hollywood cinema. Are title sequences an entirely different medium from the films they introduce, or does their failure to conceal their artifice and their frequent promotion of non-narrative pleasures represent an intensification of a more widespread mode of film practice in which a narrative structure and apparently seamless diegetic construct exist merely as an organizational principle in which other pleasures are contained?' (Allison 2006). Allison is interested in visuals, particularly in sequences that introduce credit text into the diegesis, but it would not be difficult to complement her observations with musical ones. In his study of paratexts in film, Alexander Böhnke makes the same point (2007a: 17–23).

shameless commercialism of a film released five weeks before Christmas, at the same time of the year when its story starts (as superimposed text informs us, driving home the point): postmodern auto-irony at its crassest.

The self-referentiality goes further: In *Love Actually*, 'Christmas Is All Around' is supposed to be based on Billy Mack's earlier hit 'Love Is All Around'. In the real world, 'Love Is All Around' (written by Reg Presley and first performed by The Troggs in 1967) was covered by Wet Wet Wet and used for the end credits of *Four Weddings and a Funeral* (1994), scripted by Richard Curtis, the director and scriptwriter of *Love Actually* – art and life collapse into one, across levels of narration and films, and the entertainment industry uses the exposure of its mechanisms as yet another source of entertainment.

Example 4: *Eyes Wide Shut (& The Blair Witch Project, The Truman Show* and *Bridget Jones's Diary)*

The Holiday takes a shortcut from extrafictional space into the diegesis by having music that turns out to be part of that diegesis masquerade as (nondiegetic) theme music – a relatively frequent twist in title sequences, because it leaves start and end points unaffected, and projects the narration as a strongly guiding one. Such sequences 'cut out' a standard element of extradiegetic narration (the theme music), or rather fulfil its formal function by 'borrowing' music from the diegesis. (A more disruptive version of this intrusion of the diegesis is exemplified by the title sequences of *The Court Jester* [1955] and *Will Success Spoil Rock Hunter?* [1957], which is discussed in ch. II.iii. The difference is that in these films, the diegesis invades not just the extradiegetic, but the extrafictional level, foregrounding fictionality in a manner typical for the transgressiveness of comedy.)

What is funny and playful in *The Holiday* can serve other purposes as well: *Eyes Wide Shut* (1999) begins, after the soundless Warner logo, with basic company, star and director credits over the second waltz from Dmitri Shostakovich's 'Jazz Suite'.[20] The music continues across cuts on the image track: from the black credit background to a shot of Alice Harford (Nicole Kidman) undressing, to the title of the film, to an external shot of an apartment building (which we assume contains the Harfords' flat) and back into the flat, where the Harfords are preparing to go out.

So far, so normal. The music binds together credits and shots of different diegetic spaces and thereby contributes to the transition into the fiction. Slightly unusual is only the use of pre-existing music, to which in most cases we would impute particular narrative purpose. But by the time of *Eyes Wide Shut*, Kubrick had been famous for using pre-existing music for three decades, so that any spectator with basic Kubrick knowledge would take this for

---

20 The opening is discussed from the slightly different angle of authorial (or indeed auteur-ial) control in Gorbman 2006: 7–9.

another example of the director's customary technique. The music continues to underscore the Harfords' preparations, but when they are about to leave, Bill Harford (Tom Cruise) goes to the CD player and switches the music off.

Reveals of the diegetic origin of music we at first assume to be nondiegetic are a common comedy effect in film, but usually the music revealed to originate in the diegesis does not really belong there – e.g. the Count Basie Orchestra in the middle of the desert in Mel Brooks' *Blazing Saddles* (1974). *Eyes Wide Shut* is different. The music is anything but implausible, is indeed just what an urbane, educated, ever so slightly superficial couple like the Harfords might have in their CD player. When the music is switched off and thereby stands revealed as diegetic, we have to reassess: it is not just another case of Kubrick's preference for pre-existing music in his films, but pre-existing music plausibly integrated into the film's diegesis.

The music is different things at the same time. It is typical for Kubrick in being pre-existing, but untypical in that its use is 'explained' by the diegesis. It functions conventionally as a theme music framework for different strands of the title sequence, but unconventionally it is not unambiguously nondiegetic, but quickly withdraws into the diegesis. It contributes to the transition from credits to fiction, but does so through the shock effect of the diegetic reveal. (It also is music by a composer working in the Soviet Union, but taking his cue from the light music of the capitalist West.) In its multifaceted ambiguity, it aptly announces a film about false impressions and assumptions, about tricks being played on people, about surfaces and what lies behind them. It is a good example for 'the title sequence as paradigmatic anticipation of the cinematic syntagm to follow', and more specifically of the condensation of such anticipation into a 'single metaphor' observable since the mid-1950s (see Stanitzek 2009: 53–54), but it is unusual for using music to create that metaphor – though it makes sense that it is used in this way by a director as musically aware as Kubrick.

The film stabilizes the effect of its precipitate descent into the diegesis by not using any manifestly nondiegetic music for the first 20 minutes. At the Christmas party the Harfords attend, we only hear implicitly diegetic music, and the status of Chris Isaak's 'Baby Did a Bad, Bad Thing' when they are back in their bedroom, naked, kissing and touching, is ambiguous. It could be music in the room, a choice fitting the situation; but it could also be understood as a narrative comment on Alice's flirting at the party, and a premonition of her affair. When the film uses the first clearly nondiegetic music, it does so with another volte-face: it is the waltz from the 'Jazz Suite' again, but now as nondiegetic music accompanying Bill Harford's coming into work the following day.

Particular narrative structures can engender yet shorter shortcuts. An extreme example is *The Blair Witch Project* (1999), which allows *no* space outside the fiction of its own authenticity. The film begins with company credits for Artisan and Haxan Films, immediately followed by the title and text informing us of the disappearance of three student film-makers and the discovery of their footage. Since there are no cast or crew credits, the implication is that what we are about to see *is* that footage, and it is at least possible to understand the company credits as being inside the fiction as well, as the companies responsible for bringing the footage to us.

That there is no music reinforces the implication of authenticity: since we are supposed to see found footage and not a finished film, where would the music come from? In the light of this, it makes sense that the end credits *do* use music, because here the real-world origin of the film is admitted unequivocally. A similar strategy is used in *The Truman Show* (1998), though even more blatantly, because the film seems to start with a normal title sequence which quickly turns out to be that of the TV series at the centre of its story (more about that in ch. V.ii).

The Truman Show, and to a lesser extent *The Blair Witch Project*, fulfil our basic expectations of a title sequence, but on a deeper level undermine them and only deliver pseudo-title sequences. In *The Blair Witch Project*, that is part of the game, of the pretence of authenticity. In *The Truman Show*, the yawning gap left when we realize that we are not seeing the title sequence for the film *The Truman Show*, but only those for the TV series *The Truman Show* within the diegesis of the film, fits its project of playing with our media awareness. Another means of toying with our expectation of a proper and paced induction into the film are pre-credit sequences: the most extreme way of plunging the audience directly into the narrative. But such films (e.g. the James Bond or Indiana Jones franchises) have to make up for it later; in James Bond with especially elaborate title sequences, to reassure the audience that all is well with this film.

Though taking metaleptic shortcuts into the diegesis, the title sequences of *The Holiday*, *Eyes Wide Shut* or *The Truman Show* still conform – at least on the surface – to the template of music as a frame for disparate filmic elements (company logos, title, credits, nondiegetic or diegetic images; extrafictional, nondiegetic or diegetic music); just one of many examples of music in film as structural glue. This unifying role of music against the dissociative tendency of other elements is so typical for title sequences that disassociation can be introduced artificially, as a mark of a 'proper' title sequence. *Bridget Jones's Diary* (2001) provides a fleeting example (see Heldt 2012). We are introduced to Bridget Jones (Renée Zellweger) in a pre-credit sequence set at her mother's annual Christmas turkey-curry buffet. After the failure of her mother's (Gemma Jones) plan to get her together with eligible bachelor Mark Darcy (Colin Firth), Bridget contemplates her future as a lonely spinster, before dying alone and being 'eaten by Alsatians'. This is the cue for the title and opening credits of the film, but the relationship between music and images is subtly surprising.

We see Bridget on her sofa, watching an episode of TV series *Frasier* with the sound switched off and listening to Jamie O'Neal sing 'All by Myself'. But then, in a move pre-empting her decision to take control of her life (another title sequence presenting a metaphor for the film's trajectory), she gets up and starts to mime to the song, using a rolled-up journal alternately as microphone and drumstick. The music does what a unifying element needs to do and runs through the scene uninterrupted. It would have been easy to match Bridget's miming to the music, but that is not what happens. Twice, the image track shows fade-outs/fade-ins of Bridget (she gets up from the sofa, and she briefly leaves the frame and returns); in both cases the images imply a brief temporal gap between fade-out and fade-in. We understand both images and music as diegetic, but their respective timelines do not quite match – and crucially, do not match because the film has introduced a mismatch that seems to fulfil no other purpose than to artificially dissociate image and soundtracks; we are, after all, in a title sequence, where things do not yet quite hang together, and if they do, they have to be made not to. That is important in a film whose title sequence follows an introductory scene that is not a relatively separate entity (like the pre-credit mini-films in James Bond movies), but simply the first part of the story. With the credits unobtrusively sliding into the film, the film uses its little play with narrative structure as a marker for a title sequence.

Example 5: *Breakfast at Tiffany's*

While music that is part of a company logo is clearly extrafictional, it is less clear whether the theme music of a film can be categorized as wholly intrafictional, because it occurs at a point at which the fiction is only beginning to establish itself, and because in many title sequences it underscores credits that refer to the extrafictional world. The grand manner of much movie theme music, its 'tone of […] enthusiasm' (Adorno and Eisler 1994: 60), could lead one to hear such music less as narratively functional and more as 'advertising', a proclamation of the spectacle to follow.

At the other end of title sequences, music often stresses their transitional nature. The theme music of many (especially classic Hollywood) films leads harmonically and/or motivically into the music underscoring the following scene, acknowledging that the borders of the fiction are rarely hard and fast, and that their fuzziness helps to induct the audience into the right frame of mind.

Breakfast at Tiffany's (1961) provides an example, but also an example of a title sequence that seems to try to underplay the acknowledgement of extrafictionality, or rather, to integrate it into the unfolding of the storyworld[21], both through music and through the interaction of credits and images.

The film begins with around five seconds of the Paramount logo, already set to the accompaniment of the theme song, 'Moon River', which after a fade to black continues into the first shot, showing us the empty street in front of Tiffany's, a taxi with Holly Golightly (Audrey Hepburn) approaching. The acknowledgement of Paramount is kept to a minimum, and our attention is immediately taken over by the music, which leads into the shot establishing the storyworld. The music envelopes the entire title sequence, overwhelming any distinctions between levels of narration.

The suppression of extrafictional elements is reinforced when the melody of 'Moon River' starts on a harmonica, without a title or credits appearing: the images establishing the diegesis and the music establishing the narration are on their own. The first lettering we

---

21 In this, *Breakfast at Tiffany's* is not untypical for its time. Will Straw points out that '[m]ore and more, by the 1960s, theme music specific to a film will replace studio fanfares over a studio logo, for example, or animated elements which are part of a film's specific presentation of information about itself will come to interact with studio logos' (Straw 1999: 216).

Detail from the screenshot on the left

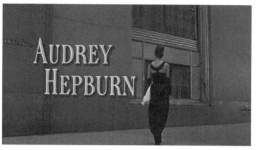

Figure 6: Introducing Tiffany's and the heroine in *Breakfast at Tiffany's* (1961).

see is diegetic too: when Holly alights from the taxi (at around 28 seconds), we see 'Tiffany & Co.', fairly small, next to the door; then (around 36 seconds in) we see the big sign above the door when Holly looks up. Only after this does the first credit appears: 'Audrey Hepbun', while we see Holly Golightly from the back, walking towards the shop window – the credits are just confirming what we see (Figure 6).[22]

After the name 'Tiffany's', the second part of the title, the 'Breakfast', is diegetically prepared when we see Holly take a croissant and coffee-to-go out of her paper bag; only then (around the one-minute mark) does the lettering 'Breakfast at Tiffany's' appear on the screen (Figure 7).

The title only appears after both Tiffany's and the breakfast have been introduced, and when the repeat of 'Moon River', now with strings instead of the humble harmonica, has begun. The music bows to the tradition of musical grandeur for the film title, but only after it has established a more intimate tone first.[23]

---

22 The name of male co-star George Peppard is the only credit for more than the first minute of film that is not just a reinforcement of something we are seeing before us.

23 One could see the pre-empting of title and star in the diegesis as a more subtle variant of the inscription of credits onto ostensibly diegetic objects (see Allison 2006). If Allison's examples 'diegeticize' the extrafictional presentation, other films 'narrativize' the diegesis by having characters address the audience at the beginning of a film (see Hartmann 2003: 19–38).

Figure 7: The breakfast in *Breakfast at Tiffany's*.

At the end of the credits, on the penultimate chord of 'Moon River', the image cuts to a shot of Holly's street, and the last two notes are sequenced upwards to form the underscore for the first proper plot event: Holly running across the street and entering her apartment block to evade the man waiting in a car in front of the house. Memorable as this title sequence is, it leads into the storyworld both quickly (by slotting the credits into the unfolding of the diegesis) and smoothly by gliding out of the title sequence into the beginning of the plot proper. *Breakfast at Tiffany's* is a radical example of a title sequence that from its beginning is integral to the film. Other title sequences are much more self-enclosed, not so much leading into the narrative as setting the scene for it. But in their transitional nature, many title sequences are at least as much text as paratext.

*

Title sequences are not the only point at which the real world enters a film, and one major avenue of real-world intrusion shows a methodological limitation of narratology. Like other primarily ahistorical theories, it tends to isolate film from its moorings in the empirical world and to transform it into a 'text' (etymologically a 'weave'), an abstract formation of elements of a symbolic code, in order to enable analysis of the rules and routines organizing that particular formation. Such abstraction may be necessary for a focused look at film from one perspective, but it closes off others – such as the fact that films are not just *made* by real people, but that the reality of their making leaves traces in the text, and that the audience is aware of many of them, even if they do not occur in as overt a form as credits.

The most obvious example are well-known actors. If we recognize an actor, what we know of him and his previous roles will impinge on our consciousness, and the nature of the role as a temporary mask becomes more noticeable: the made-ness of the fiction moves further into the foreground, and the willing suspension of disbelief becomes a bit more difficult: 'Due to the star's iconic status, he or she can be grafted only tangentially onto a fictional persona' (Mulvey 2006: 173). On the other hand, the roles typical for a star can cue our understanding of a story (who the good and the bad guys or gals are, who may or may not survive, etc.), and film studios work on the fusion of public star personae and roles (see Böhnke 2007: 101).

A variant of this is the presence of famous musicians. Zofia Lissa has pointed out that in *My Song for You* (1934), with famous tenor Jan Kiepura playing famous tenor Riccardo Gatti, the viewer can focus either 'on the singing of the depicted hero or on the reproduction of the singing of Kiepura', and that in such cases 'only for a very naïve audience [...] the film world prevails over the reproduction. Most viewers fluctuate between the two perspectives of perception, depending on the degree to which they are interested in either the story or the musical performance' (Lissa 1965: 167; my translation). Other films import reality without even that minimal fictional gloss. *Carnegie Hall* (1947), for example, parades a host of classical musicians appearing as themselves: conductors such as Bruno Walter, Fritz Reiner or Leopold Stokowski, instrumentalists such as Gregor Piatigorsky or Jascha Heifetz, singers such as Lily Pons or Jan Peerce. They are attractions in themselves, but they are also 'reality props' for the fictional story, vouching for its credibility.

While the real-life presence of people may be the most obvious example for the intrusion of extrafictional reality into a fiction – because we are biologically geared to the recognition of faces and voices – the same applies, in principle, to other kinds of recognition: that of the style of a particular director or composer, for example. The contemporary pop songs and instrumentals for part of the nondiegetic music of Sofia Coppola's *Marie Antoinette* (2006) accentuate the difference between the heroine and the routines of the French court she finds herself thrown into, but it is also a reminder of the musical style of two previous films directed by Sofia Coppola, *The Virgin Suicides* (1999) and *Lost in Translation* (2003). What stands out against the genre norms of music for a costume drama contributes to the formation of a norm on the level of this particular histocial author.[24]

Even if intertextual references do not become strategic on a textual level, they may be part of someone's self-marketing, and even if personal style is not consciously foregrounded, intertextuality may be hard to avoid because creative work often has a personal signature. However perfect a score may be integrated into film, and however well it may serve its purpose, it also drags the real world of its creation into the film.

iii. Extrafictional narration and audience address

What Edward Branigan calls 'extrafictional narration' (1992: 88–90) does not become overt in film very often, but when it does, music can add to the way the narration addresses its fiction and extra- and intrafictional 'space' relate to each other.

---

24 It is not just nondiegetic music, though. When, at the mid-point of the film, Marie Antoinette is trying on shoes, we see a pair of modern plimsolls among the period footwear: pop modernity breaking through the historical cocoon she is stuck in. Shortly after this scene, Marie Antoinette and her friends escape from Versailles to attend a masked ball in Paris, and the historical fissure widens: contemporary pop music (Siouxsie and the Banshee's 'Hong Kong Garden'; implicitly also Bow Wow Wow's 'Aphrodisiac') is shown to be music at the party. The breakthrough does not last; with her and Louis' coronation a few film minutes later, she is dragged back into her courtly life and role.

Extrafictional narration issues from a point we understand as being outside the fiction, but is *about* that fiction, and often about the way in which it is fictional. Foregrounded extrafictional narration occurs most often as audience address, usually near a title sequence. (A less overt aspect of extrafictionality is described by the concept of the implied author and is discussed in ch. II.iv.d.)

Occasionally, an extrafictional level is inserted into a film by on-screen characters we are cued not to construe as part of the primary diegesis. In *Head-On/Gegen die Wand* (2004), for example, the story is interspersed with scenes showing clarinettist Selim Sesler and his orchestra and actress and singer Idil Üner perform Turkish folk music by the Bosphorus. One could describe this music as 'non-diegetic and visualized' (Merlin 2010: 73; my translation): we do not understand the interludes as part of the main story.[25] They do not interact with that story, but rather comment on it, and remind the audience of the problematic ties the fictional protagonists, Turks living in Hamburg, have with Turkey. The effect is paradoxical: we can understand the interludes as comments on the fiction, underlining its fictionality by stepping out of it. On the other hand, our awareness of the reality of the musicians and the meaningful connection between music and story insists on the real-world relevance of the story – stories like this might really happen. Seen from that angle, the categorization of the music as nondiegetic is problematic. The film makes us aware of the fact that the musicians sing and play in the same world as the characters, even if they are not part of the same story, but rather about it.

Different is the two-man Greek chorus in *There's Something About Mary* (1998), which is also about the film's story, but is placed in the same space as the characters and interacts with them to a limited degree (or indeed to the not-so-limited degree of a chorus musicians being metaleptically shot in an altercation between primary characters).

*

If extrafictional narration appears as an audience address, like title sequences it can be kept separate from the fiction or lead into it. Of the examples discussed below, three are from title sequences, while the last one is from a trailer using the same format.

An audience address issuing from outside the fiction necessarily draws attention to the borderline between that outside and the fiction, and to the fictionality of the latter. One reason for using such overt narration can be a particular claim about the relationship of story and reality (e.g. a truth claim); another reason can be comedic self-consciousness.

Since title sequences inevitably reference the extrafictional by pointing out the made-ness of a film, one strategy of dealing with this residue to be left behind is to take the bull by the horns and turn the admission of fictionality into an attraction. *The Court Jester* (1955) does

---

25 James Buhler, David Neumeyer and Rob Deemer use the concept of 'nondiegetic-onscreen' music in a different sense, for scenes in which 'an onscreen character imagines or remembers speech or music and the performance of that music is visualized' (Buhler, Neumeyer and Deemer 2009: 72). Such a case I would understand as internal focalization (or metadiegetic narration) (see ch. II.v.).

Figure 8: Opening credits of *The Court Jester* (1955).

that in a form typical for what Steve Seidman has called 'comedian comedy' (Seidman 1981). After the company credits the title sequence shows the eponymous jester (Danny Kaye) introduce the film and its (mock-)medieval setting in the song 'Life Could Not Better Be', while increasingly interacting with the credits by moving letters around, conjuring up credits, etc. (Figure 8).

The song addresses the clichés of a 'medieval spree', i.e. of the kind of film we are about to see: there are 'knights full of chivalry, villains full of villainy' (the latter with the credit for Basil Rathbone), and 'You'll see, as you suspect, maidens fair, in silks bedecked/Each tried-and-true effect for the umpteenth time we resurrect'; Kaye sings about the research that went into the film (and the dust that ensued), and when the song 'brings us to the plot', we learn that 'plot we've got/Quite a lot.'

A key feature of 'comedian comedies', according to Seidman, is their 'highly artificial and transparent nature', their use of 'devices which function [...] to interrupt the smooth exposition of a "real" fictional universe. These devices constitute what I mean by extrafictional features' (Seidman 1981: 3). 'Life Could Not Better Be' shows such features: the focus on the comedian's performance, including the audience address that is part of such performance; the enunciatory stance (in the sense of Christian Metz's or Geoffrey Nowell-Smith's appropriation of Emile Benveniste's concept), acknowledging the act of narration, the enunciator and the audience addressed; and the self-referentiality of cinematic entertainment broaching tropes of cinematic entertainment.

Acknowledgement of the artificiality of film may be not just typical for 'comedian comedies', but more frequent in comedies in general, because here the effect is the end that justifies means that in other films might address the machinery of fiction too openly; in this, comedies are similar to horror films (more in ch. IV; see also Allison 2006).

*

The Court Jester prefigures the playful Hollywood title sequences 'of the late 1950s and early-to-mid 1960s' with their 'proliferation of possible relationships between extradiegetic

Figure 9: Tony Randall and the company logo in *Will Success Spoil Rock Hunter?* (1957).

elements (such as graphics, lettering and music) and diegetic worlds' (Straw 1999: 213). *Will Success Spoil Rock Hunter?* (1957) is similar to *The Court Jester* in one sense, and very different in another. *The Court Jester* uses the closed form of a theme song, frequent in title sequences on both sides of 1960: a mini-film before the film. The audience address even takes hold of individual credits, adding a layer of extrafictionality on which the film not just shows, but comments on its made-ness. The frame for the film's status as an artefact, however – the company credits – remain outside the self-referential curlicue. *Will Success Spoil Rock Hunter?* goes a step further with its extrafictional, but homodiegetic narrator, who is on-screen even for the company logo: before the 20th Century Fox logo we see a tiny Tony Randall (playing the titular Rock Hunter) behind a drum kit, with trumpet and double bass, playing along with the company fanfare while the visual logo enters to his right (Figure 9).

He remains on-screen after the logo has faded, and introduces the film, though rather confusedly, calling up his own credit when describing female co-star Jayne Mansfield, and trying to remember the film's title and coming up with *The Girl Can't Help It* – a Jayne Mansfield film directed by director Frank Tashlin and released half a year earlier, which also opens with its male star, Tom Ewell, introducing the film and his role on-screen. The film never recovers to find to a proper title sequence: Tony/Rock has to be reminded of the title by an apparition of the three female stars (Jayne Mansfield, Joan Blondell and Betsy Drake), and the credits are interspersed with parodies of television ads introducing the film's theme. But there is no continuous music, no theme tune: the musical shock of the beginning seems to have been too great to allow the film to return to title-sequence normality. At the end of the beginning, Tony Randall also guides us into the diegesis, and we hear his voice over establishing shots of Manhattan: 'This is me again – Rockwell R. Hunter. And that's Madison Avenue away down there. That's my street. My street of grey flannel dreams. I'm employed on Madison Avenue in an advertising agency.'

Most title sequences aim for an orderly transition from extrafictional space into the fiction and the diegesis. But comedy likes to play with orderliness and hierarchy, and here it has completely consumed the framework; even the most extraneous extrafictional space of the company logo has been dragged into the narrative game by Tony Randall's usurpation of the 20th Century Fox fanfare.[26] The reference to *The Girl Can't Help It*, too, is not just intertextual, but makes the film industry the subject of its own product: 'No, we've made that', he corrects himself when he realizes that he has given the audience the wrong title, alluding to the serial production of genre films, and even to the fact that *Will Success Spoil Rock Hunter?* out-metaleaps *The Girl Can't Help It*, whose opening at least leaves the 20th Century Fox logo and its music alone.[27]

*

A more straightforward example of extrafictional narration is the opening to the CBS television series *The Twilight Zone* (premiered in 1959). *The Twilight Zone* is an anthology series of self-sufficient stories with different scriptwriters, directors, actors, etc., only connected by being about the uncanny, futuristic or paranormal. The stand-alone quality of the episodes may have suggested itself to stress the anthology aspect of the series by reinforcing the envelope around the disparate material in the opening and closing narrations spoken by Rod Serling, the creator of *The Twilight Zone*. The one for the first ever episode, *Where Is Everybody?*, goes:

> You are travelling through another dimension. A dimension not just of sight and sound, but of mind, a journey into a wondrous land whose boundaries are those of imagination. That's the signpost up ahead – your next stop: The Twilight Zone.

The narration is addressing the audience directly, something that happens in fiction only in relatively rare moments that 'break the fourth wall', i.e. the illusion of a closed diegetic space,

---

26 Unsurprisingly, the idea is taken up in Baz Luhrmann's parodically postmodern *Moulin Rouge!* (2001). Here, even extrafictionality is framed: by a stage curtain that opens onto the 20th Century Fox logo, and by a (mock-)conductor gyrating in front of the screen during the company's fanfare. The curtain opens a second time onto the (flickering and sepia-tinted) credits, accompanied by a potpourri of pre-existing music, ironically starting with 'The Sound of Music' – everything is knowing, refracted, part of the entertainment and its deconstruction at the same time. The overload of framing continues with Henri Toulouse-Lautrec (John Leguizamo), singing David Bowie's 'Nature Boy', to lead us into Paris and the room of Christian (Ewan McGregor), who types lines from the lyrics and then the story the film will tell, to leave no doubt about the cardboard nature everything we see and hear.

27 *The Girl Can't Help It* is playful in other ways. When Tom Ewell mentions 'the grandeur of Cinemascope', he realizes that the screen is too small and moves its edges outwards; when he mentions the 'gorgeous, life-like colour by Deluxe', he sees that the picture is black-and-white and repeats the phrase to switch on the colour. That playfulness extends to the music when Ewell explains that the film is about 'music that expresses the culture, the refinement, and the polite grace of the present day' and his voice is drowned out by a jukebox with Little Richard singing 'The Girl Can't Help It', which continues for the credits.

and acknowledge the existence of an audience (and by implication the fact that the diegesis is an illusion created for that audience). The framing device in *The Twilight Zone* does not surprise us as much as, say, an actor looking into the camera and talking to us, because the introductory narration happens before a diegesis has been established. (For audience addresses from *within* a just established diegesis, see Hartmann 2003). We understand the voice-over as extrafictional – it talks about the fiction as something that we are about to see and that will involve imagination (ours or that of the creators of the fiction?), and it talks to us as addressees of the fiction.[28]

In *The Twilight Zone*, music helps to demarcate the extrafictional narration: Bernard Herrmann's (and from the second season Marius Constant's) theme belongs to the extrafictional frame that introduces the series to us, and consequently (and different from other TV or film theme music), it does not return within the episodes. These have their own scores, stressing the fact that they are separate fictions brought together under the umbrella of an extrafictional audience address.

*

The introduction to *The Twilight Zone* adds a layer of narration between the 'real world' of historical authorship and the fiction, but keeps it cleanly separate. Very differently, the final example creates a smooth transition between extra- and intrafictional space, and music is crucial for papering over the cracks. The example comes from a different kind of paratext, though: the trailer of Alfred Hitchcock's *The Wrong Man* (1956).

Both trailer and film use an audience address by Hitchcock. The trailer uses a longer version over a montage of images that introduce protagonist Manny Balestrero (Henry Fonda), while in the film the audience address itself is shorter, but leads into a longer introduction of Manny. What may justify the replacement of the film opening by the trailer for my purpose is that: (1) both use the same basic structure (Hitchcock's narration, the introduction of Manny and the Stork Club) and the same musical building blocks; and (2) the music in the trailer brings out a tension between its function as 'structural glue' and the definition of levels of narration that is not untypical for filmic paratexts requiring a degree of structural unity.

Edward Branigan uses the opening of *The Wrong Man* to explain extrafictional narration and introduce the concept of the implied author (more in ch. II.iv.d). He also mentions Bernard Herrmann's music, but leaves out the cue accompanying Hitchcock's on-screen appearance and focuses on the music for the Stork Club (Branigan 1992: 96–98). He points out that the same music, continuously playing, can be understood differently with regard to different elements of the sequence: extrafictional in relation to title and credits;

---

28 Opening narrations were common in 1950s and 1960s TV series, especially ones about the futuristic or fantastic, probably to underline their spectacular nature, but perhaps also not to let the audience stumble unprepared into these extraordinary worlds; see, for example *Space Patrol* (1950–55), *Star Trek* (1966–69), or German TV series *Space Patrol: The Phantastical Adventures of the Spaceship Orion/ Raumpatrouille. Die phantastischen Abenteuer des Raumschiffes Orion* (1966).

extradiegetic with regard to a montage of images of dancers in the Stork Club (the music accompanies an image montage with temporal gaps, summarizing an evening of dancing to the soundtrack of a single piece); diegetic with regard to the end of the credits, because the music now matches the images of the band playing. While the third categorization is obvious and the second defensible, the first one is problematic: the coincidence of credits and music does not necessarily mean that we understand that music as extrafictional. Were that the case, one could argue that we understand the images from the Stork Club under the credits as extrafictional as well, which seems implausible. Instead, we experience a transition into the storyworld typical for title sequences. After Hitchcock's address, we get (extrafictional) titles/credits, then images and music introducing the diegesis, albeit in a time-compression montage, and eventually we land in the diegesis, with the music now matching the images.

Branigan does not comment on the transition from Hitchcock's address to the title sequence, and in the film there is nothing remarkable about it (perhaps apart from fact that the musical cues for both follow each other attacca). But the trailer works differently. As the film, it begins with Hitchcock introducing himself and the film:

> [During picture 1] This is Alfred Hitchcock speaking. In the past, I have introduced you to many kinds of people: murderers, thieves, swindlers, many of the geniuses of business of crime. Now I'd like you to meet an entirely different person: [Cuts to picture 2] an average sort of fellow, who leads a very normal life. [Cuts to picture 3] The big difference is that his story is true. [Cuts to picture 4] This is Manny Balestrero, tucked away at the rear of the bandstand of the Stork Club in New York. He lived in a simple, routine world. When the lights went out, the fiddle was put away. [Cuts to picture 5] Then, the same subway, the newspaper, home to Rose and the kids. Yes, Manny's life was straight and narrow – until the night of January the 14th 1953, when… [Cuts to picture 6] {police officer:}'Is your name Christopher Emanuel Balestrero?'

With the 'when', Hitchcock's voice-over is replaced by the intradiegetic voice of one of the police officers stopping Manny, and we have finally arrived inside the storyworld.

If we take the images and voice-over alone, the sequence is straightforward: Hitchcock (or an actor posing as Hitchcock) appears as a backlit figure in a big empty space, casting an ominous shadow, and begins his narration, referring to his past work and promising a different kind of hero, at which point the images jump into the world of that hero. Hitchcock functions as an 'invoking narrator' (Black 1986), whose voice calls up images that show what he tells us – the trailer visualizes a mythic shorthand version of the film-making process itself, in which Hitchcock as director conjures up images for us. But the images carry the burden of Hitchcock's claim that the *The Wrong Man* is different from his previous films because its story is true. The fact that the wizard does not hide behind the curtain any more is meant to lend credibility to the claim, and the mundane nature of the street scene the first diegetic image shows supports it (though a low-key opening is a common strategy of fictional films, not least Hitchcock's).

While Hitchcock is talking about his average hero, the images home in on him, first showing his place of work, the Stork Club, then Manny himself as a bass player in the club's band. We follow him through the end of a shift and the way home, before the mundane part of the story ends when he is stopped by police officers outside the club, and at this point that Hitchcock's voice-over ends, having guided us into the storyworld, which in the trailer continues in a series of short excerpts from the film. (In the film itself, Hitchcock's address is shorter and ends with the first images of the Stork Club.)

It is the music, however, which makes the trailer intriguing, which ties a knot into its orderly progress, and in doing so binds it together (a common function of music in trailers and title sequences). But the music also asks questions about the credibility of the extrafictional stamp of authenticity the film receives in Hitchcock's truth claim. Music is present from the start: when Hitchcock becomes visible, we hear two loud chords played by a small ensemble, including a muted trumpet, followed by descending motives played by a plucked bass and bass clarinet at low volume. When we are introduced to Manny's world (Picture 2 of Figure 10), the music becomes richer, but still holds the tone of quietly ominous suspense music fitting for a Hitchcock opening. Only with the pictures from dancing couples at the club does the music change to a Latin dance number, as if to prove the words of the voice-over ('his story is true') by replacing nondiegetic with 'realistic' diegetic music. The music remains a reflection of what we see for shots of the band at work, and reverts to its ominous thriller tone for Manny on his way home.

Yet despite the change of style the sections are not discrete musical units. The ensemble is the same throughout, and what we hear is, in effect, one long musical cue (with a brief interruption for 'the fiddle was put away') that changes style back and forth in accordance with the images. Hitchcock's narration helps to unify the sequence, but so does the music, and even its details stress continuity. One bass line runs through the sequence, and the stylistic change is introduced merely by a brief accelerando to Manny playing the bass line in the club. The chameleon nature of the music, changing style but not suspending continuity, helps to unify the stages into one smooth transition from extrafictional narration into diegetic space. This may be particularly important in a trailer that combines disparate levels of narration, but still has to appear as a textual unit. But the musical unity plays havoc with the hierarchy of levels of narration:

- Least confusing is the fact that the same music is used for Hitchcock and for images of Manny after work. This is music setting the ominous tone for what we expect to be a thriller, and the images of Manny are invoked by Hitchcock speaking about him, which justifies the recurrence of the music. The return of the music as underscore for Manny on his way home and with his family may make us retrospectively reconstrue it as displaced music for Manny's story from the start, but that is a minor point.
- The musical connection between suspense music and dance music is more surprising. It is as if Manny's band is underscoring from the start the sequence introducing us,

Picture 1: 'This is Alfred Hitchcock speaking.'

Picture 2: '...an average sort of fellow'

Picture 3: 'The big difference is...'

Picture 4: 'This is Manny Balestrero...'

Picture 5: 'Then, the same subway, the Newspaper...'

Picture 6: 'Is your name Christopher Emanuel Balestrero?'

Figure 10: *The Wrong Man* (1956), first part of trailer.

among other things, to this very band, with a convenient change to the music they play in the club for a few shots in the middle of the sequence. Alternatively, we might understand the music as a nondiegetic layer that adapts stylistically to the required function: suspense music for Hitchcock's narration and the images invoked by it; dance music that mirrors the music played in the club when the images call for it.

But however we understand the music, the loop it establishes between diegesis and extrafictional narration also implies a higher level of authorial control, a level on which Hitchcock's on-screen appearance is as much a piece of fiction as the rest. We are, of course, aware of the fact that Hitchcock's truth testimonial is just another narrative trick of the trade. But the music points that out subtly, but clearly enough for those who listen, and in this self-consciousness becomes part of the fun of the trailer.

While not everyone in the cinema may notice the loop in the narrative hierarchy, it is there to attest to the artifice of fiction and as a potential source of aesthetic enjoyment, and it is at points like this that David Bordwell's claim that '[f]or the viewer, constructing the story takes precedence; the effects of the text are registered, but its causes go unremarked' (Bordwell 1985: 48) has to be accepted with caution. There are different kinds of entertainment in narrative, and immersing oneself in the story is only one of them. Causes for textual effects may be part of the entertainment equation for more people then some narratologists like to believe; otherwise, the inventiveness of so many films not just in organizing their discourse to allow story construction, but also in organizing their discourse in ways that are interesting in themselves would be hard to explain (see also ch. I.iii, point 5).

iv. Nondiegetic and diegetic music

The boundary between diegetic and nondiegetic music has so far been the main attractor for film music narratology, but also – to mix metaphors – its main bone of contention. For that reason, the two levels are considered in a joint section. Its purpose is to outline their relationship; much else in the book has to do with these concepts and how they have been used in films.

The career of 'diegetic' and 'nondiegetic' (or 'extradiegetic') music in film musicology goes back to Claudia Gorbman's adoption of the terms from Gérard Genette (Gorbman 1987: 11–30). But they are only the two most recent of a long list of terms practitioners and scholars have used for the distinction they mean: 'source music' and 'score' (or 'underscoring') are just the best-known of them.[29] The widespread adoption of the diegetic/nondiegetic distinction rides on the success of the concept of the diegesis in narratology. But while (film) narratologists seem to agree, by and large, that the differentiation between diegesis and nondiegetic elements of a narrative is useful, film musicologists have not stopped worrying about it.

They have pointed out the fragility of the distinction (R. Brown 1994: 67–91); they have compared the dichotomies diegetic/nondiegetic and source music/scoring (Kassabian

---

29 Claudia Bullerjahn lists such terms (see Bullerjahn 2001: 19–21): on the diegetic side (roughly; the terms do not match exactly), scholars have used 'realistic (film) music', 'naturalistic music', 'source music', 'szenische Musik', 'immanente Musik', 'aktuelle Musik', 'Musik in ihrer natürlichen Rolle', 'Inzidenzmusik', 'musique objective', 'musique justifiée ou légitimée par l'image', 'musique d'écran' and 'livello interno'. Corresponding terms on (again roughly) the nondiegetic level are: 'Musik außerhalb des Bilds', 'Irrealmusik' and 'außerszenische Musik', 'transzendente Musik', 'stoffführende Musik', 'underscoring', 'background music', 'unrealistic music', 'functional film music', 'musique subjective', 'musique d'accompagnment', 'musique de fosse' and 'livello esterno'.

2001: 42–49); they have explored the subtleties of the relationship between diegetic and nondiegetic music, the fuzzy areas or movements between them (Chion 1994: 66–94 for film sound in general; or Biancorosso 2001; Buhler 2001; Stilwell 2007; or Binns 2008), or tried to re-systematize certain types of fuzziness (Smith 2009); they have discussed the diegetic/nondiegetic distinction in the context of other terminological systems (Neumeyer 1997 & 2009), suggested alternative terminological lines between concepts (Winters 2010), or set film music narratology into a wider theoretical and aesthetic context (Yacavone 2012); they have problematized the application of the terms to film music on the basis of a discussion of the meaning of 'diegesis' (Cecchi 2010; and Merlin 2010) or 'narration' (Winters 2012), or have reformulated the relationship between diegesis and narration (Davis 2012); they have analyzed scenes that demonstrate particular options of diegetic or nondiegetic music or their relationship (Levinson 1996 on the implied author; Kassabian 2001: 42–49 on 'source scoring', i.e. the use of diegetic music as if it were underscoring; Holbrook 2005a & 2005b on 'ambi-diegetic music', i.e. diegetic music used to further story development; Norden 2007 on 'diegetic commentary', i.e. diegetic music commenting on the storyworld; Biancorosso 2009 on sudden reversals of our interpretation of the narrative status of music).

To engage directly with all of these contributions to the discussion would take up as many pages again as this book is long. Instead, this sub-chapter tries to sketch a coherent account of 'diegetic' and 'nondiegetic' music, and of some questions around the concepts, and refers to the literature where necessary or helpful:

- Section (*a*) considers the distinction itself and music's relationship with it.
- Sections (*b*) and (*c*) look at examples *within* the conceptual horizons of diegetic and nondiegetic music respectively.
- To develop the discussion of diegetic music, section (*d*) interrogates the concept of the implied author with regard to features scholars have described as 'diegetic commentary', 'source scoring' or 'ambi-diegetic music'.
- Section (*e*) discusses less basic examples of using diegetic music, some following on from the implied author, others leading into section *f*.
- Section (*f*) itself looks at examples of music that crosses or straddles conceptual boundaries (including displaced diegetic and supradiegetic music, explored at greater length in Chapter III).

a. Narratology, the diegesis and music – some considerations

The diegesis in the terminological field

'Diegetic/nondiegetic' is one among other sets of terms that describe the relationship between, in Seymour Chatman's terms, the 'what' and the 'way' of narrative (Chatman 1978: 9). More common in literary studies is story/discourse (French: *histoire* and *discours*; see Todorov 1966, who introduced the terms): 'The what of narrative I call its *story*; the way

I call its *discourse*' (Chatman 1978: 9). Gérard Genette borrowed 'diegesis' (French: *diégèse*) from Etienne Souriau as an alternative to 'story' (*histoire*) (see Genette 1980: 27, footnote), while he uses 'narrating' (*narration*) 'for the producing narrative action' (Genette 1980: 27), i.e. that what a narrator does and what happens on an extradiegetic level (Genette 1980: 228), and '*narrative* for the signifier, statement, discourse or narrative text' (*discours* or *récit*) (Genette 1980: 27). So actually we are dealing with the paired terms diegesis/narration, which are located on the diegetic and nondiegetic levels respectively.

Despite the narratological relaunch Genette gave Souriau's 'diegesis' (discussed above, p. 19), and despite the confusing relationship between this use of the term and its origin in Plato and Aristotle (see e.g. Shen 2005; Fuxjäger 2007), it proved handy:

- 'Diegetic' and 'nondiegetic' (or 'extradiegetic') are not weighed down by the connotations 'story' and 'discourse' carry from everyday speech, but are specific to narrative theory.
- The common core allowed Genette to develop the terms into a system for nested levels of narration, with 'metadiegetic' as a level internal to the diegesis (see Genette 1980: 228–29), and 'homodiegetic' and 'heterodiegetic' – for narrators who are or are not part of the storyworld – to further differentiate the relationship between narration and diegesis. (That 'diegesis' easily forms the adjective 'diegetic' makes the term linguistically handy as well.)
- From everyday speech, 'story' inherits the implication of a sequence of events, while 'diegesis' rather implies a story*world*, which fits our understanding of stories as taking place in a (fictional) world of its own, similar to the one we know, but (fictionally) autonomous: 'the surrounding context or environment embedding storyworld existents' (Herman 2005: 570)[30], which includes the possibility of further stories happening in the same storyworld (important for film franchises).

A different angle is taken by the 'fabula/syuzhet' distinction of Russian formalist literary theory. While 'fabula' matches 'story', 'syuzhet' is not the same as 'discourse', but rather 'the story as actually told by linking the events together' (Chatman 1978: 20), the order of events as presented in a narrative text. But events are presented by the means specific to a medium – a novel has other ways of presenting a scene than cinema, though it can tell broadly the same story, cast into the same syuzhet. For medium-specific means of storytelling,

---

30 The idea of a storyworld, though, weakens the sense of a story as a sequence of events. Genette pointed out that 'story' and 'diegesis', while on the same side of the distinction, are not synonymous, though he had suggested their equivalence in *Discours du récit* (1972) (see Genette 1980: 27, footnote): 'Souriau proposed the term *diégèse* in 1948, contrasting the diegetic [*diégétique*] universe (the place of the signified) with the *screen*-universe (place of the film-signifier). Used in that sense, *diégèse* is indeed a *universe* rather than a train of events (a story); the *diégèse* is therefore not the story but the universe in which the story takes place […]. We must not […] substitute *diégèse* for *histoire*' (Genette 1988: 17–18). For the relationship between diegesis, fabula and story, see also Fuxjäger (2007: 20–21).

David Bordwell introduced the term 'style' (Bordwell 1985: 50) and arrived at a tripartite terminological system of 'fabula/syuzhet/style'.

All of these sets of terms[31] encapsulate the relationship between something that is manifest and something that is not: the words on the page of a novel, the image frames and soundtrack of a film are manifestly there.[32] But the story or fabula, and the diegesis as the fictional world in which it takes place, are mental constructs, (re)constructed by the reader, spectator and listener. To mentally construct the diegesis of a film, the information provided by the film itself is not enough. We understand films on the basis of three sources of knowledge (see Ohler 1994: 32ff):

- the cues provided by the film;
- our knowledge of conventions of narration in general and of filmic narration in particular (we can read, for example, the filmic signs for a dream sequence, or know how to understand music that indicates a character's mood);
- our general knowledge of the world (we expect, for example, physical objects to obey roughly the same laws as those in the real world, if not cued by the film to readjust our expectations, in a fantasy film, for example).

In the Bordwellian tripartite distinction, what is manifestly present is only the 'style' of a particular narrative medium, while both syuzhet and fabula are constructions, though on different levels of abstraction. The text of a film or book is understood by the recipient to suggest scenes; the order of scenes as presented by the text (i.e. the syuzhet) then has to be translated into a chain of causes and effects (the fabula).

The diegesis as a mental construct

That the diegesis (or story or fabula) is constructed by the viewer, that it only takes place in her or his mind is a basic fact of narrative fiction: 'the "reality" of fiction (the concept of the diegesis) [is] a reality that comes only from within us, from the projections and identifications that are mixed in with our perception of the film' (Metz 1974: 10).[33] The idea has been frequently reiterated by film scholars:

> It would be an error to take the fabula, or story, as the profilmic event. A film's fabula is never materially present on the screen or soundtrack. (Bordwell 1985: 49)

---

31 'Diegesis/narration' also echoes distinctions such as 'signified/signifier', 'content/form' or 'matter/ manner', which have been applied to different texts or artworks, not just narratives.

32 One must not, however, confuse the physical object (the book with its pages with ink on them, the celluloid strip, etc.) with the text of the 'aesthetic object' (in Roman Ingarden's term) (see Chatman 1978: 26–27).

33 Chapter 1 of Metz's *Film Language*, where the quotation is found, was originally published as an article (Metz 1965).

Diegesis is not something that the film either possesses or lacks, but rather a way of describing an interlocking set of judgments we make about the presentation of sensory data in the film at a particular moment. (Branigan 1986: 44)

To read a text, to see a film as a fiction, means first of all to construct a world: to diegetize. (Odin 2000: 18; my translation)

Especially the fragility of the diegesis points to the fact that it is not received passively, but *actively* constructed [...]. The diegetic comprises more than what the image shows. The diegesis is the product of a *synthetic effort*, which is produced in the appropriation of the text [...]. (Wulff 2007: 46; my translation)

One needs to be cautious, though. The synthetic effort that produces the diegesis is based on cues given by the film (plus our knowledge of narrative and of the world), and in that sense the construction is presupposed by the film. The interplay between the two aspects is captured by Souriau:

Diegetic is everything we take into account as being represented by the film, and as part of the reality *presupposed* by the signification of the film [...]. (Souriau 1951: 237; my translation)

On the one hand, there is the 'we', the audience, who take things into account as being represented; on the other hand, there is the signification of the film presupposing a (fictional) reality – both go hand in hand. While the construction of the diegesis is subjective, it is not arbitrary, but guided by the organization of the film text.

The constructedness of the diegesis would seem to be obvious. But recent publications by film musicologists have tried hard to reclaim this insight from a different understanding of the diegesis, which they take to be widespread, at least in film musicology. Alessandro Cecchi starts from the proposition that 'that the concept of diegesis is based on objective configurations of on screen reality, and that the diegetic/nondiegetic distinction corresponds to immediate perceptive data' (Cecchi 2010: 1), and that 'the act of inference confronts us with knowledge of an objective and coherent world (diegesis), while what appears on screen (the narration) is merely a subjective and partial perspective on this' (Cecchi 2010: 3). He then sets out to disprove these assumptions to arrive at the antithetic conclusion:

Diegesis is based on an act of inference which cannot lay claim to any kind of objectivity: it is a subjective act, and hence merely hypothetical. [...] [D]iegetic and nondiegetic aspects cannot be distinguished at the ontological level; rather, they cooperate in the audiovisual narration, within which they are constantly interacting. The fact that in many cases (but not – "always") the traversing of the boundary – "does [...] *mean*" (Stilwell 2007: 186) depends strictly on the theoretical construction applied to the particular audiovisual situation, and not on the claimed perceptive objectivity of the diegetic/nondiegetic threshold. (Cecchi 2010: 7–8)

That is true, but narratologists have never doubted it – the 'claimed perceptive objectivity of the diegetic/nondiegetic threshold' is a straw man.[34]

In similar fashion, Didi Merlin (building on Fuxjäger 2007) goes back to Souriau's definition of 'diegesis' (see above). Crucial for Merlin is Souriau's statement that the diegesis is that 'which we take into account as being represented by the film', which posits the spectator as actively engaged in constructing the diegesis. It is this idea that Merlin defends against the 'ontologization of the diegetic reality' (Merlin 2010: 70) he sees at work in, for example, Christian Metz's 'conception of film as text, in which the diegesis can be determined independently of the spectator, as a function of the text' (Merlin 2010: 70; see Metz 1971: 14[35]). Merlin's critique of an ontologizing understanding of the diegetic/nondiegetic differentiation comes to the conclusion that:

> [...] pairs of terms frequently used in film musicology – *onscreen vs. offscreen, diegetic vs. nondiegetic* (or *intradiegetic vs. extradiegetic*), *internal diegetic vs. external diegetic* – are not sufficient for a precise description of the temporary results of the interactive processes taking place on the perceptual, cognitive and emotional level between audiovisual input and the recipients. (Merlin 2010: 96)

While it is true that the dichotomies suggested by the paired terms are incapable of capturing all the subtleties and ambiguities of the examples Merlin uses to interrogate the concepts[36],

---

34 The same is true of Alexander Binns' discussion of the diegetic/nondiegetic distinction in films by Wong Kar-Wai (Binns 2008). The 'rigid distinction between diegetic and non-diegetic' that, according to Binns, is 'no longer tenable' (Binns 2008: 128), describes a misuse of the concept that has never been part of its narratological remit (or only in the practice of those who think the distinction to be a cut-and-dried way of categorising music in films).

    In his claim that 'music, especially music conventionally recognized as non-diegetic, is not located in any one place of a film's visual world' (2008: 130), Binns summarizes Lawrence Kramer's idea that 'film music collapses the distance between the screen and the spectator' and 'extend[s] to the image the real, emotionalised backdrop that we experience in life' (2008: 130; referring to Kramer 1995: 112–13). While Kramer's idea may provide part of the answer to the question why there is (nondiegetic) music in film at all, it does not say anything helpful about the diegetic/nondiegetic distinction, because Kramer's point concerns the relationship between music and spectator, not that between music and other elements of film.

35 Merlin is not quite accurate, as Metz does not define film as text, but writes that the defining criterion of a semiology of film is to treat films as texts. In the preceding paragraph, however, he makes clear that he sees semiology only as one among other approaches to film (see Metz 1971: 14).

36 Merlin's examples for ambiguities not captured by simple dichotomies are problematic in themselves. One is the opening scene of *Battle of Algiers/La battaglia di Algeri* (1966), which uses the opening of J.S. Bach's *St Matthew's Passion* in a scene involving a tortured Algerian rebel. Since a source for the music is neither manifest nor implied, we would normally characterize it as nondiegetic. But Merlin asks if it could not be seen as diegetic (or as 'internal diegetic' in the sense of Bordwell and Thompson 2010: 190–91), because we can imagine it to be part of the 'inner reality of perception' of the rebel, and because the music 'lends a voice to the emotional and cognitive development that takes place in the

his conclusion forgets that he himself argued in favour of Souriau's definition of the diegesis as a mental construct. As such, it is open to readjustment, reinterpretation, ambiguousness and intersubjective difference; that is part of the concept, not a defect that would mean classificatory categories derived from it are useless.

But Cecchi's and Merlin's attempts to prove the obvious show a key aspect of the relationship between diegesis and narration. On the level of narratological analysis, we know that the diegesis is a mental construct: there are only words on the page, frames of film, there is only music coming out of the loudspeakers in the cinema; the rest happens in our minds. But that is not how we *experience* narratives, and David Bordwell's warning of the 'error to take the fabula, or story, as the profilmic event' (see above) is a reaction to this problem. Most films cue us to construct dieseses that are more or less coherent most of the time (occasional winks indicating the fictionality of fiction notwithstanding), dieseses that allows us to suspend our disbelief and entertain, however provisionally, the fiction that they originate in an autonomous, profilmic reality. (Examples that break that pretence are discussed in the section on the implied author.) It is this pretence that is responsible for the illusion of the 'reality' of the diegesis and the boundary between what is diegetic and what is not, and for the resulting illusion that music is located on one side of the divide or other, and that it can move across it in a variety of ways – the spatial metaphor underlying, for example, Robynn Stilwell's image of the 'fantastical gap between diegetic and nondiegetic' (Stilwell 2007).

Nick Davis (2012) recently suggested the Klein bottle as an image for the interconnectedness of narration and diegesis or discourse and story: a non-orientable surface curved back onto itself, a more complex variant of a Möbius strip. Like Cecchi's, Davis' critique of the story/discourse distinction hinges on its (supposed) essentialism:

---

inner reality of the tortured man. This voice is audible to the Algerian, but also to those spectators who are connected to the Algerian by an *empathising* process' (Merlin 2010: 86).

There are two different questions here, which must not be confused: (1) The question whether the Algerian *hears* this music with his inner ear, which is not impossible, but unlikely; (2) the question whether the narration of the film 'lends a voice' to his suffering: 'a voice', not 'his voice'. It is the difference between music as the representation of an inner voice ('internal focalization [depth]', in Branigan's terms; see Branigan 1992: 87), and music as an external voice singing for or about the tortured Algerian. Both interpretations tell us something about the emotional import of the situation (both for the Algerian and for the audience), but the supposed source of the music is different. The emotional import is the most relevant aspect of the scene and the use of music in it, and so the difference may not be the all that interesting, but it is nevertheless the difference relevant for an understanding of the narrative construction of the scene: the difference between music heard from someone's perspective (as aural perception or mental imagination), and music that is *about* someone, even if it is about someone's inner state (and that is far from certain here).

The choice of music itself problematizes Merlin's interpretation. The use of European art music distances its voice from the diegetic character, and may lead us to construe it as commentary: the narration mourning the Algerian with music that fits the European production and reception context of the film. In that sense, the music speaks of what is a very European view of the Algerian struggle for independence.

Broadly, the story/discourse type of distinction posits a 'story' that subsists as a logical construct independently of 'discourse', while at the same time acknowledging that 'story' is generated specifically through 'discourse'. [...] The Klein bottle analogy reveals that it is distinctly unhelpful to treat 'story' and 'discourse' as if they were formally separable for purposes of analysis. (Davis 2012: 10–14)

But the story/discourse distinction does not really posit one as logically independent of the other: a story is a mental construct on the basis of discourse. The distinction between fact and fiction may clarify the point. If in real life someone tells us what happened to him that day, we indeed assume that the facts of the matter are logically independent from the discourse (his report) – at least if we believe him. Discourse does not generate the facts, but gives us (mediated) access to them, and 'story' is the name we give to that mediated access. In fiction, discourse *does* generate the entire story and storyworld, but – at least in most realist fiction – it *pretends* to give us access to story facts, or rather, gives us access to pretend story facts (exceptions that show this construction for what it is notwithstanding). Strictly speaking, a fiction film does not represent fictional characters in a fictional world: its images and soundtrack represent actors and props, but it pretends to represent diegetic characters and objects.[37]

To substantiate this point, I would need a theory of fiction this book does not have the space for. But we should keep in mind both perspectives when thinking about the place of music in the hierarchy of levels of narration. The illusion of music being located in diegetic or nondiegetic 'spaces' and of its occasional movement from one to the other – a quasi-ontological understanding of the diegetic/nondiegetic relationship – explains important features of our experience of films, of our reaction to many of the tricks of the trade of slotting music into them; these often rely on our (provisional) assumption of the stability of the diegetic/nondiegetic boundary. But from a narratological perspective, we must not forget that at ground level there is just music. It is our mental construction of the diegesis that assigns it to different levels of narration, and that assignation is open to revision, and occasionally discussion.

Diegesis or diegetization?
In order to avoid the dangers of 'ontologizing' the diegesis, and to underline the process character of our constrcution and reconstruction of its features, some narratologists prefer to speak of 'diegetization' and to think of the diegesis as a provisional construct that develops according to cues provided by the film (see Odin 1983; Hartmann 2007; Hartmann and Wulff 2007; and Wulff 2007).[38]

---

37 Most of the 'tropes of narrativity' (Davis 2012: 12) Davis proposes are indeed rather tropes of fictional narrativity than of narrativity as such.

38 The idea of 'diegetization' allows a defence of the diegetic/nondiegetic distinction against Anahid Kassabians critique. To put music in a film firmly into either the 'diegetic' or the 'nondiegetic' box, according to Kassabian, presupposes a diegesis established independently of the music, which illogically excludes music from the construction of the diegesis (Kassabian 2001: 42). Like Jeff Smith

Obvious, and indeed ostentatious, examples of diegetization at work are the many 'reveals' of the diegetic source of music that could initially be construed as nondiegetic, such as the opening scene of *The Holiday* discussed in ch. II.ii. When we see the kissing couple under the tree, we begin to form an idea of the film's diegesis as their world – but then we realize that they are just a metadiegetic insert in the primary diegesis, the world of Miles (Jack Black) and his film-music studio. The music we at first take to be a conventional marker for the 'romantic' genre world outlined in the metadiegetic scene turns out to be part of the primary diegesis as well, and in the process of diegetization it becomes a genre marker for (self-reflexive) 'romantic comedy' (more 'reveals' are discussed in ch. II.iv.e; see also Hartmann 2007: 56).

Part of the problem some film musicologists have with the diegetic/nondiegetic distinction may lie in basic features of film music. One such feature is that music is usually relatively peripheral and narratively flexible, often appearing on both sides of the diegetic/nondiegetic divide. While non-experimental narrative films may cue the spectator to construct fairly coherent and stable diegeses, music can slip through the structure and show its constructed character from a position marginal enough not to topple the entire edifice.

Another feature is what one might call the structural obstinacy of music. 'A photographed kiss cannot actually be synchronized with an eight-bar phrase', Theodor Adorno and Hanns Eisler aver in *Composing for the Films* (1994: 8), but because composing for the films is done by professionals brought up with the science of the eight-bar phrase, they insert partially independent structures into films. When in *The Sea Hawk* (1940) the lonely Doña Maria sings a song to her beloved Geoffrey Thorpe, the song she sings in the diegesis is musically developed out of 'her' nondiegetic theme. It was natural for composer Erich Wolfgang Korngold, brought up in the traditions of Austro-German symphonic music, to structure the music by recurring, varied and developed themes and motifs – that was how one did such things. It does not matter much the spectator might wonder where Maria would know her own leitmotif from, and that the thematic link produces a metalepsis: a short-circuiting of levels of narration (for the concept see, for example, Genette 1980: 234–37;

(see Smith 2009: endnote 17), I am not sure what Kassabian means, because the same applies to other elements of a film. Written text, say, can be diegetic because it appears on an advertising hoarding the protagonists are passing in a car, or nondiegetic because it appears on an intertitle between two shots (or overlaid over a landscape without us assuming that the letters are floating in the air); spoken text can be part of a dialogue between characters or part of a heterodiegetic voice-over narration. Every element of a film text has to be interrogated by the audience as to its role in 'producing the diegesis' (Kassabian 2011: 42); music is no different from other elements of film style in that respect.

Kassabian's criticism would be a challenge to the validity of the diegetic/nondiegetic distinction only if the categories were conceived as fixed for the duration a film. Music can easily be thought of as being involved in the production of the diegesis if we think of the diegesis not as a stable space that textual elements are either inside or outside of, but as something established only in the act of watching and listening, and of using the cues a film provides to construct its storyworld and the rules of its narration.

Abbott 2008: 169–74; and Pier 2005).[39] It is a welcome effect, as the motivic recurrence strengthens the association of motif and character precisely *because* it crosses the narrative boundary. Through the transcendence, the leitmotif is no longer just tacked onto Maria, but pours out of her and proves her yearning by becoming diegetically embodied. But the metalepsis is only allowed to sneak into a kind of narrative not normally keen to break the coherence of the diegesis because music has a special dispensation, because it has only a supporting role, and because it is (considered as) an art a bit apart with its own rules, which, if they do not interfere too much with the basic structures of a film, can override them sometimes.

Imaginary borders, fantastical gaps – the topology of the boundary
The double nature of the diegesis – a mental construct that nevertheless seems to produce stable quasi-spaces – shapes our understanding of moments that call the integrity of the spaces into question. We have an intuitive understanding of the dividing line and react when it is crossed.

One criticism of the diegetic/nondiegetic distinction is that it is crudely dichotomous: 'grossly reduced as either *in* (diegetic) or *out* (nondiegetic) of the narrative world of the film' (Kassabian 2001: 42). '[I]f this border has been crossed so often, then the distinction doesn't mean anything', as Robynn Stilwell casts this view in rhetorical exaggeration (2007: 184). Stilwell points out that the crossing of the border does not invalidate it, but draws attention to the act of crossing and derives meaning from it, and others have supported that (e.g. Neumeyer 2009). Audiences laugh when the organ chords underlining the vicar's speech in *Wallace & Gromit in 'The Curse of the Were-Rabbit'* turn out to issue from the village organist (see pp. 3–6), or when the snake charmer in *Octopussy* (1983) plays James Bond's signature motif (see pp. 80–81). The laughter shows that we have an intuitive understanding of the border and react reflexively to its violation.

Such border violations are well-studied in narratology, especially in literature, and range from simple linguistic shortcuts such as free indirect discourse (the narrator speaks with or for the character) to proper metalepses. Artists play with their media, which includes the transgression of seemingly natural categories. The search for a terminological system accounting for all cases is pointless; the only one to fulfil that condition would be 'anything goes'. Concepts need to point out salient features of a phenomenon, but that does not preclude those features from becoming the stuff of creative play. The feature of film that allows that creative play is the fact that on the other side of the conceptual coin, on a purely textual level, there *is* no boundary between the diegetic and the nondiegetic: anything can

---

39 In this case of a descending metalepsis (i.e. from embedding to embedded level), the narration, which Maria's leitmotif originally belongs to, enters the diegesis to aid her characterization. An alternative explanation for some descending metalepses is the idea of a 'retrospective prolepsis' (see ch. V.iii).

happen to the music at any point in a film; the borderline is only conceptual and offers no resistance to being crossed.[40]

One of the most elegant demonstrations of this occurs in the film from which this book borrows its subtitle: *Step Across the Border* (1990), Nicolas Humbert's and Werner Penzel's documentary of experimental improviser Fred Frith. While my study is mostly concerned with fiction film, the excursion into documentary may be allowed: while fiction and documentary differ with regard to the reality status of the diegesis, the boundary between diegetic and nondiegetic is similarly permeable in both.

After the graphics montage of the credits and a brief scene showing Frith humming a few tunes, the first extended scene is an 80-second 'urban symphony' to introduce New York as one of its locations. We see the camera glide along a bridge, we see cars on the road and boats on the river, but do not hear any diegetic sounds. We hear only music, a dense soundscape layering hardly identifiable instrumental sounds, spoken language and wailing voices, structured only by widely-spaced drum beats. After about 20 seconds, we realize that some of the sounds in the mix now might be attributable to the cars, and others to the horn of a ship gliding along on the river; but we cannot be sure if they are not still meant to be understood as part of the music.

After a cut showing the bridge from below, out of a moving car, the spoken language in the texture is replaced by voices that sound as if coming from a radio; there are also sounds of a siren and someone tuning a radio to a station. Other sounds are still continuing the initial musical texture, but they are slowly overwhelmed by the (real or imitated) 'real-world' sounds.

Finally, after another cut, we see images of traffic-filled streets, and what we hear now is almost completely attributable to what we assume to be the 'realistic' soundscape of this scene: cars moving, horns honking, the radio voices that belong to the reality of the city scene at least implicitly, as the representation of what drivers might hear in their cars; and only the slow drumbeats remind us of the musical starting point of this journey – only to be the element that leads us into the next scene, which starts with filmmaker Jonas Mekas banging his hand on an escalator door to hear what sound it makes.

Within less than one-and-a-half minutes, the music has, step by step, transformed itself from a musical accompaniment to the images without implied or plausible diegetic source into an almost realistic soundscape of what we see, with only a minimal reminder of the original music. The film has indeed stepped (or rather slipped) across the border – from outside the city right into its middle, and from musical accompaniment (and experimental music) to 'real' sounds; but it has done both so smoothly that we willingly follow the acoustic sleight of hand. The careful way the transition into the diegesis is effected acknowledges the borderline at the same time as its seamlessness nonchalantly treats it as if it did not exist – which, of course, it does not outside of our own minds.

---

40 A concentrated illustration of that fact can be found in the discussion of border crossings and ambiguities in films scored by Nino Rota in Dyer (2010: 81–100).

This is a problem of Stilwell's metaphor of the 'fantastical gap'. The gap provides a handy space to put in many of the examples of music in film that do not fit a simple diegetic/nondiegetic dichotomy. But the image of the gap implies that there is something between the categories, a 'third way', a discrete space (an implication Stilwell confirms when she writes of the gap as 'this liminal space' [2007: 187]). Yet what separates the categories is nothing but our imagination.

An image that may be helpful in illustrating the point is that of a borderline between two territories on a map. There is normally no geographical feature to mark the dividing line in the physical world; the border between two countries is purely conceptual, too. It can, however, quickly become practically relevant if one tries to cross it illegally and is caught by the border patrol. The narratological border patrol is made up of our assumptions about narrative and what it 'normally' does (though the definition of 'normally' may be very different for different film genres – a comedy can get away with border violations that would seem bizarre in, say, a costume drama).

The one-term-fits-all quality – while contributing to the success of the image – is its other problem. It lumps together different ways of using the diegetic/nondiegetic distinction into a synthetic category: supradiegetic fantasy in *Dames* (1934) (Stilwell 2007: 188); the integration of diegetic into nondiegetic music in *King Kong* (1933) (2007: 189); 'reveals' of music as diegetic in *The Winter Guest* (1997) and *Holy Smoke* (1999) (2007: 189–90 & 197–98); ambiguity between internally focalized and displaced diegetic music in *I Know Where I'm Going!* (1945) (2007: 193–94); diegetic music as 'source scoring' (see pp. 95–97), indicating a character's inner state or a psychological link between characters in *The Killing Fields* (1984) and *Manhunter* (1986) (2007: 194 & 198–99); and nondiegetic music as internal focalization in *The Insider* (1999).[41]

Jeff Smith's critique of Stilwell (Smith 2009) also hinges on the over-generality of the fantastical gap, though his attempt to put the rabbit back in the narratological hat generates its own problems. He shows that candidates for the fantastical gap can be classified as varieties of diegetic music (music with varying degrees of aural fidelity;

---

41 Over-generality also affects Anahid Kassabian's use of the term 'source scoring' (Kassabian 2001: 43–47), borrowed from Earle Hagen, who understands it as music that is 'like source in its content, but tailored to meet scoring requirements' and 'matches the nuances of the scene musically' (Hagen 1971: 200; more on the concept on pp. 85–87). Of Kassabian's examples, only the first, from *Dead Again* (1991), matches Hagen's defintion: implicitly diegetic music from a neighbouring flat becomes the underscore to an altercation between characters. Her other examples play with the diegetic/nondiegetic boundary in other ways. The example from *Mississippi Masala* (1991) is a case of displaced diegetic music (though displacement is often, as it is here, used in a way that approximates Hagen's understanding of source scoring). The example from *Moonstruck* (1987) uses diegetic music and diegetic images, but dissociates their temporal connection, resulting in a montage bound by diegetic instead of nondiegetic music. The victory celebration from *Star Wars* (1977) refuses to define the music as either diegetic and nondiegetic, leaving it in an ambiguous state that can be understood as a variant of what I call 'would-be-diegetic music' (see pp. 68–69): the film sings or plays with or for the characters.

displaced diegetic music; diegetic music whose source is initially disguised). While he successfully differentiates between ways of playing with our idea of the diegesis, Smith downplays their effects: by displacing diegetic music, for instance, or by holding back and revealing its source. Whether we understand the music as in some way or at some point diegetic is less relevant than *how* a film (mis)leads us to understand it. The interesting aspect of Stilwell's interrogation of the diegetic/nondiegetic distinction is not the image of the fanastical gap itself, but the idea that the crossing of the mental borderline produces meaning.

Narrative agency and the range of diegetic and nondiegetic music

Another bone of contention has been that the categories of diegetic and nondiegetic music seem to gloss over important differentiations in the use of music within either category. But this, too, is a feature rather than a bug. The diegetic/nondiegetic distinction is about 'where the music comes from', about the question 'Who speaks?' (Genette 1988: 64). That does not restrict what the music can speak *about*, and to confuse the questions would be a category mistake. That does not mean that it is not worth exploring what diegetic and nondiegetic music have been used to speak about in films. But the internal differentiation does not call the validity of the distinction into question.

Dissatisfaction with the umbrella quality of 'diegetic' and 'nondiegetic' informs several attempts to refine the conceptual arsenal. Morris Holbrook's 'ambi-diegetic music' (2005a & 2005b) differentiates on the diegetic side, between music that serves 'realistic depiction' of the storyworld and music that serves 'dramatic development' (Holbrook 2005b: 49; more in ch. II.iv.d). In his exploration of the implied author, Jerrold Levinson (1996) focuses on the nondiegetic side of things and distinguishes between different kinds of nondiegetic music: nondiegetic music that makes 'something fictional in a film' (an idea based on Kendall Walton 1990), i.e. music that informs us about something we accept as a storyworld fact, such as a character's emotion at a certain moment; and nondiegetic music that comments on the diegesis 'in a mode of distanced and reflective juxtaposition to the story narrated' (Levinson 1996: 272). While the distinction is sensible, Levinson's assignation of the former kind of music to the 'cinematic narrator' and the latter to the 'implied filmmaker' (1996: 252–53) misunderstands the concept of the implied author (further discussed in ch. II.iv.d).

Levinson's distinction was recently taken up by Ben Winters (2010), who argues against too clear a conceptual division between storyworld and nondiegetic music. About Anton Karas' zither music in *The Third Man* (1949), Winter asks:

[D]oes it make sense to distinguish the 'non-diegetic' zither music [...] from the rest of the narrative: is it not just as essential to the fictional world of post-war Vienna presented in the film as the image of the Ferris Wheel in the Prater, or the characters of Harry Lime and Holly Martins? (Winters 2010: 224)

But that confuses narrative and diegesis. The music is essential to the *depiction* of the fictional world (and both depiction/narration and diegesis are parts of the narrative[42]), not to the fictional world *as depicted* in the film, because the music is not a part of the fictional world, but a means of its depiction. That also applies to Winters' critique of Gorbman's use of 'extradiegetic': 'Gorbman did not seem to consider the possibility that her extra- or non-diegetic music might be part of the narrative as it unfolds (in the same way as other parts of the *mise-en-scène*), not an intrusion that signals an external level of narration' (Winter 2010: 226). But being part of a narrative is not the same as being part of the diegesis, a much narrower concept.

To arrive at a more integral understanding of nondiegetic music, Winters suggests a model that retains the distinction between diegetic music 'heard by the characters "as music"' (2010: 237), and music that is not part of the characters' world. The latter he differentiates into 'extra-diegetic music' and 'intra-diegetic music'. 'Extra-diegetic music' comprises music 'whose logic is not dictated by events within the narrative space' (2010: 237), e.g. music accompanying montage sequences, or music that 'seems distanced from the narrative action' (2010: 237) and expresses a reaction to it, such as Samuel Barber's 'Adagio for Strings' in *Platoon* (1986). 'Intra-diegetic music' is music that:

> [...] exists in the film's everyday narrative space and time [...]: it may be considered to be produced by the characters themselves (either as a result of their physical movements, as with mickey-mousing, as an expression of their emotional state, or as a musical calling-card), or by the geographical space of the film – as with the zither music of *The Third Man*. (Winter 2010: 237)

One problem of the distinction is that it proposes fixed categories for fluid phenomena. The 'distance' of a musical cue to the 'narrative action' is not a matter of either/or, but, as the term says, a point on a scale (or rather in a complex field of relationships) between narration and diegesis. But the more crucial problem is that the distinction misconstrues the relationship between narration and diegesis. The narration of a film is indeed 'part of the narrative' and not 'an intrusion' because it furnishes us with information that allows us to construct and interpret diegesis and story: information ranging from the fully mimetic (shots of the action) via the partly mimetic (a map with the line of flight of an airplane to indicate a journey, for example, or music to indicate someone's emotion) to the reflective (a voice-over, or Barber's 'Adagio' in *Platoon*).

---

42 This presupposes a definition of narrative as 'the narrative statement, the oral or written discourse that undertakes to tell of [...] a series of events' (Genette 1980: 25). Genette also mentions a second meaning, which identifies narrative with 'the succession of events [...] that are the subjects of this discourse' (1980: 25): the story (or, more specifically, since Genette points out that this understanding of the term ignores the medium, the fabula). If Winter understands 'narrative' in this sense, then it makes a lot of 'sense to distinguish the "non-diegetic" zither music [...] from the rest of the narrative' (Winters 2010: 224), because then 'the rest of the narrative' would be located on the diegetic level.

The comparison with narration in a novel may clarify the issue, even if it should be made with caution, as narration works differently in both media. A novel has few options for presenting information mimetically: dialogue, letters and other written documents, perhaps drawings, etc. The narrator has to supply the rest, and is personalized in the voice telling the story. Film has manifold mimetic options, both visual and aural, but the narration rarely has a voice of its own, and chiefly operates by *arranging* bits of (mostly mimetic) information through framing, camera movements or zooms, cuts, etc. (see Gaudreault 2009, especially pp. 81–100 for narration in film[43]). Nondiegetic music is one of the exceptions, because it can indeed appear as a 'voice'. But what can narrating voices say? A narrator in a novel can provide story information (e.g. tell us what a landscape looks like or what character feels, and thereby make the landscape or the emotion 'fictionally true'), can comment on diegetic facts (describe the impression the landscape makes on him, or mock the emotion), can use language to imply the atmosphere of a landscape or a character's mood, or can move further out from the diegesis and muse philosophically about landscape or emotions, leaving it to the reader to figure out the relevance of this to the story. The range is wide, but all of that is narration, and while the specific narrative capabilities of music are different, we should grant it its own range.[44] (That point is developed in ch. II.iv.d.)

It is important to retain the insights contained in Holbrook's, Levinson's or Winters' differentiations without overtaxing the concepts of diegetic and nondiegetic music with tasks they cannot fulfil. The question of what level of narration the music is on has to be kept apart from the question of what it says and does, and by what means it says and does it. Nondiegetic music can function as a distancing comment, but also evoke a mood or give insight into the inner state of a character; diegetic music can provide 'realistic depiction' (Holbrook 2005b: 49), but can also be blatantly unrealistic, and can structure and inform a scene as well as nondiegetic music (which is why 'underscoring' is used in this book next to 'nondiegetic music': not as an alternative term for the same concept, but to describe

---

43 Gaudreault identifies narration with editing and sees the camera image itself (including movements, zooms, etc.) as part of filmic 'monstration' (Gaudreault 2009: 81–89), whereas I understand as part of the narration of a film any decision about the selection and presentation of (fictional) story facts, including image framing, camera movements, etc.

44 Winters' reluctance to identify some nondiegetic music with narration is based on his understanding of that term: '[W]hile the majority of music in film might be usefully be thought of as part of a narrative, it does not usually narrate and therefore cannot be said to occupy an extra-diegetic level that is removed both temporally and spatially from the characters' (Winters 2012: 40). It is unclear why the extradiegetic level would be temporally and spatially removed from characters: neither would be a present-tense narration in a novel. 'Extradiegetic' means another level of narration: a different category altogether. It is also unclear what is meant by 'narrate'. Elsewhere, Winters equates narration with 'imparting narrative knowledge' (2012: 40), and prefers terms such as Igor Stravinsky's 'wallpaper music' or Aaron Copeland's 'atmosphere' to describe what much film music does: 'Such descriptions emphasise the way in which music is utilisied to define the shape and character of a narrative space' (2012: 40). That is inaccurate because the music defines the shape and character of a *diegetic* space, and defining the diegesis means to impart narrative knowledge.

a function rather than a level of narration, to describe music that provides background, atmosphere, and sometimes pace and structure for a scene).

The diegetic/nondiegetic distinction is only one of many that can be applied to music in film, and different categories only provide certain kinds of information and not others. David Neumeyer has discussed the diegetic/nondiegetic distinction in the context of other categories for music in film (Neumeyer 1997, 2000 & 2009): on-screen/off-screen, vocal/instrumental, synchronized/non-synchronized, sound levels, continuous/discontinuous music, closed/open musical structures, thematic or motivic referentiality, formal interaction of music and editing, motivation for or narrative plausibility of music (see Neumeyer 1997: 16–17). He argues against treating the relationship of analytical categories as 'a simple hierarchy crowned by the source/background pair' and in favour of treating them as 'a field or network where this pair is one item' (Neumeyer 2000: 40). The list of categories one deems relevant is open to discussion (and the questions of narrative agency Levinson, Holbrook and Winters ask are conspicuous by their absence from Neumeyer's models, though one could see them located on a higher level, to which the analysis of basic distinctions and their interaction contributes). But the warning against prioritizing the diegetic/nondiegetic distinction as fundamental is important.[45]

---

45 Neumeyer is not immune to the lure of hierarchy, though. In Neumeyer 1997, he locates the diegetic/nondiegetic distinction on a low level of a hierarchy based primarily on Bordwell. Music appears as a subcategory of the soundtrack, which is subordinated to film style (in Bordwell's sense as medium-specific means of narration), which is subordinated to the distinction between systems of narration, which Neumeyer distinguishes from story and 'excess' (narratively non-functional features of a narrative; see Thompson 1981: 287–303; and Bordwell 1985: 53). The systems of narration are subordinated to the distinction between processes of narration and sources of narrative agency. Music itself Neumeyer differentiates into 'codes': cultural, formal and cinematic conventions; the diegetic/nondiegetic distinction is classed as one of these 'codes' (Neumeyer 1997: 14–17). But the hierarchy is problematic: to relegate music to a subcategory of style overlooks that it is often crucial for 'excess', and overlooks that diegetic music features on plot and story levels. That also applies to Neumeyer's system of 'interplay of style and plot'. Crucial for the latter is the relationship between diegetic and nondiegetic music, but music in Neumeyer's model only appears as a subcategory of style. The idea of a 'field or network' Neumeyer suggests elsewhere may work better than a tree-like hierarchy. (He is also inaccurate with regard to Bordwellian terminology, and categorizes plot and style under 'systems' of narration and distinguishes them from story and style. In Bordwell, 'syuzhet' and 'fabula' are 'systems' of narration, while style is the medium of syuzhet construction and excess is beyond the systemic part of the model; see Bordwell 1985: 50.)

The problem also applies to the model in Neumeyer (2009). Its first two levels are unproblematic: on the first, a spectator distinguishes sounds in the real world of the cinema from sounds that are part of the film; and on the second level, between diegetic and nondiegetic sounds/music. But the next level, which Neumeyer calls 'narration', is not a subcategory of one of those concepts, but describes different ways to construe the relationship between diegetic and nondiegetic sounds/music: as oppositional (or dialectically related), as a continuum or series of intermediate stages, or as an opposition that also includes the 'fantastical gap'. Yet this third 'stage' is not a subordinate level, but something categorically different: a description of the assumptions we make to distinguish between diegetic and nondiegetic in the first place, and as such a condition for the second 'stage' of Neumeyer's model rather than its subcategory.

This study is not concerned with the integral analysis of film music, but singles out levels of narration. From that perspective, Neumeyer's categories can be passed over here. The question of narrative agency within the horizon of diegetic and nondiegetic music, however, is relevant because it asks what 'narration' on those levels can mean. Music can be used on the diegetic and the nondiegetic level in very different ways, some of which are explored in the following sections of the chapter.

b. Nondiegetic music and narrative agency

The main sense in which nondiegetic music encompasses different options concerns its functions, a category only partly connected to that of narrative agency, which this study is about. That can include formal structuring (music to unify a montage, music providing continuity across a change of scene, music as formal punctuation, etc.); it can mean to evoke place, time, milieu or mood; it can mean clues for the audience (the indication of danger or deliverance, for example); it can mean underlining the trajectory of a scene, etc. None of that is relevant here; what is relevant is how nondiegetic music can imply different kinds of narrative agency.

Music as voice or as emanation

Nondiegetic music can be placed at varying 'distances' to diegetic facts, and establish different relationships between narration and diegesis. At one end of the scale, it can function as commentary, can speak about events. One of Ben Winter's examples for his definition of 'extra-diegetic music', Samuel Barber's 'Adagio for Strings' in *Platoon*, represents this option. When Oliver Stone used it in 1986, the 'Adagio' had become, in effect, identical with its reception history (see Howard 2007). It had been used to announce the death of F.D. Roosevelt in 1945 on the radio, and later became the unofficial US funeral anthem, employed in connection with, among others, the deaths of Ohio senator Robert A. Taft I in 1953, Albert Einstein in 1955, John F. Kennedy in 1963 and Grace Kelly in 1982. Barber had made a choral arrangement to the text of the 'Agnus Dei'

Elsewhere in the article, Neumeyer hits upon a more interesting problem when he discusses the interplay of the diegetic/nondiegetic distinction and narrative agency. Diegetic music can be a realistic element of the storyworld, but nondiegetic music necessarily raises the question of its function: Why is it used in a scene? But if we look at the constellation from the perspective of narrative functionality, nondiegetic music is the less problematic category because it is functional in any case. Diegetic music, on the other hand, requires interpretation because 'it provokes the question: Is this environmental sound or does it have [is it meant to have] narrative significance?' (Neumeyer 2009). In ch. II.iv.d I suggest an approach to narrative agency that distinguishes between (implied) author and narrator, between narrative agency in the presentation of supposedly 'given' story facts (including nondiegetic music) and implied authorial agency to account for the those story facts (including diegetic music). This may provide a simpler account of diegetic music that is not just 'environmental sound', but narratively significant.

in 1967, confirming the quasi-sacred aspect of the piece; an aspect perhaps less to do with its musical features than with the history of its use. In *Platoon*, that reception history is tapped into to say that the American soldiers who had died in the war deserve the national music of mourning, alongside Roosevelt, Einstein or Kennedy. We could assign the music to different sources: to Stone as the author of a 'message movie'; to an abstract cinematic narrator; or to Chris (Charlie Sheen), from whose retrospective perspective the story is told. Whatever assignation we prefer, crucial for its effect is that the music is pre-existing, and that it carries its reception history into the film.

The *Platoon* example relies on the historical charge of the Barber music, but the impression of an independent musical voice can be achieved by original music as well. An example is the central battle of Akira Kurosawa's *Ran* (1985), when the combined forces of Great Lord Hidetora's sons Taro and Jiro ambush their father's troops. One of Hidetora's guards, shot through with arrows, tells him that all is lost, and after that we see images of the slaughter. But the diegetic sound has cut out completely and has been replaced by the lament of Tôru Takemitsu's nondiegetic music; the narration refuses to stand the horror of war any longer and mourns it instead. The impression of a voice with its own message relies on the surprise effect: the abrupt switch from diegetic sound to nondiegetic musical lament avoids the 'naturalization' of the music as an integral part of the scene, and seems like a *decision* that makes us aware of the narration as agency, with its own voice and perspective on story events.[46]

A musical comedy voice is achieved in *Sixteen Candles* (1984), when music gives Sam's (Molly Ringwald) experiences with fellow students or her grandparents a drastic, comic book aspect by quoting well-known TV themes: *Dragnet* (1951–59), *The Twilight Zone*, *Peter Gunn* (1958–61). The use of pre-existing music with a high recognition factor means that the music muscles into the foreground, and gives mundane events an intensity we might associate with the adolescent experience the film is about. Even though Sam is present in all the scenes, we do not understand the TV themes as representing her perception: *Dragnet* and *The Twilight Zone* precede the moments when she comes into play, and *Peter Gunn* only starts after the image has cut away from her to a parade of bizarrely dressed teenagers at a party. It rather as if the narration gives us its own gloss on Sam's experiences.

At the other end of the spectrum, nondiegetic music can seem to be an emanation of something within the diegesis rather than something added by a narrating agency (part of what Winters calls 'intra-diegetic music'). When Doctor Cochrane (Edward Platt)

---

46 We could link the change in sonic perspective to Hidetora's realization that the battle is lost (and his realization of his sons' treachery), but the vignettes from the battle accompanied by the music are not shown from his visual point of view; they show random scenes of killing and seem to survey the events overall rather than from Hidetora's perception.

 Wolfgang Petersen's *Troy* (2004) copies Kurosawa's and Takemitsu's ploy for the storming of Troy, but is too timid to go all the way. Diegetic battle sounds continue at low volume below the keening, clichéd 'ethnic' voice singing the lament, and the sonic doubling weakens the effect.

tells Kyle Hadley (Robert Stack) in *Written on the Wind* (1956) about his fertility 'weakness', and Kyle abruptly leaves the café, only stopping for a second to look at a young boy on an electric horse, the music, with its ostinato around an augmented second and its massive crescendo, so clearly represents his inner agitation that it might indeed seem strange to place it outside the diegesis, since it so clearly concerns the diegetic fact of Kyle's emotional state. We do not assume that the music speculates about that state from the perspective of an external onlooker, but that it informs us of something that is fictionally true. One can make the case for locating such music on the lowest of Branigan's levels of narration: 'internal focalization (depth)' (Branigan 1992: 87) (see more in ch. II.v.) But even as an example of internal focalization, the music is still not diegetic: it is not a *musical* part of the storyworld; it is music that *represents* a part of the storyworld to us (in this case an emotion). Again the comparison with a novel can clarify the point. There are different ways of indicating a character's inner state:

a. The novelist can write: 'She sat down on the bed and wondered: "When did it all start to go so wrong?"' (tagged direct style, 'She [...] wondered' being the tag).
b. Or 'She sat down on the bed, wondering when it had all started to go so wrong' (tagged indirect style).
c. Or 'She sat down on the bed. When did it all start to go so wrong?' (free indirect style) (for the concepts, see for example Chatman 1978: 201; Genette 1980: 169–85; Bal 2009: 48–55; and Fludernik 2009: 66–69).

The informational content about diegetic facts is the same in all cases, but in example (*a*) the character itself provides the information in mimetic interior monologue, while in examples (*b*) and (*c*) the (extradiegetic) narrator's voice provides the information *for* the character (in example *c* even speaking *as* her), but from her perspective – cases of internal focalization (see ch.II.v). The source of the information is in all cases the character's mind – an element of the diegesis. But the narrating voice is different, located on different levels of narration, and that is the difference relevant here – and with regard to the question how to categorize music that is not a *musical* part of the diegesis, but closely aligned to something within that diegesis.

Which level of narration provides the information in the three sentences is less interesting than the information itself. A film-maker can invoke 'cliché Paris' by having a musette accordion play in a corner of the frame, and she can do the same by having the accordion play without visible or implied storyworld source. The informational content would be (almost) the same, and the same purpose of underscoring the scene with musical local colour would be served, but the music would nevertheless come from different levels of narration – the difference would just not be very interesting: But that the differentiation between diegetic and nondiegetic music may not always tell us something interesting does not make it superfluous; we should just not expect more from it than it is made to do.

Nondiegetic music, diegetic control

However, commentary function and closeness to a character are not mutually exclusive: nondiegetic music can comment *and* be aligned with a character. The opening of *Ferris Bueller's Day Off* (1986) shows Ferris (Matthew Broderick) trick his parents (Cindy Pickett and Lyman Ward) into believing that he is sick and has to stay in bed, only to get up and have his day off when they have left. While his sister (Jennifer Grey) sees through him, the parents fall for Ferris' hammy acting – acting supported by an underscore of sweetly sentimental American family-movie music. It is the music Ferris would want to play if this were not his life, but a movie (which on another level it is), or the music he would want to play in his parents' minds. But that makes it blatantly ironic if heard from his own perspective – and from ours, who are made complicit in his trick. We are faced with music that is not diegetic (we cannot even link it to the parents' perception, because it continues when they have left the room and we see only Ferris), but seems under Ferris' control. The film confirms that at the end of the scene, when Ferris breaks the 'fourth wall' by looking into the camera and saying: 'They bought it.' The music in *Ferris Bueller's Day Off* parodies a range of film scoring clichés, and in this it is a good fit for Ferris' way of seeing the world. We can easily imagine the music as his choice – events in his life are as much under his control as the narration of the film, including its nondiegetic music, which becomes part of Ferris' extrovert and extravagant self-performance.

Nondiegetic music that seems to be controlled by a diegetic character is particularly suited to characters a film wants to show as manipulative: benignly so in *Ferris Bueller's Day Off*, a little more deprecatorily in a scene from *The Brothers Grimm* (2005) that shows the younger brother, Wilhelm (Matt Damon), and his snake oil business of promising clueless villagers deliverance from supernatural scares (organized by the brothers, who then proceed to get rid off them in spectacularly staged action). When Wilhelm tells the citizens of Marbaden that with his and Jacob Grimm's arrival their problems are as good as over, his speech is accompanied by triumphantly swelling music, which breaks off suddenly when he switches rhetorical register to come to the practicalities of their work. The music follows the trajectory of his speech so closely that it seems to be under Wilhelm's control as much as his words, and the rhetorical effect of his performance transmits itself to the audience (though its ludicrous aspect may come through more strongly for us than for the Marbadeners).

The scene shows a variant of the 'psychological parallelism' discussed in Chapter IV: the music does something to us that puts us in the shoes of diegetic characters. The music takes on a double nature. It is not diegetic, nor is there reason to assume that Wilhelm or his audience hear this music in their minds. The music presents an aspect of the story to us in the cinema: the effect of Wilhelm's sales pitch. But at the same time it seems to be under Wilhelm's control – his rhetorical performance seems to wave the baton that conducts the music, as if, quite magically, he has the ability to wrest control of nondiegetic music from the narration (albeit in a manner as over-obvious as his verbal rhetoric). The tension between interpreting the music as a representation or as a parody of his hyperbolic rhetoric cannot be resolved, but therein lays its ironic effect.

Such moments are close to Mickey Mousing: music that mimics features of diegetic action in its texture, or rhythmic or melodic contour. Such music can seem like an emanation of the diegetic event rather than something that informs us about that event. In Sergio Leone's *Duck, You Sucker!/Giù la testa* (1971), the music introducing the Irish ex-terrorist Sean (James Coburn) begins exactly when he has taken off his motorbike goggles, and a guitar chord Mickey Mouses his hand adjusting his coat. The musical exaggeration of his movements reproduces the larger-than-life effect Sean's appearance has on Juan (Rod Steiger), but also adds to the comic-book hyperbole of the film as a whole: the sublime and the ridiculous, as we know, are neighbours. In a postmodern western such as *Duck, You Sucker!*, the parodistic effect is intentional, while Mickey Mousing in older films may today seem like unintentional parody not least because of changes in film style and taste. But the effect may also be inherent in a technique that produces tension between different levels of narration that nevertheless seem to conspire to produce a unified audio-visual phenomenon.

Whether to understand music as parody of an on-screen event or as an intimation of its effect can also be a question in cases that lack the audio-visual mirroring of Mickey Mousing. When in *For a Few Dollars More/Per qualche dollari in più* (1965), El Indio (Gian Maria Volonté) steps up to he pulpit to tell his parable of the iron safe and the wooden chest disguising it, the film accompanies him with sweet, pseudo-religious music that is as playfully cynical as Indio himself. We may hear the music as an emanation of his performance, an evocation of its effect on the diegetic audience, or we may hear it as parody, and as in *The Brothers Grimm*, the tension is crucial for the ironic effect.

Would-be-diegetic music
A special case of nondiegetic music speaking for diegetic characters is what one could call 'would-be-diegetic music': music that does not have a diegetic source, but that we can imagine *could* occur in the diegesis at this point. The ur-example – at least in sound film, while the technique is more natural for silent film accompaniment – is Hanns Eisler's 'Solidaritätslied'/'Song of Solidarity' at the end of *Kuhle Wampe or: To Whom Does the World Belong?/Kuhle Wampe oder: Wem gehört die Welt?* (1932). The song pervades the third 'chapter' of the film. It already casts its shadow when material from the song is used as instrumental accompaniment to the montage of factories and machines that opens the chapter. It enters the diegesis as a song sung by communist workers during a sports and theatre festival in the countryside. But for the end of the film, it is used differently. After the train journey back to Berlin that forms the (musicless) fourth chapter of *Kuhle Wampe*, we see the worker-athletes walk through a long tunnel heavy with symbolic import, and again we hear the 'Song of Solidarity', but now without diegetic source: we do not see the workers sing. It has detached itself again from its diegetic anchoring, and the film's narration takes over the choral, solidary voice of the workers and sings for them, positions itself on their side.

This was to become a common technique to express 'a kind of fantasy collectivity through music that transcends the individuals', as Richard Dyer describes it (Dyer 2010: 96) with regard to *Treno popolare* (1933) and *Sing As We Go!* (1934).[47] Such fantasy collecvtivity can be understood to imply that the narration takes sides in a diegetic conflict. When Geoffrey Thorpe (Errol Flynn) and his crew in *The Sea Hawk* (1940) escape Spanish captivity and sail home to England, the rousing chorus 'Strike for the Shores of Dover' – derived from the fanfare theme that opens the film – has no visible source: we do not see the sailors sing. Instead we hear a choir singing what we might imagine the sailors could be singing in this situation. As in *Kuhle Wampe*, the narration of the film sings for the characters whose side it is on.

Claudia Gorbman points out that at the end of *Kuhle Wampe*, Eisler leaves distancing Brechtian alienation behind and is unashamedly affirmative, with musical means that 'make the heart swell with uncritical emotion – not unlike the male chorus on the soundtrack as the cattle drive begins in *Red River* (1948)' (Gorbman 1991: 280). Affirmation was no problem for Eisler if it was used for the good fight. To laud the solidarity of the Czech against Nazi occupation in *Hangmen Also Die!* (1943), or to underline and transcend the toil of the Dutch people in Joris Ivens' documentary *New Earth/Nieuwe Gronden* (1933), is described as unquestionably positive in *Composing for the Films* (Adorno and Eisler 1994: 25–26). That is the point of the technique, which distinguishes between diegesis and narration, but reaches out into the diegesis and implicates the narration in its events. (More on Eisler and narration in Heldt 2008b.)

c. Diegetic music: storyworld attachment and narrative agency

Modes of storyworld attachment
In what ways can music in a film be diegetic, that is, part of our mental construction of the storyworld? A first set of distinctions describes how music can be attached to the storyworld:

- On-screen/off-screen: The most straightforward case is music visibly made on-screen and audible to us and (we assume) to characters. But if the camera moves and thereby removes the source of the music from our view while the music continues, in most cases we will still assume the music to take place in the storyworld, only off-screen (but in a space contiguous with the one we can see).
- Sonic/non-sonic: Music need not be audible to lay claim to diegetic presence. It can be shown to take place without giving us access to the sound itself (a musician seen to be

---

47 Dyer also shows that in films about 'folk' cultures, the distinction between diegetic and nondiegetic music can break down altogether, and music can be shown to pervade that culture's world so thoroughly that its source is immaterial (see Dyer 2010: 96–97).

playing through a window, for example; for such cases, Claudia Gorbman has suggested to distinguish between 'on-track' and 'off-track' sound; see 1987: 144–150). Music can also be introduced by proxy: through musical notation or the visual presence of records or CD, or by report, e.g. through characters talking about music; if they mention pieces we know, our musical imagination can fill in the gap.[48]

- On-scene/off-scene: A third distinction is suggested by Jonathan Godsall in a forthcoming study on pre-existing music in film (Godsall n.d.). It is less straightforward because it touches upon our basic understanding of 'diegetic' as that which is part of the 'narratively implied spatiotemporal world of the actions and characters' (Gorbman 1987: 21). *Goodfellas* (1990) is a good example. The film is pervaded by pre-existing songs contemporary with or older than the time the story is set in, some with manifest or implied sources in scenes and some without (and some of unclear status). But is it correct to say that *any* of the songs are nondiegetic? After all, all of the songs do exist in the world the characters inhabit; any character could know any of them. The question is particularly relevant for films with 'realistic' diegeses and pre-existing music, but in principle for any music a film implies could plausibly be played in its world.

A further distinction is necessary for this. Godsall suggests a distinction between diegetic music that is 'on-scene' (i.e. has a source in the scene in question, either on- or off-screen) and diegetic music that is 'off-scene' (i.e. is part of the storyworld, but not of the scene in question). It is unlikely that this wider usage of 'diegetic music' will supplant the current one, which tends to use the scene rather than the diegesis as a whole as its frame of reference.[49] But even if we accept that in most cases in which we label music as 'diegetic', we refer to the scene in question, we should not forget that 'nondiegetic music' that is part of the wider world of the characters can also be described as diegetic,

---

48 An elaborate example occurs in *Léon/Léon: The Professional* (1994). Bent cop Norman Stansfield (Gary Oldman) takes a pill that makes him ready for a bit of the old ultra-violence, and says to accomplice Malky (Peter Appel), 'I like these calm little moments before the storm. It reminds me of Beethoven. [Cut to the inside of the flat of Mathilda's family.] Can you hear it? [He makes conducting movements.] It's like when you put your head to the grass and you can hear the growin' and you can hear the insects. [Cut to inside of Leon's flat.] Do you like Beethoven?' Malky replies, 'Couldn't really say.' Stansfield: 'I'll play you some', while he takes Malky's gun and shoots open the door. While he walks through it, he makes further conducting movements, but we hear unrelated music on the soundtrack. To Mathilda's father (Michael Badalucco) he says, 'We said noon. I've got one minute past. [He snaps his finger, at which the nondiegetic music ends, as if he had been conducting it.] You don't like Beethoven. You don't know what you're missing. Overtures like that get my juices flowing. So powerful', etc.

The film restricts itself to external focalization (see ch. II.v), but shows us that music *is* going through a character's mind – the film just refuses to make it audible, which is irritating, because we expect internal focalization at this point.

49 Similar to Godsall's distinction is Michel Chion's, who uses the terms 'son in' (diegetic on-screen sound), 'son hors-champ' (diegetic off-screen sound), and 'son off', which he defines with reference to the individual scene as 'sound emitted from an invisible source that in addition belongs to a time and/ or place different from the space-time of the action shown in the image' (Chion 2009: 249–50).

if in principle rather than in scenic actuality. More important than the terminology is awareness of the twist in the system itself.

Diegetic music and narrative agency

A second range of options for diegetic music concerns, as for nondiegetic music, narrative agency. At one end, it can realistically furnish the diegesis.[50] At the most neutral, this means what Michel Chion calls 'ambient sound': 'sound that envelops a scene and inhabits its space, without raising the question of the identification or visual embodiment of its source' (Chion 1994: 75) – muzak in an airport, a jazz piano in a bar, etc.[51]

But music appearing in 'its natural role' is not precluded from 'simultaneously fulfilling additional tasks' (Lissa 1965: 166; my translation); even seemingly non-significative music can become meaningful. In David Lynch's *Wild at Heart* (1990), the orchestral prelude from Richard Strauss's 'Im Abendrot' for the credits is followed by Glenn Miller's 'In the Mood' for the first scene at the Cape Fear Hotel. The volume of the music drops when the camera tilts down from its worm's eye view of the ceiling of the hotel staircase to show us the guests, and we can imagine the music as diegetic, coming from an off-screen room. That is confirmed when, after the horrific altercation in which Sailor Ripley (Nicholas Cage) batters Bob Ray Lemon (Gregg Dandridge) to death, 'In the Mood' continues unperturbed: a classic case of musical anempathy, typically provided by diegetic music because the diegetic status naturalizes its lack of affective appropriateness. But though 'In the Mood' is plausible diegetic music for the situation, dramaturgically it is a foil for the brutal scene and for the music around it: the hyper-romantic Strauss and the speed-metal piece 'Slaughterhouse' (by the band Powermad) that accompanies the fight (either fittingly brutal nondiegetic music, or, since the band is one of Sailor's favourites, a representation of music in his mind). In that neighbourhood, 'In the Mood' seems not inoffensively neutral, but glaringly insipid, music that represents the opposite of the world of emotional and musical extremes Sailor and Lula (Laura Dern) inhabit, a world in which late Strauss, speed metal and the crooner Elvis Presley of 'Love Me Tender' are linked by their courting of emotional extremes and their refusal to bow to good taste – music that is wild at heart.[52]

'In the Mood' in *Wild at Heart* is diegetic music that is relatively realistic, but has an obvious purpose. But even the least conspicuous diegetic music can be understood as a purposeful choice on the level of 'historical authorship'. How we understand diegetic music, and how clearly a film foregrounds authorial agency to account for it, depends

50 This option is described by Holbrook's 'realistic depiction' (2005b: 49) or Neumeyer's 'environmental sound' (2009).

51 Barbara Flückiger calls soundtrack elements that characterize locations *Orientierungslaute* ('orientation sound', Flückiger 2001: 305–306). Sound complexes that characterize a space are usually called background, ambience or atmosphere.

52 The function of radically different music as expressions of Lula's and Sailor's love has been pointed out by Annette Davison, referring to an observation by Michel Chion (Davison 2004: 176–79).

on the question if that purpose is *meant* to be noticed: if music is put where it is in the diegesis to make a point, and in a way that betrays the intention to make a point. In such cases, films show up the fictionality of the diegesis and the difference between story*telling* (the presentation of fictitiously given facts) and story*making* (the invention of a story).[53]

In *Wild at Heart*, 'In the Mood' functions within an overall musical design and is not necessarily meant to be understood as self-conscious commentary. A step further goes *Little Voice* (Mark Herman, 1998). Billy (Ewan McGregor) is waiting outside of LV's (Jane Horrocks) house, waiting to speak to her despite her reclusiveness. Without having seen him, LV puts on a record with Cole Porter's 'My Heart Belongs to Daddy', sung by Marilyn Monroe – an 'accidental' juxtaposition that neatly summarizes what he has to overcome in his cautiously budding romance with her: LV's devotion to her dead father and his record collection she has so deeply internalized. The lyrics comment on the situation, while the music is still diegetically plausible: it is the kind of music LV listens to. But it is the irony of fate that puts it is its place, or rather the conscious irony of authorial agency.[54] The nature of that agency is discussed in the following section.

d. Diegetic commentary and the implied author

The concept of the 'implied author' has been reasonably successful in general narratology, controversial in film narratology, and has hardly ever been applied to music in film. But it can provide a theoretically more deeply-rooted account of what film musicology has described as 'diegetic commentary' (Norden 2007) or 'ambi-diegetic music' (Holbrook

---

53 My understanding of such moments differs from what is covered by Holbrook's 'ambi-diegetic music' (Holbrook 2005a & 2005b); more in ch. II.iv.d. Neumeyer does not elaborate his concept of 'narrative significance' (2009) enough to say if it is closer to Holbrook or to the implied author.

54 *Little Voice* is full of diegetic commentaries, but not all of them function in the same way. When LV's mother (Brenda Blethyn) is canoodling with Ray Say (Michael Caine) on the sofa, LV plays 'That's Entertainment' (sung by Judy Garland) as an ironic comment on her mother's behaviour, with lines such as 'The clown with his pants falling down' (referring to Ray), 'The lights on the lady in tights' (her mother), 'Or the ball where she gives him her all' or 'The plot can be hot, simply teeming with sex' (their behaviour). Her mother hits back with 'It's Not Unusual' (sung by Tom Jones) to claim her right to have fun.

In such scenes, the characters themselves use music to communicate and comment on their lives. But other scenes employ blatant ironies of fate that introduce authorial agency, e.g. when LV is listening to 'The Dicky Bird Hop' (sung by Gracie Fields) and right after the line 'I hear them saying early ev'ry morn, "Get up! Get up! Get up!"', her mother bursts into the room and rudely says 'Get up, you! Ray wants you downstairs', unwittingly, but precisely puncturing the bubble of popular songs in which LV tries to hide. The blithe mixture of diegetic commentaries by the characters and others that betray authorial agency could be seen as confirming the status of the film as a musical one (if not as a film musical). Music is central to the film, at whatever level of narration.

2005a & 2005b), and can clarify the status of narration in film and its relationship with the distinction between diegetic and nondiegetic music.

The implied author in (film) narratology

When Wayne Booth invented the implied author in *The Rhetoric of Fiction* (1961), his main concern was to hold the real author at arm's length and to look at the text as text: his question was 'not what an author wanted to say but only what his text means' (Kind and Müller 2006: 162). Booth wanted to study how the idea of authorial agency became part of a text and our construal of it, rather than to refer textual features back to authorial intention, biography or other factors grounding a text in the real world that had produced it. In this light, the concept of authorial agency we have in mind when we are reading, say, a novel is not about actual authorship, but part of the rhetoric of fiction: 'The "implied author" chooses [...] what we read; we infer him as an ideal, literary, created version of the real man; he is the sum of his own choices' (Booth 1961: 74–75). One problem with the real world is that it is knowable only imperfectly; readings on that basis are reliant on the chance availability of contextual information. A second problem is that it is difficult to reverse-engineer how authorial intention or historical conditions have informed a text. A third problem is that a fictional text can be read and interpreted even if we know nothing of its author: the manuscript of a novel found in a suitcase on a skip, without any clue as to its author, would be a feasible object of literary analysis.

But that does not make the idea of authorial agency pointless. Fiction is, by definition, invented, made-up. Yet even if one is not interested in the process of invention, but only in the text itself, it may still be interesting to ask how its inventedness becomes 'a principle recorded in the text' (Chatman 1990: 81). In inventing a story and the procedures of its narration, an author can wear any number of masks – can, in fact, not *not* wear a mask. The same empirical author could take the same story kernel and fashion utterly different texts from it, with different implications, messages, effects:

> It is a curious fact that we have no terms either for this created 'second self' or for our relationship with him. None of our terms for various aspects of the narrator is quite accurate. 'Persona', 'mask', and 'narrator' are sometimes used, but they more commonly refer to the speaker in the work who is after all only one of the elements created by the implied author and who may be separated from him by large ironies. (Booth 1961: 73)

Booth tried to steer a course between the biographism of old and the 'desiccated' pieties of New Criticism, which had reduced literature to 'verbal and symbolic interrelationships', but excluded authors, audiences, ideas, beliefs and 'narrative interest' (Booth 1977: 84–85), and for that he distinguished between real and implied author. But he also makes a distinction on the other side: between implied author and narrator, between the voice that *tells* a story, the voice that says 'she said' and 'he said', and the agency that steers the 'choice of character and episode and scene and idea' (Booth 1961: 74), the agency that invents the story *and* the rules of its presentation.

The distinction between real and implied author is one of epistemological interest. There is nothing wrong with researching what relationship a text has with the conditions of its production; it is just a different perspective from one that asks how a text works as text. Both questions can be asked equally well for literary fiction and fiction film. Despite the career of auteurism in a phase of film studies and journalism, the collaborative nature of film-making means that the shadow of the author was never as long here as in literary studies, which dampened the need for a narratological construct to account for the fictionality of fiction film.

But the other distinction, between implied author and narrator, works more smoothly in literature than in film, and because of that the implied author, while not uncontroversial in literary studies (Kindt and Müller 2006 summarize the discussion), has had a much more chequered career in film studies, in tandem with the concept of a cinematic 'narrator'. (David Bordwell has been the chief detractor of 'narrators' and 'implied authors' in film narratology, while Seymour Chatman has been their main proponent in a virtual discussion over three decades; see Chatman 1978: 147–51, Bordwell 1985: 61–62, Chatman 1990: 74–108 & 124–38, and Bordwell 2008: 121–30.[55])

In a literary text, the narrator is manifest in the voice that tells a story, inscribed in the verb forms in the parts of the text that do not represent direct speech.[56] Filmic narration works differently, and usually without a strong sense of such a narrating voice. There can be direct narration, of course – a voice-over, for example, or scrolling text. But these are nowhere nearly as pervasive in film as narrating voices in novels. There may be nondiegetic music, but the semantic elusiveness of music makes it difficult to understand more than a few instances of this as the equivalent of a personalized, narrating voice.

The more important narrational task in a film is the organization of our access to information: the framing of images, camera movements, cuts – the structuring of the bits of 'monstration', of the direct 'showing forth' of events in the seeming immediacy of the camera image (and seemingly synchronous diegetic sound).[57] This means that in film, we find an impersonal system of narration. And for pragmatic reasons it is easy to think of that system as encompassing both the means for presenting story 'facts' *and* the story it allows us to (re)construct: Booth's 'character and episode and scene and idea'.

---

55 Booth briefly contributed to the debate as well (2002).

56 The exception would be a novel consisting only of 'documents', without a narrating voice connecting them, historically important in epistolary novels particularly popular in the eighteenth century.

57 For the concept of 'monstration' see Gaudreault 1987 and Gaudreault 2009. One need not subscribe to Gaudreault's line of division between 'monstration' (roughly, the camera image) and 'narration' (roughly, editing) for the distinction between recorded (or seemingly recorded) information and its selection and editing to make sense. (For a concise critique of Gaudreault's use of the two concepts, see Stam, Burgoyne and Flitterman-Lewis 1992: 116–17.)

That is, roughly summarized, David Bordwell's critique of burdening film narratology with 'narrators' and 'implied authors': while there *can* be personalized narrating voices in films, they are not a *conditio sine qua non*. Even if an audience becomes aware of the intentionality of narrational techniques in 'self-conscious passages, we don't characteristically attribute them to a narrator. For ordinary audiences, the relevant agent or agents are the filmmakers, commonly known as *they*' (Bordwell 2008: 122). 'They' can invent a clever way of showing us an event as easily as they can invent a clever event itself. This makes sense from the perspective of a poetics of cinema, of cinema as craft. But 'they' are still a problematic concept, however we understand 'them':

- Either 'they' are taken literally as the historical film-makers. That would fall back to a naïve identification of the reality of film production with the effects produced by the result of that production – the methodological mistake Booth wanted to get away from. While there is nothing to be said against studying the former, one must not confuse it with the latter interest (even if some films reference extrafictional conditions of their existence), which is not delegitimized by audiences not sharing it.
- Or 'they' are just a demotic word for Booth's or Chatman's 'implied author': the idea of an authorial agency we construct to account for the inventedness of story and narration.

At the bottom of Bordwell's position is his critique of a communication model of narration, of the idea of a 'message' being 'passed from sender to receiver' (Bordwell 1985: 62). Instead, he describes film narration as 'the organization of a set of cues for the construction of a story. This presupposes a perceiver, but not a sender of a story' (1985: 62). Bordwell's interest in story construction in the mind of a perceiver is shared by Edward Branigan, who does use terms such as 'nondiegetic narrator' and 'implied author' (Branigan 1992: 87), but strictly as pragmatic shorthand for the way a perceiver understands a narrative:

> My claim is that 'narration' exists whenever we *transform* data from one to another of the above [levels of narration]. Whether we are an 'author' or a 'reader' is no longer pertinent: the central activity of narration is the redescription of data under epistemological constraint. (Branigan 1992: 112)

This is the core of a perceiver-centred theory of narration developed from cognitive narratology (for a summary, see Jahn 2005a). From this perspective, a narrative text is of interest with regard to our ways of making sense of it. A problem of this approach, however much it can tell us about the mental assemblage of cues into stories, is that it is counterintuitive with regard to the basis of narrative in mental mechanisms and of storytelling in everyday life. Our mind is an as-if machine: a machine for mental simulations of potential consequences of events and actions. That makes fiction possible: we can think about it as if it were real, while we know that it is not – that is precisely what our mental activity consists of most of the time anyway. The basic situation of storytelling is that of someone telling us about something that happened: a communicative situation. Because we are geared to mental simulations, we can simulate that communicative situation with invented stories: that is fiction.

But even a narrative form such as film, which has no real equivalent in everyday communication (holiday videos excepted) can still be understood in the terms of that basic communicative situation: as a 'guided reading' (Gaudreault 1987: 33) of information about a fictional world, rather than 'a way of understanding data under the illusion of occurrence; that is, a way of perceiving by a spectator which organizes data as if it were witnessed unfolding in a temporal, spatial, and causal frame' (Branigan 1992: 115). If we take out 'illusion', which accounts for the fictionality of fiction, Branigan's definition does not just apply to our making sense of narrative as a selection and arrangement of information about the (real or simulated) world, but also to how we may make sense of (a bit of) the real world. But understanding 'data [...] unfolding in a temporal, spatial, and causal frame', i.e. understanding events, is not the same as understanding a narrative as an *intentionally organized* system of cues for the (re)construction of events (even if we may, on occasion, make sense of real events by transforming them into a narrative).

Crucial is the question of intentionality: not the actual intentionality of the historical author(s), but intentionality as a principle that governs the relationship between a narrative as an organized set of cues and the (re)construction of a story and its narration by the perceiver. In that respect, standard-issue fiction films are the polar opposite of a tragedy structured according to the Aristotelian unities, which obviate the need for narrational decisions about what we see and hear. Films are full of structural features betraying intentionality – not just the specific intentions inscribed in a particular film narrative, but intentionality as a principle of the form. Chatman points out the problem of Bordwell's perspective:

> What does it mean to say that a film is 'organized' but not 'sent'? Who or what organizes it – not originally, of course, but right there on the screen during projection? Bordwell does not tell us. [...] If we argue that 'narrator' names only the organizational and sending agency and that that agency need not be human [...] much of Bordwell's objection seems obviated, and we are spared the uncomfortable consequences of [...] a creation with no creator. (Chatman 1990: 127)

But even if we accept Chatman's defence of a communication model of narration, the question remains what the distinction between implied authorship and narration may yield for our understanding of film (and film music), even if we talk not of an 'implied author', but of '"text implication" or "text instance" or "text design"' (Chatman 1990: 86). Like Bordwell, Chatman insists that this is not a matter of principle: 'My defense is strictly pragmatic, not ontological: the question is not whether the implied author *exists* but what we *get* from positing such a concept' (Chatman 1990: 75).

In the end, the difference between their positions may not be so big: 'The organization of a set of cues for the construction of a story', Bordwell's definition of film narration, contains 'organization' *and* 'construction'. It is in the dance of these two around each other – an organization of cues that takes the knowledge, expectations, preferences and reactions of the perceiver into account, and the perceiver's reaction to the cues to (re)construct what they imply – that narrative comes to fruition.

The implied author and film music (I)

The only major attempt to import the implied author into film musicology is Jerrold Levinson's article 'Film Music and Narrative Agency' (1996), but Levinson construes the concept in a way that is neither true to its origin nor helpful for film musicology.

He starts with the basic distinction between narrator and implied author (or implied film-maker; see Levinson 1996: 251). For the narrator, the story is real, and he observes it and shows it to us; the implied film-maker, on the other hand, is responsible for the construction of narration *and* story, and is 'aware' of its fictionality (Levinson 1996: 253).[58] The next distinction also makes sense: that between music that makes something 'fictional' or 'fictionally true' (1996: 259), and music that comments on the story from the outside: 'Something is fictional in a film […] if it is *to be imagined to be the case* by viewers' (1996: 259; based on Walton 1982). To make something fictional means to inform the audience that it is true: the swell of strings that tells us that a character is in love, or the tremolo that warns us about impending danger (to use two trite, but typical examples). The love and the danger are fictional facts of the storyworld. We may not always be sure about the exact nature of the fictional truth thus suggested: the tremolo may tell of danger objectively impending or of a character's fear of danger, and the dividing line can be fine or nonexistent. But in any case such music claims that what it says is 'the case'.

The other option is music that does not serve the construction of the storyworld, but comments on it 'in a mode of distanced and reflective juxtaposition to the story narrated' (Levinson 1996: 272), as Levinson says about the xylophone music from Carl Orff's and Gunild Keetman's 'Schulwerk' in the feedlot scene in *Badlands* (1973), one of his key examples for music he attributes to the implied film-maker.

Levinson's main reason for not assigning this music to the 'cinematic narrator' (Levinson 1996: 273) is that he cannot see what it might contribute to our understanding of the story or the perspective from which the story is shown:

> […] Orff's score […] [has] no obvious connection with, or fittingness to, gritty scenes of cows being force-fed and almost expiring in the heat. That is to say, there is nothing in the character of the state of affairs depicted that the music could plausibly be thought to second, nor anything indeterminate about those states of affairs that the

---

58 The two can be congruent: narrators who invent a story in the process of telling it, i.e. narrators manifestly aware of the fictionality of the story. In this context, Levinson mentions Kendall Walton's distinction between 'reporting narrators' and 'storytelling narrators', the latter signalling the fictionality of the story they tell (see Levinson 1996: 279, endnote 11; and Walton 1982: 368–72).

music might plausibly be thought to specify. [...] Could it be narrative in the sense of expressing the cinematic narrator's view of the situation depicted? This seems unlikely, if only because it is rather unclear what sort of attitude could be signalled by such music in relation to the events shown. (Levinson 1996: 273)

But not to know what a narrational technique achieves in a film is not a good reason not to understand it as a narrational technique. And neither can Levinson say why the implied film-maker may have used it:

This leaves as the only [...] possibility the assignment of the music to the implied filmmaker who, from a point both outside the story and its narration, has apparently added this music as a kind of counterpoint to the fictional drama. But to what end? It is hard to say [...] but possibly one of aesthetic embellishment, or derangement of the viewer's moral compass, or refraction of the story's content in a distorting mirror, or external meditation on the film's happenings. (Levinson 1996: 273)

This leaves the implied film-maker the role of a dumping ground for difficult-to-explain elements of the text – not a helpful idea.

Levinson's general point is correct: the dichotomy of diegetic and nondiegetic music (or 'paradigmatic film music', as he calls it [Levinson 1996: 248]) makes a crude distinction. To say that music issues from within or without the storyworld does not tell us what it *does*: what purpose it serves, what kind of information it provides (more about that in ch. II. iv.a–c). Nondiegetic music can tell us about the inner state of a character (or seem to emerge from that state); it can inform or mislead us about the significance of events; it can comment; it can structure etc. Diegetic music can be a naturalistic part of the storyworld, but can also provide blatantly ironic commentary.

Levinson makes a valid distinction between nondiegetic music providing essential information (making something fictionally true) and nondiegetic music commenting on a scene in a way that does not affect our understanding of the 'facts' of that scene. But given the range of what music can do on different levels of narration, that difference alone is not sufficient reason to assign different options to different narrative agencies.

The comparison with a novel may help to clarify the issue. The manifest presence of the novelistic narrator as the grammatical subject of sentences not assigned to diegetic characters is a major difference between novels and the rather organizational nature of filmic narration. But that presence also makes it easier to see what nondiegetic narration can encompass. Depending on the kind of focalization (see ch. II.v) and therefore on the 'knowledge' of the narrator (see Bordwell 1985: 57–61), (s)he can do different things: when the narrator of Thomas Hardy's *The Return of the Native* (1878) tells us that Eustacia Vye 'was in person full-limbed and somewhat heavy; without ruddiness, as without pallor' (Hardy 1985: 118), he characterizes her exterior, and that is how we will imagine Eustacia to look – the narrator's voice makes her looks fictionally true. When he tells us that '[t]o be loved to madness – such was her great desire' (1985: 121), he tells us something about her inner life, and again we do not doubt the truthfulness of the description. When he tells us that '[o]n Olympus she would have done well with a little preparation. She had the passions and instincts which make a model goddess, that is, those which make not quite a model woman' (1985: 118), he characterizes and satirizes her, but also lets us know about the narrator's own ideas about goddesses and women, which we may agree or disagree with. And when he muses that '[i]n heaven she will probably sit between the Héloïses and the Cleopatras' (1985: 124), we have to use our knowledge of Héloïse and Cleopatra, and what we have learned about Eustacia and about the allusion-rich and (at least in this chapter) ironic voice of the narrator to figure out what the remark is meant to tell us.

Different narrative functions and relationships between character, narrator and reader do not in themselves require the level of narrative agency to change. While the approach of the narrator may change from one section of a novel to the next, we do not doubt that the same voice speaks throughout. Not just the comparison with narration in a novel, but also Occam's razor should advise us not to assign bits of narration in film to different agencies without reasonably clear criteria for the differentiation.

Though David Bordwell has been critical of the implied author, the gap between his ideas and a communication model may not be insurmountable (see above). We can perhaps clarify the issue by recourse to his distinction between syuzhet, style and fabula (Bordwell 1985: 48–57): the sequence of story events as presented on screen (i.e. the syuzhet); the means the medium has to present story events (i.e. the style); the implied sequence of events the audience can reconstruct from the syuzhet (i.e. the fabula). If we construct the implied author to account for the inventedness of the fiction, then (s)he is responsible for all three levels. If the narration is what presents a story to us (whatever its origin), it accounts for syuzhet and style: the agency that 'decides' what of the story facts we see and hear, and when we see and hear them from what perspective. The narration, however, would not be responsible for devising the story implicit in the syuzhet, i.e. the fabula (nor for the rules and limitations of its own operation).

If the narration presents the story, we cannot find the implied author in that presentation, and if nondiegetic music is part of the style of film – its arsenal to present a story – we cannot hear the implied author in nondiegetic music. But if we construct an implied author to account for the invention of story facts, we may catch a glimpse of the shy creature in diegetic music. This becomes obvious in moments in film that foreground their fictionality and show us that a story fact has been put there for a purpose, especially if it strains credibility if measured by the yardstick of a 'realistic' diegesis.

The implied author and film music (II)
Film musicology has used different terms for music that is locatable in the diegesis, but goes beyond storyworld furnishing and provides added narrative value: 'diegetic commentary' (Norden 2007); some instances of 'source scoring' (diegetic music coordinated with a scene as if it were nondiegetic; see Hagen 1971: 200; and Kassabian 2001: 43–49); and, to some

extent, 'ambi-diegetic music' (Holbrook 2005a & 2005b). Problems of 'source scoring' as an umbrella term are mentioned in footnote 41. The problem of Morris Holbrook's approach is that he uses reductive definitions of diegetic music (i.e. 'realistic depiction') and nondiegetic music (i.e. 'dramatic development') (Holbrook 2005b: 48–49; echoing Roger Manvell's and John Huntley's distinction between 'realistic' and 'functional' music, see Manvell and Huntley 1957: 59). This distinction ignores the range of functions to which diegetic and nondiegetic music can be put (see ch. II.iv.b & c). On this basis, Holbrook defines 'ambi-diegetic music' (ambiguously diegetic music) as 'cinemusical material that (like "diegetic" music) appears on-screen as performed by one or more actors but that (like "non-diegetic" music) advances dramatic development of plot, character, or other important cinematic themes' (Holbrook 2005a: 153). There are two problems with this:

- The status of music as diegetic is not made ambiguous by the function to which it is put: that would be a category mistake.
- That diegetic music fleshing out a character may help 'dramatic development' is not surprising even if we assign, with Holbrook, 'realistic depiction' to the diegesis. That and how Susie Diamond (Michelle Pfeiffer) in *The Fabulous Baker Boys* (1989) sings Richard Rodgers' & Lorenz Hart's 'My Funny Valentine' certainly characterizes her (see Holbrook 2005b: 54–56), but it does so in a realistic way – of course a certain type of character would choose a certain kind of song, and sing it in a certain way.

More interesting is the distinction between plausible diegetic facts and diegetic facts that point out their own inventedness, undermining the illusion of a self-contained diegesis originating in a (fictitiously) autonomous pre-filmic reality. Of course, we know that fictional stories are invented and do not originate in an autonomous reality. The issue is not what they *are*, but how they *function*: whether they allow us to construct the illusion of a self-contained diegesis or lift the curtain and show their own fictionality (more or less clearly: it is not a matter of either/or, but of gradations).

To differentiate further, the 'plausibility' of a fictional story cannot be measured against the real world, but only against the unwritten rules of different genres. We usually know what to expect and accept in a story, not primarily because of our knowledge of the world, but because of our knowledge of fiction. But there is a difference between diegetic facts that go to the limits of what is plausible in a given genre context and those that go beyond. The end of *Octopussy* is a fight to the death in and on an airplane. It is a typical Bond climax, and though Bond's feats of dexterity and endurance go far beyond what would be plausible in the real world, they still obey the laws of nature of Bond world (however unnatural they may be on occasion).

But not all scenes in *Octopussy* obey them. A generic element of Bond films is the 'recognition scene': Bond has to establish contact with a fellow agent, and in order to make sure that both are talking to the right person, they have to exchange meaningless phrases. In *Octopussy*, the template is musicalized. Bond is in India, alighting from a boat and entering a bazaar. We hear the music of a snake charmer and see a musician, instrument and snake without taking them to be anything but musical *couleur locale*. But then the snake charmer makes himself known as Bond's contact by switching from to the core motif of Monty Norman's Bond theme, inevitably raising a laugh in the audience. It is the same laughter that greets the reveal of the village organist in the church scene in *Wallace & Gromit in 'The Curse of the Were-Rabbit'* (see pp. 3–6). The snake charmer is not supposed to know the Bond theme, and neither is Bond. The nonchalant implication that Bond has seen Bond movies does not just strain credibility, as the typical Bond chase or fight scene might, but crosses it: a classic metalepsis, a shortcut between levels of narration.[59] The fictionality of the story becomes part of it; the implied author is not content to organize matters behind the scene, but becomes manifest in the text.

Bordwell would call this narrative 'self-consciousness' (Bordwell 1985: 57–61). The problem with that concept is that it covers cases on different levels of narration. Bordwell ascribes 'moderate self-consciousness' even to the grouping of 'characters for our best view' in 'most Hollywood shots' (Bordwell 1985: 58; see also 1985: 11–12). While this shows that films are artifice from the ground up – supporting Bordwell's case against 'mimetic' theories of film narration (1985: 3–15) – it hardly qualifies under his definition of narrative self-consciousness as 'a recognition that [the narration] is addressing an audience' (1985: 58). Such grouping of actors is the kind of trick of the trade audiences are not normally meant to notice. Film-makers are of course conscious of such tricks, but they are rarely foregrounded on a textual level.

But even such cases aside, Bordwell's narrative self-consciousness lumps together narrative procedures that differ with regard to their treatment of manifest fictionality. As an example, in *Kramer vs. Kramer* (1979), the Vivaldi mandolin concerto we have heard during the credits returns and marks the climax of the dialogue between Ted Kramer (Dustin Hoffman) and a colleague who tells him that he might soon be offered a partnership in the company and would take Ted 'along'. We take this to be nondiegetic music, but when Ted and his colleague are walking along the street outside the office building, we see two buskers play the music on mandolin and guitar: a diegetic reveal, making us retroactively reinterpret the music during the conversation as displaced diegetic (more about those concepts in ch. II.iv.e & f). As such, it certainly displays self-consciousness in Bordwell's sense: the film shows that it is playing with our expectations regarding the status of the

---

59 To ignore this borderline as ostentatiously as the snake charmer scene in *Octopussy* speaks of a narration as self-conscious as an audience in 1983 would have been about the pleasures of Bond. But the scene is not unprecedented. Some of the theme songs of individual films have been used in a similar way: in *Dr. No* (1962) we hear 'Under the Mango Tree' several times before Honey Ryder (Ursula Andress) sings it; in *From Russia with Love* (1963) we hear the theme song on the radio during Bond's picnic with Sylvia Trench; and in *On Her Majesty's Secret Service* (1969), a janitor whistles the *Goldfinger* (1964) tune. While *Dr. No* and *From Russia with Love* remain within the horizon of one film, the last example comes close to *Octopussy* in addressing the Bond series as a phenomenon of pop culture.

music. But that is an effect of the narration and relies on the framing of images and the sequence of shots, which conspire to keep the origin of the music hidden until such time as the narration sees fit. The presence of the music in this context, however, is not particularly surprising – there is no reason why upmarket buskers might not play a bit of Vivaldi in the right part of town.[60]

The relationship between diegesis and filmic technique is slightly different in the church scene from *Wallace & Gromit in 'The Curse of the Were-Rabbit'*. While it is not completely out of the question that a village organist would know and use the chords for her horror film effect, it is unlikely enough to make the joke work. We laugh at music which, for this scene, is both right (as nondiegetic music) and wrong (as diegetic music). The effect relies on the interlocking of narrational tactics (image framing that only reveals the organist after the fact) and diegetic 'fact' (the choice of music she plays).

If there is a remote chance that we may accept the choice of music in this scene, if not as diegetically plausible then at least not as impossible, things are different again in the snake charmer scene in *Octopussy*. Here, the bubble of diegetic self-containment is well and truly burst by Bond's signature motif; even the wide plausibility horizon of a Bond film cannot accommodate it, and the implied author winks at us.

Of course, *Wallace & Gromit in 'The Curse of the Were-Rabbit'* demonstrates that diegetic 'facts' and their filmic presentation can be flip sides of the coin of a particular narrative strategy. In such cases, Bordwell's summary category of 'them' makes sense. This is especially true of films defined by their intended effect, e.g. comedies or horror films. Again it is Bordwell's interest in the poetics of cinema, in the craft of making a film work, that informs his narratology. But that ignores the distinction between fictitiously (more or less) self-contained stories and stories foregrounding their inventedness. The implied author as a construct that accounts for a particular kind of narrative self-consciousness can help to make that distinction.

To summarize with reference to the hierarchy of levels of narration:

- All films have historical authors, but most of the time we can blank out our awareness of that fact because historical authors normally become manifest only in particular moments: in the credits, but also when, say, a famous actor has a cameo appearance and we know that we are meant to recognize him as his real-world self.
- All films also have a narrating agency; or rather, cue us to construct one to account for the organization of the film: image framing, camera movements, cuts, nondiegetic music, but also larger-scale aspects such as syuzhet construction.

---

60 We do remember, of course, that we have heard the music during the credits and assume that it is not just a random bit of realistic diegetic music, but has added meaning. This is confirmed when after the reveal the music underscores a shot of Joanna Kramer (Meryl Streep) about to leave the flat and her family. But these, too, are narrational effects: the music is being used by the narration of the film in a meaningful way and throughout the film. Its presence in the diegesis, however, is not remarkable in itself, and does not call the fiction of an autonomous pre-filmic reality into question.

- Most films also cue us, at least to some degree, to construct a narrative agency on the level of the implied author. Some externalize that authorial agency in the form of an extrafictional audience address (see ch. II.iii). But usually, the realm of the implied author is story construction: the selection of the 'facts' of diegesis and fabula. In most cases, our awareness of authorial agency will be confined to typical fabula patterns: we know how fictional stories go (though it is possible to try to evade that by aiming for a 'realistic' story). But sometimes films foreground authorial agency more locally, in moments that show their fictionality on the level of diegetic 'facts' (and not just on the level of narrational tactics, as in the typical 'uncommunicative' image framing and cutting for the purposes of a diegetic reveal): when James Bond recognizes his own leitmotif, the storyworld itself is exposed as a cardboard construction. We may be aware of that fact anyway, but in narratological terms the relevant question is whether (and if so, how strongly) the film text cues our awareness of the fact.

Using the concept of the implied author in the context of this study is not about 'proliferat[ing] theoretical entities without need' (Bordwell 1985: 61). Its purpose is to distinguish between meanings of 'narrative': between storytelling and storymaking. To become narratives, all invented stories need to be told, ask us to construct a mediating agency that selects, arranges and presents the story to us. But not all told stories have been invented – we can tell someone what actually happened to us that day.

The distinction does not directly apply to fiction, which is, after all, the art of inventing stories. But it applies indirectly: one can tell a story in a way that suppresses its made-ness. Other stories (or moments of stories) foreground their inventedness, and implied authorial agency peeks through the cracks. The author is implied because the issue is not historical authorship, but effects organized by the text. In many, perhaps in most, films we understand these aspects as two sides of the same coin of Bordwell's 'them': our construction of an agency responsible for story facts *and* story presentation. But the conceptual distinction can still be made, and while proliferating theoretical entities (or distinctions) may be a sin against common scholarly sense, ignoring conceptual distinctions is no lesser sin. Nothing is lost in making one distinction too many (nothing but clarity, at worst), but occasionally insights may be won.

It is a narrow use of the implied author, one that leaves out a lot of the concept's potential, because it focuses on the distinction between implied author and narrator and ignores that between historical and implied author.[61] In this reduced form, it mainly helps to differentiate between different ways of using music in film self-consciously.

---

61 It is not, for example, about the implied author as a 'narratological guarantee that meaning, which equals intent, is walled in' (Verstraten 2009: 128). But the idea of the implied author as a shorthand for the 'meaning' of a text is problematic. Since reception theory, the idea that authorial intent equals

Diegetic commentary

While a metalepsis like the one *Octopussy* implies authorial agency in a particularly forceful manner, the more common case is 'diegetic commentary': music located in the diegesis, but used to comment on the story from a perspective that is not itself locatable in the diegesis (as would be the case if a character used music to comment on, say, the actions of another character). If the commenting music is sufficiently plausible in its diegetic context, such scenes can achieve a fine balance between diegetic self-sufficiency and (implied) authorial intention. *The Blue Angel/Der blaue Engel* (1930) provides an example: we are in Professor Rath's (Emil Jannings) school and hear a girls' choir somewhere in the grounds sing the folksong 'Ännchen von Tharau'/'Little Anne of Tharau'; this precedes the moment when Rath will take away from one of his pupils a postcard with a picture of nightclub singer Lola Lola (Marlene Dietrich), with whom he will fall hopelessly, tragically in love. And that is what the lyrics of the song are about: someone who has fallen hook, line and sinker for the beloved. The first stanza goes (with my unpoetic and fairly literal translation):

> Ännchen von Tharau ist's, die mir gefällt,
> Sie ist mein Leben, mein Gut und mein Geld.
> Ännchen von Tharau hat wieder ihr Herz
> Auf mich gerichtet in Lieb' und in Schmerz.
> Ännchen von Tharau, mein Reichtum, mein Gut,
> Du meine Seele, mein Fleisch und mein Blut.

> Little Anne of Tharau is the one I like,
> She is my life, my possession, my money.
> Little Anne of Tharau once more has her heart
> Aimed at me in love and in pain.
> Little Anne of Tharau, my treasure, my possession,
> You, my soul, my flesh and my blood.

From financial and material metaphors, the text proceeds to the fusion of lover and beloved, spiritually and in the flesh; the kind of fusion Rath will hope for with Lola Lola, though he will find only his own annihilation, while she remains coolly aloof.

The example also shows that the issue is not plausibility as such, but perceived intentionality: 'Ännchen von Tharau' could well have been sung by a German school choir around 1900; in that sense it fits its diegetic context. What is not as plausible is the juxtaposition of the song and Rath's incipient downfall: the irony of fate or the irony of the implied author? The latter interpretation makes particular sense since 'Ännchen von Tharau' is only one of three diegetic pieces in *The Blue Angel* that provide an ironic counterpoint

---

meaning has become unsustainable, and perhaps the idea of 'the meaning' of a text does not make much sense in any case.

to Rath's slide into sexual servitude[62] (set against Friedrich Hollaender's songs in the Blue Angel nightclub with their merciless frankness about sexual politics).

The 'diegetic plausibility' of songs whose lyrics seem to comment on the action can vary, usually in inverse proportion to the directness of the commentary. In German comedy *Sun Alley/Sonnenallee* (1999), Doris Ehrenreich (Katharina Thalbach), the mother of hapless hero Micha Ehrenreich (Alexander Scheer), is preparing to flee from the GDR to West Germany, while her husband Hotte (Henry Hübchen) and visitors from Dresden are watching TV – the West German game show *Am laufenden Band* (literally *By the Conveyor Belt*, a format similar to *The Generation Game*), the climax of which consisted of candidates trying to remember consumer goods parading past them on a conveyor belt; those they could remember they were allowed to keep. In the bit of the show Hotte and the guests are watching, host Rudi Carrell sings 'Eine Insel für mich allein' ('An Island for Myself'), a song about an office worker who wins the lottery and buys himself an island. The crass exhibition of western consumerism and the song about escaping to a better place show us what the Ehrenreichs lack and what Doris is dreaming of, and we have no doubt that the film is not aiming for a credible diegesis but for comic effect.

Source scoring
Ostentatiously deliberate construction of the diegesis can imply authorial intent even if the aim is not musical commentary. An example for a scene that goes even further in using diegetic sound that is plausible in itself and yet shows the authorial hand is the cat-search scene in *Alien* (1979) (see ch. IV.ii, pp. 190–91). At the other end of the plausibility range lies, for example, the famous reveal of the Count Basie Orchestra playing 'April in Paris' in the middle of the desert in *Blazing Saddles* (1974). Here, the reveal of the music as diegetic has no commentative value – it only says that the film is not even trying to establish a coherent diegesis, but that diegesis and narration are both at the service of making jokes, and nothing else.

What Earle Hagen called 'source scoring' involves the arrangement of diegetic music in a way that echoes typical uses of nondiegetic music: 'like source in its content, but tailored to meet scoring requirements' (Hagen 1971: 200).[63] The term comes from a different terminological tradition, but is handy as a label for something that could only be said

---

62 The other pieces are: (1) The mechanical clock of the Garnisonskirche (Garrison Church) in Potsdam we hear several times play 'Üb' immer Treu und Redlichkeit'/'Always Practice Loyalty and Probity', ironic because Ludwig Hölty's text from 1775 is sung to the melody of 'Ein Mädchen oder Weibchen' from Mozart's *Magic Flute*, in which Papageno sings about his desire for a woman; (2) 'Es war einmal ein treuer Husar'/'There Once Was a Faithful Hussar', which issues from a pub when Rath is walking towards the Blue Angel nighclub. The song tells about the hussar's love for a girl who falls ill while he is away and dies in his arms when he returns (whereas in *Der blaue Engel* Rath himself will die in nobody's arms, because his love is anything but faithful).

63 Irene Kahn Atkins uses a different definition of 'source scoring': 'music […] heard first as source music and subsequently as background music, usually reorchestrated' (1983: 14). Transitions from source to score are part of the use of source scoring as Hagen understands it, but not the defining aspect.

cumbersomely on the basis of the terms 'diegetic' and 'nondiegetic'; for that reason it is used in this book as well.

Source scoring often just means congruity of ostensibly diegetic music with other elements of a scene, rather than commentative value as such. The simplest case is diegetic music that coincides with other diegetic action: unlikely coincidence as a minimal form of the irony of fate. In *Laura* (1944) the implicitly diegetic background music at a party ends exactly after detective Mark McPherson (Dana Andrews), who is phoning his superior, has said, 'I said I'll bring in the killer today' and everyone stares at him in shock – a shock the music seems to share, even though we assume that it has come from a record player.[64]

What is a rhetorical effect in *Laura* can also have a purely formal function. In *The Big Lebowski* (1998), The Dude (Jeff Bridges) and Donny Kerabatsos (Steve Buscemi) attend an amateurish, but pretentious ballet performance to the 'Gnomus' movement of Modest Mussorgsky's *Pictures from an Exhibition*, when Walter Sobchak (John Goodman) comes in and starts to talk to them. The conversation ends with Walter saying, 'Our fuckin' troubles are over, Dude', promptly followed by the emphatic final gesture of the music. There is no good reason that conversation and music should end as emphatically and at the same time, or rather no good reason in terms of a realistic diegesis. In terms of formal satisfaction, the coincidence makes sense, and is reinforced by a cut confirming the double closing gesture: two strands of diegetic events and the editing of the scene work in concert. As in many cases of very overt narrative filmic structures, this happens in a comedy context, in which effect reign supreme and justify the obviousness of the technique.[65]

While there are many examples of this minimal version of source scoring, the idea of music shown or implied to be diegetic that 'matches the nuances of the scene musically' (Hagen 1971: 200) comes into its own when it fulfils more complex functions. In *Fame* (1980), Leroy's (Gene Anthony Ray) fit of rage – because his English teacher claims that he is unable to read – is accompanied by the furious end of Rossini's 'Stabat mater'. The music with its slightly clunky piano accompaniment sounds as if it could come from a rehearsal in the building, but it takes roughly 30 seconds until the image track switches to that rehearsal and we see the choir which, we assume, is singing at the same time as Leroy is smashing

---

64 *Laura* is a difficult example for arguments involving story construction, however, because its convoluted structure makes it difficult to clearly assign authorial or narrative agency anyway. But the ubiquity of David Raksin's 'Laura' theme on different levels of narration supports the film's attempt to dissolve the boundaries between levels of narration and between fiction, fact, imagination and invention.

65 The genre that exploits such diegetic coincidences is the cartoon, and no subtype more than the concert cartoon. When in the *Looney Tunes* episode 'Baton Bunny' (1959) Bugs Bunny conducts Franz von Suppé's 'Morning, Noon and Night in Vienna', the cufflinks he has lost in the struggle fall back into place precisely in time with two celesta chords – one of numerous instances of diegetic actions following the music, which becomes a kind of programme (or, rather, ballet) music for the scenes it has inspired. It is another kind of narrative self-consciousness, one that reflects the clichés of image-music relationships in film back at us in a mirror image. It is not the music that nestles up to the images and follows their contours, but the images that fit the music as the cartoon's backbone.

glass cabinets in the corridor. As in the *Blazing Saddles* example (see above), there are two components that make the effect: on the one hand, the editing that holds back the reveal of the diegetic origin of the music; and on the other hand, the choice of music that fits the moment and coincides with another diegetic action, which by chance (or implied authorial fiat) takes place at the same time.

A less obvious example of this type of dramatic (rather than formal) source scoring occurs in *None But the Lonely Heart* (1944): Ernie (Cary Grant) is tuning the piano of his neighbour, Ma Chalmers (Eva Leonard Boyne), while one floor below Jane Snowdon (Queenie Vassar) is trying to talk Ernie's mother (Ethel Barrymore) into 'fencing' and argues that the money she could make from this would also benefit Ernie – the same Ernie who throughout the scene is kept in the spectator's mind via the irregular piano tones that provide an disquieting underscore.[66] Ernie's non-music becomes an effective background for the tense dialogue between the two women; a reminder of Ernie himself as a crucial part of what they are talking about, and a pointer to the authorial agency that has set up these events to make its effect.

Unlikely coincidence

Diegetic commentary and source scoring rely on diegetic coincidence. Such unlikely coincidences (unlikely against the yardstick of realism) can be exploited in different ways beyond the examples mentioned above.

The simplest way is exploited in scenes in (often) musical films that show music to be diegetic, but coordinate it in a way that would be highly unlikely in a realistic storyworld. Classic examples are songs passed from one singer to the next in early sound films such as *Under the Roofs of Paris/Sous les toits de Paris* (1930) (see Gorbman 1987: 142–143) or *Love Me Tonight* (1932). Similar are scenes that coordinate diegetic music and other diegetic events (e.g. movements of people), even if there is no realistic reason why the music should organize those events.[67] One of the early scenes of *Cry-Baby* (1990) uses a combination of diegetic commentary and temporal coordination: 'Cry-Baby' Wade (Johnny Depp) switches on his car radio, so the song we hear ('The Flirt', sung by Shirley & Lee) is manifestly diegetic. But while volume and sound quality throughout the scene are plausible for music from a car radio, implausibly the song is neatly coordinated with the action: to start with simply because it starts when Wade switches on the radio (as if he had control over the programme as well); then when Wanda (Traci Lords) is mortally embarrassed by the patter of her bus-driver father (David Nelson), and his longed-for departure is followed in the song by the line 'Oh look, Daddy, you're so cool'; then when the line 'Are you thinkin' 'bout marriage?' exactly coincides with Wade looking at 'square' Alison Vernon-Williams (Amy Locane), who will become his girl by the end of the film; and further when the line 'Do you have plenty money?' accompanies Wade looking at Alison walking towards him, etc. The song of course also ends precisely when Alison has left and Wade and his fellow Drapes have got in

---

66 See Kassabian (2001: 45–46) for a similar example of source scoring from *Dead Again* (1991).
67 See, for example, Gorbman's discussion of the end of *Hangover Square* (1945) (1987: 161).

their car. But diegetic plausibility is not what we expect from musical films, and while *Cry-Baby* is not a film musical in the narrow sense, its rock 'n' roll movie parody is generically close enough.

The *Cry-Baby* example shows Wade in control of the music. Another character in control of music is Sailor Ripley (Nicolas Cage) in *Wild at Heart* (1990), a quality he proves when he and Lula (Laura Dern) are on the road, and all Lula can find on the car radio are news items ranging from the horrible to the ludicrous. Disgusted, she tasks Sailor with finding her some good music, and as if by magic he finds Powermad's 'Slaughterhouse', one of the couple's favourite pieces (more in Davison 2004: 177–79).[68]

A slightly weaker version of such quasi-magical coincidences (appropriate, given the fairy-tale features of *Wild at Heart*) is the organizing principle of many scenes in *Fame*: the editing places two musical (or other) events back to back in the syuzhet that happen in different places (or even at different times) in the fabula:

- Ralph Garci (Barry Miller) is auditioning in the school's drama department and, standing on a chair and playing god, makes an imperious hand movement. After the cut, Bruno Martelli (Lee Curreri), who is auditioning in the music department, is playing a mighty chord on his keyboard, as if he had followed Ralph's gesture.
- When his professor interrupts Bruno, who is playing Beethoven's Fifth Symphony on a battery of electronic instruments, Martelli says that if the professor does not like it, he also could play it with a disco beat, and the film cuts to the dance auditions, where we are hearing a disco beat.
- The acting teacher asks his students to let their tongues roll in their mouths, which after a while is accompanied by music that after a cut turns out to come from the ballet class.
- At the end of the ballet scene, a group of students doing classical dance are suddenly accompanied by jazz, which after a cut turns out to originate in the jazz-dance class.

These are just a few examples of a pervasive pattern that balances diegetic plausibility and implausibility. The links between events in different diegetic locations are an effect of the editing, but they also rely on the events happening and fitting well together (Ralph's hand movement and Bruno's chord, etc.). While the film does not make clear if these events happen at the same fabula time, the editing suggests that they probably do, which extends the coincidence from syuzhet to fabula and adds the implication of authorial control over the manifold musical events in the school. Again, as with *Cry-Baby*, *Fame* is a musical film,

---

68 A diegetically slightly less unlikely demonstration is Sailor's power is provided in the early scene in the Hurricane Club: just lifting his hand, Sailor can make Powermad stop playing (when a young guy has accosted Lula), and when he suddenly launches into Leiber & Stoller's 'Love Me (Treat Me Like a Fool)', the speed metal band straight away accompany him, including perfect backing vocals.

and slightly different rules apply. It is a musical film that not only does not aim for supradiegetic transcendence, but actively avoids it and is careful to show all of its production numbers as purely diegetic (more in ch. III.iv). But even in the context of this attempt to distance the film from the tradition of the film musical, the lure to structure it by musical coincidences seems to have been too strong, perhaps especially strong, since the coincidence had to comensate for the loss of supradiegetic transcendence.

While the unlikely coincidence of diegetic events is the most typical case, other solutions are possible. In *There's Something About Mary* (1998), Ted (Ben Stiller), about to take his great love Mary (Cameron Diaz) to the prom, has gone to the bathroom in her parents' house and is dreaming of the evening to come (even though a terrible accident with his zipper will give the evening a rather different direction). Out of nowhere, we hear Burt Bacharach's 'Close to You' (sung by Sally Stevens), and after the opening line 'Why do birds suddenly appear?', we see a couple of (love)birds on the branch outside the window. The song is not diegetic; at best, it might be music going on in Ted's mind, but even for that we have no indication. The birds that suddenly appear seem to have reacted either to Ted's mind as magic wish-fulfilment, or to the narration of the film – story 'facts' and narration working hand in hand in typical comedy manner.

e. Diegetic music: further options

'Diegetic commentary' or 'source scoring' describe broad categories of music that has an identifiable or plausible diegetic source, but is nevertheless used in a surprising or less than straightforwardly realistic manner. But there are many more ways of playing with the diegetic status of music and our expectations of what that status entails. While it would be pointless to attempt to comprehensively classify such options, one can point out characteristic ones.

The diegetic reveal
The opening scenes from *The Holiday* and *Eyes Wide Shut* discussed in ch. II.ii are not just examples for managing the transition from extra- into intrafictional space, but also for a broad class of examples that use diegetic music to play with our understanding of levels of narration: what I call a 'diegetic reveal'. The church scene from *Wallace & Gromit in 'The Curse of the Were-Rabbit'* (see pp. 3–6) is a model example, as it is of the fact that comedy is the most frequent application of reveals. Giorgio Biancorosso and Jeff Smith have discussed them (Biancorosso 2009; Smith 2009), the latter only briefly in connection with Bordwell's concept of the 'communicativeness' of a film's narration, i.e. the question 'how willingly the narration shares the information to which its degree of knowledge entitles it' (Bordwell 1985: 59). That can apply to syuzhet organization – crucial in crime films or thrillers – but also to the more local information management of a reveal. (There can also be overlap between diegetic reveals and spatially displaced diegetic music. The difference is that diegetic

reveals rely on the idea of a unified space, encompassing on-screen and off-screen, with the music located in off-screen space until the reveal. Spatial displacement, on the other hand, can transform the music into underscoring for events in a non-contiguous space; as a result, we perceive it more strongly as a transition across the diegetic/nondiegetic border.)

The difference between Smith's and Biancorosso's understanding of diegetic reveals illustrates their crucial feature: Smith discusses them in the context of Stilwell's 'fantastical gap between diegetic and nondiegetic'. Stilwell herself discusses a reveal from *The Winter Guest* (1997), but Smith argues that it should be rescued from the gap, because it reveals that the music was diegetic all along, turning its initial construction as nondiegetic into an audience 'misapprehension' (Smith 2009). Biancorosso, who calls such moments 'reversals', discusses them in the context of optical illusions known as a 'reversible figures' (or 'ambiguous' or 'multistable' images), such as the duck-rabbit head, which can be seen to represent the head of a duck or that of a rabbit, or the Necker cube, which we can interpret as seen from the top or from below. Such figures depend for their effect on the reversibility of our interpretation: we cannot see the duck and the rabbit or both perspectives of the cube at the same time, but our interpretation can flip back and forth (and trying and failing to see both images simultaneously, or trying to make them flip, is part of the fun). But diegetic reveals do not work like that, because film moves in time, and time 'does not move backward [...] nor can one replay the music; as a result, the initial perception is impossible to revive' (Biancorosso 2009).

That would confirm Smith's understanding of the reveal as something that shows us what narrative status the music has had all along. Biancorosso does not concur:

> An ambiguity that is finally solved is no less ambiguous for that, however. [...] When a reversal occurs, we do respond to the sudden shift, adjust to a new perspective [...] thus recognizing, if only on the level of the fabula, our initial perception as a misreading. The experience of the shift retains its meaning, however, for it draws us in the picture [...] and is a reminder of the precariousness of our reliance on conventions. (Biancorosso 2009)

The issue is the double understanding of the diegetic/nondiegetic distinction discussed in ch. II.iv.a: the diegesis is a mental construct, but in order to facilitate story immersion, most films most of the time cue us to construct a stable diegesis. The effect of diegetic reveals consists in the layering and interaction of two interpretative conflicts:

- The conflict between our original interpretation of music as nondiegetic and our revised interpretation of it as diegetic after the reveal.
- The conflict between a 'naturalizing' understanding of the diegesis as a space (the music has been diegetic from the start, but the narration was uncommunicative until the reveal) and a 'realist' understanding of the diegesis as a mental construct based on cues provided by the film.

The first of these conflicts is not open to reversal (or only in retrospect), because once revealed, we cannot *not* be aware of the diegetic anchoring point of the music any more. The second, on the other hand, is a result of the 'double intentionality' of our understanding of representative art (see pp. ch. I.iii, point 5): a film gives us a glimpse into a fictional world, but it also a piece of artifice, knowledge we can suppress, but never completely forget.

There is a second noteworthy aspect to many diegetic reveals, especially to comic ones such as the Count Basie scene from *Blazing Saddles* (see above), or the harpist scene from Woody Allen's *Bananas* (1971), discussed by Biancorosso. Harp music on the soundtrack is revealed to originate with a harpist who, nonsensically, sits in a closet in the same room as Fielding Mellish (Woody Allen):

> [C]an the *same* music be both nondiegetic and diegetic within the same context? In the case of this excerpt, the answer is that it cannot. The harp glissandos may be plausible as nondiegetic background scoring [...] but it is entirely implausible as an occurrence in the film's story world, and that is why it cannot ultimately be anchored to a source without generating amusement, surprise, or laughter. (Biancorosso 2009)

But the point of the scene is that the music *does* occur in the film's storyworld, showing that a film can give us conflicting cues for the construction of what is and is not diegetic. The fact that harpists do not sit in closets without good reason (i.e. our knowledge of the world), and the conventions of sound quality and the semiotic appropriateness of film music (i.e. our knowledge of film style) tell us that is only makes sense as nondiegetic music[69], but the reveal shows us that it is diegetic music – it is both and neither, and in that sense the image of the fantastical gap is apt. (In a further turn of the screw, one could argue that the very ponderousness with which the scene demonstrates the diegetic/nondiegetic borderline adds to its comic effect.)

The question is what 'implausibility' means in such scenes. Does *Bananas* actually cue us to construct a diegesis that is plausible in terms of our knowledge of the real world? It is the aspect Smith fails to consider in his discussion of the equivalent Count Basie reveal in *Blazing Saddles* (Smith 2009). For Smith, 'the gag is produced as an effect of the film narration's communicativeness', not 'by the manipulation of diegetic and nondiegetic space'. He concedes that 'it is a rather unusual diegesis that motivates source music in this way', but does not pursue this. Yet the effect relies on more than management of audience access to information. What the scene shows us is that both the uncommunicative narration *and* the construction of that diegesis are aiming for jokes. Involved are narrational and implied

---

69 Sound quality is only one of the clues we use to assess the status of music, but it can become the pivot of a diegetic reveal. In one scene of *There's Something about Mary* (1998), Pat Healy (Matt Dillon) is sitting in his car, attempting to stake out Mary (Cameron Diaz). Suddenly, we are startled by loud music, whose sound quality suggests that it is nondiegetic. But Pat is startled as well, and only then do we notice that he was wiretapping Mary and was listening to the sounds from her flat with his headphones. When he reduces the volume, the sound quality changes to suggest diegetic sound.

authorial agency as two sides of the same effect-seeking comedy coin, and that is true of many diegetic reveals.

There are others, though, for which this is not relevant, especially in reveals not in comedy contexts. The Shostakovich music revealed as diegetic in the opening scene of *Eyes Wide Shut* is plausible as music a couple like the Harfords might listen to. (It is also plausible as the kind of music Kubrick might use as nondiegetic music, which produces the irony of this reveal; see ch. II.ii.) Biancorosso also discusses the purposes of diegetic reveals in serious contexts.[70] One such purpose is simply characterization: *Diva* (1981) begins with postman Jules (Frédéric Andréi) on his motorbike in front of a fence, taking off his helmet and putting on his postman cap – an utterly prosaic scene. But the soundtrack accompanies it, surprisingly, with classical music: the aria 'Ebben? Ne andrò lontana' from Alfredo Catalani's opera *La Wally* that is at the heart of the film's plot and music, music that neither seems to fit the man nor the situation. Then Jules alights and switches off the radio he has installed on his motorbike, and we realize that this is the music he listens to, and that there may be more to learn more about him than met the eye in the opening scene.[71]

A more complex reveal occurs in *The Haunting* (1963). We witness an uncomfortable, eventually acrimonious discussion between Eleanor Lance (Julie Harris), her haughty sister and brother-in-law, in whose flat Eleanor lives. The scene is accompanied by slightly unnerving, tinkly music-box music. But when Eleanor has thrown her relatives out of the room, a drum roll sounds, and she gets up and switches off the music box that was the source of the music.

The reveal of the source (before only hinted at by Eleanor's niece glancing into a corner, but without indication of what she was looking at) 'excuses' and naturalizes the anempathic music, typically for anempathic music in film. But the explanation works only retrospectively, when the music has already made its effect. It does not fit our expectations of underscoring for this scene, but its very inappropriateness adds to the tension (and makes it easier for us to feel with Eleanor, who, when she switches off the music, shows that she was as unnerved by it as we were). But the double role of the music as retrospectively diegetic music *and* as disturbing underscoring is confirmed by the drum roll. We can just about accept that it might come from the music box, and we understand that it is what makes Eleanor decide to switch it off. But it is also the ironically triumphant reaction to Eleanor's throwing her family out of the room – source scoring insisting on the double nature of music which is more than 'an effect of the film narration's communicativeness'.

---

70 For example in *The Rules of the Game* (1939), *Fanny and Alexander* (1982), or *Slow Motion* (1980).

71 *Diva* plays the same trick with skinhead Le Curé (Dominique Pinon) (see Powrie 2006: 144). See Heldt (2008b) for a similar use of the technique in *None But the Lonely Heart* (1944), here to give us the first glimpse of the musical side of Ernie Mott (Cary Grant).

Lack of diegetic realism

Another class of music Jeff Smith wants to take out of the 'fantastical gap' (see Smith 2009) concerns examples that have a manifest diegetic anchoring point, but lack the aural fidelity we would normally expect from realistic diegetic music. Smith points out that aural fidelity is only one of many features of music or sound in in a film we use to assess what level of narration they may be coming from, and hardly the most important one. One of his examples, from *La Pointe-Courte* (1955), is not about music, but about dialogue in a scene that sees the couple wandering through a landscape, shown from different perspectives and distances, while sound levels vary to allow us to hear what they are saying, not to be true to what a diegetic observer would hear. Smith is correct that films are pragmatic in situations such as this. Narratologically, this is not a very interesting case, the sonic equivalent of a film arranging actors in a shot 'for our best view' (Bordwell 1985: 58).

Smith's second examples, from *Zodiac* (2007), concerns the song 'Hurdy Gurdy Man' coming from a car radio that for the brutal climax of the scene changes its volume after the fashion of nondiegetic music. For Smith, this is no reason to assign the music to a fantastical gap, and he asks why we accept the dialogue in *La Pointe-Courte* as diegetic, but not the music in the *Zodiac* scene. The reason is that sound levels in *La Pointe-Courte* are chosen for pragmatic reasons of cinematic exhibition, while *Zodiac* changes them for expressive purposes (which Smith admits, without letting this affect his categorization of the examples as equivalent). In *Zodiac*, the unrealistic sound level *means* something, does not just assure our access to diegetic information; the volume change signals that the narration has 'taken over' diegetic music for other ends than realistic storyworld representation.

Some examples of music anchored in the diegesis, but with unrealistic sound levels do operate in slightly different ways, though. At the start of *Bridget Jones's Diary* (2001), Bridget is coming home for her mother's annual New Year's Day turkey-curry buffet. As soon as her mother has opened the door, Burt Bacharach's 'Magic Moments' (sung by Perry Como) starts, at a volume unrealistically high for diegetic music from the house. But when the volume recedes after the start of dialogue, we realize that this is indeed supposed to be diegetic party background music, indicating the tastes of Bridget's mother, 'a strange creature from the time when the gherkin was still the height of sophistication', as Bridget's voice-over explains. But both the initial volume and the coincidence of the opening door and the beginning of the music indicate that realism is only one side of the coin, that the music is not just a storyworld element, but envelopes the scene to characterize the family background Bridget has such an ambiguous relationship with. The music is both within the storyworld and about it, and image and sound editing point that out.

An obvious place for music shown to be diegetic, but also enveloping a scene, is the title sequence. The one in *Little Voice* (1998) is underscored by 'Come Fly with Me' (sung by Frank Sinatra), shown to come from the record player in LV's room. But the music is also spatially displaced to shots of LV's mother, Billy, and to establishing shots of the village. But in title sequences different rules apply. The point here is exposition of the location and some of the dramatis personae, and instead of understanding the music as diegetically anchored but with unrealistic volume, one could also see it from the other side – as title music also used for a shortcut into the diegesis, a common opening tactic in films (see ch. II.ii).

Musical quasi-rendering

A subcategory of music shown to be diegetic, but in an unrealistic way is what Michel Chion calls 'rendering'. Chion's concept is based on the idea that sounds in film are perceived as 'truthful, effective and fitting not so much if they *reproduce* what would be heard in the same situation in reality, but if they *render* (convey, express) the sensations – not necessarily auditory – associated with the situation' (Chion 1994: 109; see also Chion 2009: 488). This primarily concerns sound editing, be it the design of diegetic sounds to enhance their impact or the introduction of sounds that fit expectations contrary to reality (e.g. Doppler effects for passing spaceships even though there is no sound in the vacuum of space). The use of music for rendering a sonic impression is usually so noticeable that it breaks diegetic illusion, and is rare outside of cartoons, where fidelity to the world as we know it is of so little concern that instead of rendering, one could better speak of the musicalization of diegetic sounds and the diegetization of music.

Examples can be found in any *Looney Tunes* or *Tom and Jerry* cartoon. In the *Looney Tunes* episode 'Fast and Furry-ous' (1949), Wile E. Coyote ambushes Roadrunner with the lid of a pot, and a reverberating chord renders the moment when Roadrunner stops inches from the lid; woodwind figures render Coyote's surprised blinking; a flute trill renders Roadrunner turning around and preparing for take-off; a cymbal clash the moment when he lets Coyote crash into the lid. In the following ambush, the sounds of Coyote throwing a boomerang repeatedly into the air are part of the rhythmic structure of the music. In the *Tom and Jerry* episode 'The Yankee Doodle Mouse' (1943), dynamite sticks are thrown in time with the music, and percussion accents double up as renderings of diegetic sounds. (This is similar to the 'musical' integration of diegetic sounds in *The Prodigal Son/Der verlorene Sohn* [1934], discussed on pp. 110–11.)

In live-action films, rendering in Chion's sense is the most common case, but occasionally rendering in the cartoon sense occurs (i.e. a *musical* rendering of sounds meant to be noticed as unrealistic). A film may aim for a non-realistic effect, for example in the use of music to replace or to mask diegetic sounds in *Under the Roofs of Paris* (1930), discussed by Claudia Gorbman (1987: 141–144). Other films use music for cartoonish overemphasis. During the confrontation of Mortimer (Lee Van Cleef) and Juan Wild (Klaus Kinski) in *For a Few Dollars More* (1965), a single tone on the Jew's harp marks the moment when Mortimer takes away Wild's cigar to light his own pipe. When Mortimer shoots the hat off Monco's (Clint Eastwood) head, the flying hat is rendered by a screeching sound we would rather expect in *Tom and Jerry*. The hat makes a whistling sound when it falls back, and a timpani glissando marks the moment when it hits the ground, followed once more by the Jew's harp that seems connected to Mortimer's actions – a sonic signature of his threateningly playful behaviour, as difficult to judge as the status of sound and music in many cartoons.

In such moments, the borderline between musical and non-musical soundtrack events, and between diegetic and nondiegetic sounds, has all but disappeared. Especially in cartoons, music is often less underscore than framework, and the animation not a fictitiously autonomous quasi-space, but choreographed to the soundtrack mix, with a fluid relationship between the integration and separation of diegetic/nondiegetic sounds/music. Extreme cases are cartoons structured by a song, as in Max Fleischer's *Song Car-Tunes* or *Screen Songs* or Disney's *Steamboat Willie* (1928). But the question what 'diegetic' and 'nondiegetic' music might mean in cartoons would require its own study.

Temporal dissociation

Diegetic reveals and the unrealistic use of diegetic sound as narrational takeover leave the diegesis its own integrity. While the narration plays with diegetic facts by managing our access or distorting them for dramatic purposes, we can still imagine the music autonomously taking place in the diegesis (which is what makes Smith categorize such examples as diegetic). But other cases break up that integrity, while still binding the music to the diegesis. One is the title sequence of *Bridget Jones's Diary* (see ch. II.ii), which presents images and a song both shown to be diegetic, but presents the song as continuous while introducing temporal gaps into the image track, severing the temporal congruity between diegetic sounds and images.

In *Bridget Jones's Diary* (or in *The Wrong Man*, see p. 44), the technique can be understood in the context of the liminality of title sequences. But it occurs at other points in films, too.[72] A scene in *Stand by Me* (1986) shows the four boys sitting round a campfire, searching for 'some sounds' on their transistor radio. They find the Del-Vikings' 'Come Go with Me', a song used before in the film without manifest diegetic source. In the earlier scene 'Come Go with Me' bridges a shot of the boys wandering by a lake and a scene of the boys roasting potatoes over a fire: shots with an ellipsis between them, which would suggest to us that the music is nondiegetic. By the campfire it is manifestly diegetic, but then the scene develops its own elliptical structure; we hear snippets of dialogue with six temporal gaps, all bridged by the song. The dialogue bits, held together by the fact that they all concern the question what kind of animal Goofy is, represent a longer stretch of time, but the montage of diegetic dialogue is overlaid by the uninterrupted song which had also been shown to be diegetic at the start of the scene.

One could simply say that the song starts as diegetic music and then becomes nondiegetic for the remainder of the scene. But that would misrepresent the interplay of cues and potential explanations. Apart from the temporal incongruity, there are no other signals to tell us that the narration has 'taken over' diegetic music. Its sound quality does not change, nor does the camera move out to encompass the scene, as in other cases of the de-diegetization of music (see pp. 113–15). Image framing and the sound of the song are consistent with the

---

72 David Bordwell analyzes its use in *Playtime* (1967) and *The Spider's Stratagem/Strategia del ragno* (1970); see Bordwell (1985: 82 & 97).

interpretation of the music as diegetic. The effect is rather that of two strands of the diegesis that have parted company for a while: an intervention of the narration into the diegesis, which is no longer presented perfectly mimetically, while the diegetic status of images and music is kept in our consciousness throughout. The audio-visual arrangement of the scene involves different factors:

- The sound quality and volume in relation to the framing of images, which do not point to a change in the narrative status of the music.
- The 'structural obstinacy of music' (see pp. 56–57). We readily accept ellipses in a series of images (or rather, we can mentally construct a coherent sequence of events from an elliptical series of images), but ellipses within music are problematic because most music relies for its coherence on a precise rhythmic, metrical, harmonic and phrase structure that cannot be taken apart at will without making the music incomprehensible. That particulary applies to a song with its simple structure.
- The echo of the earlier use of the song, which suggested we hear it as nondiegetic. After the diegetic anchoring point, the temporal dissociation reminds us of our previous construal of the song as nondiegetic.
- The integrity of the diegesis is overlaid by the convention of wrapping a montage sequence into a piece of music. The dialogue is realized as a montage of related but discontinuous snippets, and the only difference between this and other montage sequences is that here the narration does not use nondiegetic music as a frame, but 'borrows' music from the storyworld.

The scene combines elements of film style in a way that suggests a comprehensible diegesis sufficiently clearly, but prevents them from cohering completely, and thus makes us realize that the integrity of the diegesis is not 'natural', but depends on the careful arrangements of cues for our construction of the reality (or not) of the storyworld.

Stand by Me is full of little suspensions of the 'diegetic effect' (see Burch 1990: 43–47), but its narrative framework provides a naturalizing explanation. The story is told from the perspective of the adult Gordie Lachance remembering his youthful adventure, and we can understand what we see and hear as filtered through his memories, which may include narrative freedoms taken with the songs which make up the majority of the soundtrack. It may be no accident that more cases of such 'temporal dissociation' of diegetic images and music can be found in films with a subjective, retrospective narrative perspective. An elegant one occurs in *Milk* (2008): Harvey Milk (Sean Penn) meets Scott Smith (James Franco) in the subway; they go home to his flat and have sex. The music playing in Harvey's flat – we see him put the needle on the record – is the Swingle Singers' version of the E^b major prelude from J.S. Bach's *The Well-Tempered Clavier*, book 2 (BWV 876). The piece runs through without interruption, but suddenly we see Harvey and Scott post-coitally sitting in the bed – the temporal ellipsis in the syuzhet dissociates diegetic images and (still?) diegetic music. Once the diegetic link between music and images is broken, the film runs with the idea. Next we see images from a later phase of their relationship: a road trip, filmed as if with a Super-8 camera. But the music is still the continuing Bach piece that has now become completely de-diegeticized, has become music that frames their relationship as a whole (and as such is part of a more consistent strategy of scoring Harvey's life with art music – Bach, Mozart, Puccini).

But as in *Stand by Me*, the story of Milk is told in retrospect by Harvey Milk himself, who is speaking his memoirs – the memoirs dramatized in the bulk of the film's screen time – into a tape recorder shortly before he is killed by political opponent Dan White (Josh Brolin). Again what we see and what we hear can be understood as being filtered through Harvey's memories, providing an 'explanation' for rifts in the integrity of the diegesis. In *Milk*, these rifts also fit the editing style, which is all about fluidity, about the smooth flow of linked textual elements. The film consists of a range of image types (some pseudo-documentary, presenting 'historical events'; others closely linked to Harvey's experiences) and often short snippets from different phases of Harvey Milk's life, and the editing helps to make it into a coherent whole. In this context, film style occasionally overrides diegetic consistency in order to make the whole comprehensible (and, indeed, make it seem like a whole).

f. Transitions, transgressions and transcendence: Displaced diegetic music, supradiegetic music and other steps across the border

As with the internal ranges of diegetic and nondiegetic music, the options for crossing the borderline or making it fuzzy or ignoring it can be systematized only to a degree. The first two sections of this sub-chapter deal with major classes of music not firmly locateable on either level of narration: displaced diegetic music and supradiegetic music (the latter is more extensively discussed in Chapter III). The last section looks at a few of the countless other options films have for stepping across the border.

Displaced diegetic music
Strictly speaking, the term 'diegetic music' only indicates that the film cues us to construe music as a (physical) element of the diegesis, but does not say how it relates to other diegetic elements. The standard sound film case is that music and its source are shown or implied to coexist in in the same diegetic space-time. But as other diegetic sound, music can be detached from its diegetic source in different ways:

- The most common case is a 'sound bridge' involving music: an overlap of music from one scene to the next (Bordwell and Thompson 2010: 296–97). The music (or other sound) can precede the image it 'belongs' to ('sound advance'), lag behind ('sound lag'), or link several shots ('sound link') (see Buhler, Neumeyer and Deemer 2009: 92–97). A variant is a 'sound match': similar sounds on both sides of a cut (2009: 97). While sound bridges are pervasive in narrative film, they are not normally particularly interesting from a narratological point of view, because they rarely add meaning or produce an effect beyond that of musical continuity editing.

- Strictly speaking, 'off-screen music' means any music whose source is not visible in an image frame, including sound bridges and displaced diegetic music. But in the interest of differentiation, it makes sense to speak of 'off-screen music' if the source of the music is not visible, but implied to be in a space contiguous with the space we have visual access to in the frame, and happening at the same time as the other diegetic action in the scene.[73] Off-screen music does not affect our sense of a coherent audio-visual representation of a diegetic event – we just assume that we cannot see every part of it, and that some parts are only accessible to us aurally.

- To be distinguished from musical sound bridges and from off-screen music is 'displaced music': music that has a shown or implied diegetic source, but is used with images in relation to which it cannot be understood as diegetic.[74]

  - Music can be *spatially displaced*, e.g. if the film cuts between scenes taking place in different locations, but implicitly at the same time, and in one of the locations diegetic music occurs that also underlies the action in the other place;

---

73 Michel Chion further distinguishes between 'mental off-screen sound' ('a sound we hear only mentally or logically as offscreen, as its source is absent from the image, when in fact its source is the same loudspeaker as the sounds that are onscreen or nondiegetic') and 'real off-screen sound' (a sound that is 'truly acoustically heard emanating from a speaker situated outside the borders of the screen, when its fictional source is supposed to be situated "in the wings" of the screen space'; Chion 2009: 481). While the difference is important for film production and exhibition, and badly integrated 'real off-screen sound' can disrupt the impression of a coherent diegetic space, narratologically the distinction is not relevant.

74 'Displaced diegetic sound' has become an umbrella term for spatially and temporally displaced sound, though in Bordwell's and Thompson's *Film Art: An Introduction*, which contains the most systematic account of displacing sound, the term itself is not used. Instead, they distinguish between:

  - 'diegetic' and 'nondiegetic' sound (see Bordwell and Thompson 2010: 284–85): sound that is manifestly or implicitly part of the storyworld;
  - 'on-screen' and 'off-screen' sound (see Bordwell and Thompson 2010: 285): sound whose source is inside or outside the frame (but implicitly in a contiguous space, which is how I use the term, though that means that Bordwell and Thompson do not have a term for what I call spatially displaced music);
  - 'external' and 'internal' diegetic sound (see Bordwell and Thompson 2010: 289–91): sound that is a physical feature of the diegesis and sound that is heard/imagined inside a character's mind;
  - 'synchronous' and 'asynchronous' diegetic sound (see Bordwell and Thompson 2010: 294): the manipulation of sound/image synchronization on the micro-scale of (pretend) film projection;
  - 'simultaneous' and 'non-simultaneous' diegetic sound (see Bordwell and Thompson 2010: 294–97): sound and image showing the same or different moments in story time, with the further distinction between sounds referring to an earlier moment of story time than the image they are shown with, and sounds referring to a later moment of story time: both cases of what I call 'temporally displaced music'.

- music can be *temporally displaced*, typically if a scene involving synchronous diegetic music ends with a cut implying a temporal leap, but the music continues across the cut and also underscores the following scene;
- music can be *spatially and temporally displaced*: many examples involving temporal displacement also involve spatial displacement, if a scene cuts to another one at a different point in story time and a different location.

While displaced diegetic music would seem to be merely a subcategory of displaced diegetic sound, there is a difference. The most common case of temporally displaced diegetic sound is a 'sonic flashback' (Bordwell and Thompson 2010: 295): a sound we have heard previously (as synchronous diegetic sound) is used at a later point together with images with regard to which it cannot be understood as diegetic. The sound points back to its origin, and we are asked to make a connection between the present and the moment of its origin. The moment of origin may also be part of the connotative and affective charge of diegetic music that later returns on the nondiegetic soundtrack, but the link tends to be weaker than for nonmusical diegetic sounds. The little tune Cockeye plays on his flute before the youthful gang rob a drunk in *Once Upon a Time in America* (1984) becomes one of the leitmotifs of the film (see ch. V.i.c), but we do not understand it as a reminder of this particular moment every time it reappears. Instead, it becomes associated with the friendship of the gang more generally, and acquires its charge by picking up meaning every time it is used, within or without the diegesis.

The difference lies in the fact that the nondiegetic reappearance of originally diegetic sounds is rare and therefore claims our attention. That diegetic music is 'taken up' by the narration, on the other hand, is the most frequent case of a transition between the two levels, and while we normally take it to be meaningful to some extent, it is not a particularly conspicuous technique. A flashback involving music is usually arranged as a flashback a *character* experiences, and so remains within the diegesis (but since what we hear in such a case occurs at the same moment of story time, albeit mentally, it is not displaced diegetic music in the above sense; see also Bordwell and Thompson 2010: 296). That means that what we experience as a displacement of diegetic music in the strong sense normally requires the displacement to happen during a single cue – the editing has to make clear that something happens to this particular bit of diegetic music. The examples discussed in this section show this kind of displacement.

*

Jeff Smith has argued against an overly liberal use of Robynn Stilwell's 'fantastical gap between diegetic and nondiegetic' (Stilwell 2007) as a holdall for film-musical techniques than can be described more precisely in other ways. He discusses spatial and/or temporal displacement of diegetic music as one example for an alternative analytical tool (beside different degrees of aural fidelity and different degrees of 'communicativeness' of the narration; see Bordwell 1985: 57–61). The problem, according to Smith, is that 'the use of nondiegetic music is so common in fiction film-making, one usually assumes that any music not clearly located in the storyworld is likely to be nondiegetic' (Smith 2009), when it might actually be something more specific, e.g. displaced diegetic music. The problem with Smith's attempt to narrow the 'fantastical gap' by pulling examples back out and assigning them to a more specific category is that the issue is not categorization, but explanation. The 'fantastical gap' is problematic because it lumps together different ambiguities, transitions and transgressions, but it does preserve a sense of the effect such ambiguities have on our experience of a film – the effect on our understanding and expectations of the kind of narration we see and hear at work. To say that displaced diegetic music is, after all, diegetic, and therefore not a candidate for the fantastical gap, does not explain much if it does not explain what is achieved by the displacement.

The problem is borne out by Smith's example for spatially and temporally displaced diegetic music: the Volcano scene from *Trainspotting* (1996), showing the meeting of Renton (Ewan McGregor) and Diane (Kelly Macdonald) in the Volcano nightclub (Figure 11). The scene is held together by a cover version of Blondie's 'Atomic', performed by Britpop band Sleeper. Smith's analysis distinguishes five phases (Smith 2009):

1. The music begins as diegetic music in the club. (We do not see a source, accurate with regard to the setting.)
2. The music becomes off-screen when the action moves outside the club and we (and the characters) hear just the muffled sound of the song through the walls and doors, while diegetic sounds of the scene outside the club are in the foreground.
3. The volume of the music swells when Diane leaves the cab door open for Renton, effectively inviting him home with her, and he runs towards the cab.
4. The music continues at the higher volume in Diane's and Renton's cab ride, and can now be described as spatially displaced diegetic music. We can assume that it is still continuing in the club (no temporal displacement), but we hear the music in a space where the characters cannot hear it, at least not physically.
5. The music accompanies cross-cutting between Diane and Renton, Gail (Shirley Henderson) and Spud (Ewen Bremner) and Tommy (Kevin McKidd) and Lizzy (Pauline Lynch). Now the music has also been temporally displaced, as the series of shots of the three couples implicitly covers more story time than the song at its diegetic point of origin.

Phases 1 and 2 are unproblematic: the music can be understood as accurately rendered diegetic music (more or less, see below). What we hear is what we see, or expect to hear. But Smith's phases 3 and 4 fails to capture what happens in narratological terms:

Figure 11: Renton in the Volcano chaos in *Trainspotting* (1996) and Diane's appearance.

> The music continues at this volume over the shot of Diane and Mark [Renton] kissing inside the cab [...]. The music's level in the mix implies the norm for nondiegetic sound within the syuzhet, but [...] it is really a manipulation of the music's fidelity for expressive purposes. Moreover [...], the shift in space does not negate the music's original location within the diegesis; it is here an example of spatially displaced diegetic sound. (Smith 2009)

The problem is the 'but': 'a manipulation of the music's fidelity for expressive purposes' may not 'negate the music's original location within the diegesis', but it changes the music's original location in the narrative structure. Music that began as an element of the film's 'monstration', of its showing of diegetic facts, transforms into an element of its 'narration' (see Gaudreault 2009); the narration has appropriated the diegetic music and uses it to underscore a scene with regard to which it cannot be considered diegetic. We do not expect Diane and Renton to be able to hear 'Atomic' in the cab, not even when they are still close to the club, certainly not at the volume we hear the music on the soundtrack. That is reinforced when the displacement also reaches the music's temporal aspect. From something located within diegetic space, the music has become something that envelopes the scene, but also defines it (which, given the lyrics inviting the addressee to have sex with the 'I' of the lyrics, makes perfect, if unoriginal sense).

The starting point for Smith's introduction of displaced diegetic music into his argument was that it offers a way out of the fantastical gap; even displaced diegetic music is still diegetic music. But the tension between diegesis and narration is the issue: the fact that the music gets further and further removed from its place in diegetic space and time.

There are two further aspects to the scene Smith fails to mention, though they have a bearing on the way it can be understood:

1. While 'Atomic' is presented as diegetic in the Volcano, its entry is unrealistically perfectly coordinated with Diane entering Renton's world. The music in the club cuts sharply from Heaven 17's 'Temptation' to 'Atomic' exactly when Renton's eyes fall on Diane. While not impossible, the coincidence strains credibility, and we more likely understand it as an instance of implied authorial agency. The coincidence has been put there in order to make 'Atomic' from a random song into 'our song' for Renton and Diane (or rather for Renton), even if only for this one night. The appropriation of the diegetic song is already pre-empted by using it in a way that prepares us for its role as the signature song for the night's further developments.
2. The second aspect applies to the whole film. Renton is its homodiegetic narrator, his voice-over invokes the images we see; some realistic, some anything but. We can understand everything we see as filtered through his perception and memories. That also applies to 'Atomic' and its positioning at the right point in time, and it applies to the later use of 'Atomic' as music that moves further and further away from its diegetic anchoring point to surround the scene. The narration uses this song as emblematic for the night – a narration that is, after all, Renton's own.

This is supported by the way the scene in the club is filmed. Far from being a realistic portrayal of the goings-on, the images clearly show Renton's perspective: his increasingly frantic search for a woman, any woman, who will hold his gaze for more than a split second; his looks at the friends who are shown to be groping, smooching, taking drugs in an exaggerated manner consistent with understanding the images as Renton's perception. His perception also seems to inform the contrast between the chaos and the clarity that reigns once Diane enters the scene – the gap in the swirling mass of people that opens when Renton looks at her. If what we see is internally focalized, then 'Atomic' is not just music that happened, but also music focalized through Renton's experience and memories, which also connect the 'diegetic' song at the beginning of the scene and its displacement later on.

What makes the displacement of music interesting is how it allows diegetic music to be used both (more or less) realistically and as part of the 'voice' of a narrating agency. The possibilities are manifold, and the following examples just indicate a few options.

The Volcano scene demonstrates one potential of displaced diegetic music: to show that music that is part of a diegetic event can represent that event as *pars pro toto* on a higher level of narration. Several examples of this can be found in *Muriel's Wedding* (1994) in connection with its eponymous (anti-)heroine, ABBA fan Muriel Heslop (Toni Collette). When she is flying to Hibiscus Island for a mini-holiday with her terrible clique of friends, we hear Blondie's 'The Tide Is High' when the plane is approaching the island, before the song is 'revealed' as diegetic music, sung by Muriel's gang: the song is part of their fun (though not, at this point, for Muriel) and labels the entire holiday. More symbolic meaning is extracted from a displaced diegetic song when Rhonda, the new and true friend Muriel meets on Hibiscus Island, puts Muriel's nasty friends in their place with a withering put-down, and 'Waterloo' starts, telling us what the nasty friends have just experienced and celebrating Rhonda's victory (and Muriel's liberation), before we see the two perform the song on the stage in the holiday colony.

A more complex displacement occurs in a scene close to the beginning of the Finnish composer biopic *Sibelius* (2003). After the opening sequence showing Sibelius' funeral in 1957, the image changes from black-and-white to colour, and we see the old Sibelius and his wife observe a flock of migratory birds. The birds link to the next scene, which shows Sibelius as a little boy, running to reach the edge of a marching column of soldiers. We hear marching music, but do not (yet) see a diegetic source; only after a while do a few soldiers with instruments pass through the frame. But the music we hear is the 'Alla marcia' from Sibelius' *Karelia Suite* op. 11 from 1893, written more than 20 years after the scene we see. It is a double bluff. When we first hear the music, we have not yet seen the marching soldiers but just the little boy, accompanied by music we know (if we recognize it) he would later write himself. With the soldiers, and especially with the military band marching through the frame at one point, the music acquires a diegetic anchoring point, but it is a paradoxical one. This, clearly, is not the music little Janne would have heard on that day; that music we do not get to hear at all. What we get instead is the music the film implies the experience triggered in Sibelius: the scene reconstructs Sibelius' biography in the light of the man the narration knows he would become.[75] (If we include the preceding images showing the old Sibelius and his wife, we could also understand these images as Sibelius' own retrospection.) The same trick is repeated with other pieces in subsequent scenes and helps to define the film's perspective as one of retrospection, typical for biopics, many of which look back over the career of their subjects from the perspective of their status as monuments of cultural history (for other examples of that perspective see Heldt 2009).

Displacement of music is frequently employed in musician biopics because it allows them to do two things at once: to build longer pieces of music into the film without having to clear the space for extended diegetic performance scenes (though these are common as well); and use music implied to play a biographical role (whether historically accurate or

---

75 The idea may have been borrowed from a scene in Ken Russell's *Mahler* (1974). Mahler is at work in his studio in the countryside, while his wife Alma is rushing about in the attempt to quieten the sounds around them (their screaming baby, cowbells, folk musicians and drinkers at a pub, etc.), sounds which all find their way into Mahler's symphonies, excerpts of which we are hearing at the same time.

not) to tell the story of that life, feeding a loop between life and work. A classic example occurs in the German Mozart biopic *Whom the Gods Love/Wen die Götter lieben* (1942) (more in Heldt 2009: 39–41). Mozart visits the Weber family in order to further his budding relationship with Constanze; at the same time, musicians in the imperial palace prepare a string quartet rehearsal in which the emperor will participate. Mozart is out of favour, and his friends' plan is to sneak in one of his pieces without telling the emperor by whom it is, in the hope that he will like it and perhaps commission music from Mozart. The plan works: the emperor, after some grumbling, accepts the music placed before him, and they play the first movement of Mozart's quartet K575 (written for the cello-playing Prussian king, not the Austrian emperor).[76] But in bar 61, the film's syuzhet shifts to the Weber household, while the music continues at lower volume, and in effect becomes underscoring to the domestic scenes unfolding: cookies have burned in the oven, and the disorienting opening of the development section in bar 78 fits the mild upheaval. With bar 86 and its arrival of clear G major, Mozart himself arrives at the door, and some further light-hearted confusion concerning an ash streak on Constanze's cheek is also appropriately underscored by the music. Then we return to the palace, where the music comes to its end.[77]

The implication is clear: the two scenes happen at the same time, and they have parallel import for Mozart's life – in the palace, his professional fate hangs in the balance, as does his private fate at the Webers'. All's well that ends well: the emperor will commission *The Abduction from the Seraglio*, while Constanze will become Mozart's wife. But there is also a meta-message in the parallelism under the umbrella of Mozart's music: biographical construction is more important than plausibility in this (kind of) film. *Whom the Gods Love* foregrounds its capacity for 'self-conscious narration' (Bordwell 1985: 57–61) and for myth-making, and foregrounds its identity as a film (in)formed by music.

Spatial displacement of diegetic music for scenes implicitly taking place at the same time is common, but again the point is the meaning derived from these parallels. In *Cabaret* (1972), displacement of diegetic music allows a musical film that studiously avoids the supradiegetic state typical of classic Hollywood musicals; musical numbers can spread out beyond their performances, but the music stays tethered to the diegesis (more in ch. III.iv). Other examples are the musical scene-links in *Fame* discussed in the section on the implied author (pp. 88–89). While the point made by these displacements is not as heavy-handed as in *Whom the Gods Love*, there certainly is a point as well: to show the restless activity of different groups in the music academy the story is set in – the fact that everyone is involved in different activities, but that all of those activities

---

76 The music has been edited for the purposes of the film. It starts not at beginning of the movement, but in bar 32, and there are other cuts later on.

77 In another alteration to the actual music, the performance ends not with the end of the movement, but with the *stretta* of string quartet K465.

happen in pursuit of artistic excellence (or fame, as the film's title has it in a rather more disillusioning way).

Earlier I have described what I call 'would-be-diegetic music' (see pp. 68–69) as a way of implicating the narration in a conflict in the diegetic world by making it seem to sing for characters. There are others ways of making music in a film take sides though, and the displacement of diegetic music is one of them. The first sequence of *The Wind that Shakes the Barley* (2006), a film about the birthing pains first of the Irish Free State, shows a group of British soldiers barging into an Irish village and rounding up the men. One of the villagers, young Micheail (Laurence Barry), gets lippy, is taken into a barn and beaten to death. The scene ends with the British soldiers leaving the village again, while on the soundtrack we first hear a drone and then a voice sing Robert Dwyer Joyce's song 'The Wind that Shakes the Barley' (about a young Irish rebel in the revolt of 1798). There is no visible or plausible source for the music, but then the image cuts, and we are in the house where Micheail is laid out, and where an old woman sings the song for him (confirming, by the choice of song, his involvement with the Irish resistance against British rule). But the drone that opens the music is visually unaccounted for, and even without it, the effect of the temporal displacement of the music to a point *before* its anchoring in the fabula (in addition to the spatial displacement) makes it seem for a moment as if this were not just the old woman's lament, but one the narration of the film sings to state its partiality to the perspective of the Irish villagers.

What scenes such as those in *Whom the Gods Love* or *Fame* do beyond projecting messages through film-musical syntax is project that syntax itself; they structure the films by formal means, foregrounding their genre identity as musical films. *Step Across the Border*, Nicolas Humbert's and Werner Penzel's Fred Frith documentary (1990), uses the displacement of diegetic music for the same purpose: to delimit sequences linked to Frith's journeys around the (musical) world, to indicate inspiration derived from different musical cultures, and to structure the film into arcs centred on diegetic music, but spilling over into preceding and subsequent scenes.

At one point during a tour of Japan in 1988, we see images of old Japanese people and hear voices and diegetic sounds. But the relationship between sounds and images is puzzling, because we never see a clear source for any of the presumably diegetic sounds, while the voices do not match the shots of people opening their mouths. Already the soundtrack, while seemingly linked to the images, is semi-autonomous, and since Frith's music works so much with environmental sounds, it is both part of the diegesis shown and something else; connected to it, but partly abstract.

Then a song starts (entitled 'After Dinner' on the soundtrack CD), sung in Japanese, but the relationship to the shot of the old man it coincides with is unclear. Twenty seconds later we see Japanese singer Haco sing the song, and when the image cuts to her, in a completely different space, the diegetic sounds finally cease. The displacement of the music is at an end; image and sound finally go together. But their loose relationship is confirmed when, at its end, the song accompanies Frith sleeping on a train: the locking of image and soundtrack

Figure 12: Beginning, core part and end of 'After Dinner' in *Step Across the Border* (1990).

was only intermittent, and they separate again, completing the arc and confirming that the soundtrack, appropriately for the film's subject matter, is more than the sonic flipside of the image coin (Figure 12).

The same happens when music from a concert ('Houston Street' on the soundtrack CD) is displaced onto preceding and following images of New York, matching their shabby, melancholy atmosphere, but without explanation of the relationship between music and images. More important is the formal principle of music that seems to start as atmospheric accompaniment to the images, but is then 'revealed' as diegetic, suggesting its reconstrual with regard to the preceding images as displaced diegetic music, before the music confirms that construal by becoming displaced again in the end (Figure 13).

In a nice dialectic twist, the structural displacement of music contributes to its cultural placement: its localization as music that 'belongs' to Japan, or to the New York shown by the images. It is a minimal, but because of that minimalism more effective, audio-visualization of musical ideology *Step Across the Border* is so rich in.

Supradiegetic music

'Supradiegetic music' is used by Rick Altman (1987: 62–85; he spells it 'supra-diegetic', but for consistency I use the contraction) for the relationship of diegetic and nondiegetic music in the numbers of film musicals: transcendent spaces where normal diegetic logic is suspended, music takes over, and the genre reaches its purpose in displays of pure performative

Figure 13: Beginning, core and end of 'Houston Street' in *Step Across the Border* (1990).

bliss.[78] Supradiegetic music is often reached by what Altman calls an 'audio dissolve' (in conjunction with 'video' and 'personality' dissolves), the transition from diegetic sounds via diegetic singing and/or dancing to its melding with nondiegetic accompaniment.

That transcendent space seems so specific to the film musical that the main discussion of Altman's concept takes place in Chapter III. But it is worth considering whether it may not be transferable to other situations. Its genre-specificity has prevented the term from having much of a career in film (music) scholarship, even in literature on musical films. We should be cautious, though. Altman's term means not just any fusion of diegetic and nondiegetic music. Such moments are common, allowing the highlighting of diegetic music-making. When Holly Golightly (Audrey Hepburn) sits on the window sill in *Breakfast at Tiffany's* (1961) and sings 'Moon River', we take the orchestra that softly enters after the first stanza in our stride. The narration lends support to the film's un-heroic heroine and marks the moment as important.[79] But the primacy of the diegetic event is not in question, there is no indication that 'the events of the diegesis change motivation' (Altman 1987: 70). To qualify for consideration as supradiegetic, more is required: at least some sense that the filmic moment goes beyond diegetic self-containment and falls under the spell of the music, is organized by it more than by the logic of diegetic causes and effects.

Points in narrative film where changes of motivation or organization are common are beginning and end – special cases because the diegesis is often not yet self-sufficient, or not any more (for title sequences, see ch. II.ii). The ends of the narrative parts of films (before end credits) often use music as punctuation: a marker that we have arrived at the edge of the story. That can be done by nondiegetic music, often a song commenting on the story. The conclusion can be particularly effective if the music grows out of the diegesis. At the end of *The First Wives Club* (1996), club members Brenda (Bette Midler), Elise (Goldie Hawn) and Annie (Diane Keaton) give a triumphant rendition of 'You Don't Own Me' (by John Madara and Dave White Tricker), and are soon joined by a nondiegetic orchestra that leads into the end credits. The crossing of the borderline between diegetic and nondiegetic music coincides with the crossing of the borderline between story and peritext, strongly marking that point.[80]

A more complex example occurs in *Sun Alley* (1999), a comedy about a group of youths in the GDR in the 1970s. Products from the West are coveted possessions, and Wuschel

---

78 'Supradiegetic music' is not to be confused with the terms 'supradiegetic narrator' or 'supradiegetic agent', which are sometimes used for what is more commonly called an implied author; see Neupert (1995: 61) or Gaudreault (2009: 4) (the latter term is based on Danielle Candelon).

79 There is more to the relationship between nondiegetic and diegetic music in this particular moment, however, though in a very different sense (see ch. V.iii).

80 Such musical punctuation is a time-honoured tradition: Italian eighteenth-century *opera seria* used ensemble pieces only sparingly, and usually only with diegetic justification (an acclamation for the king, chanting priests, etc.). But the last number was commonly an ensemble of all singers, celebrating the usual happy end. The breach of the rule not to use ensembles save diegetically made the point that the space where such rules applied, i.e. the story space, had been left behind.

(Robert Stadlober) is particularly keen on Rolling Stones' *Exile on Main Street* (1972), the title an obvious allusion to the teenagers' view of their life in the GDR. Towards the end of the film, he believes to have bought *Exile on Main Street* on the black market, but when he puts it on his turntable he realizes that he has been ripped off with anaemic Eastern Bloc pop. But Wuschel and his friend Micha (Alexander Scheer) refuse to be disappointed by reality any longer, and join in by playing air guitar and air bass. As soon as they start, the diegetic sound from the turntable ceases, and we hear what we assume they think they are playing. They rock out onto the balcony, people in the street notice them, and the two, fired up by the recognition, launch into an air-music rendition of Wayne Carson Thompson's much-covered 'The Letter',[81] which everyone else seems to be able to hear too, because people are swaying and dancing to the music, including a police officer and two officials from their school. At this point, diegetic plausibility dissolves. In the flat, we could still imagine the music to be internally focalized through their musical imagination, but now that imagination has found its way into the diegesis – their inner life has taken over GDR reality. Eventually, the people begin to dance off towards the border to West Berlin; a border guard plays air guitar on his Kalashnikov and fires a few

Exile on Main Street?

The music of the mind

'My baby just wrote me a letter'

Popular movement

Figure 14: 'The Letter' scene at the end of *Sun Alley* (1999).

---

81 The song was performed by the band Dynamo 5, which had been put together for the film.

celebratory shots; Micha and Wuschel join them by jumping down from the balcony, and over the music carrying everyone towards freedom (even if only in their imagination, more than a decade before the fall of the Berlin Wall), Micha begins his concluding voice-over narration (Figure 14).

It is a good example for an Altmanian audio dissolve, beginning with diegetic action and proceeding via diegetic music to a musical state connected to, but also transcending the diegesis. And transcendence is the point, biographically, psychologically, politically and structurally: Micha's and Wuschel's refusal to bow to the reality of having been ripped off with the wrong music; their magic ability to make real music by playing air guitar; the infectious effect of the music on the people, including the stern wardens of the GDR system; the people's bid for freedom at a point in history when this was in no way on the political cards; the nonchalant relationship of the scene with diegetic logic.

The empty border guard hut in the last images of the film could be seen to indicate that the people managed to escape into more than just their musical fantasies, foreshadowing the counterfactual end of Quentin Tarantino's *Inglourious Basterds* (2009), which blithely ends another German dictatorship before its time. But these images are already overlaid by Micha's concluding narration and by another song (Michael Heubach's 'Du hast den Farbfilm vergessen' ['You've Forgotten the Colour Film'] from 1974, sung by Nina Hagen, an authentic piece of GDR pop culture), and could be seen as an acknowledgement that the preceding fantasy was indeed just that. But, as in *The First Wives Club*, more important is the fact that this leads into the end of the film; the dissolution of diegetic and historical plausibility has a 'syntactic' justification.

More interesting are moments at the core of films where normal rules do apply. An example that toys with transcending the diegetic/nondiegetic division, but keeps this side of it occurs in *King Kong* (1933). The interweaving of nondiegetic and diegetic music is part of the basic musical strategy of the film. The mystery space of Skull Island is marked by the return of nondiegetic music after roughly 20 musicless minutes after the credits, but into that music is soon integrated the sound of drumming, drumming the dialogue tells us to understand as diegetic (see also Stilwell 2007: 189). Such integration of narration and diegesis is typical for horror films and their often clear implied authorial presence in the service of the implicit contract to horrify the audience (see Chapter IV). It can also, again as in other horror films, be understood to indicate the more-than-natural realm our heroes have entered. That nondiegetic music in *King Kong* only starts once the ship has reached the fog surrounding Skull Island fits that reading.

But the integration of diegetic and nondiegetic music continues when the crew enter the island, and culminates when – guided by drumming, the sound of a horn-like instrument and chanting ('Kong, Kong'), but also by the slowly crescendoing support of the nondiegetic orchestra – they have reached the place of the terrible revelry. Film director Cal Denham (Robert Armstrong) parts the reeds, and a blast of brass marks the sight of islanders in gorilla costumes dancing in front of the gigantic gate in the wall that separates their realm from Kong's, while others surround them in elaborate costumes. 'Holy mackerel, what a

'Holy mackerel …   … what a show!'
Figure 15: The Skull Island musical number in *King Kong* (1933).

show!', Denham comments; as an entertainment professional, he knows a good show when he sees and hears one, and the dance continues with the full support of the nondiegetic orchestra (Figure 15).

It is not quite supradiegesis, not quite like a number in a film musical, but it shares some of the characteristics: there is the integration of diegetic and nondiegetic music to give the scene an impact neither of the elements would have had on their own; there is the internal audience film musicals like to use to validate the entertainment value of what the external audience in the cinema is seeing (and hearing). Here, the internal audience has the added advantage of consisting partly of film professionals, who can attest to the cinematic qualities of the scene, and there is the sense of 'what a show' on both levels: a show for the hidden diegetic spectators, and a show for the cinema audience, who enjoy both the diegetic spectacle and the supra-spectacle the film develops out of it by using its techniques of framing and cutting images and of reinforcing diegetic music by a nondiegetic orchestra. That the supradiegetic effect is not quite there makes sense in a film that has its *raison d'être* not in the magic of music, but in that of monsters.

Closer to the structure and effect of supradiegetic music comes a scene in *The Prodigal Son* (1934). In the early part of the film, Tonio Feuersinger (Luis Trenker) lives in South Tyrol, ensconced by the traditional world of his mountain community, summarized by a scene that shows the woodcutting team Tonio is part of get into the 'flow' their work[82], and again diegetic 'facts' and filmic presentation are two sides of a coin. The woodcutters work rhythmically and support themselves by singing a song; and the film cuts rhythmically and supports their singing both by reinforcing diegetic sounds (trees falling, tree stems rushing down a wooden chute and splashing into the river etc.) with percussion[83] and by nondiegetic

---

82 The term 'flow' for this kind of mental state was coined by Hungarian psychologist Mihaly Csikszentmihalyi (see Csikszentmihalyi 1975).

83 This is not quite the same as Michel Chion's 'rendering' of sounds. Chion's term means the unrealistic (re)production of sounds to achieve a realistic overall effect not just of that sound, but of the complex sensory experience that sound was part of, of the effect of an event (see Chion 2009: 237–45 & 488). In *The Prodigal Son*, the reinforcement of the sounds is perceptibly unrealistic; the percussion effects are clearly audible as what they are. The point seems to be to add something to diegetic sounds to

accompaniment. The effect of the scene comes strikingly close to that of a musical number (at a time of film history when the dividing line between musical and non-musical films was more fluid than later). The point of the supradiegetic effect is not to evoke a narrative space beyond the diegesis, though, but a psychological space of men fully immersed and in control of their work.

That feeling of control becomes important as a foil for the second part of the film, which shows Tonio as an immigrant in the USA, an experience characterized by a loss of control over his life; like an uprooted tree, he cannot grow into the new situation (and at the end returns). But the film takes up the woodcutting scene and shows Tonio in the USA in a complementary situation that gives him, for a moment, the feeling of being back in control. He has found work in the construction crew of a skyscraper, and we see him high up on the half-finished building, surrounded by a symphony of clanging and hammering. In addition to the sounds of work, we hear nondiegetic music, and during the scene the two sonic and narrative levels increasingly merge, the hammering becomes more and more rhythmic and musical. Once more Tonio experiences the 'flow' of being at one with his work, reminding him (and us) of his old life in Tyrol (and naturally the film capitalizes on the mountain/skyscraper simile when, at the transitional point of the two halves of the film, the image of one dissolves into that of the other).

Another example for a merging of diegetic and nondiegetic music not in a film musical (though in a musical film) occurs in the Mozart biopic *A Little Night Music/Eine kleine Nachtmusik* (1940), loosely based on Eduard Mörike's novella *Mozart on the Journey to Prague* of 1855 (see Heldt 2009: 41). The film's semi-tragic heroine is Countess Eugenie of Schinzberg, about to be married off to boring country squire, but dreaming of Vienna and its culture, and Mozart's music embodies that dream for her. And then Mozart, on the journey to Prague and the *Don Giovanni* premiere, passes by the Schinzberg estate and stops at the village inn. Eugenie is standing by a window when the orchestra starts to play (seemingly) nondiegetic music. But then she joins in and sings 'Deh, vieni, non tardar' ('Oh come, do not tarry') from *The Marriage of Figaro*, completing the music with her diegetic song of love-longing. The moment's message is brought home to us when the music (the melody now in the violin) reaches across the cut to Mozart and Constanze at the inn: Mozart admires the landscape beyond the palace park visible through the window, where Eugenie is looking out of her own window at (we assume) the same time.

The transcendence of a narrative boundary in the supradiegetic fusion echoes Eugenie's yearning to transcend her prescribed and predictable provincial life, a yearning she acts out in singing Mozart. The link with Mozart across the cut also has a double dimension: it shows the spiritual connection between Eugenie and Mozart. But it is also bit of magic realism: in the text of the aria, Eugenie calls out to a 'beloved soul' to come to her, and Mozart duly

---

evoke the sense of hyperreality the men have in their 'flow'. The technique may also be a residue of the silent-film practice of using music instead of diegetic sound that made it into early sound film (see, for example, Claudia Gorbman's discussion of *Under the Roofs of Paris*, Gorbman 1987: 140–150).

comes, even if at the end of the film he has to continue on his way to Prague, to fame and early death, while Eugenie has to stay.

Into the wild – further options

Beyond displaced diegetic and supradiegetic music, systematization of transitions and transgressions of the diegetic/nondiegetic distinction becomes tenuous. The starting point for the following survey of some of the options can only be Cole Porter's (and Paul Feyerabend's) insight that 'Anything goes': anything can happen to and with music at any point in a film; the borderline is purely conceptual and offers no resistance. What may offer resistance is our understanding of the narration/diegesis relationship, and the question is what such moments of transition or transgression mean: mean for our understanding of a film, our (re)construction of the diegesis and our expectations of the workings of the narration.

Summarizing the relationship between source music and score, Fred Karlin and Rayburn Wright point out that 'source music […] can also change its function at any time and continue as score' (Karlin and Wright 1990: 511). They nevertheless order the possibilities into five options (see 1990: 511–12), and these options may help to clear a path at least into the outer parts of the wilderness:

1. Source music can function as score;
2. source music can change into score;
3. source music can crossfade into score;
4. source music and score can be used simultaneously;
5. source music can play the underscoring theme.

Examples and theoretical implications of option 1, 'source scoring', are discussed in ch. II.iv.c–e. Option 3 is not relevant for this study, because it only concerns a technique of continuity editing, a momentary blurring of cues otherwise (normally) clearly assigned to diegesis and narration respectively. An example is the opening scene of *Wild at Heart*: the implicitly diegetic 'In the Mood' is swamped by speed metal track 'Slaughterhouse' for Sailor's fit of murderous rage, and resumes after it has passed (see pp. 78–79). It is an example for what Michael Chion calls 'masking' (2009: 480), though here nondiegetic (or possibly internally focalized music) masks diegetic music.

The same applies to option 4: simultaneity of diegetic and nondiegetic music does not confuse levels of narration; the multichannel medium film can present information on different levels of narration at the same time. More interesting are examples of musical *integration* of levels in one cue, e.g. the *King Kong* moment discussed above (pp. 109–10), when the dialogue tells us to understand the drumming in the orchestral texture underscoring the ship's approach to Skull Island as diegetic music from the island. The trick makes us share the surprise of the people on the ship. We assume that the entire musical texture is nondiegetic and have to revise our assumptions along with the crew who identify the vague noise they are hearing not as the sea breaking on a beach, but as drumming – a case of psychological parallelism (see pp. 180–81). Integration is also used in *Planet of the Apes* (1968), when the ramshorns blown by the apes during their hunting of humans are part of an orchestral cue. Here, the point of the integration is to surround the horn calls with the halo of orchestral musical excitement for the action scene.

Another case of diegetic/nondiegetic integrations are musical soundscapes too dense to be aurally analyzed. This occurs especially in (recent) horror films, where the uncertainty produced by the attempt to untangle such soundscapes can be used to put the audience in the shoes of diegetic characters trying to use sonic clues to alert them to danger; examples of this are discussed in Chapter IV.[84]

That leaves Karlin's and Wright's options 2 and 5. Option 2 addresses one of the principal classes of diegetic/nondiegetic border-crossings, while option 5 names a subgroup of another class: transitions from diegetic to nondiegetic music on the one hand, and transitions from nondiegetic to diegetic music on the other. Before a look at examples, a few words on the meanings of 'transition' and of 'music' in this context.

- 'Transition' can mean a change in our understanding of the narrative status of the music in the syuzhet – in the order of events as presented on-screen. It can, however, also mean a change in the fabula we construct on the basis of the syuzhet. The relationship between syuzhet and fabula can be complex, and there is no point in trying to systematize them in relation to music crossing from one level of narration to another. (Ch. V.i, on *Once Upon a Time in America*, presents a case study of a film for which this is relevant, though.)
- 'Music' in this context can mean different options: a single, unbroken musical cue that for part of its duration we construe as diegetic and for another part as nondiegetic; a cue that is used several times in the same way, but on different levels of narration; and musical material that is used on different levels of narration, but in slightly different, varied forms. It is crucial that we perceive only a sufficient degree of identity – that we understand a bit of music on one level as the same music as a bit on another level, however flexible our understanding of 'the same' may be.

Transitions from diegetic to nondiegetic music & de-diegetization

Transitions from diegetic to nondiegetic music are usually less conspicuous, at least if the diegetic instance comes first in the fabula. This allows the film to retain the illusion of an autonomous pre-filmic reality in which the music originates. That may apply to individual

---

84 Films such as *The Boat/Das Boot* (1981) use the same technique for the same purpose: together with the submarine crew the audience listen for sounds that betray an approaching destroyer, or the imminent failure of the structural integrity of the submarine's hull.

scenes only: most films imply that their story is being told with the benefit of hindsight. We know that the narration knows what is going to happen and arranges what we see and hear to guide us through the events. But we can suspend that knowledge and follow a story as if it happened as we see it, and in that context we can understand diegetic to nondiegetic transitions as 'natural': music occurs in the storyworld, is 'noticed' as relevant by the narration and taken up. (The first part of ch. V.iii develops this idea further.)

The development of the first 38 bars of Franz Liszt's 'Étude de concert' no. 3 in *Letter from an Unknown Woman* (1948) is an example for music originating in the diegesis, but moving out of it. In the first of the flashbacks that make up the bulk of screen time, the letter from 'unknown woman', Lisa (Joan Fontaine), tells of her initial attachment to musician Stefan (Louis Jourdan), which began with his practicing the Liszt piece. But his playing breaks off after 38 bars (in itself presaging the relationship between Lisa and Stefan) and becomes the core of the film's nondiegetic music, which develops the plot and psychological motifs sown in the initial scene (more in Laing 2005: 77–98).

If such transitions are common in leitmotivic scores because they naturalize the link between leitmotifs and diegetic referents, transitions within a single cue can bring out plot implications. If they also involve temporal ellipses, their effect can be close to that of displaced diegetic music; in many cases a distinction may be impossible to make. A potential difference lies in the management of sound quality. If the sound does not change meaningfully throughout the displacement, we are more likely to experience the music as a stable element of the audio-visual nexus that has been recombined with (or displaced onto) other images. If sound quality does change in a way we are meant to notice, we may rather experience it as narrational 'appropriation' and de-diegetization.

Sound quality is also a marker of transitions in scenes that do not involve temporal ellipses, but distance the music from its diegetic origin in other ways. In both cases, we understand what happens as the narration doing something with/to the music; what differs is our understanding of that intervention. In displaced diegetic music, the music is left intact, but reassigned to other images; in a digetic to nondiegetic transition, the music itself is affected, is de-diegeticized to a larger or smaller extent, and can in that de-diegeticized form either be moved as well or left in place.

Almost Famous (2000) uses a transition that affects both the music and its synchronization with the images: 18-year-old Anita Miller (Zooey Deschanel) explains to her mother (Frances McDormand) and 11-year-old brother William (Patrick Fugit) why she is leaving home by playing Simon & Garfunkel's 'America' on the record player. When the song reaches the vocal part, the image cuts, and we are in front of the house, watching Anita pack her possessions into her boyfriend's car. The temporal relationship to the previous scene is unclear, but since the music has also become louder and has lost the record-player crackle it had at the start, we do not assume that it is still playing inside the house. Instead, the music now explains *to us* what is happening: she is going to 'look for America' like the speaker of the song, for an America beyond the confines of her suburban home and her controlling mother. That is developed when the music goes over onto William, in a double sense. Before she hops into the car, Anita looks into his eyes and says, 'One day, you'll be cool.' Then she advises him to look under his bed, where – still accompanied by 'America' – he will find Anita's record collection: the beginning of his interest in rock and pop and his career as a music journalist. Her music is his now, and 'America' is acting that out on the soundtrack.

An example of a diegetic to nondiegetic transition within a continuous scene is the use of B.B. King's 'Better Not Look Down' in *Thelma & Louise* (1991). The song plays on Thelma's and Louise's car radio (we even hear B.B.King announce it), and the two move in time to the music. But when they have overtaken the truck driver who had made lewd gestures at them earlier and have asked him to follow them (with the aim of shooting up his truck), the camera moves away from their car, the song gets louder and seems to change from something located within the diegesis to something enveloping the scene and commenting on it via lyrics such as 'Better not look down, if you want to keep on flying/ Put the hammer down, keep it full speed ahead/Better not look back, or you might just wind up crying/You can keep it moving, if you don't look down'. Not looking down is just what Thema and Louise have to do if they want to keep on flying on their increasingly mad rush away from their former lives. The change of status is confirmed when the song simply fades out after the truck driver has alighted, without any indication that the radio has been switched off. The song has done its duty for the narration and can be dispensed with without worries about diegetic plausibility, because by this point we do not understand it as diegetic any more.

Transitions from nondiegetic to diegetic music
Transitions from nondiegetic to diegetic music can be more striking, because they either require us to construct a more complex relationship between diegesis and narration, or they can seem to break the 'integrity' of the diegesis.

Nondiegetic to diegetic transitions across wider spans of film time and involving leitmotif systems (Karlin and Wright's category no. 5, 'source music can play the underscoring theme') can imply that a story is being told in retrospect. The narration knows that a piece of music will play a role in the diegesis and already uses it before that point ('before' with regard to the fabula). While films can imply hindsight – that the narration knows what is going to happen – in all sorts of ways, such a motivic transition into the diegesis is a strong way of doing that. (Examples are discussed in ch. V.iii.)

Local nondiegetic to diegetic transitions can be more disconcerting because in such cases we usually do not look for overarching explanations involving the temporal relationship of story and narration. The snake charmer scene in *Octopussy* is a drastic example (see pp. 80–81). *Almost Famous* provides a hardly less perplexing example, but one engineered more smoothly. Elton John's 'Tiny Dancer' starts on the soundtrack when William and the band take their leave from Aaron (Chris McElprang) and the other teenagers at his house, and we assume it to be nondiegetic (the departure of the tour bus is synchronized with the start of the vocal part). But in the bus, the song gradually changes sides. At first, everyone is sitting quietly in their seats, reflecting on the events of the night. We have no indication that the music might have (acquired) a diegetic anchor, but we could imagine it to come from a radio or cassette player. Then the drummer of the band starts to tap the rhythm at the point when the drums set in in the song, then everyone moves in time with the music, and then they all start to sing, and the song has become fully diegetic.

One could see this, too, as a case of displaced diegetic music, temporally displaced in this case onto a time before its diegetic anchoring point. But the film avoids making a diegetic source manifest before the band members start to play and sing the song themselves. The effect is that the music seems to have been in the air, on their minds, and from there finds its way into physical reality. And this is the function of the song: it does not just bind together the scene and inject a crescendoing trajectory into it, but also (re)binds the band into a community, after the previous night had threatened that. William says to Penny Lane (Kate Hudson) 'I have to go home', because he has been on tour with Stillwater for too long. But she replies: 'You are home', and the communal singing of 'Tiny Dancer' is the embodiment of that, an embodiment that attests to its strength by becoming diegetized.

In such a scene, *Almost Famous*, though primarily a fictionalized (auto)biography, aspires to the condition of a musical film, where music has more licence to overwhelm the division of levels of narration than in other genres. Because of this, such transitions are more typical for films about music. *Dazed and Confused* (1993) contains several scenes in which music we originally construe as nondiegetic enters the diegesis: songs begin without diegetic source and the sound quality of nondiegetic music, but change to sound as if coming from a car radio; teenagers sway in rhythm with or sing to music introduced without plausible diegetic source. In such moments, music acquires quasi-magical properties, which makes sense in a film about teenagers and their intense relationship with music as the soundtrack to their lives: audio diaries for their highs and woes, always in the literal and metaphorical air, not accidentally in a film that is a generational update of *American Graffiti* (1973), itself defined by the ubiquity of music in the diegesis and in the narrative structure.[85]

Anything goes

Beyond such broad types, a survey of transitions between diegetic and nondiegetic space (or construal) cannot but be a list of curios from a limitless list of possibilities. Since Chapters III–V discuss examples in detail, general remarks may suffice.

While anything musical can happen at any time in any film, it is not equally likely to. Narrative contexts provide conditions for certain kinds of transitions between levels of narration. As mentioned above, music as a topic, as a core feature of diegesis *and* narration, is one such condition. Elsewhere I have discussed climactic scenes in two Mozart biopics,

---

85 The other main reason for (supposedly) nondiegetic sound or music entering the diegesis is of course the 'rhetoric of revealing the workings' of the sonic conventions of cinema, 'in the mode of the gag or parody or in a poetic manner' (Chion 2009: 211): the unmasking of the artifice of film.

Whom the Gods Love (1942) and *Amadeus* (1984), which use complex knots of transitions and ambiguities to bring conflicts central to the films to a head. *In Whom the Gods Love*, this concerns the scene centered on the *Don Giovanni* premiere, the Mozarts' marital crisis and the identification of Mozart with Don Giovanni; in *Amadeus* it concerns Salieri (F. Murray Abraham) helping Mozart (Tom Hulce) with the Requiem, and Salieri's fervent wish to get in on Mozart's creativity (more in Heldt 2009: 41–44).

Transitions can also be naturalized in films with homodiegetic narrators. If what we see and hear is filtered through the subjectivity of a diegetic character, 'illogical' uses of music (illogical by the measure of our experience of external reality) can be 'explained away' as subjective perception; we do not see and hear what happened, but how it appeared to the narrator. Early on in *Trainspotting* (1996), we hear the 'Habañera' from *Carmen*, without any indication that it could be diegetic music, while Renton explains that for drug withdrawal, one needs 'soothing music' (which the 'Habañera' is, compared to the music heard up to that point in the film), dragging the music into our imagination of diegetic reality. But since Renton features both in the diegesis and as its narrator, the distinction between the levels collapses. The same is the case later, when we hear a dance track for another of Renton's attempts to withdraw. There is no plausible diegetic source for the music, but neither is there one for the image of Diane appearing in front of him and singing. All of this happens only in his mind (as the distorted images confirm).

Goodfellas (1990) is pervaded by songs from the time its story traces, but whether these songs appear in the diegesis or nondiegetically hardly matters, and in several cases our construal of their status changes within a scene (e.g. for 'Roses Are Red' or 'Pretend You Don't See Her'). However we understand the songs, they contribute to the film's period flavour, and the division of levels of narration is crossed by character-narrator Henry (Ray Liotta) anyway, whom we can understand as the agency controlling the nondiegetic music, for which he uses the music of his times.[86]

A different context is set up in *American Graffiti*. Most of the songs in the film can be understood to issue from Wolfman Jack's radio show the teenagers are listening to all the time. But they move with utmost fluidity between diegetic anchoring points (mostly car radios) and the function of sonic envelopes around scenes (a function they have for their teenage audience). The songs are what Peter Larsen, taking his cue from Edward Branigan, calls 'chameleon music' (Larsen 2005: 164–65). In this, *American Graffiti* provides a textbook illustration of what Michel Chion calls 'on the air' sounds: sounds whose 'diegetic source is shown to be some electrical mode of transmission (radio, telephone, intercom, amplifier, etc.) that allows them to go beyond the so-called natural laws of sound propagation and travel freely in space yet still remain anchored in the real time of the scene' (Chion 2009:

---

86 This control also applies to other aspects of the narration: 'Not only does Henry govern space, he also controls time. All visual action – and even most musical placement – is cued and concatenated by the very phrasing of his words. At moments, the film even goes into freeze-frame, demonstrating the authorial power with which he is recalling his past' (Brophy 2004: 115–16).

482). The magic of music, the magic of technology and the unfathomable teenage mind combine to overcome space and narrative structure.

But the film is very precise in its treatment of physical, technological and narrative space, and the radiophonic origin is crucial for the way the film uses songs. This becomes obvious in the case of songs that are *not* in the air, but played live, at the school dance. 'At the Hop' is clearly diegetic, and when the image track cuts away from the dance hall to the girls' toilet, we hear the music only muted, in realistic acoustic perspective. The same applies to the following song, 'She's So Fine'. This is music not on the air, and so it does not partake of the magic of technological ubiquity.

What is true of films with homodiegetic narrators applies even more to films with recursive narrative structures, such as Federico Fellini's *8½* (1963). We see the film being made within the story of the film we see, and the relationship of diegesis and narration loops back onto itself. Every bit of nondiegetic music is also part of the storyworld, while every bit of diegetic music is also part of the world of Guido Anselmi (Marcello Mastroianni) as the auteur of the film we see, i.e. of its narration. While the image of the Klein bottle to describe the interconnectedness of story and narration in narrative (see Davis 2012) is helpful, but needs to be applied with caution (see pp. 54–55), here it fits perfectly: *8½* is indeed a film version of Klein bottle or Möbius strip. For most points on the surface of a Möbius strip or a Klein bottle we can say with reasonable confidence whether they are rather on the inside or the outside; and most musical cues in *8½* we can assign to a level of narration in their local context. But there are also fuzzy zones of inside-becoming-outside and vice versa, and in the end it is all only one surface.

If film music is full of curious crossings of the diegetic/nondiegetic borderline, it may be appropriate to end with an example that consists of nothing but the standard ingredients of classic Hollywood film-making of the golden age, but combines them to an effect that – if my reading is not too fanciful – is as playfully transgressive as anything in film music. The scene from *The Sea Hawk* (1940) shows the attempt of the English sailors imprisoned by the Spanish to capture a ship to flee back home. They manage to escape from the bowels of the ship, but still have to overcome the guards on deck. And overcome them they do, with the assistance of a series of musical stingers courtesy of Korngold's score. Five times, the English jump onto a guard and pull him to the ground, and each time their pounce is accompanied by a stinger, followed by hushed diegetic sounds for the approach to the next guard.

That is common action-adventure practice. More remarkable are the practicalities of the scene, in the diegesis and in the relationship between film and audience. What we see would obviously not work in reality, because the noise the guards' metal armour would make when they are pulled to the ground would alert their colleagues only metres away. Lack of plausibility is no reason for an adventure film to not show something, but *The Sea Hawk* shows it with a twist: what covers up the noise the armour should be making are the stingers, pouncing with the English, but from outside the diegesis.

There are two ways of reading the audio-visual cooperation: (1) It plays with the psychology of perception. The stingers prevent the audience from realizing that the ambush would not work in the cold light of the day outside the cinema, but the fact that they are such a conventional means of film music helps, because stingers are what we expect in such a scene. (2) We could also see the scene as another – albeit outrageously transgressive – example of the narration taking sides (see pp. 68–69 & 105). The stingers help the good guys to escape, in a scene that ties action-adventure excitement and the comedy aspect rarely far from the film's surface into a tight sailor's knot.

v. Music on my mind: Metadiegetic narration and focalization

The third term imported into film musicology by Claudia Gorbman that has become common, though slightly less so than 'diegetic' and 'non-' or 'extradiegetic' music, is 'metadiegetic' music: music we understand as 'narration by a secondary narrator' (Gorbman 1987: 22). This, too, stems from Gérard Genette (see Genette 1980: 228–34). But Gorbman's use of the term is problematic. While her definition is in line with Genette, her example is not (and that applies to most uses of 'metadiegetic' in film music literature). Gorbman's hypothetical example concerns musical memory: diegetic character X remembers a piece of music that played a role in his past life, and 'a change comes over X's face, and music swells onto the soundtrack, the melody that had played early in the film on the night X had met [Y]' (Gorbman 1987: 23).

But when he coined 'metadiegetic', Genette was thinking of (usually larger-scale) embedded narratives. Antoine-François Prévost is the historical author of the *Mémoires et aventures d'un homme de qualité qui s'est retiré du monde* (1728–31). The *homme de qualité* is the Marquis de Renoncourt, the extradiegetic narrator of his own *Mémoires*. One of the characters in volume seven of Renoncourt's pseudo-autobiographical narration is the Chevalier Des Grieux, and within the diegesis of that volume, Des Grieux tells the story of his adventurous and tragic life with Manon Lescaut[87]: a story within a story, and 'the events told in Des Grieux's narrative, a narrative in the second degree, we will call *metadiegetic*' (Genette 1980: 228; italics in original). The crucial point is that Des Grieux is the narrator of this story; it is his voice that tells it.

There are film music examples that fit Genette's use of the term, e.g. the 'Broadway Melody' ballet in *Singin' in the Rain* (1952). Don Lockwood (Gene Kelly) explains his idea for a number for the rejigged sound film *The Dancing Cavalier* to Cosmo (Donald O'Connor) and studio boss Simpson (Millard Mitchell). By way of illustration, he points to the screen, and we see and hear his idea as a (very stagey) bit of film text.

---

87 The story was also published separately in 1731 as *L'Histoire du chevalier des Grieux et de Manon Lescaut*, and inspired operas by Daniel-François-Esprit Auber, Jules Massenet, Giacomo Puccini and Hans Werner Henze, as well as several films.

Figure 16: Transition into the 'Broadway Melody' sequence of *Singin' in the Rain* (1952).

A diegetic character in *Singin' in the Rain* becomes the narrator of the embedded narrative of the 'Broadway Melody' sequence with its metadiegetic (stage) world. The example demonstrates a major difference between literature and film. While we assume that Don explains his idea to Cosmo and Simpson verbally (and Simpson says that he cannot quite visualize it and has to see it on film!), for *us* this explanation takes the form we imagine it to have in Don's mind – a difference difficult to realize in a novel. As in Gorbman's example, we get an insight into a character's mind. But the point that justifies the term 'metadiegetic' is that it is a story told by Don (to Cosmo and Simpson and to us). That is not necessarily the same as a glimpse into someone's mind, at least not for Genette.

Crucial is the difference between the question 'Who speaks?', i.e. the identity of the narrating voice, and the question 'Who sees?' (later expanded to 'Who perceives?', see Genette 1988: 64), i.e. the perspective from which narrated events are being perceived (see Genette 1988: 64). The novelistic narrator speaks, but she can speak what a character sees, feels, thinks, etc. To return to one of the sentences used before (in ch. II.iv.b): 'She sat down on the bed and wondered when it had all started to go so wrong.' The voice is that of the narrator, the grammatical subject of the sentence. The perspective from which things are seen, though, is that of the 'she' of the sentence, that of the diegetic character.

In Genette's terms, this is 'internal focalization'. The character's mind is the lens that 'focalizes' the narration, without the narration abrogating control over the telling. The character does not become a narrator, just the focal point of the narration's attention. This may be a better match for Gorbman's example: the 'forty-piece orchestra that plays' (1987: 23) is the voice of the filmic narration, but what it plays is focalized by X and his memories.

For Genette, narration and focalization belong to separate aspects of narrative: narration to 'voice' (*voix*), and focalization to 'mood' (in the grammatical sense, *mode* in French; see Genette 1980: 29–32). The former concerns the agency controlling the presentation of

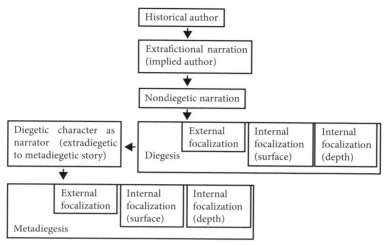

Figure 17: Branigan's levels of narration with integrated types of focalization.

information; the latter the source of information the narration has access to (the 'point of view' of older literary theory; see Genette 1980: 185–89).

In Edward Branigan's levels of narration (see p. 22), 'metadiegetic' does not feature, but it is present implicitly via the fourth level: the diegetic narrator. (The diegetic narrator should, strictly speaking, appear on the same level as the diegetic character; only what he narrates is located on a metadiegetic level.) Below the diegetic character, Branigan lists different types of focalization. From Genette's perspective, that is inaccurate; focalization does not describe a level of narration, but types of access to diegetic facts. If one wanted to integrate the perspectives into one model, one would have to place the different types of focalizations on the diegetic level (Figure 17).

Genette distinguishes between three types of focalization (1980: 189–211):

- Nonfocalized narration (or zero focalization): the narrator knows more than any particular character, and has access to physical and mental data (the traditional omniscient narrator).[88]
- Internal focalization: the narrator knows and says what a particular character knows.
- External focalization: the narrator is in the situation of diegetic characters (in general, not in the position of any particular character) and has access only to external diegetic facts, not to mental states and events (therefore knows less than any particular character).[89]

---

88 Genette's use of the term differs from that of film narratologists such as Branigan or Kuhn, for whom 'nonfocalized narration' or 'zero focalization' is the non-subjective representation of events as they would appear to an unspecific diegetic observer (see Branigan 1992: 105–07; Kuhn 2011: 122–40).

89 Relational categorization of focalization is not unproblematic, however. In external focalization, the 'less' the narration knows means mental data characters have subjective access to, while the narration

Focalizations can be stable or change over the course of a narrative, and in internal focalization, the perspective can remain the same for a narrative (fixed internal focalization), can move between characters (variable internal focalization), or can present the same event from different perspectives (multiple internal focalization, e.g. in *Rashomon* [1950]). In the practice of narrative, concept boundaries can be fuzzy, though. Highly variable internal focalization can be close to nonfocalized narration, for example, and in film, the internal focalization of a point-of-view shot may not be very different in informational content from an over-the-shoulder shot (a shot that shows both a character and what he sees).

Since Genette introduced this system in *Discours du récit* ([1972] 1980), narratologists have discussed and refined it, especially Mieke Bal (2009: 145–65), but also Shlomith Rimmon-Kennan, Manfred Jahn, David Herman, Manfred Niederhoff, Markus Kuhn and others (see Genette 1988: 64–79; and summaries in Jahn 2005b; Niederhoff 2011; and Kuhn 2011: 119–22), while Seymour Chatman uses the terms 'slant' and 'filter' for narrator and character perspectives respectively (1990: 139–60). Most of the discussion is based on literature and not relevant for the question whether 'focalization' may be a helpful concept for music in film.[90] One refinement I use, however, is the distinction between 'focalization *on*' and 'focalization *through*', based on Mieke Bal's revision of Genette. Bal points out that focalization is not just about *who* perceives, but also about *what* can be perceived (see 2009: 145–63). From that perspective, Genette's question should not have been 'Who perceives?', but 'Who perceives what?' Zero and external focalization both do not take the perspective of any particular character, but differ with regard to the information accessible (mental and physical, or only physical data); external focalization is focalization not through a particular lens, but *on* the outside of things. Zero and internal focalization, on the other hand, entail access to mental data, but in zero focalization the perspective of perception is neutral, while internal focalization perceives events *through* the lens of a particular character (but see also Niederhoff's critique of Bal, summarized in Niederhoff 2011: §13–16).

*

Genette's 'narration' and 'focalization' were developed for the analysis of literature and work better for literature than for film. In, say, a novel, the voice ('Who speaks?') is grammatically inscribed into the text and normally clearly distinguished from the focalizer ('Who perceives?'). In film, narration is not necessarily personalized. It can be, of course, for example in the case of a diegetic character verbally telling a story: an externally focalized

---

has not. But the narration may have access to a wider range of external information than any individual character, so that it is rather a question of kinds than one of quantity of knowledge. For internal focalization, the relational formula becomes problematic with the additional distinction between 'internal focalization (surface)' (i.e. perception) and 'internal focalization (depth)' (i.e. thoughts, feelings, etc.). If the narration has access to perceptual data, but not to thoughts, feelings, etc., it would not know as much as a character, but less.

90 Peter Verstraten provides subtle discussions of filmic focalization in *Film Narratology* and briefly writes about music (Verstraten 2009: 153-60), but does not bring the two together.

metadiegetic narrative[91], like a story told in direct discourse by a character in a novel. But beyond such simple cases, clarity gets lost. Even in a film that does establish a voice (by an initial voice-over, for example) and is understood as the acting-out of that narration, we tend to forget the voice in the audiovisual machinery of filmic narration.

With regard to mental states, things are more difficult yet. In the cinematic representation of mental states, there is no clear distinction between a 'direct' utterance (e.g. a character thinking something that in a novel could be rendered as direct discourse) and an 'indirect' one (the narrator telling what the character is thinking in the narrator's own voice). Do we understand the flashback showing the killing of Harmonica's brother in *Once Upon a Time in the West* (1968) as Harmonica's mental self-report (metadiegetic in Genette's sense, with Harmonica as the narrator of an emebedded analeptic narrative), or do we understand it as the primary narration of the film showing us the sights and sounds from Harmonica's reminiscing perspective (i.e. internal focalization)? There is no way to decide, nor does it matter much. The more an episode is a clearly demarcated embedded narrative, and the more clearly we understand a diegetic character as *controlling* the presentation of information in it, the more appropriate the term 'metadiegetic' might be. But conceptual boundaries are fuzzier than in literature.

Embedded narration does not, of course, have to mean actual storytelling to diegetic narratees. 'Broadway Melody' in *Singin' in the Rain* is a story Don tells Cosmo and Simpson (though we see and hear not his verbal account, but the audiovisual ideas in his mind). Its companion piece, the ballet in *An American in Paris* (1951), is a daydream Jerry Mulligan (Gene Kelly) dreams of Paris and Lise Bouvier (Leslie Caron). But it is equally metadiegetic, because it functions like a story, to Jerry and to us, even if he only tells it to himself: he is in control of its presentation, and it takes over the narrative for its duration.

Given that Mieke Bal has warned narratologists against fetishizing the idea of the 'voice', even in literature, its application to film music needs to proceed with caution. Categorization itself may be less important that using narratological concepts as tools to understand the effects of a scene: 'To ask, *not* primarily where the words come from and who speaks them, but what, in the game of make-believe, is being proposed for us to believe or see before us' (Bal 2009: 229).

Michel Chion, David Bordwell and Kristin Thompson avoid such problems by simply labelling Gorbman's 'metadiegetic music' 'internal' or 'internal diegetic' music (Chion 2009: 479; Bordwell and Thompson 2010: 290–91), while James Buhler, David Neumeyer and Rob Deemer use the term 'imagined diegetic sound' (Buhler, Neumeyer and Deemer 2010: 78). Film has different means of representing interiority: voice-overs, visual clues implying transition into a dream or memory, etc. Music can be both means and object of such techniques, and the link between music and interiority need not, from this perspective, be singled out as special. The problem of 'internal diegetic' or 'imagined diegetic' music is that the terms gloss over the fact that audience access to a character's inner state is not the standard case in film, but requires stylistic means that stand out. 'External focalization' is the

---

91 Externally focalized on the level of the film's primary narration.

default setting of film. We see and hear what happens in the physical storyworld. Film *can* show other things, but only by means that are less common, and therefore show more of the machinery of filmic narration. Gorbman's 'metadiegetic music', however problematic with regard to Genette's original concept, at least preserves the sense that something narrationally conspicuous happens in such moments.

I am not sure how satisfactory an alternative 'focalization' can provide without generating its own problems. It is less handy than 'internal diegetic music' or 'imagined diegetic music', and it is unlikely that 'metadiegetic music' in Gorbman's sense will fall out of usage any time soon. But focalization may allow a more integral discussion of the representation of subjectivity through music in film, perhaps the least theorized of the narratological problems discussed in recent film musicology (although Gabriel 2011 attempts an overview). The following summarizes such a model. It is based on Genette, but in Branigan's differentiated hierarchy (see Branigan 1992: 87 & 100–07), which distinguishes between 'internal focalization (surface)' and 'internal focalization (depth)'. The distinction applies the question *what* is perceived in different focalizations to film. In a novel, internal focalization usually (though not necessarily) means that the narrator knows what a focalizing character sees and hears, *and* what she feels and thinks. In film, however, that makes a difference, because film (as we know it) can show physical events more easily than mental ones. It is easy to show something from someone's point of view or audition – 'internal focalization (surface)'. But to show someone's thoughts or feelings – 'internal focalization (depth)' – requires different filmic means, and it makes sense to recognize that in the model.

1. *Nonfocalized narration.* What is easy to do in a novel would be so difficult in film that it does not happen for any length of film time, and needs not to be considered here.

2. *External focalization.* While external focalization restricts *what* the narration can perceive and not its perspective of perception, the narration can still operate in different ways. It can represent different characters even-handedly or focus its attention on a particular character, either through an entire narrative or for a part of it, can follow him (rather than others) and make him a conduit for our learning about the storyworld.

    Musically, this can mean to show what music a character makes, listens to, likes; characterization through the establishment of diegetic facts. Though narratologically seemingly straightforward, this can provide a wide range of information about characters and the situations they are in, but also make intertextual links or structure scenes (Claudia Gorbman has shown this for the mode of 'artless singing' in films; see Gorbman 2011). Such focalization on the actions of a character may also involve singling her out in a scene, underlining her presence and relevance, which may involve nondiegetic music as well (e.g. a leitmotif that tells us whom in a scene the film is paying most attention to).

3. *Internal focalization (surface).* For this, the topology has to change to 'focalization *through*' – through a character's sensory perception. A film can show us what a character sees or hears. 'Point of view' is a common concept; that the visual metaphor proves

unsatisfactory when applied to literature brought Genette to focalization in the first place. But we can also, with Michel Chion, speak of a 'point of audition', the filmic representation of auditory perspective (Chion 1994: 89–94; and Chion 2009: 85–86).

Our ability to identify the spatial origin of sound is much less precise than our ability to pinpoint the source of light falling into our eyes, so the identification of points of audition is rarely as clear (or relevant) in film. The problem is exacerbated by dissociation of the actual sources of images and sounds in cinema. While we can forget the dissociation when watching a film, it makes it difficult to represent points of audition, or in any case very dependent on the capabilities of recording and projection systems.

Because of the difficulty of implying a point of audition with sufficient clarity, drastic applications are the most obvious examples, especially the depiction of deafness. The most famous example may be Abel Gance's *The Life and Loves of Beethoven/Un grand amour de Beethoven* (1936), which in the Heiligenstadt sequence switches between representing diegetic sounds and music objectively (birdsong, a stream, a blacksmith, the music of a fiddler) and demonstrating Beethoven's perception by cutting off diegetic sound or by replacing it with shapeless din. To let a film, only a few years after the breakthrough of sound film, fall silent again, even if only for moments, may have been a particularly striking way of impressing Beethoven's terror at his deafness on the audience.

Michel Chion is interested in Gance's mediation between sonic perspective and 'the subjective suffering of the hero' (see Chion 2009: 298 & 210). But the film does that not just by moving smoothly from 'objective sound' to Beethoven's subjective sonic isolation. The most interesting moment comes at the end of the scene: Beethoven is staring into the stream, contemplating suicide (the mirror image shows what we know will be his death mask). But suddenly we hear the birds, water, blacksmith and fiddler again, while we see Beethoven in close-up. Though he cannot hear the sounds any more, so the implication, he can still remember them. And then we hear the opening of the 'Pastoral Symphony' and its invocation of happiness, and understand that Beethoven is hearing the music in his mind (confirmed when he accompanies the orchestral crescendo with conducting gestures). Beethoven realizes that though deaf, he can still compose, and the film makes this palpable by slipping from internal focalization on Beethoven's sensory (non) perception to internal focalization on the music he is imagining, descending further into his subjectivity (for a close reading of the scene, see Wulff 2010).

The difficulty of clearly implying points of audition means that this further slide into subjectivity is an attractive option for film. A scene in *Beyond Silence/Jenseits der Stille* (1996), a film about the hearing daughter of deaf-mute parents, uses the same trick as Gance's film. On Christmas Eve, Aunt Clarissa (Sybille Canonica) plays her clarinet for the family, accompanied by her father. Lara (Sylvie Testud), the daughter of Clarissa's deaf-mute brother Martin (Howie Seago) and deaf-mute Kai (Emanuelle Laborit), is so captivated that she forgets to use sign language with her father. Martin stares at the scene, and the volume drops and is briefly replaced by a humming sound, which may imply his (non-)auditory perspective. But quickly, the focalization of Martin's auditory perception descends further to the focalization of memory, a subjective flashback to Martin's youth. At another Christmas party, Clarissa also played the clarinet, also accompanied by her father, while Martin stares at her, unhearing (and by implication uncomprehending the appeal music has for everyone else, as it will later have on his own daughter, who will become a musician). The flashback is dissolved in an instant when Martin's brother-in-law lights a match – an *optical* intrusion shocks Martin out of his reverie.

4. *Internal focalization (depth).* This means focalization through a character's mind. The category can be divided into two ways of representing subjectivity, the first of which is much less problematic than the second:

   a. Focalization of music through a character's *internal* experience or imagination of it. This is what Gorbman's example for 'metadiegetic music' describes and what Bordwell and Thompson call 'internal diegetic music': music in someone's mind.

   In *The Glenn Miller Story* (1954), the eponymous hero is searching for the right sound for his band – the search that organizes the trajectory of the film. Because a trumpeter has cancelled for a concert, he has to replace him with a clarinettist and is sitting at home at night, rearranging the 'Moonlight Serenade'. He is writing notes onto paper, but at the same time we hear the music in its full arrangement, without a diegetic source – this is the music as he is hearing it mentally. Occasionally he tries out a chord on the piano, completing the skills triad: he produces physical sounds on the piano; he can imagine music in his mind; and he can write it down (unlike some of the black jazz musicians from which he learnt). He is the complete musician, a depiction that fits the film's overall construction of Miller as the one who melds different aspects of American music-making into a mix that conquers the world.

   As focalization through someone's point of audition, internal focalization through someone's imagination is particularly effective if a film transitions from objective to subjective depiction of music. *Love Actually* (2003) provides an example. The Prime Minister (Hugh Grant) has just been elected and enters 10 Downing Street. On the radio, the Pointer Sisters' 'Jump' is played, especially 'for our arse-kicking prime minister', who begins to move in time to the music, at first tentatively, then increasingly boisterously. The music also becomes louder and fuller, while the Prime Minister dances out of the room and downstairs, where he crowns his performance with a slow pirouette while pointing his finger and miming singing. But when he has turned full circle, he suddenly becomes aware of a secretary staring at him, and with a screech of shock, the music breaks off, and he says, as if this had been on his mind all the time: 'Yeah, Mary, I've been thinking….' Finally, it has become clear that what we have heard was the music as he heard it in his mind. While that was a possibility from the start, we could not be sure. The music with its scene-enveloping sound quality could have been a representation of his inner ear, but also the narration taking up the PM's enthusiasm – not least because the scene briefly dissociates music and images:

the song runs through, while there are small ellipses in the images, which could be understood as a de-diegetization. But the end clarifies the assignation of the music with its comedy of embarrassment (it is, after all, an English British prime minister).

The same trick is used to more disturbing effect in *Happiness* (1998). After a painfully embarrassing meeting with his neighbour Helen Jordan (Lara Flynn Boyle), Allen (Philip Seymour Hoffman) is alone in his apartment. In the background, we hear 'Soave sia il vento' from Mozart's *Così fan tutte*, without any hint of a source. Allen, in is underpants, is looking for Helen's number in the phone book, fantasizing about making an obscene call to her. The first Helen Jordan he calls is the wrong one. He tries again, and indeed the right Helen is at the other end of the line, and afraid of his own courage, he hangs up – and at the same time 'Soave sia il vento' breaks off, too. Up to this point, we could have construed it as diegetic music playing in his flat (or as nondiegetic, though it is difficult to see why the narration would make such a wilfully perverse choice). But when the music cuts out with the phone connection, we have to reassess, and find ourselves facing the possibility that this, the most tender music imaginable, a heartfelt wish of good luck to lovers (supposedly) leaving for war, has been playing in his mind while he was fantasizing about 'fucking' Helen 'so hard it'll come out of your ears'. In a split second, Allen has become a mystery to us, and while the juxtaposition of his sexual and his musical imagination does not make him any less disturbing, it certainly makes him a lot more intriguing.

b. Focalization of a character's inner state (via music as medium of narration). This is the more problematic category: music as representation or intimation of a character's mental states or processes. It is connected to the examples of nondiegetic music not as external 'voice', but as an emanation of something diegetic (see ch. II.iv.b), and can be understood in comparison with the idea of a character's inner experience focalizing novelistic narration: 'She sat down on the bed and wondered when it had all started to go so wrong' (see above). The idea of nondiegetic music as a means the narration has for internal focalization may address some of the dissatisfaction with the broad remit of 'nondiegetic music' that has prompted, for example, reformulations by Jerrold Levinson and Ben Winters (Levinson 1996; and Winters 2010, discussed in ch. II.i.b).

An example from *For a Few Dollars More* (1965): El Indio is with his gang. We hear high-register strings while he touches his throat, gesticulates to his men and says, 'Now'. He is given a cigarette and calms down with every drag, while the string sounds recede. The music is not a physical part of the diegesis, but it is clear that it represents an internal state: Indio's drug dependency. It is unlikely to be 'metadiegetic' in Gorbman's or 'internal diegetic' in Bordwell's and Thompson's sense; we do not assume that Indio is hearing these sounds in his mind, rather that the sounds represent something similarly shapeless, insistent and painful in his mind.

In a narrative context defined by focalization, such an interpretation comes particularly naturally. *Lady in the Lake* (1947) shows us its storyworld through the eyes and ears of Philip Marlowe (Robert Montgomery). Conventional nondiegetic music is used occasionally, but when Philip is punched in the face or falls unconscious, we hear angelic singing that it would be hard *not* to understand as a representation of something inside him in those moments: a cartoon representation, but still understandable as music indicating something non-musical in the character's mind.

Other cases are less straightforward. In *The Sea Hawk* (1940), the lyrical variant of the main theme, linked to the 'romantic' rather than the 'heroic' side of Geoffrey Thorpe (Errol Flynn), is used, for example, when he enters the cabin on the Spanish ship his crew are boarding in the first battle, the cabin in which Doña Maria (Brenda Marshall), her father and her maid are hiding. The theme returns when Maria sees Thorpe at an audience with Queen Elizabeth. In both scenes, the music is synchronized with the images so that we can understand it as establishing a link between Maria and Thorpe-as-love-interest (see p. 230 and R. Brown 1994: 97–120). But do we understand it as an attempt to suggest Maria's subjective view of Thorpe, embodied by the music to suggest her inner state in looking at him: a translation of the female gaze at the romantic hero/male star? Or do we understand it as a pointer courtesy of the narration that we should be aware of this side of Thorpe (or Errol Flynn's star persona), and not one about Maria's view of him? The difference may be slight, and there is no way of deciding. But the diegesis and its relationship to the narration are only constructed in our subjective processing of the film's cues, and while cues are usually clear enough to make a particular construction more likely than another one, there can be room for ambiguity.

Ambiguities, of course, are possible in literature as well. 'She was tired and distracted' could be understood as saying, 'She *felt* tired and distracted': the narrator informs us of the inner state of the character (internal focalization). But it could also be understood as saying 'She *seemed* tired and distracted': the narrator describes the impression the characters makes on her, judged by external appearance (external focalization). While the ambiguity inherent in the neutral 'was' can be used consciously, it would be easy to avoid by choosing either 'felt' or 'seemed'.

Film has other options and other problems. A film could show us an actress that seems tired and distracted – external focalization is the default setting of most narrative fiction films. If the film wanted to switch to internal focalization, it could use a homodiegetic voice-over – the inner voice of a character telling us that she is tired and distracted. Or the film might use nondiegetic music to imply the character's inner state. But in film and its use of music, precision is difficult to achieve, and its often vague position between being a voice *about* and a voice speaking *for* is weakness and strength. One cannot achieve the precision of narrative perspective achievable in language, but one can (or, rather, cannot not) generate ambiguities that can be intriguing in themselves, and give the audience a say in how to understand a moment in the story and its narration: where to locate the point of view of a scene.

That may be responsible for our reaction to music as a medium of the focalization of interiority. If we understand it as speaking *about* a character's inner life, we may experience it as manipulative; the most common charge against classic uses of music in film. If, however, we understand it as a means of cinematic language to express truths about a character's inner life, we may experience it as a powerful tool.

A summary of the categories might look like this:

	Who 'speaks'? (= Source of music?) → Narration	Who perceives what? (= How is information restricted?) → Focalization	What is focalized?
'Realistic' diegetic music	Character/object in the diegesis	Physical sound of music (as heard by diegetic characters in general) Branigan: External focalization [focalization *on*]	Music (in its physical reality)
Diegetic music from particular point of audition	Character/object in the diegesis	Sensory perception of a specific character Branigan: internal focalization (surface) [focalization *through*]	Music (as heard by a particular character)
'Metadiegetic music' (Gorbman) 'Internal diegetic music' (Bordwell & Thompson)	Narration of film (relating a character's mental music)	Character (mentally) Branigan: internal focalization (depth) [focalization *through*]	Music (as imagined, remembered etc. by a character)
Nondiegetic music as representation of interiority	Narration of film (using music as its medium)	Character (mentally) Branigan: internal focalization (depth) [focalization *through*]	The character's inner states or processes

Figure 18: Summary of categories for music and focalization in film.

It is a tentative suggestion, and questions abound. Not relevant for the categorization, but intriguing is that in cases of internal focalization (depth), music is rendered in a form it would not actually have in dreams or memories, because the music of our dreams or memories is, in its vagueness, unrenderable: 'In dreams and visions lie the greatest creations of man, for on them rests no yoke of line or hue' (Lovecraft 2007: 364). But film has to use the yoke of line or hue, and the music that is supposed to represent a character's imagination is necessarily rendered with the stylistic means of film (which may include defamiliarizing manipulations such as reverb); perhaps an equivalent to the voice of a novelistic narrator who speaks the thoughts of a character.[92]

---

92 Branigan takes a different stance: 'In *internal* focalization, story world and screen are meant to collapse into each other, forming a perfect identity in the name of the character: "Here is exactly what Manny

If the relative vagueness of film in defining agencies of perception and narration is one major difference to, say, a novel, the multichannel nature of film is another.[93] While this means different possibilities, it also means medium-specific ambiguities. Film can do things simultaneously that in a novel have to happen consecutively, including switches between focalizations. Novels can do this in a very small space: 'He roared with laughter, but his heart was not in it' – external and internal focalization happen in quick succession on the discourse level, but the events are simultaneous on the story level. A film could show the laugh and indicate the feeling through nondiegetic music simultaneously, but the difference to the novel would be minimal.

Simultaneity of different focalizations can also apply to one sense alone. Towards the end of *Rose-Marie* (1936), Marie de Flor (Jeanette MacDonald) sings in a production of Puccini's *Tosca*, but her singing is again and again disturbed by snatches of the 'Indian Love Call' that reminds her of Sgt. Bruce (Nelson Eddy) – music on her mind, competing with her performance and resulting in her breakdown (see also Lissa 1965: 186–188).

A scene from the Robert Schumann biopic *Reverie/Träumerei* (1944) shows another way of using multiple channels. His wife Clara visits Robert in the mental asylum where he lives after his attempted suicide, and he shows her a piece of music he has composed: wild and spidery scribblings, without rhyme or reason. But on the soundtrack, we hear the 'song of a bird, for flute and small orchestra' he tells her he is working on perfectly lucidly: the split between internal focalization in the music and external focalization on the image track shows us that something has broken in Schumann, that he cannot communicate his musicality to the world any more.

But there are questions. When a film visualizes a retrospective homodioegetic voice-over (e.g. in *Goodfellas*), it is not necessarily clear if the images we see are filtered through the subjectivity of a character-narrator, or if we see objective images (external focalization on the image track; potentially also on the soundtrack if voices and other sounds can be

---

sees [in *The Wrong Man*]: these shapes and colors are in his head'" (Branigan 1992: 102). But do mental images exactly replicate the look of objects they refer to, and do inner sounds exactly like real music? 'Perfect identity' may not be achievable, and is not necessary to make the audience understand what the shapes, colours and sounds are meant to represent.

    The problem is wittily acknowledged in *The Seven Year Itch* (1955), when in one of his daydreams (accompanied by Rachmaninoff's Second Piano Concerto), Richard Sherman (Tom Ewell) imagines his wife Helen (Evelyn Keyes) mocking his 'tremendous imagination': 'Lately, you have begun to imagine in CinemaScope – with stereophonic sound.' The necessary cinematic realization of mental sights and sounds is re-cast as a feature of the mental process itself.

93 The multichannel nature of film has led some narratologists to distinguish between focalization as a term for relations of knowledge, ocularization for relations of visual perception, and auricularization for relations of auditory perception (see, for example, Kuhn 2011: 127–31, based on work by François Jost and Sabine Schlickers). That alone is not enough to account for the options of the medium, though. Not only does film combine visual and auditory information, it can also simultaneously present different strands of visual and auditory information (through split screens, for example, or through the layering of different images or of sounds and music).

heard), while we hear the character-narrator's take on events (internal focalization on the soundtrack).

Ambiguity is also possible when different filmic channels are narratively defined with differing degrees of clarity. *Black Swan* (2010) charts the descent of ballet dancer Nina Sayers (Natalie Portman) into delusional paranoia, and is increasingly shot through with images we understand as internally focalized through her perceptions and visions. But what about the music from Tchaikovsky's *Swan Lake* we hear on the soundtrack? Is it to be understood as nondiegetic? Or do we imagine that Nina, who increasingly sees her story as an echo of *Swan Lake*, also mentally hears *Swan Lake* as the soundtrack to her life, and that what we hear is in fact internally focalized through her delusion?

On a smaller scale, the same question arises in *Cabaret* (1972). At the end of the forest excursion, the camera shows Sally's (Liza Minelli) eyes, and we assume that the images of past events we see represent Sally's memories. On the soundtrack, we hear 'Welcome'. But is the music also internally focalized through her memories? Or do we understand it as a means the narration has to hold the montage together and to remind us of the beginning of Sally's and Brian's (Michael York) love story?

Another question leads us back to the Gorbman's appropriation of Genette's category of the metadiegetic, and concerns cases that *are* metadiegetic in Genette's sense, i.e. embedded narratives. In a novel, a voice is all it needs (and all there is) to identify a character-narrator. In film, things are less clear. In an embedded filmic narrative, do we understand *all* aspects of the narration as controlled by the diegetic narrator? *Bride of Frankenstein* (1935) uses a classic framing narrative. On a dark and stormy night, Mary Shelley (Ella Lanchester) tells the continuation of the Frankenstein story to Lord Byron (Gavin Gordon) and her husband (Douglas Walton), the story that forms the core of the film. Mary is a character in the primary diegesis and the narrator of the metadiegetic story of Frankenstein, the monster and the bride, with regard to which she is extradiegetic. But what about the extradiegetic music of that embedded narrative (i.e. the bulk of Franz Waxman's music for the film)? Is that part of Mary's narration as well? Do we imagine that *all* the filmic means that present the embedded story to us are under her control? How do we deal with the fact that the music is based on a nineteenth-century idiom the historical Mary Shelley could not have known and hardly imagined? Do we understand the music as a stand-in for the powers of her narrating voice? Or do we imagine an impersonal narration – presenting both framing and embedded narrative – that takes its cue from Mary and presents her verbal story to *us* as a film? Or is that distinction pointless (a view that would support Bordwell's scepticism regarding the construction of agents such as narrators)? Literature knows what Genette calls 'reduced metadiegetic' or 'pseudo-diegetic' narration: 'the metadiegetic way station, mentioned or not, is immediately ousted in favour of the first narrator, which to some extent economizes on one (or sometimes several) narrative level(s)' (Genette 1980: 237). The primary narration takes over the embedded narrative as well, to avoid having to refer to the hierarchy of levels all the time. But as in other cases, the conditions of narration in novels and in film are so different that the comparison is on shaky ground; what is a choice in a novel is a hardly avoidable ambiguity in film.

An example for the difficulties that films involving metadiegetic narratives can pose for our understanding of musical agency is the use of musical allusions in *Bonjour Tristesse* (1958), based on the eponymous novel of 19-year-old Françoise Sagan, published in 1954. The film has a framing and an embedded narrative. In the black-and-white frame, we see 18-year-old Cécile (Jean Seberg) in Paris with her father Raymond (David Niven), wistfully remembering the previous year on the French Riviera; the embedded narrative, shown in colour, matching Cécile's perception of her current life as sad and empty, and of the recent past as exciting and colourful.

Cécile is shown to be the narrator of the embedded narrative, which begins with a shot of her face, while her voice-over introduces the flashback that makes up the main section of the film. But, as in *Bride of Frankenstein*, it is not clear how we understand the agency controlling the music in this embedded narrative, both (meta)diegetic and (meta)nondiegetic. But the question is relevant, because composer Georges Auric builds musical allusions into the score that provide covert commentary.[94] In a scene in which the protagonists, among crowds of tourists on the Riviera, are dancing exuberantly outside the Café de Paris, the music alludes to the German song 'Die Gedanken sind frei' ('Thoughts are Free'), written in the late eighteenth century and, with obvious political implications, stating that no one can guess the thoughts in one's head, that thoughts cannot be shot 'with powder and lead', and that even in a dark dungeon thoughts can tear the walls apart.

At this point, there is no discernable sense to the allusion. It becomes meaningful, however, when it returns as (meta)nondiegetic music in a scene crucial for Cécile's intrigue to separate her father from his new lover, Anne Larson (Deborah Kerr). She has persuaded his previous lover, Elsa (Mylène Demongeot), to pretend to be in love with Philippe (Geoffrey Horne), in order to make her father jealous and make him return to Elsa. In the scene in question, Elsa excitedly tells Cécile that the plan has worked. Yet she has no idea that Cécile does not want to help her, but to get Anne out of the picture – as she will, when the disappointed Anne has a car accident that may or may not be suicide. This secret agenda is alluded to in Auric's use of the song, which tells us that no one, certainly not naïve Elsa, can guess Cécile's thoughts. In retrospect, this moment also makes sense of the use of 'Die Gedanken sind frei' outside the café, as an earlier stage of Cécile's inexorably unfolding intrigue.

But how do we account for the clever use of music (if we notice it at all, which seems unlikely for non-German-speaking audiences)? As (covert) musical commentary in the Café de Paris scene, it is a case of source scoring, and as such we could understand it with regard to implied authorial agency. We can also see it as a way for Auric to write himself and his musical knowledge into the score. The third option is to understand it as an aspect of Cécile's narration of her own story. As she is controlling the lives of those around her with her schemes, we can understand the music as being controlled by her. That would mean that

---

94 The allusions were pointed out in a paper on music and (jazz) dance in *Bonjour Tristesse* given by Hanna Walsdorf (University of Heidelberg) at the conference 'Jazz and Film', 30th Sept. – 1st Oct. 2011, University of Kiel, Germany.

we would have to understand the (meta)diegetic music in the Café de Paris scene as filtered through her retelling of the story: we do not hear the music that actually played there and then, but the music Cécile puts there in retrospect to effect the allusion. The windmills of her mind provide the music both within and without the diegesis of the embedded narrative.

To link 'Die Gedanken sind frei' to Cécile makes sense because the framing narrative, too, is crucially linked to her thoughts. When, at the start of the film, we see her dancing with Jacques (David Oxley), the camera shows her looking straight at us, while her voice-over tells us that she experiences her life as empty, is bored by Jacques' attention and is living in the past. Here, too, those around her cannot guess her thoughts. And here, too, source scoring makes an appearance, when Juliette Gréco appears on the diegetic stage to sing 'Bonjour Tristesse', a song that voices Cécile's thoughts. But how do we account for this? While it is clear that Cécile is the narrator controlling the embedded narrative, does this suggest that we should also understand her as the narrator of the framing narrative, including the irony of fate of Juliette Gréco's song fitting her perception of her own life so perfectly? The extensive use of source scoring usually shows that a film is happy to present itself as an invented story. Here, however, the inventedness can be tied to Cécile, who tells her own story, and seems to be in control of the means of narration and of story facts both on the metadiegetic and the primary diegetic level. The film is all about inventing one's own life (and in the process playing havoc with that of others), and about an all-encompassing self-stylization that may have been part of the very idea of the French *jeunesse dorée* (*et blasée*) of the 1950s the film parades before our eyes and ears.

Chapter III

Breaking into Song? Hollywood Musicals (and After)

i. Supradiegesis

The characteristic feature of classic Hollywood musicals is not that there is a lot of music in them (though there usually is), nor that singing and dancing is central to their stories (though it often is, especially in backstage musicals). The characteristic feature is the form of at least some of that music: the form of musical numbers that showcase the stars and their talents, ingenious choreographies, and sometimes extravagant set design and costumes. Characteristic in turn for many such numbers is what Rick Altman calls 'supra-diegetic music', often reached by what he calls an 'audio dissolve' (Altman 1987: 62–74):

> The most common form of audio dissolve involves a passage from the diegetic track (e.g., conversation) to the music track (e.g., orchestral accompaniment) through the intermediary of diegetic music. This simple expedient, perhaps more characteristic of the musical than any other stylistic trait, has long been sensed as a typical – and somewhat unrealistic – musical technique. Here, for example, is Otis Ferguson's description of what he sees as the chief problem in the musical, how to bring in the first number: 'Somehow, before the film has got many feet, somebody has got to take off from perfectly normal conversation into full voice, something about he won't take the train he'll walk in the rain (there is suddenly a twenty-piece band in the room), leaving everybody else in the piece to look attentive and as though they like it, and as though such a business were the most normal of procedures' (*New Republic*, October 2, 1935). (Altman 1987: 63)

Usually, audio dissolves go hand in hand with 'video dissolves' and 'personality dissolves' (Altman 1987: 74–89): the transformation of a realistic diegetic space (realistic by the yardstick of the genre) into the ideal space of a faraway time or land or dream; and the transformation of a character into a hidden self that can only come out in musical performance. More than that, though, dissolves also effect 'a leveling of representational levels' (Altman 1987: 80): audio dissolves meld diegetic and nondiegetic music into the soundtrack for a performance, and video and personality dissolves transform diegetic space into a stage for the number and a diegetic character into a star. When Fred Astaire has fully entered into a dance number, we see no longer Jerry Travers (in *Top Hat* [1935]) or 'Bake' Baker (in *Follow the Fleet* [1936]) in a bandstand in a London park or in a San Francisco nightclub – we see Fred Astaire dance on a stage the film provides for him.

While the three dissolves normally go together, for this chapter the musical side is the most interesting, and I will focus on audio dissolves, though in most cases video and personality dissolves are also (unmentioned) parts of the equation.

What is reached via an audio dissolve is not really a state *between* diegetic and nondiegetic music, but one *beyond* the categories, indeed beyond the very distinction they make: a transcendental space of performative bliss that musicals rely on to (dis)solve their characters' problems. There's nothing, we learn time and again, that cannot be put right by transcending reality into performance. (There is more to the performative utopianism of film musicals, though; see Dyer 2002: 19–35.)

It has been argued that musical numbers are moments of particular emotional intensity, 'when the need for emotional expression has reached a particularly high point [...] which can no longer be contained by the character(s)' (Laing 2000: 7; building on Feuer 1993: 49–54). But though many numbers are triggered by overflowing hearts, to understand them primarily as performance of emotion would be reductive. Other genres (e.g. the melodrama) have other ways of showing and evoking emotion. In musicals, it is not so much the number that is a function of the plot, but the plot that is a function of the numbers: the scaffolding for the numbers it has to frame and motivate, however flimsily, 'a showcase or even a bad excuse for the ultimate end of the spectacular intermissions' (Verstraten 2009: 178). What musical numbers show off is first and foremost themselves: their own inventiveness, virtuosity, joyful abundance of extrovert skill (in singing, dancing, but also in film-making). That this usually takes place in supradiegetic space, beyond the confines of a 'realistic' storyworld, may be only partially due to the fact that their virtuosity would be difficult to do in the storyworld – some films (e.g. *Fame*) do just that. The reason may rather be that such confinement would 'functionalize' the numbers and deny them the self-sufficiency of sheer performativity.

*

How do film musicals reach this transcendental space? Altman describes a gradual mediation. The audio dissolve begins by positing diegetic music. Music then begins to adjust other diegetic elements to its own state: characters sing instead of speaking, dance instead of walking, and an internal, diegetic audience may begin to sway in time to the music. Then nondiegetic accompaniment fades in and merges with the diegetic music.[95] At this point, 'non-musical' diegetic sounds may fall away, and 'the normally dominant image track now keeps time to the music track, instead of simply being accompanied by it. The music and its rhythm now initiate movement rather than vice versa' (Altman 1987: 69). Altman illustrates that convincingly with examples from *Till the Clouds Roll By* (1946), *Words and Music* (1948), *Blue Hawaii* (1961), *Top Hat* (1935), *Oklahoma!* (1955) and Busby Berkeley choreographies.

---

95 For Altman, this is the main difference between Hollywood and Broadway. In a stage musical, numbers normally start with the orchestra, or with orchestra and soloists simultaneously. The number is a structurally separate entity, and not reached by transcending the diegesis (Altman 1987: 66).

But as often as this sequence of events occurs, Altman's account ignores the wider range of techniques Hollywood musicals have used to transcend into the supradiegesis. Of course such techniques are not historically invariant and have developed over time. Despite its generally chronological discussion of films, this chapter cannot chart film-musical history, but only pick out examples that show interesting aspects. It starts with the mediation between diegesis and supradiegesis in some classic musicals: *Top Hat, An American in Paris* and *Singin' in the Rain*, with supporting roles for *Show Boat* (1936), *42nd Street* (1933) and *Love Me Tonight* (1932). After a look at *Cabaret* (1972) and its renunciation of supradiegetic transcendence, the chapter concludes with two films whose claims to be musicals may be contentious (for a discussion of genre assignations, see Feuer 2010), but which reference the Hollywood tradition, albeit in consciously postmodern ways: Woody Allen's *Everyone Says I Love You* (1996) and Lars von Trier's *Dancer in the Dark* (2000). The discussion focuses on the idea of the supradiegesis throughout, and in that sense it is consciously reductive. Much more could be said about any of the films, but that would be beyond the chapter's remit.

ii. Superabundance: *Top Hat* and the 1930s

Audio dissolves make us glide from one construal of music to another, across the conceptual borderline between storyworld and musical stage, diegesis and supradiegesis. *Top Hat* (1935), one of RKO's Fred Astaire/Ginger Rogers musicals, shows as wide a range of techniques for integrating numbers as any film musical of its time. But even that only represents part of the range of options for integrating numbers into a musical, especially for the 1930s, when studios were exploring the possibilities of the genre.

At one end of the range are numbers barely integrated at all, when characters just 'start to sing and dance all of a sudden', as a skeptical Jeff (Peter Stormare) in *Dancer in the Dark* summarizes one idea of the musical (more below). After the title sequence and a first shot of the showboat on the Mississippi, *Show Boat* (1936) shows the people of Natchez at work, singing 'Cotton Blossom', the song that started in the title sequence, like a chorus in a stage musical: no mediation, instead the acknowledgement that in a musical, people just sing. The next number, 'Cap'n Andy's Ballyhoo', can be understood as a broadly realistic calling card of the show troupe, but in the third we are beyond diegetic realism again when Gaylord Ravenal (Allan Jones) strolls through town and without any transition sings 'Where's the Mate for Me'. It may be no accident that musically, the song is closer to the operetta tradition than others in *Show Boat*, a tradition whose distance to the storyworld may be accentuated by this unmediated introduction.

At the other end of the range are purely diegetic numbers, naturally typical for backstage musicals, and particularly defining Warner's 1930s musicals such as *42nd Street, Gold Diggers of 1933* (1933) or *Footlight Parade* (1933). While there is nondiegetic music in *42nd Street*, its musical numbers can all be understood as taking place on actual stages in the storyworld, and all of the music in those numbers as being made in those diegetic spaces: 'It Must Be

June' is sung by the rehearsing ensemble; 'You're Getting to Be a Habit with Me' is sung twice by Dorothy Brock (Bebe Daniels) during rehearsals; and, in the 'backloaded' structure typical for the Warner musicals, 'Shuffle Off to Buffalo', 'Young and Healthy' and '42nd Street' represent the show the story had been working up to. But while the film is about the hard work of making entertainment, at its end it acknowledges the need for transcendence, albeit with a media-historical twist. At no point is there 'suddenly a twenty-piece band in the room' (see above) that could not be understood to be in the theatre, but step by step the three final numbers transform that theatre into the space of fantasy. Performative bliss is reached not through crossing the boundaries of the diegesis, but by stretching them to breaking point. That stretch is even expanded in *Gold Diggers of 1933* and *Footlight Parade*, in the latter especially with 'Honeymoon Hotel' and with the paroxysms of spectacle in 'By the Waterfall'. Crucially, this means not just elaborate staging, but spaces impossible to show in live theatre (the complex interior of the 'Honeymoon Hotel'), film-editing tricks (the stop-motion animation showing the wedding in 'Honeymoon Hotel'), and Busby Berkeley's geometric arrangements of dancers, seen from angles that would not work for an audience in the theatre, but rely on – and thereby show off – the work of the film camera. In a second transcendent movement, films showing stage performances transform them into filmic performances, in the process foregrounding film as a medium that transcends the limitations of live theatre.

An early sound-film musical that combines methods of introducing musical numbers from both ends of the spectrum is *Love Me Tonight* (1932), a film playfully experimental in a way one might call postmodern, were that stance not typical for much art in the 1920s. The film opens with a 'city symphony' (Altman 1987: 152) of the sounds of a Paris morning, patiently layered into a composition: a worker with his pickaxe, a snoring drunk, a housewife with her broom, a steam engine, an alarm clock, a crying baby, someone sharpening a saw, the raising of shopfront shutters, a woman shaking out a sheet, shoemakers hammering in different rhythms, someone operating a grinder, bike bells, a woman beating a carpet, car horns… nothing in the sound mix is *not* shown as part of the scene, but the layering builds the sounds up into a quasi-music that becomes more than sonic representation – a form of de-diegetization in spite of the visual evidence of the origin of the sounds. Eventually, gramophone music is added to the mix, but the gramophone is soon moved off-screen – a second kind of de-diegetization. Then Maurice Courtelin (Maurice Chevalier), the gramophone's owner, says that Paris is too loud for him, closes the window and, to the continuing music, sings 'That's the Song of Paree' (starting with the words 'It's not a sonata by Mozart').

On a content level, the opening links *Love Me Tonight* to big-city films of the time: Walter Ruttmann's *Berlin – Symphony of a Great City/Berlin – Die Sinfonie der Großstadt* (1927), Dziga Vertov's *Man with a Movie Camera/Chelovek s kino-apparatom* (1929) or Alberto Cavalcanti's *Nothing But Time/Rien que les heures* (1930). As music history, it shows that in the twentieth century, music can mean things other than 'a sonata by Mozart'. In that, it is close to the radiophonic experiment of Ruttmann's *Weekend* (1930), a collage of sounds of a

Berlin weekend that prefigures later composition with found sounds by almost two decades. As an example of filmic narration, the deliberate arrangement of diegetic 'facts' foregrounds authorial agency. And as an element of a film musical, it is a number in its own right, but also introduces the first song through its paradoxical de-diegetization of on-screen sound, approximating an Altmanian audio dissolve in an unusual way.

The other chief method used in *Love Me Tonight* to introduce a number is not to introduce it at all, but here, too, the film uses a twist. When his car breaks down in the countryside, Maurice encounters the princess, who is riding in her horse-drawn carriage and loudly and with orchestral accompaniment singing 'Lover', 'as though such a business were the most normal of procedures' (see above). But the film disabuses us of the idea that this is a musical-specific kind of utterance not to be confused with real singing in the real world when, in the ensuing banter, the princess asks Maurice if he is 'a little insane', he replies by offering to sing for her, which leads her to the conclusion that he is indeed insane, to which he replies that she did sing for him, too. Singing is something that people just do in *Love Me Tonight*, but also something worthy of comment, and even slightly deranged: a fine balance between singing as musical-normal and really strange.

*

Top Hat avoids such demonstrations of the strangeness inherent in the genre, and instead mediates carefully between storyworld and numbers. To do that, it uses Altmanian audio dissolves, but also others. It is a backstage musical, but the backstage aspect is less important than in other 1930s musicals. Instead, informal musical stages come to the fore: a bandstand, a hotel ballroom, a hotel suite, the alleys and squares of (a very stagey) Venice – locations for a range of ways of getting musical numbers under way.

The very first number, 'Fancy Free', shows one variant of Altman's model. Instead of reaching the supradiegesis gradually from a position of diegetic realism, nondiegetic music sets the stage and invites Fred Astaire's performance. Apart from its method of mediation, 'Fancy Free' is interesting for the way it plays with audience expectations of genre identity. The music for the credits (conventionally a potpourri of tunes to come) briefly carries over into the fiction by accompanying a shot of top-hatted gentlemen in front of the Thackeray Club in London. But as soon as we have entered the club, the music falls silent, a sudden hush triggered by the *Silence* sign we see – the narration takes its cue from the diegesis and is as observant of the rule as the club members, who react furiously (if silently) to any noise in their *sanctum sanctorum*. In a musical, such ostentatious silence is perplexing and, dialectically, raises the expectation of music to come. But the film protracts the process of establishing itself as a musical: The silence is followed by dialogue when Jerry Traver's (Fred Astaire) manager Horace Hardwick (Edward Everett Horton) enters. (Nondiegetic) music only starts again when Jerry and Horace enter the latter's hotel suite. But it takes more than three minutes of further, musically underscored dialogue between Jerry, Horace and Horace's valet Bates for more to happen. Only when Jerry explains that he can do without long-term relationships with women does he slip from normal prose into alliterative, then rhythmic speech and then into singing and a little later dancing 'Fancy Free'.

Altman is not very precise in his description of this as an audio dissolve:

> In the first song/dance of *Top Hat* (*Fancy Free*), Astaire slides from conversation with Edward Everett Horton into song simply by rhythmifying and melodizing his voice patterns. [...] The entrance of the orchestra is rendered equally imperceptible by the simple expedient of fading the accompaniment in behind Astaire's voice. (Altman 1987: 67)

But the accompaniment has already been there for over three minutes. True enough, it pauses for three seconds when Hardwick talks about wifely schemes, but it restarts before Jerry slips from speech into song, and we experience the interruption as just that: a brief pause in a stretch of continuous music that carries over into the song. Elements of an audio dissolve are there, but with an important difference: the scene does not sneak into the number out of a 'realistic' situation (whatever that means in a musical), but sets the stage with music that makes us wait for the number to begin, and makes us wait rather eagerly. After the almost silent opening of the music, we do get music, but still not a musical number, for which we have to wait for three more minutes.

'It's a Lovely Day to be Caught in the Rain' follows Altman's model more faithfully, and is indeed another example Altman uses to illustrate an audio dissolve:

> [Astaire] walks into a dance, trying to impress her, but she is having none of it. Yet she cannot help beating time with her cane, which soon becomes beating time with her feet as she walks around the band shell mocking Astaire's every move. But to mock his movements she must imitate them, and so, imperceptibly once again, rhythmical movement has led to dance. The band shell, which was once just a band shell, has now become a stage, so much so that the number concludes with a bow to the camera. By this point all diegetic sound has been either exclude or assimilated to the music's rhythm. The thundering storm which brought on the rain has now abandoned its realistic function in order to serve as accompaniment for the couple's song-and-dance number. (Altman 1987: 67)

Altman's analysis is correct, but passes over the fact that this is just one phase in a longer dissolve into the number. The transition begins around four minutes earlier, when Dale flees from thunder, rain and lightning under the bandstand. Jerry also enters the bandstand, with a little skip in his step that foreshadows that we are in for another performance (if the bandstand has not already alerted us to the fact). They exchange banter, but another peal of thunder drives her to seek shelter in his arms, and we begin to suspect that the thunder is not quite neutral. Jerry capitalizes on the situation by telling a little parable about 'a clumsy cloud from here' and 'a fluffy little cloud from there': 'She cries a little – and there you have your shower; he comforts her – they spark: that's the lightning. They kiss: thunder.' Again it thunders mightily, and music starts up and brings on Jerry's song.

Almost from the start the thunder appears in anything but 'its realistic function' (see the Altman quotation above), but is drafted into the transition. The thunder is a conspicuous part of the music as its grand opening chord; but to do this it has to 'react' to Jerry's tale and peal at the right moment – the implied author (see ch. II.iv.d) arranges a bit of musico-magic realism in a genre-appropriate version of the pathetic fallacy. On the one hand, the scene is a variation on the gradual de-diegetization typical for an audio dissolve; on the other hand, it foreshadows the imminent number: with the bandstand as its ominous location, with Jerry's little skip, with the increasingly partisan and increasingly musical thunder. The second phase then proceeds as described by Altman and leads into the dance proper. Eventually another peal of thunder interrupts the music, again at the right moment, and signals the *stretta*, after which the two sit at the edge of the bandstand, ready to take the applause for their performance.

*

This integration of diegetic sound into the music can also be observed in other scenes, albeit less conspicuously, and is part of a strategy of blurring the distinction between diegesis and nondiegetic music and between residually 'realistic' diegetic logic and musical logic in *Top Hat*. One example are sound matches between scenes spatially or temporally disconnected in the fabula, but consecutive in the syuzhet. They are variations of a sound bridge (see ch. II.iv.f). Sound bridges briefly pull apart sounds and images 'belonging' together in the fabula and put them in different time frames in the syuzhet. Sound that should be simultaneous with an image begins under a preceding image, or continues into the next shot. The sound matches in *Top Hat* instead use similarities between sounds across a cut. In one scene, a hotel maid knocks a vase on the rim of a dustbin to clean it out, and her four knocks are echoed after the cut by four knocks of the conductor calling his musicians for attention before the start of the show (Figure 19).

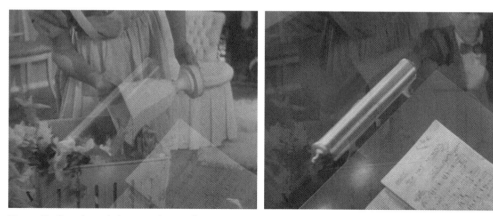

Figure 19: Sound match from maid to conductor in *Top Hat* (1935).

Figure 20: Musical match from theatre to Venice in *Top Hat*.

What one might call a 'music match' occurs at the end of the show introduced by the vase/conductor echo. The band begins an instrumental recapitulation of *Top Hat*, and after the first line the film cuts to a small band on a balcony in Venice, playing the same music (though with different instrumentation, fitting the visible band) (Figure 20).

The difference to a standard sound bridge is that in both cases the diegetic integrity of the scenes before and after the cuts remains unaffected; there is no pulling apart of sound and image. All sounds and music are diegetic, and all coincide with their putative sources on the image track. Instead of sound being carried over from one scene to the next, the scenes after the cut echo or continue the ones before on the soundtrack, even if the images show very different things. Musical logic takes over from diegetic plausibility: the maid knocks the vase on the dustbin the same number of times and at the same speed as the conductor knocks his baton on his stand; and the mock folklore band in Venice 'accidentally' plays one of the songs from Jerry's new show in London.

As in the church scene from *Wallace & Gromit in 'The Curse of the Were-Rabbit'* (see pp. 3–6), storytelling and storymaking are integrated in these echoes. Narrational agency positions spatially and temporally distant fabula events next to each other, and implied authorial agency aligns the number of knocks and the Venetian band's choice of music. Of course we do not think in this way as spectators. The distinction between narration and authorial agency becomes well-nigh meaningless in a musical, because the idea of an autonomous pre-filmic reality reported by the narration is, if not outright inapplicable, at least strongly compromised: that events be plausible in an everyday sense is not on the genre agenda.[96]

---

96 In the terms of Juan Chattah's taxonomy for sound-design analysis (Chattah 2007), these sonic echoes might be categorized as 'intra-diegetic transference': aspects of diegetic sonic events from one scene are transferred to the other; first the number and rhythm of knocks, then the identity of the piece of music played.

The two sonic echoes are minor events, but they contribute to the same strategy as 'It's a Lovely Day'. The diegesis is taken hostage by musical logic, a logic that builds thunder into the bandstand number, looks for or generates musical rhythms in everyday activities and pursues sonic parallels across time and space. While the supradiegetic space of the production numbers may be the most prominent arena for the reign of musical logic, it is by no means confined to them, but is an undercurrent throughout the film.

∗

'Dancing Cheek to Cheek' provides another variant of Altman's model, tipping the scales toward the diegetic side without losing the transcendent effect. The number begins inconspicuously, with the song played instrumentally as dance music in the hotel in Venice. As in 'Fancy Free', the accompaniment for the number is not snuck in after the song or dance has started, but is there all along. But while in 'Fancy Free' the musical stage makes us wait for a song-and-dance to fulfil its promise, in 'Dancing Cheek to Cheek' the invitation is concealed as plausible diegetic music, even if we suspect its purpose.

As expected, Jerry asks Dale for a dance, which begins realistically. But then he cannot be contained any longer by the constraints of ballroom dancing and breaks into song, though none of the other dancers and onlookers around seems to notice anything unusual: indication that we are in supradiegetic territory now, though intriguingly without any music not construable as diegetic.[97]

Jerry leads Dale away onto an empty terrace, though the music does not change its acoustic perspective – another indication that the music is not to be understood as strictly diegetic any more, but has become supradiegetic. The two dance ever more extravagantly around the terrace, and the music point out its supradiegetic nature. Already when Jerry leads Dale onto the terrace the music becomes richer. Towards the end of the number, it seems to follow the inspirations of the choreography rather than the other way round. No longer is the music the stable ground on which the dancing is built, but just one element in an all-encompassing virtuoso performance of movement.

The transformation of the music away from its origin in the ballroom continues when, after having ceased for about six seconds after the end of the dance, it starts again when Dale opens the doors to a balcony. But now it underscores the ensuing dialogue between Dale and

---

97 Richard Dyer explains the lack of reaction by Jerry's singing: 'Fred Astaire's light voice and deft delivery creates an intimacy that envelopes just him and his partner – no-one notices when he croons 'Cheek to Cheek' to Ginger Rogers on a crowded dance floor in *Top Hat* […] before gliding her away to a secluded area' (Dyer 2000: 25). But even a light voice would be noticeable by other dancers only a metre away – if diegetic plausibility were the issue here. But it makes more sense to say that the supradiegetic bubble envelopes just Jerry and Dale, while the other dancers continue to dance in the reality of the diegesis. This is supported by the fact that once Jerry and Dale get up to dance, we only hear their voices and the music, but no other diegetic sounds anymore (see Altman 1987: 173). To avoid the strangeness of a supradiegetic bubble within an otherwise 'realistic' diegetic space, the choreography soon removes the couple onto a terrace architecturally fantastic enough to clarify that we are not in the real world any more.

Jerry, a status clarified when Jerry, very suddenly, proposes to Dale, she slaps him, and the music stops for a moment just before the final cadence in order to make acoustic space for the slap, and then finishes after Dale has stormed off in a huff: the music has now become a means of narration, highlighting dramatic events.

'Dancing Cheek to Cheek' produces supradiegetic transcendence by a step-wise transformation of 'realistic' diegetic space into an ideal stage – insofar it fits Rick Altman's model of an audio dissolve. But it circumnavigates the core of that model. It does not reach the supradiegesis by fusing diegetic and nondiegetic music, but by gradually 'de-realizing' diegetic music. The point at which the music ceases to be diegetic ballroom music and becomes something else it not definable; there is a seamless transition – that is the point. After its transition, the music returns as conventional underscoring, not any longer part of the supradiegetic space, but beyond it on the other side of the scene.

*

For obvious reasons, musicals normally sport a grand number towards the end. The fantasy ballets in *Singin' in the Rain* and *An American in Paris* are examples, like cadenzas in classical solo concertos: outpouring of sheer virtuosity and fantasy, centred on the soloist. In these sequences, theatricality beyond what is normal even in musicals reigns supreme, and the films still seem to aspire to the condition of the Broadway stage. But the metadiegetic ballets in *Singin' in the Rain* and *An American in Paris* also set up spaces where theatricality can flourish with a modicum of plausibility: a way of containing them in a safe, derealized space. Jane Feuer claims that '[t]he secondary, the unreal, the dream world holds at bay the imaginative excess to which musicals are prone. In the musical, as in life, there are only two spaces where we feel secure enough to see so vividly: in the theatre and in dreams' (Feuer 1993: 68). It may not be so much about feeling secure (who feels secure in a dream?), but rather that dream sequences and embedded stage performances provide ready-made bubbles of unreality, an unreality musical numbers otherwise have to generate via audio dissolves and other means of building supradiegetic distance from the 'reality' of the diegesis.

Busby Berkeley's big ensemble numbers in 1930s Warner musicals are another example, but they do not demarcate a separate sphere for the performances. Rather like 'Dancing Cheek to Cheek' in *Top Hat*, they reach performative transcendence in a double way. They are set apart as stage performances in the diegesis, and within that diegetic frame, they greadually move into a hypertheatricality in which the camera becomes as much a part of the dance as the bodies of the dancers and the sets they move in.

Top Hat, too, has its grand finale, one that incorporates a final show of virtuosity and the resolution of the plot. Once more it is not introduced by a proper audio dissolve. 'By the Adriatic Waters' begins as nondiegetic underscore for a brief scene with Jerry and Dale on a restaurant terrace in Venice; but it soon becomes the accompaniment to an ensemble dance in the streets of Venice – a Venice so ostentatiously stagey that it has 'grand finale' written all over it. The musical scenario still has some diegetic anchoring, because it is the beginning of Carnival, which naturalizes the dancing and music in the streets, though the film makes

146

no attempt at verisimiltude. When Dale finally sings 'By the Adriatic Waters' herself, all the ingredients of the number have been assembled, and as in 'Fancy Free' and 'Dancing Cheek by Cheek', there is no proper audio dissolve: the musical accompaniment is already there, inviting the solo singing and dancing onto its stage.

iii. The classical style: *Night and Day, An American in Paris, Singin' in the Rain*

Such variations do not invalidate Altman's ideas about 'dissolves' and supradiegetic music, but rather differentiate them. In any case, his definition does not try to cover all possible cases, but constructs and exemplifies a prototype. Yet neither 'Fancy Free' nor 'It's a Lovely Day' from *Top Hat*, both used by Altman as examples, provide perfect examples for an audio dissolve as gradual transition from diegetic plausibility to supradiegetic transcendence; both are more complex than the smooth curve of this transition. But of course there are examples of audio dissolves in Hollywood musicals that match Altman's model. They rather seem to be found in later musicals, though, as if the genre needed time to develop a 'classical style'.

It is easier to effect the transition into supradiegesis if the setting for a number is inherently musical, since that effortlessly motivates (diegetic) music, whereas breaking into song in a non-musical context foregrounds the unrealism of the genre. But such artificiality can also be a challenge. To see how the film motivates singing in a scene that does not suggest it can be part of the fun of watching a musical.

The scene around 'What Is This Thing Called Love?' in the Cole Porter biopic *Night and Day* (1946) is an example for a 'musical' musical scene. Porter (Cary Grant) works as a song plugger for a sheet music publisher and has to plug material that is not always top notch. At the start of the scene, he and singer Carole (Ginny Simms) present the desperately generic waltz 'I Wonder What's Become of Sally' to an unenthusiastic audience. After the song, the two have a short break, which Carole fills with banter and double entendres as she tries to hit on Porter (and her lack of success plays with Porter's – and possibly Cary Grant's – homosexuality). She complains about the poor quality of much of the music they have to sell, tells Porter that his own stuff is much better and asks him to play 'What Is This Thing Called Love?' He does, she sings, and immediately musical magic is in the air – people start to listen, gather round the platform, form an audience in the emphatic sense. After the first verse, the orchestra creeps in and realizes the magic the scene could only imply before. Everyone goes wild for the song; people ask to hear it again and want to get copies of it. The internal audience is another feature of many musical numbers, showing the audience in the cinema how to relate to the song – usually enthralled – and like supradiegetic music works on two levels: for the characters in the diegesis and for the audience in the cinema.[98]

---

98 Another genre context for which the internal audience is crucial is the musician biopic; see Claus Tieber's analysis of the 'obligatory scene' in such biopics (2009).

147

Night and Day is only partly a musical: it integrates elements of the musical into a biopic, and the supradiegetic transcendence of the scene is carefully limited not to overwhelm the biopic purpose of the whole. But it represents an audio dissolve of a type that had spilled over from the musical into other genres if musical intensity and meaningfulness were required.

*

Not accidentally, two classics of the Hollywood musical, *Singin' in the Rain* (1952) and *An American in Paris* (1951), also provide some of the most careful audio dissolves in the Altmanian sense. 'Moses Supposes' may come top of the list – a number that (almost) seems to have been made to illustrate the idea. Don Lockwood (Gene Kelly) has to take elocution lessons for his forthcoming sound film career. His friend Cosmo Brown (Donald O'Connor) comes to pick him up. The teacher makes Don say test sentences to practice specific sounds; one of them is: 'Moses supposes his toeses are rose, but Moses supposes erroneously/Moses, he knowses his toeses aren't roses, as Moses supposes his toeses to be.' Don does as he is told, and Cosmo joins in, but after a short while they add rhythm to their speaking, begin to dance around the teacher, throw the book with the exercises away, begin to play with the words – 'A moose is a moose/A rose is a rose/A toese is a toese… hup-di-doody-doodle' – and away they are into the number, now accompanied by the orchestra. A supradiegetic state has been reached by a seamless transition from normal to rhythmic speech, to rhythmic movement, to playing with the musicality of words, to singing. The only step left out is that from unaccompanied to accompanied singing.

'Make 'Em Laugh' is hardly less careful in managing the transition, though it falls back on a musical prop. Cosmo exhorts Don not to mope about the fact that he cannot get Kathy Selden out of his head. During his exhortation, he slips into rhythmic speech, makes musical allusions ('Ridi, pagliacci [sic], ridi'), begins a kind of recitative, accompanying himself on the piano, before the half-spoken, half-sung recitative leads into song. Again, though, the beginning of the orchestral accompaniment coincides with the beginning of the song proper, and does not sneak in behind the singing as in 'What Is This Thing Called Love?' from *Night and Day*.

Similarly, 'Tra-la-la' in *An American in Paris* in introduced with a classic audio dissolve on the basis of a musical situation. Jerry comes home happy because Lise has agreed to a date, and finds Adam composing at the piano. He seems to know the music because he identifies the snippets Adam plays as 'Tra-la-la', and starts to sing it (so is Adam only arranging a pre-existing song, or is such logic meaningless in a musical?). At first, Jerry only sings textless interjections into Adam's playing, who tries to shoo him away. But after the first fragmentary stanza, the song comes together, the piano is complemented by the orchestra, and we are in the number.

'By Strauss' shows another careful audio dissolve, but one that continues the move away from diegetic 'realism' even after supradiegesis has been reached. Adam Cook (Oscar Levant) sits in the café and fools around on the piano, playing snatches of jazzy music. His friend Henri Baurel (George Guétary) complains about that, Cook and Jerry identify Baurel as a lover of waltzes, and they all sing – still fooling around and realistically diegetic – Gershwin's 'By Strauss'. Only with the start of the chorus does the orchestra lift the number into a supradiegetic state. (To underline the moment, just before the orchestra comes in, we see an internal audience gathering in the street; later they applaud after the triumphant close of the music.) The orchestra, though, remains modest until 'the emperor' enters – the café proprietor, mockingly hailed by the others. At that point, the piece lifts off into fantasy, the orchestral accompaniment becomes ever more elaborate, and the piano, until then anchoring the music to the diegesis, is now fully integrated into the orchestral texture.

But *An American in Paris* does not just carefully structure dissolves into individual numbers; it extends that care to the way music is introduced in the film. After the credits and the conventional underscore for establishing shots of Paris with Jerry Mulligan's voice-over but before any of the numbers, music enters the diegesis when Adam Cook introduces himself in his own voice-over, while we hear and then see him play the piano in his little upstairs room. Next, Henri Baurel introduces himself, and after that introduction we see him walk towards the café, while we still hear Adam's piano (or rather, while we hear piano we assume to be played by Adam). Then, to show Adam that he has arrived, Henri starts to sing in the street a couple of phrases from 'Nice Work If You Can Get It', and Adam matches his playing to the song.

The scene introducing Levant and Guétary orderly layers the different musical elements that could be used for an audio dissolve. But everything remains diegetic, albeit in a carefully structured sequence. We first hear the piano, then see it; then it is used acousmatically, because it now implies its diegetic anchoring point; then diegetic singing is added, but only for a while, and not for a complete number – this, the scene tells us, is only an *amuse oreille*, a preparation for the musical numbers to come.

Only after this preparation does the film dare to introduce its first proper number; but again it procrastinates and offers us no singing, only dancing, nor a proper transition into supradiegesis. Henri tells Adam about Lise (Leslie Caron) and describes her many facets (Figure 21), and we see illustrations of these danced by Lise (to arrangements of the Gershwins' 'Embraceable You') in the mirror in the café, realizing Henri's voice-over.

Images and music tied to Henri's invoking voice, are meta- rather than supradiegetic, acting out of his eulogy of Lise's charms. The containment of the number as embedded narration of metadiegetic images is symbolized by the fact that Lise's fantasy dances take place within the frame of the mirror, even if the frame is not visible during the dances; transcendence is hinted at in the miraculous apparition of the dances, but is not fulfilled, but encased by the mirror and in Henri's (and/or Adam's) mind. That changes only with 'By Strauss', carefully built on the model of layering diegetic piano music and diegetic singing pre-empted by the brief snatch of 'Nice Work If You Can Get It'.

*

Figure 21: Lise's charms in *An American in Paris* (1951).

Dream interludes

But metadiegetic embedding of a number does not necessarily lower its claim to transcendence. The great ballets before the end of *An American in Paris* and *Singin' in the Rain* are just such metadiegetic fantasy sequences, as is the one in *An American in Paris* in which Adam Cook imagines himself play his (i.e. Gershwin's) piano concerto. The metadiegetic nature does not affect their transcendental quality, even though they are enclosed on a level of narration nested within the diegesis – in principle in the way *Dancer in the Dark* (2000) locks its musical numbers away inside Selma's mind (see below). But *Dancer in the Dark* makes the dream of transcendence embodied in the musical numbers seem pathological, while the 1950s ballets aim for a space where the imagination of virtuoso musicians grants the numbers a degree of virtuosity that overrides any sense of narrative subordination.

That 'Broadway Melody' in *Singin' in the Rain* is not about inner imagination, but about clearing a space for an extravagant display is indicated by its visual set-up. Don tells Cosmo and

Simpson of his idea for the big number for the 'modern part' of *The Dancing Cavalier*. He points to the cinema screen in the room by way of illustration, so that we have to construe the following images and music both inside his head and on the screen his imagination is prefiguring.

The suspension of narrative order is caught up in a dialectical relationship between interiority and exteriority. On the one hand, it is the part of *Singin' in the Rain* that most clearly aspires to the condition of the Broadway stage it eulogizes. On the other hand, that stagey-ness is justified as the imagination of a Broadway dancer imagining the story of a Broadway dancer, and the extroversion and lack of (filmic) realism is balanced by the tumble through layers of narrative embedding: Don's 'story of a young hoofer who comes to New York' contains an internal performance of the young hoofer in a nightclub – the same dancer and the same type of sets, costumes, etc. serve both for his primary story, shown as a Broadway stage show, and for his performance in the club, which within this embedded narrative *is* a stage show (with the following dance with the green-clad Cyd Charisse occupying an uncertain space between both levels). The doubling of levels of performance continues through the part of the sequence that show the hoofer's rise to fame, but the tumble continues when his second dance with Cyd Charisse is realized as a dream sequence – an embedded narrative within an embedded narrative, all taking place on the same (kind of) stage, and in Don's head, and (as far as the sequence foreshadows the finished film) on the screen in the projection room, and on the cinema screen.[99] Jane Feuer compares what Peter Wollen called the 'multiple diegesis' (Feuer 1993: 68), the 'interlocking and interweaving plurality of worlds' (Wollen 1972: 11) in musicals with that of Godard films:

> In a Godard film, multiple diegesis may call attention to the discrepancy between fiction and reality, or fiction and history. In the Hollywood musical, heterogeneous levels are created so that they may be homogenized in the end through the union of the romantic couple. In the Hollywood musical, different levels are recognized in order that difference may be overcome, dual levels synthesized back into one. (Feuer 1993: 68)

It may be (and certainly may have been in 1982, when Feuer wrote her study of the Hollywood musical) an academic reflex to engage in Hollywood ideology critique. But things may be not quite as pat as that. While Feuer is correct about Godard's aims in un-nesting and criss-crossing levels of narration, and while she is also right about the thrust of Hollywood musicals to resolve their narrative complexities at the happy end, the dramatic trajectories of the films and the happy ends themselves are formulaic enough to be recognized for what they are even by viewers not on the hunt for ideology: 'As has often been reiterated, what may be memorable about melodrama is not the recuperative end but the dust which it raises on the way the near inevitable, "forced" closure. Similarly, the resolutions of musical

---

99 For background on 'Broadway Melody' see Wollen (1992: 41–43). A further level is that of historical authorship, with Gene Kelly responsible for planning the dancing in the sequence (see Fordin 1996: 359).

narratives are discardable' (MacKinnon 2000: 45). The happy end does not make what went on before go away, and what remains is the exhibition of artifice: all the world's a stage, and while the Hollywood musical does rarely critique that idea, but celebrates it (and in the process itself), the idea still informs the ways the films destabilize the diegesis. What may remain more profoundly than the generic resolutions is the idea that fiction films are rickety constructions, made-up make-believe, and that is not so very far from Godard.

*

After the interlude on interludes, back to *An American in Paris* and *Singin' in the Rain* and their integration of musical numbers. The patient long-term structuring characteristic of *An American in Paris* also informs 'Our Love Is Here to Stay'. It is introduced by Jerry breaking into song after he has dragged Lise onto the dance floor of the Café Flodair. But the surprise is tempered by the fact that they are already dancing and that Jerry just slots his voice into the music – the band had already slipped into 'Our Love Is Here to Stay', very inconspicuously more than half a minute earlier, when Jerry was ambushing Lise at her table, so that we do not really notice it as a marked musical event.

After that underhand way of introducing the song, it is developed as a theme song of the blossoming love affair between Jerry and Lise. Jerry sings a few bars in the car that brings him and Milo home after the Café Flodair scene, and appropriately she gets angry, because the song reminds her – and us – of the fact that he has hit on another woman while he was in the café with her. The confirmation of the diegetic importance of the song retrospectively colours our understanding of the café scene. In typical musical fashion, no one in the café reacts when Jerry starts to sing, and we assume that this is 'musical singing' rather than diegetic singing. But the row in the car implies that Jerry 'really' sang the song in the Café Flodair, and indeed there is no element in the café scene that could not, with a bit of suspension of disbelief, be construed as diegetic. Then Jerry sings a snatch of the song when he sits with Lise by the Seine on their first date – this is 'their song' now, quite realistically, as an element of the diegesis reinforced by repetition. But that is not enough in a musical, and moments later Jerry sings the song as a number, carried by nondiegetic orchestral accompaniment. This supradiegetic version of the song crowns a development across more than 15 minutes of screen time; and in retrospect it seems as if the song had aspired to this supradiegetic condition from the start.

*

But important as audio dissolves are in *An American in Paris* and *Singin' in the Rain*, there are also other options. Some numbers join singing and nondiegetic accompaniment from the start, e.g. 'I Got Rhythm' and 'S'Wonderful' in *An American in Paris*. (More precisely, 'S'Wonderful' is introduced by a minimal version of an audio dissolve: Henri Braudel and Jerry Mulligan, both madly in love – albeit with the same woman – call out 'C'est formidable! C'est magnifique! Ah!', before they launch into the song, as if words were not enough to give expression to their overflowing emotions, so that a song is required to top their cries of delight. That far into the film, it may no longer necessary to elaborately mediate between diegesis and supradiegesis.) Other numbers are fully diegetic, such as 'I'll Build a Stairway to Paradise' in *An American in Paris* or 'Beautiful Girl' and 'You Are My Lucky Star' in *Singin' in the Rain* (perhaps because after the climactic 'Broadway Melody' further attempts at performative transcendence would not have had much impact).

Other numbers, especially in *Singin' in the Rain*, reach transcendence via a nondiegetic track inviting the number – most self-consciously 'You Were Meant for Me', which uses a song to let a character say what words cannot, but also disabuses the audience of the idea that numbers are outpourings of overflowing hearts. The dialogue between Kathy (Debbie Reynolds) and Don preceding the song is softly underscored from the moment they walk through the studio lot alone. The music only ceases for a few seconds to mark the moment when Don, lost for words, thinks of other means to convey his feelings and enters what at the time in film history the story is located in cannot yet be called a sound stage. When he slides open the hangar doors, the underscore continues while he shows her the apparatus of film illusion: lights and painted backgrounds, vapour and wind machines, '500,000 kilowatts of stardust'. When all has come together, he begins to sing, still on the foundation of the nondiegetic music that surreptitiously has carried the scene and mediated between dialogue and song. The scene plays with the fabrication of emotion in a self-conscious way characteristic for much entertainment cinema. The machinery of illusion is shown in all its tackiness, but the film insists that there is truth in the illusion, and the tackiness becomes the guarantor of that truth: the truth of the musical, the truth of putting on a show.[100]

But there's an elephant in the hangar, the crucial ingredient of the fabrication of emotion, but one never mentioned: the music. When Don resolves to use a quasi-film setting for his romantic confession, he says 'Kathy, I'm trying to say something to you, but I... I'm such a ham. I guess I'm not able to without the proper setting'; and when he has prepared everything, Kathy asks him, 'Now that you have the proper setting, can you say it?' They both say 'say', not 'sing' – in musicals singing is as natural as speaking (albeit one reserved for special moments), and singing is often just a special form of saying.[101]

But though musicals as a matter of course reflect on the tricks of their trade, in 'You Were Meant for Me' *Singin' in the Rain* refuses to address the foundation of its genre identity. It can discuss the machinery of *film-making*, and has to, because it is part of a film about film-making. But it has to remain silent about *music*, or it would cut too close to its own heart. This glaring gap in the self-reflexive discourse is made more telling by the fact that music bathes the dialogue between the film's central couple in a romantic glow from the start, and makes the onset of the song seem quite natural – or rather, musical-natural, because musicality if the default state of a musical (underlined by the fact that the first line of 'You

---

100 'The demonstration of how the illusion is produced and how it *can be done*, does not expose the illusion, but rather transfigures the instruments that produce it' (Brustellin 2003: 28; my translation).

101 'So when [...] Joe sings 'You Wonderful You' to Jane [in *Summer Stock* (1950)], it is not a song [...] that he is singing, but a musically-embodied version of his feelings' (Laing 2000: 7).

Were Meant for Me' is 'Life was a song'). Numbers that invite song or dance onto a stage of nondiegetic music point this out particularly clearly, which makes the technique apposite for 'You Were Meant for Me', the number that speaks of the musical condition of the musical by not speaking about it.

But the technique is used for other numbers as well: 'Good Mornin'' is foreshadowed visually when we notice that the clothes of Cosmo, Don and Kathy are colour-coordinated – that might prove handy for a number. The allusive strategy continues when Cosmo and Kathy talk more rhythmically when they suggest to Don what he could do after the end of his film career, and when Cosmo sings a few bars from an old vaudeville number and dances around the kitchen. The real bridge into supradiegesis follows a moment later: nondiegetic music starts just before Don mockingly wonders if he should have danced and sung in *The Dueling Cavalier*, and Kathy and Cosmo suggest that the film ought to be made into a musical. The music begins *before* Don makes his mock-suggestion and *before* Kathy says 'musical'; it pre-empts developments, once more indicating the fundamentally musical state of the genre.

The trick is repeated when nondiegetic music starts during the planning session with Don, Cosmo and Simpson just before the latter mentions 'music' in connection with *The Dueling Cavalier*. The music is suspended for a while, but starts again when Cosmo has hit upon the solution for the integration of modern dance numbers into *The Dueling Cavalier*. The same music then bridges the cut to the next scene and leads into Kathy's 'He Holds Me in His Arms' – and here the film plays another trick with narrative perspective. Beyond the cut, the music is suddenly all diegetic, sung by Kathy in the studio, accompanied by a visible orchestra. The ubiquity of music in a musical makes such playfulness seem natural, but tricks like this add to the richness of the experience even if they are not consciously perceived. Finally, 'Singin' in the Rain' itself begins on a musical stage of nondiegetic music 'left over' from the kiss between Kathy and Don, connecting the song to the plot development that motivated it.[102]

*

The music-as-platform model is similar to that of an Altmanian audio dissolve; it paves the way into the number, provides a slope for the ascent into a supradiegetic state. That nondiegetic music can fulfil that purpose, whereas in a classic audio dissolve it is almost the last thing to happen, is unsurprising; we are so used to having nondiegetic music sneak into a film below our threshold of consciousness that we accept it in a musical as well. Almost always is such music-as-platform musically not very interesting to begin with; but it 'musicalizes' the scene sufficiently to allow the number to slide in.

On a different level of functionality, the 'How?' of integrating numbers into a musical – via audio dissolve, via music-as-platform, as purely diegetic music, as metadiegetic fantasy – is itself part of the fun. Not just what happens in the numbers is performance, there is also the performativity of the film itself, and the way numbers are motivated and integrated is part of the filmic performance of music. As much as Cyd Charisse, Fred Astaire or Donald

---

102 For a close-reading of the scene, see Wollen (1992: 25–29).

O'Connor play with body movement, movement in space, rhythm, partners, props, etc., do the films play with their own structure.

iv. Transcendence lost and regained: The aftermath of the classical style

This chapter is not a historical survey of supradiegetic music in film musicals; it only uses examples to demonstrate some of its options. But historical perspective becomes highly relevant for the aesthetics and poetics of the musical number beyond the 1960s. Like the other quintessential genre of studio-era Hollywood, the western, the musical did not weather the breakdown of that system in the 1960s unscathed, though old-style musicals were still made in the first half of the 1960s, e.g. *Mary Poppins* (1964), *My Fair Lady* (1964), *The Sound of Music* (1965) or *Hello, Dolly!* (1969). But the rise of the rock 'n' roll film since the mid-1950s had already begun to redefine the idea of a musical film, and though musicals (and westerns) were still made after the 1960s, they tended to be – and had to be – conscious reactions to or reflections of the end of an era. This is only a very crude account, more an indication of the historical fracture and a setting of the scene for the discussion of films that can be called musicals, but that do not fit the classic models: films that look for a different aesthetic for musical films or film musicals.

Cabaret (1972)

The most direct reaction was to make ostentatiously anti-classical films. *Cabaret* (1972) is yet another backstage musical; but the genre tradition only serves to throw the difference into relief: politics and promiscuity, pre-Nazi-Berlin and a *ménage à trois* instead of the Broadway and wholesome boy-meets-girl stories. But the distancing strategy also affects how music is built into the film: *Cabaret* avoids supradiegesis. It is not about transcendence, it is at best about temporary distraction through music. But if the film was not meant to rely on diegetic music alone, another way of integrating the numbers with the rest of the film had to be found. The primary one in *Cabaret* is to displace diegetic music onto other sections of the syuzhet, often with clear commentative function. The music spills out of the Kit Kat Club onto the streets of Berlin and into the lives of the protagonists, becomes the (often quite cynical) soundtrack to the travails of the characters and to the headlong rush of Germany into the Third Reich.[103]

---

103 While the diegetic anchoring of the songs in *Cabaret* as performance in the Kit Kat Club or coming from gramophones is important, it oversimplifies to claim that the '[o]ne of the film's most striking features is indeed that all the music is diegetic – no one sings while taking a stroll in the rain, no one soliloquizes in rhyme. The musical numbers take place on stage in the Kit Kat Klub [...]. Ambient music comes from phonographs or radios; and [...] a Hitler Youth stirs a beer-garden crowd with a propagandistic song. This directorial choice thus draws attention to the musical numbers *as* musical numbers in a way absent from conventional film musicals, which depend on the audience's willingness

Otto Dix, *Portrait of the Journalist Sylvia von Harden* (1926).

'Welcome' in the Kit Kat Club.

Brian's train arriving to the displaced diegetic 'Welcome'.

Figure 22: Opening sequence of *Cabaret* (1972).

The first number, 'Welcome', announces the displacement strategy straight away. We see and hear the number diegetically in the Kit Kat Club with its loving recreations of 1920s New Objectivity paintings; but it also underscores Brian Robert's (Michael York) arrival in Berlin, welcoming him into the city. The displacement is spatial as well as temporal. The music underscores events that happen far from the club, and it underscores events that in the fabula would take up much more time than the song (Figure 22).

A similar musical comment is made when Michael and Sally leave the club together one night, but now music *and* dialogue are displaced. First we hear Sally's voice while we still see Michael in the club's toilets, surprised by a transvestite next to him at the urinal. She wonders if he wonders why she works 'in a place like the Kit Kat Club', and he confirms that 'it is a rather... unusual place', a fact proven in the toilet. Then both are outside, and Sally talks about her penchant for 'unusual places, unusual love affairs', while we still hear the music that played in the club. It has not changed its acoustic perspective; we are clearly not to assume that it spills out physically into the street. Instead, it is another case of displacement (definitely spatial, potentially temporal). Only when Sally changes tack and says, 'Now – tell me all about you', does the jazz from the club fade, and we hear the accordion player we see next to them in the street. On one level, the transition is musical continuity editing, connecting the two scenes; on another level, the music highlights the course of the conversation between Sally and Brian.

In other scenes, the commentative function of displacement is stronger. When the club manager is beaten up outside by a gang of Nazis, inside the club a parody of a *Schuhplattler* is given, and the cross-cutting parallelizes the movements of the mock-Bavarian dancers

---

to overlook, say, why a gang member would sing his way through a street fight. In *Cabaret* [...] the songs announce themselves as aesthetic entities removed from – yet explicable by – daily life' (Belletto 2008: 609). This misrepresents the manifold ways older musicals motivate musical numbers, and it overlooks that in *Cabaret* the music detaches itself readily from its diegetic anchoring points to underscore the lives of the characters. This seems to have been part of the plan of the film from the start (see Gottfried 1990: 206).

and the Nazi thugs – the performance in the club acts out the political tensions of the day (with the Bavarian costumes and dance alluding to the fact that for the Nazis, Munich was the *Hauptstadt der Bewegung*, the 'capital of the movement').

A similar effect is achieved when a dance number in the club (including Joel Grey's Master of Ceremonies in drag) is intercut with images of Nazis laying a dead dog at the door of the Jewish Landauers and writing 'Jews' onto the pavement in front of their gate. There is no connection between the slapstick dance and the Nazis; but when the dancers, after a dramatic drum roll, turn around their hats, which suddenly resemble Germany army helmets, and start to goosestep, the dance-on-the-volcano motif on which the film is built is illustrated clearly.

Commentative juxtaposition also colours the private side of the story. When Sally sings 'Maybe This Time', the song about hope for a lucky love story is intercut with images of her in the bedroom with Brian – the love story for which she has the hopes she sings about in the club. The bedroom scenes fall precisely into the gaps between the widely-spaced phrases of a song that seems written with exactly this filmic treatment in mind (it was not part of the stage musical, but written by John Kander and Fred Ebb for the film). Such commentative relationship between diegetic music and other diegetic events is also employed without (or only with minimal) displacement of music. For 'Money Makes the World Go Round', sound and image tracks go together, as the number happens in the club. But the song begins precisely when Sally first sees the grand car of Sebastian von Heune. The one-second overlap is enough to establish the relationship – again a combination of continuity editing and narrative pointer.

The displacement of diegetic music is used not just for numbers in the Kit Kat Club, but also for other music, particularly music that issues, ex- or implicitly, from gramophones. The motif of the gramophone is established when, during Brian's first encounter with Sally, she puts a record on; later, we hear music in her room that sounds as if it comes from a gramophone even if we do not see it; she uses recorded music to seduce Brian; and there is a gramophone in the house of Sebastian von Heune. Only later does the preparation bear fruit. When Brian and Sally talk about their future after he has proposed to her, we hear Greta Keller sing 'Heirat' ('Wedding') and see the gramophone it comes from. 'Heirat', with the same scratchy sound quality, also underscores Brian's and Sally's conversation about their future during a forest outing, though now the song can also be retroactively applied to the marriage of Fritz Wendel and Natalia Landauer. But there is no gramophone in this scene; where the music comes from is unclear. It is imaginable that Sally and Brian have a portable one, but we can also understand the music as nondiegetic, outlining another step in the decline of their love story – an interpretation confirmed when the song appears again, with the same sound quality, during their farewell at the station, now without even a plausible implicit diegetic source.[104] At the end of the story, the narration has taken over through music focuses on their doomed love affair.

---

104 The repeat of 'Welcome' during the forest scene, though connected to images from Sally's and Brian's love story, but also other images we have not seen before, is identified as metadiegetic because it starts when the camera shows Sally's eyes in close-up when the songs begins.

The peculiar ways of meshing music and narrative in *Cabaret* are not just due to the fact that supradiegetic transcendence would not have suited this story. To keep the music entirely diegetic would have been too severe a restriction. The commentative displacement of diegetic music also allows the use of music to contribute to the bitter wit of the film; and it establishes a parallel between the Kit Kat Club and the film: both use music to comment upon the follies and tragedies of human relationships and upon the political tragedy of Germany in the early 1930s.

Fame (1980)

Another film using elements of the tradition in a consciously un-classic way is *Fame* (1980). One may hesitate to call it a musical, but the fact that the term does not quite fit marks the film's place in genre history. Occasionally a musical seems to try to break out from the episodic coming-of-age teen drama, but with a crucial difference. There are three big song-and-dance numbers in *Fame*, and all three have the exuberance, virtuosity and sheer showmanship of traditional musical numbers: first the improvised jam session in the school cafeteria ('Hot Lunch Jam' on the soundtrack record); then the collective dance mania in the street when Bruno Martelli's father parks his car in front of the school and plays one of his son's songs over the megaphones ('Fame' on the soundtrack record); and finally 'I Sing the Body Electric' at the end-of-year concert. Apart from being proper virtuoso performances, the three scenes also have the length that befits a major musical number, and at least the first and especially the second have a degree of unlikelihood that would fit comfortably into a 1950s musical. In the 'Fame' scene, the kids not only effortlessly come together in a seemingly semi-chaotic, but in fact immensely tight, complex group choreography, they also jump and dance across car bonnets and roofs in the street with no more than token complaints from the drivers. This is not the real world, only pure show with a shabby gloss of grittiness.

But in one sense, all three numbers are completely diegetic – there is no music that could not, with a hefty dose of suspension of disbelief, be attributed to the students themselves. They stop at the gates of the supradiegesis. Two reasons suggest themselves for this curious combination. Firstly, it is another distancing strategy. *Fame* plays with injecting 'social realism' into teen drama, and to wander off into the great supradiegetic yonder might have seemed escapist in a bad sense. (In that sense, the film may hark back to the 1930s Warner musicals with the Great Depression backdrop and their intradiegetic transcendence.) Secondly, the relationship between performers and performance is different in *Fame*. Musicality, the ability to dispense performative bliss at the drop of a top hat, was a given for Astaire/Rodgers or Gene Kelly and for the characters they played. The numbers provided merely an appropriate space for their transcendentally dazzling talents. But the young would-be performers in *Fame* still have to acquire that self-assurance. They may crackle and pop with musicality, yet performance is still what they are trying to learn to do. In that light, their numbers – the first two spontaneous, born of bursting energy, the last one planned, professionalized – *are* the transcendental space they aspire to, beyond their doubts, fears, inhibitions.

Everyone Says I Love You (1996)

A very different post-classical musical is Woody Allen's *Everyone Says I Love You* (1996). If *Cabaret,* or other Bob Fosse films such as *Sweet Charity* (1969) or *All That Jazz* (1979), are post-musicals, still recognizably related to genre tradition, but ostentatiously departing from it, then *Everyone Says I Love You* could be called a post-post-musical (a term unlikely to become a success). It pays homage to the classics instead of trying to show their datedness; but its homage does not try to recreate classical aesthetics. By its very distance from its models, it signals that the tradition cannot be recreated, but only lovingly gazed back upon, in line with other recent musical films: '[T]hey affirm the spirit if not the letter of classic Hollywood musicals. But they do so with an acknowledgment that that our love for old musicals cannot be anything but a form of nostalgia' (Feuer 2010: 56).[105]

Actors who are not professional or not even very good singers are only one aspect of that perspective of the amateur (in the literal sense) as the 'lover' of something, and not the crucial one; but it is one with resonance in more recent musical films. Films such as *Love's Labour's Lost* (2000), *Moulin Rouge!* (2001), *Chicago* (2002), or *Mamma Mia!* (2008) also resort to non-professionals for the main roles. *Chicago*, though, does try to recreate the exuberance of a classic film musical, even if that attempt is based on a post-classical (stage) musical itself, from 1975 and by the creators of *Cabaret*, and even though once again supradiegetic transcendence is largely replaced by displaced diegetic music and internally focalized fantasies. The use of non-professionals (though Catherine Zeta-Jones, playing Velma Kelly, is a former professional dancer) seems to have sportive aspect here: can they pull it off, can they produce the energy and virtuosity required for a 'proper' musical? But in *Everyone Says I Love You* or *Love's Labour's Lost*, non-professionalism of performances has a different effect. The films seem like labours of love, looks back at the musical not in anger, but in humble – and only very slightly ironic – admiration, an admiration that includes the admission that the days of such displays of showmanship are over. Another such look back in admiration at the great tradition is *Little Voice* (1998), which realizes its invocatory programme by having Jane Horrocks imitate the voices of famous singers of yore.[106]

---

105 Peter J. Bailey has argued, however, that Allen's view of Hollywood musical numbers is not just nostalgic, but also shaped by a 'skeptical aesthetic because they are necessarily fabrications, artifices whose capacity to reassure exists in inverse proportion to their relationship to truth' (2001: 225).

106 Feuer (2010: 55) lists as examples of 'a different kind of small-scale musicals [...] as part of an international cycle of films': *Strictly Ballroom* (1992), *Everyone Says I Love You* (1996), *Shall We Dance?* (1996), *Little Voice* (1998), *Dancer in the Dark* (2000) and *Billy Elliot* (2000). Feuer sees these films as a group quite different in its aesthetics and relationship to tradition from what she calls 'new

But more important for *Everyone Says I Love You* are other things. There is the fact that Woody Allen transplants musical elements into a typical (although fittingly light-hearted) Woody Allen story. But equally important is the way the musical numbers are integrated into the film, or rather, the way they are barely integrated. Here people really break into song in everyday situations, as if the film tried to refer not so much to actual genre practice, but to a cliché image of it.

The first number, in fact the first shot, makes this quite clear. After the simple black-and-white title 'Everyone Says I Love You', the film opens with a shot of a New York street with Holden Spence (Edward Norton) and Skylar Dandridge (Drew Barrymore), and immediately we hear a (nondiegetic) arpeggiated guitar chord that is all the preparation Holden needs to launch into 'Just You, Just Me'. No audio dissolve and only the barest minimum of a 'nondiegetic stage', instead a suddenness that may remind the audience of the beginning of *The Sound of Music*, though without the energy of Julie Andrews' iconic pastoral pirouette. The number then proceeds classically enough. After Holden's first solo stanza, we get Woody Allen-esque establishing shots of New York in spring, again ostentatiously clichéd, and then the music drags other diegetic characters into its rhythmic structure – people of all age, skin colours and social strata sing bits of the song, in a self-consciously cloying utopian version of New York; eventually even mannequins in a shop window dance to the music – despite the sudden start, supradiegetic space is established clearly and firmly.

Most of the major numbers in the film follow this model. A minimal nondiegetic opening is all that is needed to launch the songs. If there are attempts to bridge the gaps between 'realistic' diegesis and number, they are almost satirically slight. When Holden tries to buy an engagement ring for Skylar, and struggles with the price tags of the rings, he suddenly half says, half sings 'my baby don't care for rings', the first line of 'My Baby Just Cares for Me', which he duly launches into. But for a split second we are not quite sure if this is just his answer to the jeweller's 'It's an absolutely exquisite ring', and the nondiegetic accompaniment only starts after his first line. This is all that's left of the audio dissolves of old; the mode of 'breaking into song' has largely taken over. After that, the song proceeds in the same way as 'Just You, Just Me', with an increasingly elaborate dance routine that becomes properly supradiegetic.

An even more minimal bridge is used when, after Skylar accidentally has swallowed the ring, the doctor (Timothy Jerome) who is looking at the X-ray of her throat, launches into 'Makin' Whoopee', beginning with the line 'Doctors look at X-rays, but they seldom grin', which is not, of course, part of the original lyrics of the song as sung by Eddie Cantor in the 1928 musical *Whoopee* (music Walter Donaldson, lyrics Gus Kahn), nor of any of the many additional lyrics written for the song over the decades, but replaces the original first line 'Everytime I hear that march in *Lohengrin*'. Only after that replacement line does the doctor continue with Kahn's lyrics. The small textual change is all that is needed to join

---

musicals', e.g. *Chicago* (2002), *The Phantom of the Opera* (2004), *Dreamgirls* (2006), *Hairspray* (2007) and *Nine* (2009).

song and scene – again a satirical reduction of classic musical practice. 'I'm Thru With Love', 'All My Life', 'Cuddle Up a Little Closer' or 'Enjoy Yourself' are introduced in similar minimalist fashion.

Of course it is not all minimalism in *Everyone Says I Love You*; there is some wonderful playfulness at work as well with the possibilities of connecting music to storyworld. 'All My Life', sung by Vonnie Sidell (Julia Roberts) by the side of a Venetian canal, at first and traditionally seamlessly changes into the nondiegetic accompaniment to a montage of images of Vonnie and Joe Berlin (Woody Allen) on their Venetian holiday. But then, a little bizarrely, we are back not just at the same spot where she had begun the song, but also implicitly at the same time, because she sits in the same position as when Joe left her to buy her a flower, with which he now returns. There is no indication that the montage did show anything but reality, so we have to assume that the number plays havoc with linear time; a musical number, clearly, is not bound to chronologic normalcy.

Less blatantly and more locally, the reprise of 'Just You, Just Me' in the Venetian section also plays fast and loose with diegetic time (maybe time works differently in Venice?). We hear it as diegetic party music in a salsa rhythm at the ball Djuna (Natasha Lyonne) uses to introduce her intended, Alberto (Andrea Piedimonte), to her father. In the next shot, we see Joe outside the ballroom, walking down a staircase while the music continues, muted to take the change in aural perspective into account. What it does not take into account, though, is the fact that the cut also implies a gap in time – a gap the continuous music nonchalantly ignores. Such nonchalance in the non-observance of the temporal logic of the diegesis is common in film music, for two connected reasons. Firstly, while cuts on the image track are part of the elementary language of cinema, such cuts are much less part of the language of music, even in cinema, and film-makers tend to avoid them because they can be much more irritating than the attempt to achieve verisimilitude would justify. Secondly, diegetic music is very often used at least to some extent as if it were nondiegetic scoring. A piece of diegetic music can be used to frame a scene as well as nondiegetic music, but in order to do that it needs its own formal integrity, and for that continuity is essential. But there may also be a generic side to the application of the illogical temporal gap in this film: in a musical, however unusual and post-classical it may be, such nonchalance can be used with more abandon because we accept the primacy of the logic of music over that of the diegesis anyway.

The final number of the film confirms the suspension of ordinary logic, with a film-historical twist. 'Everyone Says I Love You' is played as apparently diegetic music at the Christmas party, but also serves as the accompaniment of Djuna's voice-over, in which she claims she told Skylar someone should make a film script out of the story they have all experienced (and we have witnessed), to which Skylar replies that the film would have to be a musical, otherwise no one would believe it. At the very end, the film doubles back on itself à la *8 ½* (1963), and suggests that what we have seen was not the story as such, but a version of it refracted through the lens of a musical – or rather, refracted through the lens of a film that is a refracted memory and invocation of the musical.

v. The next-to-last song: *Dancer in the Dark* (and *The Sound of Music*)[107]

Dancer in the Dark (2000) forswears old-style musical professionalism as well, and once more this could be seen as a homage to the Hollywood tradition built on its distance to the classical style. But *Dancer in the Dark* can also be seen as a strident anti-musical, an exposure of the flimsiness of its promise of transcendence.[108] How important is genre history for the film? If one wanted to dispute its relevance, one might have Lars von Trier's support. Asked if he had hoped to revive and transform the musical with *Dancer in the Dark*, he answered:

> I was trying to give it the same freshness that I think the Dogme films have, or *Breaking the Waves*. But I prefer not to start with a form or a style anymore. I'd rather start with the content of the story. (Von Trier quoted in Björkman 2003: 221)

One need not be particularly suspicious of authorial self-analysis to be skeptical. The Lars von Trier who had made *Dancer in the Dark* was used to discussions about his take on film history, and the mock-innocent retreat to 'the content of the story' is a convenient way out of such discussions – quite the opposite of the playfully arrogant call-to-arms of the Dogme 95 manifesto. But after *Breaking the Waves* (1996) and *The Idiots/Idioterne* (1998), von Trier had become a star director and may have sought shelter in (pseudo-)naïve modesty. In other statements, he leaves no doubt that *Dancer in the Dark* is a musical, nor do the reviews, which discuss it as a post- or anti-musical, positionings for which genre history is no less central.

It is clear that *Dancer in the Dark* is no exercise in genre nostalgia, but something very different – 'an anti-musical American tragedy' (Peranson 2000), 'Kafka choreographed by Gene Kelly' (Delapa 2000). The film tells of the desperate attempt of immigrant Selma (Björk) to earn money for the operation her son, Gene (Vladica Kostic), needs to escape the inherited disease that slowly turns her blind; and it tells of the tragedy that ensues and that ends with her execution just when the news reaches her that her son has been saved by the operation. It is a story that invokes another classic Hollywood genre, also identified with escapism – the melodrama (see Peranson 2000).[109]

A plot that with calculated perfidy condemns Selma to her fate has been one of the bones of critical contention: that it is either emotionally manipulative (if one accepts its machinations) or ludicrously overblown (if one does not). To castigate a neo-melodrama for being melodramatic is not a good idea; one might as well complain that horror films use tricks to frighten their audience. But relevant for this chapter is another reaction to *Dancer in the Dark*: the complaint that the musical numbers fall short of the Hollywood

---

107 This section of the chapter is based on a German-language article written in 2004 (Heldt 2005) and updated for this book.

108 The question whether the film is 'deconstruction' or 'bittersweet homage' or both is discussed in McMillan 2004 in broader terms than in this case study of the musical numbers.

109 Lars von Trier mentioned Douglas Sirk's *Magnificent Obsession* (1954) in connection with the idea of letting Selma slowly go blind (see Björkman 2003: 222).

models they reference, that they are too unprofessional, too earthbound. 'One does not whistle a happy tune coming out of this film' (Arroyo 2000), and 'even though they're the only real moments of the film when it seems von Trier attempts anything inventive [...] they never really transcend' (Peranson 2000). If transcendence is what musicals are about, this is devastating criticism – but it fails to take into account how *Dancer in the Dark* positions itself in relation to Hollywood tradition. While the plot machinations are based on a clear genre model, the musical ones are related to their genre context in a more complex way.

Since *Dancer in the Dark* ignores the plot patterns of classic musicals, the elements that refer to the tradition of the musical are slotted into the film in different ways:

- Selma's song-and-dance daydreams, which form the film's musical numbers.
- The amateur production of Rodgers' & Hammerstein's *The Sound of Music*, for which Selma rehearses the role of Maria.[110]
- The snippets from *42ⁿᵈ Street* (1933) Selma and her friend Kathy (Catherine Deneuve) watch in the cinema.
- The film's title, referencing the song 'Dancing in the Dark' from MGM musical *The Band Wagon* (1953).
- Key actors: There is Catherine Deneuve, who starred in *The Umbrellas of Cherbourg/ Les parapluies de Cherbourg* (1964) and *The Young Girls of Rochefort/Les demoiselles de Rochefort* (1967), Jacques Demy's takes on the musical, no less idiosyncratic than von Trier's. *The Umbrellas of Cherbourg* may indeed be the most radical reinvention of the genre, because in a world that is all song, music creates no transcendent space any more. There is also Joel Grey as the former Czech musical star Oldrich Novy and Selma's fantasy father figure. Grey had been the 'Master of Ceremonies' in *Cabaret* (1972), another darkening of the musical. Von Trier aligns his musical with antitheses to the late-classical style of *The Sound of Music*, the other genre reference point of *Dancer in the Dark*.
- Diegetic discourse about the musical. Occasionally, characters in *Dancer in the Dark* talk about musicals, clarifying that we are not just *in* another musical, but in an experiment with the genre:
  (1) When Selma learns about her stay of execution, she says to prison guard Brenda (Siobhan Fallon): 'You know, when I used to work in the factory, I used to dream that I was in a musical, because in a musical nothing dreadful ever happens' – an idea *Dancer in the Dark* demolishes with a vengeance. The musical we (and Selma) know is present only *ex negativo*, as dream, as refuge; just what a critical take on the genre might see as its ideological *raison d'être*, anyway.
  (2) Earlier in the film, Selma tells her luckless suitor Jeff (Peter Stormare) about her *Sound of Music* rehearsals, and he asks: 'I don't understand, in musicals, why do they start

---

110 The stage musical (1959), the 1965 film and the two films *Die Trapp-Familie/The Trapp Family* and *Die Trapp-Familie in Amerika/The Trapp Family in America* (1956 & 1958) are all based on Maria von Trapp's memoirs, *The Story of the Trapp Family Singers* (1949).

to sing and dance all of a sudden? I mean, I don't suddenly start to sing and dance.' Selma replies: 'Well... you're right, Jeff, you don't.' The dialogue is telling about their relationship, and ironic with regard to the fact that Selma shuts away her singing and dancing in her mind. But the dialogue also addresses the film's relationship with the genre. Selma avoids answering Jeff's question, but *Dancer in the Dark* gives that answer by doing what Jeff claims musicals do not. It *does* explain its numbers, and explains them psychologically, not as diegetic performance (as does *Fame*), nor as supradiegetic transcendence (as do classic Hollywood musicals). And *Dancer in the Dark* organizes this explanation with utter formal consistency, eschewing the flexibility in relating music, plot and protagonists to each other that is characteristic for Hollywood musicals.

It is in relation to Jeff's question that *The Sound of Music* (1965) becomes relevant; as a contrasting foil, as a musical that does all the things *Dancer in the Dark* studiously avoids:

- Released in 1965, the film marks the end of the heyday of the Hollywood musical. Musicals in subsequent years either tried (and failed) to continue in the old mould – e.g. *Camelot* (1967), *Doctor Dolittle* (1967), *Hello, Dolly!* (1969) or *Mame* (1974) – or tried to find new music and stories – e.g. *Cabaret* (1972), *Godspell* (1973), *New York, New York* (1977) or *All That Jazz* (1979). In *The Sound of Music*, the tradition still works, but the end is nigh.
- *The Sound of Music* presents a genre-typical 'dual-focus narrative' (Altman 1987: 16–27), contrasting and eventually uniting man and woman, rich and poor, old and young, responsibility and *joie de vivre*, strictness and leniency.
- *The Sound of Music* realizes Jeff's idea of the musical. Here, people do burst into song and dance, more ostentatiously than in most musicals, programmatically starting with Julie Andrews' pirouette on the green hill above Salzburg. Apart from that, *The Sound of Music* seems to try to present music in as many different ways as possible: grandly staged numbers (e.g. 'The Hills Are Alive'); stylized dialogue (when the nuns discuss their unruly novice in song); diegetic performances (Maria singing with the children, the family performing at the ball and the festival); audio dissolves (e.g. when Georg von Trapp [Christopher Plummer] sings 'Edelweiß', accompanying himself on the guitar before the nondiegetic orchestra comes in); nondiegetic music when motifs from the songs underscore the chase sequence. All this, *The Sound of Music* seems to say, music can do in a musical film (whose title is hardly accidental).

It is this variety that is negated by *Dancer in the Dark*, which organizes its music with the severity von Trier became famous for as one of the authors of the Dogme 95 manifesto. But Dogme 95 and other manifestos by von Trier set their rules with a dialectically playful exaggeration of severity, if not with 'the characteristics of a postmodern pastiche' (Simons 2007: 11). Typical for von Trier is not the reduction of means, but consistency: to work within self-defined rules for each film or group of films, rules that challenge his inventiveness (see Schepelern 2003). It is the idea of film as a game played with elements of film style, related to David Bordwell's idea of 'parametric narration' (1985: 274–310), but with a postmodern slant (an idea elaborated in Simons 2007).

Von Trier's 'Selma Manifesto' (reproduced e.g. in Björkman 2003: 237–240) sets out his (alleged) ideas for *Dancer in the Dark*. It describes the relationship between the 'super-realism' (Björkman 2003: 240) of the non-musical parts of the film and the musical numbers, which Selma weaves from 'her love and enthusiasm for the artificial world of music, song and dance, and her keen fascination for the real world' (Björkman 2003: 237): art made out of the fragments of her life.

But the manifesto only hints at the game that is implicit in the organization of the musical numbers. The film divides its music (almost) strictly between rehearsals of *The Sound of Music* and Selma's daydreams. The daydreams are defined by rules that are followed *almost* strictly, and the breaking or bending of the rules forms the dramatic trajectory crucial for the effect of the film. The rules are:

a. Each daydream has a psychological trigger, a moment of stress (or its release) that propels Selma into the refuge of her musico-scenic imagination. (Selma manifesto: 'A situation might be incredibly painful, but it can always provide the starting point for even a tiny manifestation of Selma's art' [Björkman 2003: 237].)

b. Each daydream has an acoustic trigger – a rhythmic sound that allows Selma to slip into the dream. It is a minimal version of an audio dissolve, but a dissolve that leads not outwards into the supradiegesis of traditional musical bliss, but inwards into Selma's deperate flight from reality. (Selma manifesto: 'She loves the simple sounds of living expression [...] the noise from machines [...] the sounds of nature [...] the little sounds caused by chance [...] She can hear music in noise' [Björkman 2003: 238–39].)

c. The daydreams use a different visual language: saturated colours (the colours of Selma's memory and imagination), high-quality film stock, and the fast montage of images from many static cameras instead of the drab colours, grainy film stock and roving handheld camera used elsewhere.

d. In her daydreams, Selma includes the people around her in her fantasy performances, as dialogue partners in songs or as a dancing chorus line. The numbers invoke a communication that does not take place in Selma's real life: the 'utopia of community' (McMillan 2004), while the numbers are really, as the Selma manifesto puts it, 'Selma's dialogue with herself' (Björkman 2003: 240).

e. The end of each daydream harshly reinstates reality, the 'transfigured world is suddenly interrupted by the world of mundance reality. Rather than being contiguous, the two realms are antagonistic' (Woodgate 2007: 396). Transcendence is but fleeting.

But while that fits von Trier's stated intention 'to give the musical a more dangerous function' (quoted in Björkman 2003: 234), the film's richness as a musical lies not just, and perhaps not so much, in its divergence from tradition, but in the variations of this schema. It is a paradoxical richness, dialectically achieved through locking its musical numbers away in

Selma's mind. It is the care with which the variations are arranged across the film that acts as a counterweight to the relentless progress of the story.

1. Initially, the schema is only pre-empted: twice (around six-and-a-half and roughly 26 minutes into the film) Selma, standing by her machine in the factory, seems to slide into a daydream. Her look becomes dreamy, and the rhythm of the machines is sonically foregrounded. But while the machines provide the acoustic trigger, there is as yet no psychological trigger; not all that is needed is there yet.
2. In Selma's first song 'Cvalda' (her nickname for Kathy), the acoustic trigger is provided by overlapping machine sounds, which in Selma's mind become a dance rhythm. The psychological trigger is her overwork. To earn more money for Gene, she works the nightshift, and has to operate two machines. But her failing eyesight makes this impossible, and she is slipping behind. In the end, Kathy helps, and the emotional release starts Selma's dream, in which the factory becomes a wonderland of movements of (wo)man and machine: the kind of interaction she cannot master any more.
3. 'I've Seen It All' confirms the pattern. Because of her worsening blindness, Selma has made too many mistakes and has lost her job. Jeff follows her on her stumbling way home along the rail tracks and realizes that she cannot see any more, and it is her realization of Jeff's realization that psychologically triggers the daydream, acoustically prompted by the sounds of a freight train rattling by.
4. 'Smith & Wesson': Selma has realized that her savings have been stolen, and deduced that her neighbour Bill is the thief. She confronts him and in the ensuing altercation kills him. In the song, she has a sympathetic discussion with Bill and his wife, Linda, and is comforted by Gene. The acoustic trigger is the needle on Bill's record player, which is circling through the groove at the end of the record.

    In this song, the first variation on the acoustic trigger occurs. After around three-and-a-half minutes, the song seems to be at its end, and with the sound of a closing door we are back in the real world. But a second acoustic trigger intervenes (the clanging of the wire against the flagpole in Bill's garden), and the second stanza starts. To reinforce the variation, a second repeated sound is built into the stanza – water that rhythmically splashes out of a pipe.
5. This structural doubling is taken up by 'In the Musicals', which is sung twice by Selma: before and during her trial. The first time, the psychological trigger is her impending arrest, when she realizes that the director of the *Sound of Music* production tries to keep her from leaving the rehearsal until the police have arrived. The acoustic trigger is the drum solo played by a new percussionist to help Selma with her singing and dancing. The second stanza follows when, during the trial, Selma's claim that Oldrich Novy is her father is exposed as a lie. The acoustic trigger this time is provided by the scratching sounds of the pencils of the court artists.
6. Up to this point, variations only affect details of the numbers. For 'My Favourite Things', the rules are broken more profoundly, but in a way that confirms the schema by offering

explanations for breaking it. Selma is in prison, awaiting news about a stay of execution, and since she is blind, the acoustic deprivation in her cell is becoming hard to bear. 'But it's so quiet here. Don't the prisoners march or something?' she asks guard Brenda. But the prisoners don't, and no rhythmic dream-trigger is available. The only sound Selma can hear is singing from the prison chapel, which almost imperceptibly comes through a ventilation shaft. The soundtrack adds a rhythmic sound without clear diegetic origin to bring the scene in line with the others. And so Selma starts, tentatively, to sing 'My Favourite Things' from *The Sound of Music*, after a while helping herself by drumming with her fingers on the wall, then with a toothbrush and a comb on the table and a shelf, and after the end of the song she jumps up and down on the floor.

The colour shift, too, is less clear than before. Only after a while does a close-up of a glowing red toothbrush and silvery water tap confirm that we have arrived in the saturated world of Selma's fantasy. But even then her singing, dancing and jumping seem so realistic that we are surprised when at the end of the scene the colours return to normal, and Brenda enters the cell and sees Selma standing on her bed, her ear pressed against the opening of the ventilation shaft.

The justification for varying the schema lies in the fact that the external factors are different. Lonely Selma cannot even muster the power for imagined communication any more. And while her anxious waiting provides a psychological trigger, the whispering sounds from the prison chapel are not enough to light up her musical fantasy. She has to fall back on *The Sound of Music* (the title names the antidote to her acoustic deprivation) and a song that speaks of what she needs: 'When the dog bites, when the bee stings, when I'm feeling sad, I simply remember my favourite things, and then I don't feel so bad' – though in Selma's case, her favourite thing is the song about favourite things itself. But Selma's dancing is now reduced to jumping up and down in her cell, and her singing is unaccompanied. Selma's imagination is scarcely capable of resisting reality any more, an idea that will be taken up by 'The Next-to-Last Song'.

The scene also helps to clarify the relationship between *The Sound of Music* and *Dancer in the Dark*. The situations 'My Favourite Things' is sung in in *The Sound of Music* are relatively pale: Maria sings it first when the Trapp children are afraid of a thunderstorm, later the children sing it when they are sad that their father is about to marry the wrong woman, and that Maria has disappeared – before she returns at just this moment, confirming the song's magical powers. Only when the song is used in the underscore for the family's flight from the Nazis does the film indicate that the historical context may offer more meaning to 'when the dog bites, when the bee stings'. In *Dancer in the Dark*, that potential is unleashed.

7. The counting song '107 Steps' is a retarding element and reinstates the schema. Her strength fails Selma when she has to go to the gallows, and Brenda, who has understood how Selma's imagination works, stomps rhythmically to trigger Selma into her dream-zone. Selma takes up the rhythm and dreams herself through the 107 steps to the gallows, on the way dancing with other prisoners.

8. Earlier, Selma had told Jeff that even as a child she had loved musicals, but disliked that they had to end: 'But isn't it annoying when they do the last song?' As a little girl, she says, she always left the cinema after the next-to-last song, 'and the film would just go on forever.' This idea is revisited by 'The Next-to-Last Song', which uses the schema, but also radically transcends it. The psychological trigger is the news, reaching Selma when she is about to be hanged, that Gene's operation has been successful; the acoustic trigger is Selma's own heartbeat. After this news, she needs no external sound to start her music. And, crucially, this time she sings her song not just 'in her heart alone', like St Cecilia, but in the execution chamber, roped to the board meant to make her hanging simpler. As in 'My Favourite Things', there is no dialogue, but now not because Selma would be incapable of imagining others, but because she does not need them any more. The board falls, Selma's neck snaps, and the film's soundtrack ends.[111] The last images are silent, with the last words of the lyrics ('They say it's the last song/They don't know us, you see/It's only the last song/If we let it be') superimposed on them.

*

So in the end, *Dancer in the Dark* does deliver transcendence. But it is a transcendence that has changed levels and leads not from the diegesis into the supradiegetic space of perfect performativity, but from the metadiegetic dreamscapes of Selma's mind into the primary diegesis, into the reality of her world: into the space traditional musicals started from.

Rick Altman has described the American film musical as a genre that parallelizes the relationship of spectator and film with that of everyday life and performance or fantasy. The musical shows, in plot and structure, what it does for its audience (see Altman 1987: 50–51 & 59–62). *Dancer in the Dark* does the same, but the issue is not the celebration of entertainment transporting the audience into fantastic suprareality, but the function of entertainment as a refuge from the impositions of an intolerable reality.

Lars von Trier's statements about his work have to be taken with a large pinch of salt, but the project of *Dancer in the Dark* to bring the musical's promise of transcendence down to earth chimes in with comments he made. His interest in Björk as the songwriter for the film was based on the hope that she 'was going to write music that would fit the idea of the film; in other words, music that would express both Selma's humanity and the inhumanity of the musical genre' (quoted in Björkman 2003: 233). He does not elaborate on the inhumanity, but *Dancer in the Dark*: (1) grounds the promise of transcendence in the psychological

---

111 The soundtrack is not at the end, however: it restarts for the end credits. Von Trier bows to the tradition of end-credit music, balancing the overture that opens the film. Björk sings 'New World', a vocal version of the overture, reconfirming the title of 'The Next-to-Last Song' and subverting its point. In the end, the film fails to honour Selma's strategy of avoiding the end and discharges us from her radical reinterpretation of the musical into the conventions of a normal night at the movies.

(and at the end physical) reality of its heroine; and (2) realizes the musical in an individual appropriation of it.[112]

The appropriation takes place on different levels: that of von Trier as the maker of an auteurist musical; that of Björk; and that of Selma. Through Selma's idiosyncratic, unprofessional dreams of the American musical, von Trier can project his appropriation of the genre. Björk fits the programme. Her music – appropriating, alienating and individualizing pop music traditions as much as Selma does those of the musical – brings a musical language to the film that provides some of the transcendence the film denies, because it makes hardly reference to the musical traditions of the genre, nor borrows it from other established styles (as do rock or pop musicals). Apart from a few allusions to the language of musicals in the arrangements of some of the songs, the music is so much Björk's[113] that her portrayal of Selma becomes musically credible: this music is as personal as it has to be to mirror Selma's personal dream of the musical, which 'like no other musical … it's a collision of splinters of melodies, folk songs, noises, instruments, texts and dances that she has experienced in the cinema and in real life', as von Trier's manifesto has it (Björkman 2003: 237).

If *Dancer in the Dark* attempts to humanize 'the inhumanity of the musical genre', one can see that work in two ways. On the one hand it works in the fact that the musical is alive in the film only in Selma's dream of it, a dream that radically reconfigures the shape of the musical. Only individual appropriation of the generic product of the culture industry would guarantee, in this view, its authenticity. But on the other hand, this appropriation, for so long locked into Selma's mind, finally finds its way into her physical world. In the end, the dream is made real.

∗

One need not share Lars von Trier's opinions to grant him that he has made an original film. But it is difficult to escape history, and von Trier's attempt, too, fits into the wave of post-post-musicals discussed above. While Kenneth Branagh grafts musical numbers onto Shakespeare's *Love's Labour's Lost* (1999), and Woody Allen hangs classic songs from the framework of a Woody Allen plot in *Everyone Says I Love You* (1996), von Trier slots his musical into a melodrama plot that recalls *Breaking the Waves* (1996). And while *Dancer in the Dark* uses a professional musician, Björk's professionalism is so far removed from the musical tradition that a similar distance ensues.

---

112 There may also be an element of appropriation involved: 'The problem with most musicals is that they're so horribly American' (von Trier quoted in Björkman 2003: 223). Again von Trier does not tell us what the horror consists in, but though *Dancer in the Dark* is set in the USA, its European stars and European immigrant protagonist could be seen as an attempt to suggest a European alternative. But von Trier's comments are inconsistent; elsewhere, he claimed that *Dancer in the Dark* was made 'from admiration for the way musicals are' (quoted in McMillan 2004).

113 This includes the 'acoustic triggers' – reminders of the fact that sampled sounds and the borderline between music and sounds had played a role in Björk's music long before *Dancer in the Dark*.

This is the point at which criticism of the lacking wow-effect in *Dancer in the Dark* runs aground. Professionalism, as in classic musical films, would only have produced another musical. But *Dancer in the Dark* wants to be a dream of the musical, even if it is a bitter dream. To lock the musical numbers away in Selma's mind seems to say that that is where the genre now resides. It cannot be revived, neither naïvely nor through the shrewd perspective of postmodern irony; but it can be remembered and invoked in a look back that is aware of the historical distance that separates us from the golden age (before films such as Disney's TV *High School Musical* series [2006–2008] showed that less ponderous – though hardly less self-conscious – solutions are still perfectly possible).

Chapter IV

Things That Go Bump in the Mind: Horror Films

To use musicals as an example for features of music in film that are genre-specific and narratologically interesting may seem like the easy way out. Other genres that use music in narratively characteristic ways are ones for which music is similarly central: composer biopics, for example (see Heldt 2009), or cartoons, which due to the malleability of their dieges often structure the image track through music. In less inherently musical genres, music's narrative profile is usually less distinctive. But a condition for a genre-specific enquiry is that a genre *has* a predilection for certain uses of music. My example for such a genre is the horror film.

The chapter is exploratory. It does not pursue one specific aspect of film music narratology, but gathers material for a catalogue of genre-typical ways of building music into the narative structure of a film – not as an exhaustive profile, but as a starting point for further study.

*

The opening scene for this chapter is the same as that for the book: the gathering in the church in *Wallace & Gromit in 'The Curse of the Were-Rabbit'*, when the village organist takes over the task of scoring the frightful climax of the old vicar's speech (see pp. 3–6). Though this is no horror film moment, but a comedy one, the scene is still a good introduction to the topic, because it shows two different aspects of horror film music.[114]

There is the semiotic side of things, here the cliché of the ominous organ chords. Most scholarship on horror film music focuses on this.[115] What kinds of music are used in which kinds of horror films, and what do they bring to the films? How do musical means articulate the monster, other characters, their emotions, or horrifying spaces? How do musical means

---

114 Broad categories such as 'horror' or 'comedy' are necessarily too wide to do justice to the actual landscape of genres, subgenres, overlaps and hybrids. Of the films discussed in this chapter, one is a horror/science-fiction hybrid (*Alien*), one falls between horror and thriller (*A Blade in the Dark/La casa con la scala nel buio*), one combines horror, teen drama and comedy (*Ginger Snaps 2: Unleashed*), one horror and melodrama (*I Walked with a Zombie*), and one horror and psychodrama (*The Haunting*). *The Night of the Demon*, *The Exorcist* and *Demons/Dèmoni* are clear-cut horror films, but the first finds horror in fear and the second in revulsion. But the films all lie at least partly within the horizon of horror as it is normally understood, and the scenes discussed all have to do with audio-visual horror. (For genre categorization and hybridity see Carroll 1990: 13–15, and Hayward 2009b: 8–9.)

115 Major contributions include: Larson (1996), Donnelly (2005: 36–54 & 88–109), Scheurer (2008: 175–204), Hayward (2009), Lerner (2010a) and Hentschel (2011).

affect the audience? How is music integrated with other soundtrack elements, particularly noises? Features discussed from such a perspective are:

a. Implements from the New Music toolbox: dissonances, atonality, glissandi, clusters, noise-as-music, soundscapes, extended playing techniques, electronics etc.[116]
b. Sensory extremes: high, low, loud, quiet music/sounds (overlapping with category a).
c. Music of innocence or sacredness: children's voices (e.g. the nursery rhyme in *A Nightmare on Elm Street* 1984]), lullabies (e.g. *Rosemary's Baby* 1968]), organs or choirs evoking religious music (e.g. *The Omen* 1976]), as signifiers for innocence corrupted or sacredness defiled or perverted (see Brown 2010; Link 2010; and Hentschel 2011: 145–77 & 182–217).
d. Especially since the 1970s, the use of pop and rock, usually in particular subgenres (see Mitchell 2009; Fitzgerald and Hayward 2009; Barron and Inglis 2009; Taylor 2009; and Tompkins 2010).

There may be more to horror film music, though, and *Wallace & Gromit in 'The Curse of the Were-Rabbit'* introduces another aspect: narrative structure. The music does something unexpected (unexpected on the 'horror' level of the film, not on its spoof level). We assume the organ chords to be nondiegetic when we hear them, but then the film tells us to reconstrue them as part of the storyworld, tells us that the villagers are not only able to produce their own monster, but also their own monster-music.

In the resulting laughter, horror is blown away, not engendered (and comedy is another genre that lends itself to the exploration of its musico-narrative techniques). But the question raised by the moment also applies to horror proper: Are there particular techniques for building music into the narrative structure of horror films, and if so, how do these techniques aid horrifying storytelling?

i. Of implied authors and implicit contracts: Six little bits of theory

Apart from scattered remarks in texts with other preoccupations, there is no scholarly discussion of narratological aspects of horror film music. This chapter is a tentative exploration; not a narratology of horror film music, just the probing of features of horror soundtracks that may contribute to such a narratology.

---

116 Comprehensively discussed in Hentschel (2011: 14–128). Not accidentally, one of the favourites of horror film music scholarship is *The Shining* (1980), which takes a shortcut to the New Music toolbox via pre-existing avant-garde music (see Lionnet 2003; Donnelly 2005: 36–54; Heimerdinger 2007: 54–68; Barham 2009; Code 2010; and Hentschel 2011: 21–28ff). To a lesser extent that also applies to *The Exorcist* (1973) with its fragments from Krzysztof Penderecki, George Crumb, Anton Webern and Hans Werner Henze, though these never become as extensive or important for the score (see Heimerdinger 2007: 46–54; Evans 2009; King 2010; and Hentschel 2011: 15–21ff).

In keeping with the heuristic programme, the examples are more important than the theory. While they cannot claim to represent the whole genre, I hope to show what they can say about the possibilities of music in filmic horror storytelling. The theory to underpin the examples is piecemeal: six ideas that, while they may not coalesce into a system, throw light on different aspects of the examples. Apart from the 'implied author' (see ch. II.iv.d), none of them can be explored at length; to delve deeper would require a dedicated study.

1. The implicit contract

The first idea is that of an implicit contract between audience and film(-makers).[117] 'Horror film' defines the genre by its intended effect on the audience. Another example is 'thriller', related to horror (and sometimes jointly discussed; see Hanich 2010); another one is 'weepie' for melodrama, which, though dismissive, points out that some genres aim for particular effects more strongly than others. Other genres are named after their settings (western, science fiction, sword-and-sandal film, etc.), the kind of story they tell (war or action movie, biopic), or their historical ancestry (melodrama). But horror films are defined by what they do to us: we expect them to try to horrify us (see Carroll 1990). Normally, we expect them to horrify us in a specific way. It would not be difficult to do that more profoundly with unedited footage from a battlefield or natural disaster. The question of the relationship between true horror and what Noël Carroll calls 'art-horror' is relevant for the consideration of horror and emotion, but can be left out in this chapter, which is concerned with fictional horror within a certain generic framework (see Carroll 1990: 13 & 27–35).[118]

A genre defined by its effect relies on an implicit contract perhaps more so than other genres, because the expected payoff is so clearly defined. The film has to do a job, and it is understood by film-makers and audiences alike that it may do what it can to achieve that goal (within the boundaries of genre traditions, or at least in ways that take such traditions as a starting point). In this respect, horror films are related to fairground ghost shows and ghost trains, which historically sandwich the invention of film. Ghost shows started in 1873 with Randall Williams at the Agricultural Hall in London, while ghost trains emerged in the late 1920s, a version of the 'scenic railways' or 'pleasure railways' on fairgrounds since

---

117 The term 'implicit contract' is used by Peter Rabinowitz (1987) in a different sense, for the unwritten rules that allow readers to make sense of textual features of narratives. My use of the term focuses on the implicit agreement that genre texts normally aim to achieve certain effects, which normally raises the expectation of particular textual strategies (while genres also have exclusion rules, defining what is not admissible). The broader idea of a 'generic contract' is common in genre theory in different arts (see for example Altman 1999: 156–165 or Grant 2003 for film, or Kallberg 1996: 4–11 for music).

118 Matt Hills refuses to 'foreclose what counts as "authentic" horror' (Hills 2005: 6), because he is interested in the emotions elicited by horror and in the way 'horror' moves through different cultural traditions; see also his exploration of 'True Horror' (Hills 2005: 129–44).

the late nineteenth century[119], all using technology to create multi-sensory experiences overwhelming their audience with sights and sounds.

One consequence of this effect-orientation is that, in horror, story and narration often work hand in hand in a way that could seem over-obvious in other genres. In any narrative, story and narration *can* be understood as two sides of the same coin of (implied or real) authorial agency. But in less effect-orientated genres, the relationship may be less obvious (cartoons and comedies are exceptions), while in horror films authorial agency can come to the fore more openly because film-makers can count on the audience seeing it as a 'contractual partner' responsible to deliver the pleasures of horror.

A second aspect of the effect-orientation is that the distinction between music and noise is often less clear-cut than in other genres (cartoons again excepted), and perhaps less relevant. Hearing is less sharply discriminatory than sight, which gives sound its potential for unsettling effects at a basic psychological level. While spatial definition is an inherent feature of visual stimuli (to see something normally also means to know where it is; misjudgement of distance is one exception), we are much less precise in determining the spatial origin of sounds; and sounds separated from the visual presence of their source can be difficult to identify. This potential lack of clarity in the localization and identification of sounds means that they can be used to engender the anxiety of uncertainty – things that go bump in the night. This makes sounds a valuable resource for the horror film-maker. The integration of sounds and more conventional music can add to the sonic confusion (a reason for the use of soundscapes in many recent horror film), as does the transgressive effect of using sounds as or with music. Because of this, I discuss the use of sounds and sound effects alongside that of music.[120]

2. The implied author

The second idea is the distinction between implied author and narrator or narration (see ch. II.iv.d). To recapture briefly the limited sense in which I use the concepts:

- Narration, for the purposes of this study, is the act of presenting a story, irrespective of its (seeming) origin, including the option that the narrative retains the fiction of an autonomous pre-filmic reality in which story facts are located (or does indeed present a story found in an autonomous pre-filmic reality, e.g. in a documentary). The narration controls the means of presentation (framing of images, camera movements,

---

119 See the website of the National Fairground Archive at the University of Sheffield, http://www.nfa.dept. shef.ac.uk, especially http://www.nfa.dept.shef.ac.uk/history/miscellaneous_articles/article15.html and http://www.nfa.dept.shef.ac.uk/history/art/painting5.html. Accessed 2 June 2013.

120 The joint discussion of music and other sound is common in recent literature on horror film music; see Hannan 2009; Koizumi 2009; Evans 2009; Coyle and Hayward 2009; Halfyard 2009; Collins 2009; Coyle 2009; Lerner 2010; Donnelly 2010; Buhler 2010; and Hentschel 2011.

cuts, nondiegetic music, intertitles, voice-overs, etc., and the temporal structure of the syuzhet), but not the (seeming) facts of the story/diegesis.

- The implied author is an agency (constructed by the spectator to account for particular features of narrative texts) that 'invents' both the rules of narration *and* the facts of the story/diegesis. When diegetic facts are arranged so that they make a point we cannot plausibly attribute to chance or diegetic causation – when, for example, someone switches on the radio and 'accidentally' hits upon a song that comments on the situation – the fiction of an autonomous pre-filmic reality breaks down; we are made aware of the inventedness of the story. Films that, in order to make sense, require us to construct an implied author show off their fictionality. While we are aware on one level that the stories of cinematic fictions are invented by definition, and while the stories of most films at least occasionally show their inventedness, different genres have their own standards of plausibility that tell us what to accept as broadly 'realistic' in that genre, and what to experience as authorial agency peeking through the façade of the diegesis.

One could suspect that such foregrounding of fictionality may be dangerous for story immersion, because it demonstrates the artifice of the story at the expense of its content. But one could as plausibly assume that in genres involving a strong implicit contract such as horror, moments of implied authorial agency can impress upon us the *raison d'être* of the genre. The film lets us know that it is out to get us, and that it will use whatever is necessary, be it the means of narration or the facts of the story.

3. Unsettling ambiguities

This is a more problematic point, because it transfers ideas developed in other contexts to the micro-level of horror storytelling. But it can account for some aspects of music in horror film. Ambiguity has been described from different theoretical perspectives as a key feature of the horror tradition; prominent contributions are those of Noël Carroll and Tzvetan Todorov. Carroll points out that the objects of fictional horror typically are not just dangerous to humans (though most of them are), but dangerous in a particular way: dangerous to the system of categories we use to make sense of the world (see Carroll 1990: 42–52). Horror, in this view, involves 'impurity', the conflation of seemingly natural categories, and so the transgression of seemingly natural boundaries.

That is true of many of the monsters of the horror tradition: the vampire, who is 'undead', i.e. neither dead nor alive; Frankenstein's monster, who is a creature (and creation) of dead bits made alive by artifice, and stands between being alive and dead, whole and fragmented, natural and technological; the *Creature from the Black Lagoon* (1954), which fuses amphibian and human features; Freddy Krueger (*A Nightmare on Elm Street*), who moves between dreams and the material world; the werewolf, sometimes human and sometimes a wild animal; or Irena Dubrovna (Simone Simon) from *Cat People* (1942), who is sometimes a woman and sometimes a black panther etc.[121]

Todorov's definition of the literary genre he calls 'the fantastic' focuses not on the ambiguity of fantastic objects, but on the ambiguity between different explanations for them (see Todorov 1975).[122] Essential is that readers (and often characters) 'hesitate between a natural and a supernatural explanation of the events' (1975: 33), even if the hesitation is eventually resolved by confirming the events as natural (the 'fantastic-uncanny' [1975: 44]) or supernatural (the 'fantastic-marvellous' [1975: 52]), with the category of the purely fantastic reserved for texts that allow no decision between (e.g. Henry James' *The Turn of the Screw* or Shirley Jackson's *The Haunting of Hill House*, basis for the film *The Haunting* from 1960, discussed below).

What links Carroll's and Todorov's ideas despite the difference in what they try to explain is the idea of ambiguity that unsettles audiences (and characters) because it militates against our expectations of the natural order of natural things (see Carroll's discussion of Todorov [1990: 16–17 & 144–57]). There are, of course, explanations for the unsettling effects of fictional horror from very different theoretical perspectives. Psychoanalytical approaches are a prominent strand of the discussion I will not consider, as are interpretations of fictional horror as allegory or covert working-through of social or political conflicts. A brief chapter does not offer space to discuss the merits of such different approaches. Matt Hills points out that a problem of theory-guided approaches to fictional genres is that they can easily reduce the object of study to illustrations of a fixed theory (see Hills 2005: 2–3) – the hammer that makes every problem look like a nail. The problem applies to Carroll's and Todorov's approaches too, but what makes them attractive for my study is the fact that the ambiguities they are interested in concern mental categories, which may be transferable to levels of narration in film.

To extrapolate from the creatures of horror or structures of 'fantastic' narratives to micro-techniques of horror storytelling may still seem like (or be) a sleight of hand. The boundaries between levels of narration seem less natural than those between life and death, dreams and things, or natural and supernatural entities. But horror films have to unsettle their audiences, and to posit unnatural or inexplicable, transgressive phenomena is only one way of doing that. It is not difficult to extend the motif of transgression through ambiguity to the way music and sound are used in many horror films.[123] The semiotic features of horror scores are an obvious example: music that goes beyond what an audience would normally expect or accept from

---

121 For Carroll, a werewolf and Irena would represent impurity not by the 'fusion' of categorically different elements into 'one unified spatio-temporal being' (Carroll 1990: 46), e.g. Frankenstein's monster, but of a 'fission' of a being into conceptually irreconcilable manifestations (1990: 46–49).

122 Todorov used the term 'the fantastic' because he was interested in a broader range of texts involving non-natural entities and events, but also because he mistrusted a genre definition dependent 'on the *sang-froid* of the reader' (Todorov 1975: 35). For a discussion of this position, see Hills (2005: 33–45).

123 Film also uses techniques of visual storytelling to articulate the 'thin line between man and monster. This weakening of boundaries […] also manifests itself in the focalizations. Classic horror contains scenes in which the monster figures as the subject of the look. By means of focalization through the eyes of the monster, films attempt to generate sympathy for its vision […]' (Verstraten 2009: 180). Ambiguities in using sound and music in 1940s RKO horror films are discussed in Lee 2012.

film music, or indeed any music, or music that misappropriated from its original context and turned on its head (e.g. children's or religious music). But such ambiguities can also be found in the ways music and sound are built into the narrative structure of horror films, and may at times be more disturbing than conventionally shocking musical moments, because they call into question basic mechanisms we use to make sense of a film.[124] Of course films use music in narratively ambiguous ways all the time. What is interesting is how different kinds of films use the possibilities of such nimbleness for their own generic purposes.

4. Music as stand-in for the numinous

Occasionally we may experience nondiegetic music not just as music, but as a 'stand-in' for something else: music as the medium to focalize a character's inner state (see ch. II.v), but with particular immediacy. The absence of a clear narrating voice in most films produces an impression of showing rather than telling, and it is easy to experience music in that way: not as an extradiegetic voice telling us something *about* the inner state of a character, but as part of the language of cinema for *showing* us that state.

In horror films, music as stand-in for something within the diegesis but different from physical objects/events that are the common case of cinematic representation, may sometimes apply not to inner states, but to supernatural entities or situations (some cases allow both construals – yet more ambiguity). Kevin Donnelly stresses the links the music for *The Shining* (1980) has to traditions of religious music, music that is part of rituals purporting to connect us to a world beyond, and stresses the status of (nondiegetic) music in film as something from 'elsewhere': 'First, its non-diegetic status sites it outside the diegetic world […], and second, film music, or music in film, can have a life in wider culture outside of the confines of the film itself' (Donnelly 2005: 41). The second aspect is particularly relevant to the pre-existing music in *The Shining*, but the first one may have wider applicability in horror soundtracks, and links up with the idea of nondiegetic music as a stand-in for diegetic phenomena difficult to convey with other cinematic means. The 'elsewhere' nondiegetic music can seem to come from is not normally particularly mysterious in film, because we are so accustomed to it. But given the right interpretative context, it may still have the capacity to become strange and fantastic[125], and what better context for unleashing the potential of strangeness than horror films?

---

124 An example is the organ music in *Carnival of Souls* (1962) with its interstitial nature that is less a narrational effect than a feature of a fantastical world (see Brown 2010: 13–17). The music for John Carpenter's *The Fog* (1980) provides further examples; see Donnelly (2010: 160–61).

125 Claudia Gorbman used this idea for the thought experiment that opens *Unheard Melodies*. She asks us to imagine that film culture had developed without nondiegetic music, with a tradition of sonic realism. 'Then one day […] we attend a screening of a film from another dimension – say, *Mildred Pierce*, with Max Steiner's lush and insistent score full of dramatic, illustrative orchestral coloration. What sheer artifice this would appear to the viewer! What a pseudo-operatic fantasy world! What *excess* […]!' (Gorbman 1987: 1). The musical means of some horror soundtracks could be seen as an attempt to capture a sense of this excess in a genre context that provides justification for it.

5. Causal listening (and psychological parallelism)

While an aesthetic appreciation of films and of their music is part of our reaction to them, it is not all, and with regard to most films not the primary one; understanding what is going on and what may happen next usually comes first. We understand films as systems of cues and clues to (re)construct, in David Bordwell's terms, the syuzhet out of film 'style', to(re)construct a fabula out of the syuzhet, and on the next level to predict the development of the fabula from clues in the film and our knowledge of patterns in particular film genres. One should be careful not to reduce watching a film to reconstructing its story; the appreciation of how films cue us to understand them (or to misunderstand them for a while) is part of the fun. Music is involved in the reconstruction of causes and consequences, and any listening to film music partly proceeds from the perspective of a 'causal listening' that searches for clues about events and environments, rather than from that of a 'reduced listening' that understands it as abstract structure.[126] This is important in horror films, which are often about threats to characters within the storyworld, and mystifying threats at that; but their aim to horrify us means that they also work as (playful) threats to us. Sonic cues and clues work on different levels of narration:

- Within the diegesis: for characters trying to figure out what is going on; but also for the audience, who may be engaged in the same attempt.
- On the level of the narration: for us, who are trying to read the cues to understand the story, but also, on a meta-level, to find out how the film will scare us.
- On the level of (implied) authorship with regard to story construction: for us, who try to figure out what clues there may be in the diegetic presence of music/ sounds.

The layering of levels of causal listening provides ample opportunity for weaving music into a film in interesting ways.

One aspect of this layering is what one might call 'psychological parallelism'. We understand the characters' horror by being put in a situation that at least echoes theirs. The mirroring effect certainly applies to the shock effects of horror films and soundtracks. Horror narratives suggest audience reactions via character reactions: '[L]ike the characters we assess the monster as a horrifying sort of being (though unlike the characters, we do not believe in its existence)' (Carroll 1990: 18). But 'the sickening realization' (Varma 1966: 130) of the monster is not the only affective activity horror

---

126   The terms are those used by Michel Chion (1994: 25–34; see also 2009: 471, 487 & 489–90), based on ideas by Pierre Schaeffer, a pioneer of *musique concrète* (see Schaeffer 1966: 103–128 and 261–278). Chion third term is 'semantic listening', i.e. listening for the meanings of coded signals (usually language).

narratives engender, there is also the 'awful apprehension' (1966: 130) preceding it, and the ambiguities characters and spectators face in comprehending mystifying goings-on and horrible creatures are another field for mirroring effects, often involving music and sound.

6. Music as shock effect

Perhaps the most pervasive aspect of horror film music is music as shock effect – not audience address, but audience attack. While not particular to horror films, nothing is as much a horror scoring cliché as a big stinger to startle the audience, and the exploitation of sensory extremes aims for the same effect, as do (often diegetic) sound effects. One of the best-known examples is the noise in *Cat People* that we fear signals the attack of Irena-turned-wildcat in her pursuit of Alice (Jane Randolph), before the shock is paradoxically whisked away by the realization of the sound source on the image track: a bus suddenly entering the frame, a trick so successful that it led producer Val Lewton to use 'bus' as a generic term for such effects (see Baird 2000; Donnelly 2005: 94–95; Wierzbicki 2009: 16–18; Lee 2012: 109–11).

The effectiveness of startle effects and other music/sound aiming for automatic or even physiological reactions (e.g. the use of low frequencies) lies in the fact that they undercut normal film perception: the reading of narrative cues and the construction of a story(world). Instead, they are based on involuntary reactions; built-in systems for causal listening take over. To some extent such moments overcome the most basic distinction we have to be able to make to understand films, the distinction between sounds that are part of the film and sounds that occur in the real space of the cinema: 'Even in the local multiplex, whatever else goes on and no matter how much we may be enthralled by the film, we must still be able to distinguish between someone yelling "Fire!" on screen and someone doing so in the theater' (Neumeyer 2009). A properly executed 'bus' drafts our involuntary reaction to startling noises into our reaction to the film, and uses the reflex to put ourselves for a split second into the frame we are watching (see Baird 2000: 18–20).

As important as this is for the generic identity and history of horror music and sound design, the practice is too pervasive to need exemplification, and is only tangentially mentioned in the discussion of examples. What is interesting narratologically is that startle effects exemplify a dimension of film music not normally central to our thinking about its narrative role. We tend to focus on the places of music on different levels of narration; but the topmost level, connecting (if we return to Branigan's model [Figure 1]) 'historical author' and 'historical audience' is rarely considered, because it is the condition for the subtler things going on. But in horror films perhaps more than in any other genre, the 'historical audience' can become part of the narrative game – another field for the pervasive working of psychological parallelism in the genre.

ii. … and thirteen examples

There is no simple way of structuring the examples; that they confuse categories is part of their nature. Broadly, the discussion starts with (more or less) nondiegetic music and moves on to more or less diegetic music, but the distinction is not hard-and-fast.

*

A title sequence is a good place to start. The title sequence of *Ginger Snaps 2: Unleashed* (2004) provides a rushed and enigmatic summary of the events and implications of the first film, *Ginger Snaps* (2000), which saw Ginger (Katharine Isabelle) – the sister of Brigitte (Emily Perkins), the main protagonist of *Ginger Snaps 2* – being turned into a werewolf despite their discovery of an antidote. The antidote, while no cure for the curse, can delay the transformation into a werewolf. The first film, in time-honoured fashion, used the process of turning into a werewolf as a metaphor for sexual awakening; the second uses Brigitte's dependency on the antidote as a metaphor for drug addiction: turning into a werewolf is the equivalent of drug withdrawal.[127]

Kurt Swinghammer's music for the credits is a fast-paced, aggressive electronic soundtrack that takes up both the idea of noise-as-music characteristic for many recent horror films, and the template of contemporary electronic dance music. At first, the soundscape aspect dominates, and the music is close to the images we see: a screeching sound accompanies the razor gliding over Brigitte' skin (in her attempt to get rid of the sprouting wolf's hairs); dripping sounds accompany images of her blood falling into the bathtub, etc. After a while the music finds its stride and organizes its sounds with a steady beat, moving closer to dance music.

The music is nondiegetic and mirrors on-screen events. But it does not Mickey Mouse: instead, it *replaces* diegetic sounds (which are switched off), and in that sense crosses the borderline between its interpretation as either diegetic or nondiegetic more profoundly than Mickey Mousing. It stands in for the diegetic sounds that would normally go with the images, but it retains some of its integrity as a separate layer, not just a sonic emanation of the images: 'the signifier is linked to its signified through onomatopoeia (or iconicity)' (Chattah 2006: 131).[128] The disturbing quality of the music lies in the fact that we are never quite sure how much we are supposed to hear it as music, from the perspective of 'reduced listening', and how much we are supposed to listen for clues the title sequence provides about the film's backstory.

The music even foregrounds this wavering between two states when, after having found a steady pulse, it suspends or rather distorts the pulse for a moment when the beat steps out

---

127   The third film, *Ginger Snaps Back: The Beginning* (2004), set in the early 1800s in a fur-trading outpost in the Canadian wilderness, uses being a werewolf as a metaphor of race: of being American-Indian in a world increasingly controlled by Europeans.

128   See also Chapter 10 of *Non-Traditional Sound Design* (Chattah 2006: 126–37) for Chattah's taxonomy of the overlap, replacement and transition of features between different planes of sonic events (voice, music and sounds) and between diegetic and nondiegetic levels.

of rhythm and Mickey Mouses the moment when Brigitte three times taps the syringe she is about to use to inject the monkshood (the antidote). There is no specific horrifying purpose to the sonic strategy of the title sequence; the most obviously horrific effect derives from the drastic depiction of blood and body parts. But there is an insistent ambiguity that prepares us for the film, which uses ambiguity as a principle: ambiguity between understanding the monkshood as an antidote and as a drug; between understanding Brigitte's sidekick Ghost (Tatiana Maslany) as a psychologically damaged girl or as a monster as scary as the werewolf; and between seeing the werewolf or the institutional machinery Brigitte gets dragged into as the worst threat to her.

There is a second side to this use of music and sounds. This is a title sequence, and title sequences can challenge categorizations such as 'diegetic' or 'nondiegetic' because they are liminal zones, in which the diegesis is not yet established and the integrity of the fictional world is still in flux (see ch. II.ii). The music for the credits of *Ginger Snaps 2* produces its ambiguity not just for horrifying purposes, but also balances the tradition of (relatively autonomous) theme music and the sonic underlining of the compressed exposition of backstory. In that sense, it shows the transitional nature of many title sequences. It inducts us into the diegesis, by using music that edges towards that diegesis, even though it is still part of the opening statement of the narration theme music normally is. That the music serves horror and title sequence purposes equally well makes it an elegant solution, fitting for one of the more inventive horror films of recent years.

*

The creation of uncertainty for the way an audience understands a musical moment (or fails to understand it unambiguously) is crucial for many strategies of horror scoring, and *Ginger Snaps 2* provides several examples. One exemplifies the soundscapes beloved of many recent horror films: sonic complexes that are neither music in a traditional sense (or even the sense of sound composition in avant-garde music), nor an arrangement of diegetic sounds, but something in between and beyond.[129]

Brigitte has left the library she is working in and is on her way home, alarmed by the premonition that a werewolf is pursuing her. She is walking down a snowy street at night, and we hear a dense collage of sounds:

- electronic or electronically distorted sounds without a plausible diegetic source;
- slamming car doors
- a hissing sound that could be caused by the wind, but that could also be part of a nondiegetic soundscape;

---

129 Frank Hentschel distinguishes between 'sound design' (the arrangement of sounds implying their [diegetic] origin, albeit going beyond realistic representation) and *Geräuschmusik* or 'sound music' (the arrangement of non-referential sounds), but points out that many horror films play with the distinction (see Hentschel 2011: 62).

- echoing laughter, with too much reverb to be quite realistic;
- a distorted growling that makes us think of the werewolf, but is not clearly diegetic;
- the flickering sounds of faulty neon lights.

As in the title sequence, the layering of sounds with sources on different levels of narration has a transgressive effect. Boundaries between sonic elements become fuzzy; the ear cannot 'read' the situation in a way that would clearly attribute all of the sounds to a knowable source. In addition to this swamping of clarity, unnerving sounds (the flickering neon tubes of film cliché, the slamming doors and false laughter) seem to bunch up, almost to conspire to make Brigitte nervous. Do we understand this as the implied author peering through the gaps in the walls of the diegesis and piling up the scares? Or as an inkling of a malevolent presence within the diegesis that is announcing itself to Brigitte? Or as a reflection of the fear that makes her perceive environmental sounds as potential threats because she already feels threatened?

Crucial for the effect is that the uncertainty affects not just Brigitte, but us as well. We are listening for clues for a potential werewolf attack with her, because the attack would frighten us as well (albeit not as much as her). It is textbook 'psychological parallelism': we are put in Brigitte's shoes, who does not know how to untangle the sonic clues of her environment. And while we are not threatened by an actual werewolf attack, but just by the movie scare of perhaps having to see/hear one, in another sense we are worse off than Brigitte, because we do not even know which of the sounds belong to the diegetic soundscape around her and which ones are courtesy of the narration of the film. Our 'causal listening' has to operate on two levels: one on which we try to untangle what might be part of the soundworld Brigitte hears, and another one on which we try to decode which of the sounds might signal a threat to her. It is a suspense strategy that relies on the doubling of the knowledge gap responsible for the suspense. We do not know what will happen in the diegesis because we cannot unambiguously analyze the diegetic soundscape, and we do not know how diegesis and narration are related to each other, and how to attribute sounds to one or the other.

*

Such tangled soundscapes are characteristic for many recent horror films. But the technique itself is quite traditional (see also Lee 2012: 111–12). In a scene in *Night of the Demon* (1957), sceptical scientist Dr Holden (Dana Andrews) returns to his hotel and seems to experience a (failing or interrupted) attack of the demonic presence that has begun to haunt him. The soundtrack moves us through several reassessments of the potential source(s) of the sounds we, and perhaps Holden, are hearing:

- The high whirring sound that starts at a low volume when he steps out of the lift could be understood as nondiegetic suspense music. But when Holden stops and looks around, we reassess. He seems to be hearing or sensing something, though we cannot be sure if we are supposed to assume that he is hearing the *sound* we are hearing, or if that sound is a representation of his growing unease at something he can feel, but the narration represents to us in this way.

- Then there are sounds of heavy footsteps on the soundtrack, at first at low volume, then crescendoing alarmingly. Was this what prompted Holden's look around in the first place? Is he hearing the footsteps as sounds, as we do, or is he sensing them in a way that is for us represented by the sounds?
- The footsteps are surrounded by a dense, dissonant musical layer, which seems to be woven through by a vaguely graspable melody. Is Holden hearing or sensing just the footsteps, and is the music a nondiegetic addition to ratchet up the horror for us? Or is he hearing, albeit only mentally, all of the sounds and the music we are hearing?

The uncertainty we find ourselves in in our attempts to interpret the soundtrack puts us in Holden's shoes. The melody weaving though the soundscape adds another layer to the mystery. During Holden's subsequent conversation with professors Mark O'Brian and K.T. Kumar (Liam Redmond and Peter Elliott), he whistles the melody to them, clarifying for us that he did indeed hear it, at least in his mind. Both professors remember that in their home countries, Ireland and India respectively, there are similar tunes, both in some unspecified way connected with the idea of the devil. What is on one level a bit of cheap mystification is also part of a consistent strategy. An element of the soundscape in the corridor, which at that point could still have been understood as nondiegetic music, has now entered the diegesis. Something is coming, echoing the gathering hints of the demon's attempts to enter Holden's reality.

*

The threat of the demon trying to enter physical reality from beyond is central to *Night of the Demon*, and provides an interpretative context that may colour how we understand its music. When Holden visits Julian Karswell, the man responsible for the demonic threat, Karswell gives him a taster of the powers Holden does not believe in. Karswell asks himself 'But how to prove my point?', while we hear a four-note ostinato figure. While he is concentrating on we know not what, the motif crescendoes and is soon joined by the beginnings of a storm and by chromatic scales rushing up and down, until we have a full-blown storm, including a lightning flash-cum-thunderclap severing a big branch from a tree, accompanied by full-blown storm music: a *tempesta*, one of the oldest clichés in the dramatic book, going back to the seventeenth century. On one level, one can understand the music as nondiegetic announcement and accompaniment of a dramatic moment, Mickey Mousing the unnatural nature conjured up by Karswell. But the film is about something entering from beyond, and one can also hear it as that: nondiegetic music as a numinous presence in itself, making the 'beyond' of nondiegetic (pseudo-)space a stand-in for the supernatural. Before he starts his demonstration, Karswell asks Holden, who claims the magic powers people have believed in for millennia are imaginary: 'But where does imagination end and reality begin? What is this twilight, this half-world of the mind that you profess to know so much about? How can we differentiate between the powers of darkness and the powers of the mind?' He might as well be speaking about the way audiences deal with mercurial medium of music as it is used in many films.[130]

*

Night of the Demon uses a range of transgressive techniques involving music/sound that threaten to split apart the integrity of its diegesis. One is the use of unlikely coincidences one might normally understand as indications of implied authorial agency. But here they acquire horror-specific ambiguity, because we are not sure whether we are to understand them as the result of (Karswell's) magical agency within the storyworld. Three times in the film, for example, ostensibly diegetic thunderclaps coincide with significant plot moments, seemingly taking their cue from the thunderclap crowning Karswell's storm. On one level, these are just startle effects; on another level, their obedient occurrence at important moments bends diegetic plausibility to suit the agenda of... well, we are not sure if it is Karswell's agenda or that of the narration of the film, or one via the other:

- The first thunderclap occurs when, after a tense dialogue between Karswell and Holden, the thunder confirms Karswell's threat of Holden's impending death on the 28th of the month.
- The second occurs when Joanna Harrington, the niece of Henry Harrington, a previous victim of Karswell, reads from her uncle's diary to Holden. They learn that Harrington noticed a day before his death on 22nd October that all the pages for dates after that had been ripped from his diary. The same has happened with Holden's diary; and when they read the passage, a thunderclap confirms its ominous import.

---

130 Musical haunting is not restricted to horror. *Three Colours: Blue* (1993) provides another example. After the death of her husband and daughter, Julie (Juliette Binoche) is sitting on the balcony of her hospital room, when suddenly she is bathed in blue light, jerks up and stares into the distance while we hear loud music – a version of the 'Van den Budenmayer' march that had been played at her husband's and daughter's funeral. But we do not know where the music is coming from, and neither, it seems, does Julie. Her stare could be understood to indicate that she is trying to locate the music in the physical space around her – a reflex reaction to the musical startle. But there is no plausible physical source, and we could hear the music as nondiegetic underlining of Julie's traumatized disorientation; internal focalization *through* music. It may make more sense, however, to understand the scene also as internal focalization *on* music: Julie hears in her mind not an active memory, but music that comes unbidden because of its association with the death of her family, like a visitation from beyond. The scene continues with an 'acousmatic intrusion' (Chion 2009: 465), an off-screen voice saying 'Bonjour', after which the musical cue is repeated, now over a fade to black that could be understood as a yet more radical representation of Julie's interiority, which now shuts out anything but the music. After its end, we see Julie again, as well as the journalist who had addressed her.

The interpretation of the music as internal focalization on music is supported by Julie's repeated musical hauntings throughout the film, but the ambiguity in the first instance is crucial to impress upon us that Julie is not retrieving a musical memory, but is ambushed by it. (In his study of the *Three Colours* music, Nicholas Reyland refuses to settle on an interpretation of the music's status; see Reyland 2012: 190–96.)

- The third thunderclaps occurs when Holden searches his briefcase for the documents into which Karswell has sneaked the slip of paper with runes written on it that will conjure up the demon.

In all of the scenes, the sound effects are storm-anchored in the diegesis, but in a way that requires us to construct an agency other than chance: either the narration of the film giving us heavy-handed hints, or Karswell's powers bending the elements to his purpose. It is this ambiguity between two different 'beyonds' that lies at the heart of the film's horror.

*

One of the more surprising examples for narratively ambiguous nondiegetic music occurs in *The Haunting* (1963). Dr Markway's (Richard Johnson) ominous voice-over tells us about the history of Hill House and the evil that seems to have resided there from the start. He is a classic invoking narrator, and the images show what Markway is telling us. We see the first Mrs Crane's coach approach the house, see the horses suddenly shy for no visible reason, see the coach crash into a tree and Mrs Crane die. The moment of the horses' panic and the crash is accompanied by an almighty, but conventional, stinger. But something is odd. The stinger does not coincide with the on-screen action (the shying of the horses), but occurs a split second *before* it. And this is not sloppy editing. It is as if the horses had shied *because of* the sudden noise – a noise we suppose to be located on the plane of the film's narration, whence it should not be able to affect physical facts in the diegesis. It is a different case of implied-authorial causation: not an unlikely or impossible diegetic coincidence, but something ostensibly located outside the diegesis, affecting something within, across the conceptual borderline between them, acquiring a quasi-supernatural quality in the process.

The narrative framing of Mrs Crane's accident, however, means that the reading needs to be qualified. What we see and hear grows out of Markway's voice-over, and we could in principle construe all the means of narration as subject to his control, not just his own words. We rarely think about what in a scene invoked by voice-over narration we are supposed to think of as being controlled by that narration (unreliable narration being an obvious exception), because the immediacy of cinematic images and sounds seem to give them a truth-claim we only question when strongly prompted to. In *The Haunting*, we could hear the music either as an element of the rhetoric of Markway's narration with its half-jokey, half-ponderous tone – a metalepsis that is part of his attempt to impress upon us the evil influence of Hill House. Alternatively, we could hear it as the representation of that influence itself – a stand-in for something the film can only represent via one of the senses accessible to it, sight or sound. But the borderline between the rhetoric of Markway's narration and the rhetoric of the film's narration is a fine one, and so is the borderline between the interpretation of the metalepsis as rhetoric or supernatural agency.

*

A more conventional ambiguity in *The Haunting* involves music that seems to cross the borderline between nondiegetic music and the subjectivity of a character, but it is an ambiguity that is central to the film. The question how much of what we see and hear can be attributed to the evil influence of Hill House, especially on Eleanor Lance (Julie Harris), and how much happens in the increasingly disturbed mind of Eleanor is at the heart of the film's monsterless horror.[131]

Towards the end of the film, Eleanor dances a lonely waltz in front of the statue of Hugh Crane, the first master of the house. The waltz develops out of a flute figure in the ostensibly nondiegetic music that begins in the preceding scene. But what music is she dancing to in her mind? The music starts when Eleanor wanders away from the group and we hear her inner voice saying: 'I'm coming apart a little at a time… a little at a time. Now I know where I'm going. I'm disappearing, inch by inch, into this house.' After the cut, we see her staring up at the statue, explaining: 'We killed her, you and I, Hugh Crane, you and I, you and I', accompanied by quiet brass chords and an insistent line of flute figures which lead into the waltz whose melody is hummed by a voice. While it is easy to associate the voice with Eleanor's interiority, the status of the flute music is less clear. Was it indicating something in her mind already before the waltz, its fast movement a musical illustration of the proverbial bee in her bonnet? But it is part of orchestral underscoring that began in the preceding scene. Was *all* of the music a representation of her interiority from the start, together with her internal voice-over? But while we can imagine her internally hearing or humming the voice that carries the waltz melody,[132] it is more difficult to imagine her hearing the flute, much less so the rest of the music. There is a difference between nondiegetic music as the medium to focalize a character's inner state and the internal focalization of music we assume a character hears internally *as music* (see ch. II.v), but that distinction is elided here.

One explanation for the elision could be that the music does several things at once: suggest the inner voice to which Eleanor dances her waltz; provide the flute that speaks of her increasing mental deterioration; and supply the orchestral underscore that sets Eleanor's interior monologue apart from the preceding scene, sets the mood, and provides the rest of the dance music. Another explanation (and the two are not mutually exclusive) would be that the musical crossing of conceptual boundaries is a feature that greatly adds to the scene's depiction of Eleanor's mental disturbance.

*

---

131 Another *locus classicus* of some of the ambiguities typical for *The Haunting*, and of horror music as a stand-in for the numinous in general, is *Carnival of Souls* (1962), perhaps not accidentally made only two years later. The film plays with the narrative status of the eerie organ music that pervades the score and becomes increasingly understandable as part of the world beyond death that is claiming Mary (Candace Hilligoss). The film has been discussed in recent film music literature and is therefore not pursued here (see Hentschel 2011: 163–68; and Brown 2010, through the latter unhelpfully focuses on the homonymy of organ [the musical instrument] and [sexual] organ, which, despite an etymological connection, does not say much about the music in the film).

132 We have been prepared for this in an earlier scene, when Eleanor is made to dance in front of the statue by the others, and we hear a hummed melody that does not issue from her mouth, but that we can imagine she is humming to herself to propel her dance.

Not all horror films are narratively or musically as subtle as *The Haunting*. The simplest way to build ambiguity into a film is to make it self-reflexive. That is exploited, for example, in two Italian horror films directed by Lamberto Bava (son of the more famous Mario) in the 1980s, in the glaring midday sun of pop postmodernism: *A Blade in the Dark/La casa con la scala nel buio* (1983) and *Demons/Dèmoni* (1985). The former is about a composer commissioned to write the score for a horror film; the latter is set in a cinema in Berlin where the term 'horror film' is taken disturbingly literally.

The key musical element of *A Blade in the Dark* is the theme music, a long series of synthesizer arpeggios. Its self-reflexiveness allows the film to revel in diegetic reveals. The pre-credit sequence – about two young boys daring a third one to retrieve a ball from a basement, with predictably horrifying results – returns soon after the credits as a scene in the film composer Bruno (Andrea Occhipinti) is working on. What in the pre-credit sequence seemed to be part of the diegesis turns out to be metadiegetic. Consequently, the theme music returns as the film score Bruno is writing. But once its double nature has been established, the direction of its movement through the narrative structure is turned back, away from diegetic realism. Repeatedly, the arpeggios are used as source scoring: Bruno finds the slashed photo of a naked woman on his desk, then walks through the house in search for the perpetrator, all the while accompanied by a recording of his own music that is still playing in the music room. Slightly later, we see him working on the music in the house, before the images shift to the outside and to an attack on Katia (Valeria Cavalli). Bruno's diegetic arpeggios are increasingly overlaid by percussion for the attack, return when Katia flees into the house, fade when she hides in the basement, return again for the second attack of the killer, and have become proper source scoring when they stop after we see Katia's throat being slit. All the while brief shots of Bruno's recording equipment remind us of the (at least partly) diegetic status of the music, insisting on the double nature inherent in the film's conceit.

*

In *Demons*, the metadiegetic horror film playing in the cinema the story is set in uses, characteristic for the time, both heavy metal music (the theme music is Mötley Crüe's 'Save our Souls') and traditional horror-scoring, such as the low-volume timpani beats we hear when one of the characters in the metadiegetic film has scratched his cheek on a mask he has found in a dilapidated manison – the mask that is the source of zombification. In the primary diegesis, Rosemary (Geretta Giancarlo) has scratched herself on a similar mask, and we see her touch the scratch while the timpani beats continue. We assume the music to still be part of the metadiegetic soundtrack, but because visually that film is now off-screen, we can also apply it to the primary diegesis.

When Rosemary goes to the bathroom to investigate the scratch, she is accompanied by electronic drones that seem to swell with her discomfort. But where do we locate those? Even in the bathroom, we still can hear metadiegetic dialogue from the film, and the electronic sounds could be part of that, but we cannot be sure. Only when the drone gets much louder when the scratch begins to bulge do the sounds move firmly into the primary diegesis. This ambiguity is exploited in several scenes, with sounds and music crossing back and forth between diegesis and metadiegesis, until eventually Kathy (Paola Cozzo) states: 'The movie's to blame for all this', and everyone around her comes to the conclusion that they have to 'stop the movie', and *Demons* reveals itself as an ironic commentary on the 'video nasties' debate of the early to mid-1980s.

*

Apart from the thunderclaps in *Night of the Demon*, the examples so far had to do with the permeable membrane between diegesis and narration, and with nondiegetic music entering the diegesis or replacing or affecting elements within it. An example from *Alien* (1979) plays entirely within the diegesis. We see Brett (Harry Dean Stanton) search the Nostromo for his cat Jones, while, as we know, the alien is already hiding on-board. For more than four minutes, there is no music at all, just a patiently developed soundscape of diegetic noises: the groaning of the ship's metal hull; faraway miaows from Jones; Brett's occasional 'Here, kitty, kitty, kitty'; his heartbeat; a brief startle when he sees the cat which escapes into another room; the rustling of a piece of discarded skin from the alien Brett picks up; Brett's footsteps on the metal floor; the faint jangling of steel chains suspended from a ceiling; the dropping of water from above, onto the floor, onto Brett's baseball cap and finally onto his face … The soundscape is its own suspense music, and its consistently low volume makes us wait for the big shock effect – which duly comes, albeit not with the almighty startle we expect when we (but at first not Brett) see the alien swing down from behind him, making nary a sound. The moment is marked by the onset of music, but this, too, is not loud, and the sonic shock follows only with Brett's screams when the alien pounces on him.

Here narrative dialectics are in full swing. The very fact that every sound we hear can be anchored in the diegesis makes us only the more aware of the artifice of the scene. Every bit of equipment has been placed where it is to add to the slowly rising suspense. The diegesis has been carefully and ostentatiously arranged to create tension *because* of the absence of nondiegetic pointers, and in that care, implied authorial agency shines though as much as it does in cases of obvious diegetic commentary (see ch. II.iv.d).

The presence of Brett's heartbeat may lead us to construe the soundscape as subjective; a representation of his perspective while he is listening for sounds to betray the location of Jones. As with the scene outside the library from *Ginger Snaps 2* (see above), we are put in his shoes and prompted into causal listening. We, too, are scanning the soundscape for clues, though for clues betraying the alien rather than the cat. But that does not change the implication of authorial agency: in a dialectic flip, the 'realism' of complete restriction to the diegetic creates the impression of extreme artifice, of cool calculation – a calculation the scene also shows in the actions of the alien, echoing an aspect of the diegesis in the narrative procedure.

In a minor dialectic reversal, the soundscape that prompts us to listen for environmental clues is also an aesthetic structure in its own right, something we may enjoy listening to for its understated, carefully controlled elegance. But the building suspense would make a 'reduced listening', a listening for aesthetic qualities alone, seem perverse, and the tension between the two listening impulses adds to our unease, which adds to the effect of the scene. In its aesthetic quality going against the grain of a tense situation, the scene resembles the opening of *Once Upon a Time in the West* (1968). In *Once Upon a Time in the West*, the tension results from two layers of waiting: the gunmen waiting for something we are waiting to be revealed – a double waiting underlined by the varied repetitions of the soundscape. In *Alien*, tension results from the divergent perspectives of causal listening, Brett's and ours.

*

Not as sparse, but no less ingenious in its use of disturbing diegetic sound is a scene early in *The Exorcist* (1973). Father Lankester Merrin (Max von Sydow) is worried by a medal of the demon Pazuzu that has been found at an archeological dig in Iran. He wanders through the ruins, towards a spot from which he can see a statue of the demon. The scene layers sounds and music. When Merrin is nearing the statue, wind comes up; at the same time we hear a low rumbling noise and high, dissonantly whirring string figures.[133] But most conspicuous is the snarling and barking of dogs fighting close by. First we only hear them, then Merrin looks around and we see them, then he turns back to the statue while the barking continues unseen, not at all in the background though, but dominating the soundtrack, and when the camera zooms in on the statue's snarling face, we cannot but reconstrue the dogs' noises as the snarling of the demon.

We can read the montage of disparate elements of image track and soundtrack into a new meaning in different ways:

- We can understand it as a purely narrational effect, if we accept the plausibility of the accidental presence of the dogs at this place and time. The camera frames images and moves in a way that invites the re-construal of the barking as the demon's snarling, but it is an interpretation the narration imposes onto the scene.
- We can understand it with regard to the implied author if we focus on the unlikeliness of the dogs being present to supply the demonic voice. The diegesis demonstrates its constructedness, and we know that the film is out to get us as much as Pazuzu is out to get the Catholic priests.
- We can interpret it as horror-specific magical realism that allows the demon to use the dogs as his voice to confront Merrin.
- We can interpret the moment as a representation of Merrin's inner state. The montage would, from this perspective, be *his* reconstrual of the scene, triggered by his foreboding after the find of the demon amulet.

What is important is not which explanation we find the most convincing, but that there are similarly plausible explanations, creating ambiguity in our engagement with the film.

*

---

133 The music has not been identified in the literature; see Heimerdinger (2007: 46–54); Moormann (2009: 195–98); Hentschel (2011: 14–21).

Ginger Snaps 2 provides another, very different meaningful sound-and-image mismatch. Brigitte, lacking a syringe, is about to drip monkshood solution into her eye to get the drug into her bloodstream. Her young friend Ghost is watching, fascinated and appalled. When Brigitte is about to let the first drop fall, Ghost says 'Uh, I can't watch', and we hear a horrible scrunching sound which we take for a nondiegetic effect, a stinger to underline what Ghost is appalled by. But a cut follows, including a spatial and temporal leap, and we find the two girls lying on the floor and Ghost contentedly munching crisps, and we reconstrue the scrunching sound as that of a crisp being eaten.

It is another diegetic reveal, a classic Val Lewton 'bus', and a good example for displaced diegetic sound. As the church scene in *Wallace & Gromit in 'The Curse of the Were-Rabbit'*, it transforms shock into joke. But there is a double displacement at work. On a spatio-temporal level, we have a sound in the 'wrong' place and time; on a narrative level, a (displaced) diegetic sound does what would normally be done by a nondiegetic musical stinger. In such moments, the film tells us that it is willing to manipulate the normal order of things to generate the little shocks a horror film has to deliver.

*

The undermining of horror can be more of momentary comic effect, however. One of the key scenes of *I Walked with a Zombie* (1943) uses the means of conventional horror film sound design to deconstruct our expectations of sounds in a horror context, and shows itself as the anti-horror film it is. Literature on the film has been more interested to see it from a postcolonial perspective (see Young 1998; and Aizenberg 1999). As crucial as that is, the film's horror credentials, and the way it plays with them, may also deserve attention. I focus on one scene, but it is indicative of the way the film plays with genre features and expectations.

Nurse Betsy Connell (Frances Dee) is taking sick (or zombified?) Jessica Holland (Christine Gordon) to the *houmfort*, the voodoo place of worship, in the hope that the priest might be able to help her, or at least tell her what is wrong with Jessica. The film turns the women's way through the sugar cane fields into a veritable ghost train ride, a series of carefully paced visual and sonic scares.[134] We first see vodoo guard Carre-Four at a crossroads in the field, immobile as a statue. Betsy leads Jessica through the sugar cane, when a moaning sound stops her. She shines her flashlight around and sees a cow skull on a stick, and understands that the wind going through the skull has made the noise. Further on their way, they see a lamb's carcass hanging from a tree. Soon, another ominous sound rises on the soundtrack, one that could – from our perspective – be a nondiegetic effect to imply the women's rising nervousness or foreshadow a shock. But the flashlight reveals a hollowed-out gourd, and again it is the wind blowing though it that makes the noise (see also Lee 2012: 115–16). The next visual starte is a human skull on the ground. By now, the sound of drums and the conch calling people to the *houmfort* can be

---

134 The original screenplay (by Curt Siodmak and Ardel Wray) differs from the finished film in many small ways. For this scene, pages are missing from the extant manuscript, and we only have the end; see http://www.dailyscript.com/scripts/i-walked_with_a_zombie.html. Accessed 2 June 2013.

heard in the distance. The women walk on, and Betsy loses, without noticing it, the patch of fabric that identifies her as one who is allowed to enter the *houmfort*. A man's foot appears in the beam of her flashlight – Carre-Four, who should not allow her to pass without her patch, but does so anyway. The drums get louder, and we can hear chanting, before Betsy and Jessica come into the clearing of the *houmfort*.

The scene is structured as a series of sight and sound surprises, questions and answers. Visually, there are the shots of Carre-Four looming, the lamb's carcass and the human skull, the lost patch of fabric, but also the fact that the dense cane fields allow the women (and us) no orientation, making dangers imaginable at every step. This is where the sonic questions come in, which add a spatial dimension to the women's progress, suggesting potential scares, which are then defused one after the other:

- the moaning sound that turns out to be the wind moving through a cow skull;
- the ominously swelling noise we eventually understand to be coming from the gourd;
- the call of the conch (which we have heard before);
- and, finally, the chanting at the *houmfort* that indicates the goal of the journey.

Crucial for the effect of the scene is that each of the sound and sight riddles turns out to have a natural explanation, and that despite the eerie atmosphere and our expectation of a lurking threat, nothing bad happens. Betsy and Jessica arrive safely at the *houmfort*, and even there nothing scary occurs. Instead, the voodoo priest turns out to be Mrs Rand (Edith Barrett), the mother of Jessica's husband, a doctor who is using her voodoo persona to get the islanders to take her advice – a condescendingly colonial solution, but also one that adds to the film's demystification of cheap exoticism.

It is as if the audience is sent on a fairground ghost train ride and then are shown how each of the scares works – enlightenment overtakes horror. Before this scene, the call of the conch and the drumming, only ever heard from afar, were eerie, vaguely scary sounds. Now, after Betsy's and Jessica's journey into the heart of darkness, they seem almost like a homecoming, something reassuring because we have learned what it is, and that it is nothing to fear – a reversal of perspective crucial for a film that uses tropes of the horror film to undermine its foundations.[135]

*

---

135 There is more to the film than its anti-horror stance, though. Gwenda Young (1998) has shown that the film is careful not to privilege science over vodoo. Both are shown to be morally ambiguous. When Betsy seeks help for Jessica at the *houmfort*, vodoo poses no threat. But Mrs Rand believes that her use of vodoo turned Jessica into a zombie (rather than let her elope with her brother-in-law), while Dr Maxwell insists it was a fever. On the other hand, Mrs Rand uses her voodoo persona to help the islanders with medical problems. At the end, the black *houngan* (vodoo priest) leads a ceremony that has Jessica killed by Wesley, who also dies, both atoning for their infidelity. But given Jessica's state as the empty shell of a human being, it is not clear if we should see her death as murder or mercy. Nick Davis also points out that the film 'tends to obliterate presumed distinctions between "European" and "African" forms of thought and agency' (see Davis 2012: 17 ; see also Lee 2012: 115–16 for a discussion of the film's competing 'explanatory systems').

While these brief case studies do not get far in developing a narratology of horror film music, they may indicate a desideratum of scholarship, not just for horror, but for other film genres as well. To describe how films typically build music into their narrative structure may add a facet to our understanding of the musical profile of a genre. That profile will not be equally distinctive for each film genre; but narratological aspects should not be forgotten in the attempt to develop such genre profiles.

Edna Aizenberg sees the problem of this and other 'zombie women's films' (Aizenberg 1999: 462) as the 'transposition from enslaved black victim vitiated by white colonization to virginal white victim menaced by black erotic rites' (1999: 462), but this simplifies the film. Jessica falls victim not to 'black erotic rites', but to the sexual competition of her husband and brother-in-law, and she dies because of events set in motion by her infidelity and by Mrs Rand's revenge for it.

Chapter V

Beyond the Moment: Long-range Musical Strategies

How a film uses music on different levels of narration can be analyzed at different 'focal lengths', from wide-angle views of an entire film to close-ups of musical moments. Music has usually been studied at close range; this book is no exception and makes most of its points through the discussion of scenes and shorter excerpts. They may be part of long-range strategies, but these have rarely been considered in the literature. This chapter uses a wider angle, in case studies of *Once Upon a Time in America* (1984), *The Truman Show* (1998), and of *Breakfast at Tiffany's* (1961) and *Far from Heaven* (2002). While musical moments are important here as well, the attention is on musical strategies across a film:

1. *Once Upon a Time in America* is interesting not just because of its complex narrative structure, but because it is the last in a series of films by Serio Leone with music by Ennio Morricone that link music to memories, and to objects fetishistically embodying such memories – one way of weaving music into the structure of a film. Briefly discussed in that context are also *For a Few Dollars More* (1965), *Once Upon a Time in the West* (1968) and *Duck, You Sucker!* (1971).
2. *The Truman Show* is a self-reflexive film *about* levels of narration and fictionality and about narrative control, and music adds a loop to that self-reflexivity – a loop that shows how even inconsistency in the use of music can become a strategy.
3. The third case study discusses music in *Far from Heaven* and *Breakfast at Tiffany's* as examples of a narrative figure I call a 'retrospective prolepsis', a figure that is interesting narratively, but also musically because it is linked to leitmotivic scores (e.g. those of the Douglas Sirk films *Far from Heaven* is modelled on).

i. Music and memory in *Once Upon a Time in America*

Sergio Leone's *Duck, You Sucker!* uses a musical metalepsis hardly less surprising than that in *Octopussy* (see p. 90), though within the horizon of the film, not reaching beyond it as *Octopussy* does. The *peon* Juan, caught up in the Mexican revolution, is about to be executed. Standing with his back to the wall, he has resigned himself to his fate when he hears a few whistled notes, then the warning 'Short fuse!' and a dynamite explosion, followed by his *compañero* Sean, former Irish terrorist and explosives specialist, who in the confusion loads

Juan onto his motorbike and escapes. We are as stunned as the Mexican soldiers, but it takes us a moment to realize why: because the motif Sean whistles is from the theme that Ennio Morricone's score assigns to him. But up to this moment it has only been heard as nondiegetic music. How does Sean (and Juan) know it?

Far from being an isolated gag, the moment is part of a web of ambiguities woven around Sean and his music in *Duck, You Sucker!*, a web centred on the memories of his Irish past and of another struggle against oppression. Memory is a theme in several of Leone's films, culminating in *Once Upon a Time in America*, and Morricone's music takes up that theme in a collaboration that may justify the auteurist angle of this chapter. To prepare the discussion of *Once Upon a Time in America*, I start with some remarks about musicalized memories in previous Leone/Morricone collaborations, to trace the development of their use of this element of their filmic world.

a. Precursor 1: *For a Few Dollars More*

In its use of music as a story element, *For a Few Dollars More* seems almost like a trial run for *Once Upon a Time in the West*: less strictly organized, but based on a similar idea. For the first time in a Leone film, music is bound to an inanimate diegetic object.

To 'bind' music to elements of the diegesis is common in leitmotivic scores, though it usually binds to characters. Such recurring musical units can be quasi-fetishistic objects themselves, especially if they fit Adorno's and Eisler's critique of the leitmotif in film as 'a musical lackey, who announces his master with an important air even though the eminent personage is clearly recognizable to everyone' (Adorno and Eisler 1994: 6): if, in other words, the leitmotif does not explain something not deducible from other aspects of the film, but merely underlines them. That critique could also be levelled against Morricone's music in Leone's films, but in a dialectic move that may have appealed to Adorno, Morricone seems to try to escape from the triteness of the lackey effect by overdoing it so much that it flips over into something else – the leitmotifs become integral to their diegetic referents (more below about this in *Once Upon a Time in the West*).[136] That they are often repeated with scant variation only adds to their fetishistic quality. In *For a Few Dollars More*, fixation on a (musical) object is central to the story and explains things not obvious from the images alone.

The diegetic object is the pocket watch the bandit El Indio uses with playful cruelty in his duels (for a summary of its role, see Brown 1994: 231). He starts its tinkling melody and

---

136 This has led scholars to dispute the applicability of 'leitmotif' to Morricone's scores, because both at its Wagnerian origin and in many Hollywood cases, motifs are strands in a complex fabric that can impart information and highlights in a flexible and, if desired, unobtrusive manner (see Leinberger 2004: 17). Morricone's motifs tend to be highly individual, hardly weave a web and are very much 'heard melodies'. But Morricone, too, uses recurrent motifs with diegetic referents, and no purpose is served by reserving 'leitmotif' for only some of its historical forms.

announces that the end of the tune will signal the start of shooting. Because he knows his watch better than his enemies, he has the edge. But the watch is more than a baroque detail, as much as it is at home in the world of ritualistic machismo the 'Dollar' characters inhabit. Indio's game is sufficiently odd to make us wonder why he uses this elaborate preparation for killing, and the film provides an answer in two flashbacks. They show us a younger Indio observing a couple on a bed. The man gives the watch to the woman as a gift. Indio kills the man and rapes the woman, who shoots herself. Indio keeps the watch as a souvenir of his (first?) act of gratuitous brutality and/or a traumatic experience, harbinger of a life of crime and mental instability. The second flashback, shortly before the final duel, is indeed triggered by the sound of the watch chime.

If that were all, however, the watch would have a limited role. But its range is wider, encompassing other aspects of the story and its telling. The first flashback is in fact connected to the watch in a more circuitous way. It follows a minute-long movement of music across diegetic spaces and, possibly, levels of narration. The movement begins when Monco (Clint Eastwood) asks Mortimer (Lee van Cleef): 'Tell me, Colonel. Were you ever young?', to which Mortimer answers, 'Yep. And just as reckless as you.' Mortimer looks at his pocket watch, and a seemingly nondiegetic cue starts: a tune like that of Indio's watch, played by a guitar against a static harmonic background (Figure 23), while Mortimer tells Monco that something happened in his past that has made life precious to him – a surprising statement for a bounty killer.

After a cut, we see Indio smoke marijuana on his bed, while the melody continues, slowing down slightly after the manner of Indio's watch, the guitar now replaced by a celesta. Jumbled electronic sounds follow (similar to those accompanying Indio's first drug haze) and lead into Indio's flashback itself.

It is difficult *not* to understand the electronic sounds that go with the images of a drug-addled Indio as internal focalization, as a musical stand-in for something shapelessly threatening in his mind. But that interpretation can easily be extended backwards to the guitar/celesta tune linking the scenes. When we hear that tune to the shots of the drugged-up Indio on his bed, we understand it as focalized through Indio's memories of the watch and the deed it embodies, an interpretation confirmed by the onset of the flashback showing that deed. But before that, the tune accompanied Mortimer looking at his watch, and we may wonder retrospectively if it is to be understood as internal focalization here as well,

Figure 23: Mortimer's watch theme (aural transcription[137]).

---

137 Transcription after DVD Paramount 2005 (GE 111319), pitch adjusted a semitone downward to compensate for the different frame rates of cinema films and region 2 DVDs.

though focalized through Mortimer's memories, not Indio's: one melody linking the two characters across space and time, via the musical echo their watches embody.[138]

But we cannot be sure. We could also understand the music for the images of Mortimer as a pointer to the link between the men, or retrospectively as a displacement of the music in Indio's mind, a different way of linking them. The differences between these readings are small and unlikely to bother us while we are watching the film; but the ambiguity they instil is integral to its musical strategy. The sights and sounds of the pocket watch suffuse the narrative in different guises.

After Mortimer has killed Wild, one of Indio's gang, the same guitar melody starts when Indio looks first at the dead man and then at Mortimer. Are we to imagine the melody going through Indio's head, telling him who Mortimer might be? Or is it a nondiegetic pointer that Indio has recognized Mortimer or suspects that he ought to know him? Or are we to read it as a clue not about the inner state of Indio, but about the plot, telling us that the connection between Indio and Mortimer is a step closer to coming out into the open? Again the differences are slight with regard to informational content about the relationship between the men; but that we can understand the music in slightly different ways adds to the mystery surrounding Indio and Mortimer.

Apart from Indio's flashbacks, the syuzhet of the film proceeds by and large chronologically, but our knowledge of the watch music does not. Long before the film allows us to guess its role, it is already there, radiating meaningfulness. We first encounter Indio when his gang spring him from prison. The men are accompanied nondiegetically by the melody that will later wander from Mortimer to Indio, a slightly altered and slowed-down echo of the watch tune (Figure 24), present before the film has established any connection between the men, even before we have seen Indio at all.

The obsessive memories of the rape-cum-murder, embodied by the pocket watch, have consumed Indio, and the narration is telling us so before we can know what it is saying – another 'retrospective prolepsis' (see ch. V.iii).

Figure 24: Indio's watch theme (aural transcription[139]).

---

138 See also Cumbow 2008: 37. Charles Leinberger points out that the music combines the watch melody 'with nondiegetic instruments', which he sees as having an 'unsettling' effect on the viewer (Leinberger 2004: 35). But nondiegetic enhancement of diegetic music is common in film and normally understood as just that: an underlining of a diegetic 'fact', not something that calls the fact into question. In cases of potential internal focalization, as here, that the instrumentation is different from the watch chime could suggest that we hear the music as nondiegetic, or could be understood as an acknowledgement of the fact that memories are not mental replicas of the original event, but filtered reconstructions.

139 Transcription after DVD Paramount 2005 (GE 111319).

As in *Once Upon a Time in the West*, and very different from *Once Upon a Time in America*, the connection is nailed down when, during the final duel, Indio's watch tune is overlaid by an almost identical one from Mortimer's watch, now in the possession of Monco. No more vagueness: all is unambiguously diegetic music, and the almost-identity of the tunes makes clear to Indio and to us that Mortimer is taking revenge for Indio's murder and rape (of Mortimer's sister, as he will explain).

Though they provide plot motivation in *For a Few Dollars More*, the flashbacks and half-remembered, half-identical tunes are not about subtle psychology. They are a framework for the obsessive qualities of Leone's plot and its crudely drawn heroes, and for the equally obsessive qualities of Morricone's music, with its incessant repetition of simple motifs and its sensory intensity: un-unheard melodies (see Gorbman 1987), music one cannot but notice and that demands to be figured into the film's narrative equations.

b. Precursor 2: *Once Upon a Time in the West*

As different as the films are, the musical similarities between *For a Few Dollars More* and *Once Upon a Time in the West* are striking. Again the music uses the by then trademark mixture of electric guitar, electronics, a *deguello* trumpet and sounds rooted in the western setting: harmonica, whistling voice, banjo, clip-clopping hoof sounds. And again the motivation for a central story strand is bound to a diegetic object: the harmonica used by Frank in cynical humiliation of a man in the film only named after his instrument, way back when Frank killed his brother. The revelatory scene is embedded in their final duel as a flashback that explains the relationship between Harmonica and Frank and the instrument's significance, hinted at by the harmonica motifs embedded in Frank's theme.

But despite the similar musical building blocks, the musical *strategies* of the films are very different. Whereas *For a Few Dollars More* is about musical ambiguity, the sprawl of allusions and echoes, *Once Upon a Time in the West* is about clear outlines, about ostentatious musical organization. Intrinsic stylistic norms (Bordwell 1985: 149–55) take over and impart a stylization to the film that may have contributed to its description as 'operatic' (see Jameson 1973: 11; Darby and DuBois 1990: 377; Brown 1994: 226 & 228; Burlingame 2000: 127; Cooke 2008: 373–74; Cumbow 2008: 203–06). The music follows a set of rules whose aim seems to be to set each musical unit as far apart from the others as possible within Morricone's style. The fixity this imparts to the music seems to extend the embodiment of music in a diegetic instrument to nondiegetic music, which acquires an almost object-like solidity.[140]

---

140 Jeff Smith has discussed Morricone's 'spaghetti' scores in the context of contemporary pop music and the marketing of soundtrack albums (see Smith 1998: 131–53, especially 136–41). While that is important for the place of the scores in film (music) history, those features also make sense within the framework of a textual analysis of *Once Upon a Time in the West*.

A meta-rule is that almost all of the music in *Once Upon a Time in the West* is indeed thematic. In earlier Leone films (and in *Once Upon a Time in America*), there is far more one-off music. A second rule is that the leitmotifs are attached to one of the main protagonists – Harmonica, Frank, Jill, Cheyenne and Morton – not to any other diegetic element. The third rule is the use of highly distinctive instruments or sounds for each theme, sharply defining them, but also linking them to the storyworld:

- For Jill, Morricone uses a harpsichord, celesta, strings, French horns and the voice of Edda Dell'Orso: opulent and exquisite, far from the world of dirt and crime she finds herself in. But the metallic sound in the 12/8 part of her theme also invokes a watch chime, and the wordless female voice can be heard as siren's song as well as a lullaby.
- Charles Bronson's avenger plays the harmonica and nothing else, fitting his single-minded pursuit of a goal.
- Frank is allocated the electric guitar, not with the Duane Eddy twang of the 'Dollar' films, but with a more massive, distorted sound. Embedded in Frank's music is also the harmonica, nondiegetically recycling Harmonica's terse motifs.
- For Cheyenne, Morricone provides different guises. The first combines a plucked banjo with menacing electronic sounds. When he is revealed as one of the good guys, clip-clopping hoofs and relaxed whistling replace menace with quaintness.
- Morton's theme combines the cultured piano with waves, the acoustic image of the Pacific he dreams of reaching with his railway. Like Jill he, another non-westerner, is musically set apart from the other male characters.

The melodic structure of the motifs is no less distinctive than their instrumentation:

- Harmonica's music consists of two aphoristic motifs, one an extension of the other.
- When Cheyenne's simple modal melody is actually whistled, the melodic shape with its repetition of a single note and the rocking figure at the end becomes recognizable as the stylization of relaxed, aimless whistling.
- The large intervals and sustained tones of Frank's theme show off the sound of the electric guitar, especially as the theme at first skirts around the third-scale degree and prefers the first, fourth and fifth degrees, resulting in a rigidity enlivened only by the pseudo-Mexican flourish at the end of the second bar.
- Jill's theme also makes use of the affective intensity of large intervals. But here it is the sixth (at one point two consecutive sixths, almost ridiculously hyperromantic). As if to underline the gender difference between the obsolete western heroes and her embodiment of 'the birth of matriarchy and a world without balls' (Leone quoted in Frayling 1981: 200), her theme is the only one that opens with an upbeat.

Further 'rules' concern the introduction of protagonists and music. They all have entries in the theatrical sense, carefully prepared and precisely executed, another aspect of the often-voiced idea that the films are operatic.

The station clock at Sweetwater (shot just before the start of the music)   Jill's watch (shot just after the start of the music)

Figure 25: Introduction of Jill's theme in *Once upon a Time in the West* (1968).

The entrances of Harmonica, Frank, Jill and Cheyenne are preceded by phases of waiting filled with diegetic sounds. Harmonica's instrument is first heard after the introduction at Cattle Corner with its patient sound collage for Frank's waiting henchmen. Frank's theme is first heard after a similar sound symphony on the McBain farm, when Frank and his men step out of the dust into the line of vision of Timmy, youngest of the McBain children. We first see Cheyenne when he enters the inn where Jill is stopping on her journey, and his entrance is preceded by a gunfight outside, which the spectator perceives from the perspective of the guests – a purely acousmatic event that offers no clues as to who will eventually step through the door.

A key feature of these entrances is the staggering of musical phases, the division into musical preparation and main event, and the coordination of musical moments with on-screen events.[141] The 12/8-introduction to Jill's theme starts between shots of two timepieces. She is at the station, waiting to be picked up by Brett McBain who is already lying dead in front of his house. She looks at the station clock, and the music starts, then she looks at her pocket watch and decides that something must have happened and that she better take her fate into her own hands (Figure 25). The idea of a watch chime makes sense of the metallic sound of harpsichord and celesta for the introduction. The core tune of her theme begins when she has made up her mind, and begins exactly with her first determined step; the first phrase ends when she goes into the station, and the first statement of melody ends when she leaves the station into Sweetwater.

At the inn the film cuts to the tense face of Jill, who like the others is waiting for the end of the gunfight, and the dissonant introduction to Cheyenne's theme starts; the first tone of the melody coincides with the first time the camera shows us his eyes (Figure 26).

The harmonica motif is first heard from the acoustic perspective of Frank's men, who are about to leave when the music makes them stop, but before we have seen Harmonica. He is still an *acousmètre* (Chion 1994: 129), and his musical voice is all the more incisive for that.

---

141 Coordination was aided by the pre-composed themes being played during filming: 'Everyone acted with the music, followed its rhythm' (Leone in *Cinéma*, 69 (1969), quoted in Frayling 2000: 280).

Beginning of introductioon to Chevenne's theme   Beginning of Cheyenne's main theme

Figure 26: Introduction of Cheyenne's theme.

When they and we finally see Harmonica on the other side of the tracks, he plays the motif a second time, and a third time when the camera shows his face (Figure 27).

The introduction of Frank's theme emphasizes the link between him and Harmonica by repeating that pattern (see also Cumbow 2008: 77). Frank's theme is first heard before we can see him and his gang, when Timmy has come out of the house and sees his murdered family. The first repetition of the theme, with orchestra and textless choir, starts precisely when Frank has stepped forward into the midst of his men and they begin their march on the house; the theme ends when the camera has circled round Frank and we recognize Henry Fonda's blue eyes (Figure 28).

The result of these 'rules' is obvious: the music wraps itself tightly around the figures, becomes a second skin. Though we know that, apart from Harmonica's playing, all of the music is nondiegetic, it is somehow close to the diegesis, but not in the way of non-diegetic music as internal focalization (see ch. II.v). The repetition of musical units is too unvaried to make sense as the evocation of individual and changing emotions, like so much music in classic Hollywood scoring. Rather, the music seems to be part of the basic constitution of the characters, something that belongs to them like their bodies or, indeed, their character (something that Ben Winters might call 'intra-diegetic music'; see Winters 2010: 236–38). In that sense, the harmonica is only the most extreme example of a pervasive musical fetishism. If there is no actual object to fixate on, the music provides sharply defined musical quasi-objects clinging to their characters.

As in other cases of close linkage of nondiegetic music and diegetic elements, the technique entails the risk that we hear the music not as close to the diegesis, but as intrusive.

First statement of Harmonica's motif: Harmonica as *acousmêtre*   Second statement of Harmonica's motif: Harmonica in the distance   Third statement of Harmonica's motif: Harmonica in close-up

Figure 27: Introduction of Harmonica's motif.

Beginning of Frank's theme: Frank invisible (to us)

Second statement: Frank and the gang start their approach in line

End of Frank's theme: Frank in close-up

Figure 28: Introduction of Frank's theme.

Ambiguities concerning the level of narration we assign music to are common in film music, but in cases of such close music/diegesis-linkage the two interpretations seem so far apart as to appear irreconcilable: a contradiction adding to the impression of theatricality *Once Upon a Time in the West* thrives on.

On a more concrete level, the music supports the film's woodcut-like starkness of characterization, which is not so much superficial as surfacial, fitting for a film that is an iconic and ironic invocation of a western, 'a nothing story with conventional characters', built out of 'the conventions, devices and settings of the American Western film' (Leone quoted in Frayling 2000: 252; another tradition Leone mentions with regard to the characters of his Westerns is Sicilian puppet theatre, see Frayling 2000: 9–10).

Harmonica and Frank are fully integrated into this construction with regard to musical distinctiveness and phased introduction of their music. And yet both stand out: Harmonica is the only character allocated diegetic music; Frank the only one whose music is not isolated from that of the others – it/he is connected to Harmonica's motif that is part of Frank's own theme. Via Harmonica, their music spills over into the diegesis and makes them the motor of the plot, culminating in the duel and the flashback that spells out the roots of their bond. Duel, flashback and bond are much like those in *For a Few Dollars More*; but musically *Once Upon a Time in the West* orchestrates them far more concisely.

c. Precursor 3: *Duck, You Sucker!*

Duck, You Sucker! stands a bit apart. Leone did not intend to direct the film, but only to produce it. Only his failure to find a suitable director (or his unwillingness to entrust the project to anyone else) brought him to direct the film himself. But though it dispenses with some staples of the previous films (the climactic duel, the musically-charged diegetic objects), there are enough parallels, especially the role of flashbacks and memories. The story's heroes, Mexican *peon* and would-be bank robber Juan and the Irish ex-terrorist Sean, who become embroiled in the Mexican revolution, have their personal themes, but the musical structure is less rule-defined than in *Once Upon a Time in the West*: there is more variation and more music not clearly attached to diegetic elements. But as in *Once Upon a*

Time in the West, the music differentiates between protagonists, and puts Sean slightly more centre stage through the way it presents his past and relates it to his present.

Morricone's march theme for Juan, one of his most striking inventions, is used as straightforward nondiegetic music. Not so Sean's theme, an oddity with the tenderly mocking repeated interjection of his name and the flowing tune that seems like a development of Jill's theme from *Once Upon a Time in the West*, rather than resembling any of the 'male' themes in both films.

An explanation may lie in the flashbacks, visualizing Sean's memories. In *Duck, You Sucker!*, the flashbacks – unlike those in *For a Few Dollars More* and *Once Upon a Time in the West*, which connect characters that drive the plots – inform us of Sean's past that, psychologically, drives only himself. We hear parts of his theme before the first flashback; but only with the flashback does it emerge fully-formed, springing from the nostalgia attached to Sean's Irish past (a nostalgia that seems increasingly bitter with each flashback), and each of the following three flashbacks repeats the theme. We learn of the woman he loved and of his best friend (who may have been jealous of Sean's happiness), of their involvement in the struggle for Irish independence, of the arrest and torture of the friend and his betrayal of the comrades, which forces Sean to shoot his way out of an attempted arrest and, we deduce, eventually forces him to flee the country.

The double use of Sean's theme in the primary diegesis and in the flashbacks is not in itself remarkable. As 'his' theme, it crosses the border between reality and mental images together with Sean. But the status of the music becomes more intriguing when we reach the execution of Juan, who is rescued by Sean, who is whistling a motif from his own theme. Either we accept this as a metalepsis justified by the formal assignation of the music to Sean, or we explain away the metalepsis by assuming a diegetic origin for the theme, which would entail the possibility that the flashbacks present not just mental images of Sean's Irish past, but also mental music.[142]

Faced with this ambiguity, we may also remember the odd first appearances of Sean's theme. Musically the film begins with Juan's march while he is waiting for a coach he wants to rob. But then we and he hear an explosion, with much reverb as if from far away, and hear a whistled motif from what will turn out to be Sean's theme. Juan is listening, but presumably for the echoes of the explosion. The 'Sean, Sean, Sean' sung under the whistling and the instrumental sounds leading into the music seem to define the whole as nondiegetic. But the reverb added to the whistling gives it a spatial quality that allows us to imagine it in diegetic space. The ghostly whistling is repeated when a second explosion occurs closer to Juan; again the music seems to be identified as nondiegetic by its accompaniment. Then out of the smoke of a third explosion, Sean emerges like an apparition, accompanied by his motif, now without reverb, but still with its nondiegetic markers. The change in reverb according

---

142 When Morricone says that the theme 'expresses the dynamiter's nostalgia for his youth' (quoted in Hubbert 2011: 335), he leaves open whether the music does this by purporting to *be* from Sean's youth or just by expresssing the sentiment.

to the distance from Juan gives the motif a spatial quality that belies its identification as nondiegetic – a narrative sleight of hand that matches Sean's (for Juan magical) abilities with explosives.[143] Even if we cannot ascribe diegetic status to the music in these scenes, the whistled motif is set slightly apart from the rest of the music and seems (as do the themes in *Once Upon a Time in the West*) like an emanation of its character.[144]

Different from *For a Few Dollars More* and *Once Upon a Time in the West*, the film never shows us where Sean's music comes from. But that is the point: surrounding him with this elusive music surrounds him, for us, with an air of mystery, an echo of the mystery he is for Juan. He is an outsider in the (South-)West as much as Jill in *Once Upon a Time in the West*, but unlike her, he never grows into this world. He remains tangential to it, but at the same time connects its political struggle to the one he fled, and makes a political point at a time when politics had reached the western in a newly overt way.

d. 'Most melancholic of films' – *Once Upon a Time in America*

For a case study of music's role in the narrative construction of a film, *Once Upon a Time in America* is almost too pat an example. The narrative knot it ties itself into entails the possibility that most of what we see on the screen is nothing but an opium-fuelled dream (see Kaminsky 1983: 62; Martin 1998: 73–80; and Frayling 2000: 423–25). But even in its unusual intricacy, *Once Upon a Time in America* is instructive, not least with regard to the degree of experimentation Leone and Morricone brought to bear on a mainstream film with strong roots in genre cinema. That not everyone deemed such daring successful became clear when the American distributor slashed it by 81 minutes and recut it into a linear tale and a parody of itself (see Martin 1998: 59–66; and Frayling 2000: 458–63).

The film tells the story of a Jewish gang in New York in the 1920s and 1930s, with an epilogue in 1968, especially the story of the gang's leaders, Maximilian 'Max' Bercovicz and David 'Noodles' Aaronson, but also of co-gangsters Patrick 'Patsy' Goldberg, Philip 'Cockeye' Stein and little Dominic, and of their confidante 'Fat' Moe Gelly and his sister Deborah, the great and only half-requited love of Noodles' life.

The boys grow up to a life of not-so-petty crime, come to blows and worse with the local competition (resulting in a six-year prison sentence for Noodles), rise to riches as alcohol smugglers and proprietors of a Prohibition-era speakeasy, and become enmeshed in a different kind of conflict through their work as hired guns for the labour union movement.

---

143 Leone seems to have taken the religious symbolism quite seriously and explained that 'the Irishman […] was really a metaphor for Christ' (quoted in Frayling 2000: 317–18).

144 Partly responsible for this impression of an emanation are precise coincidences between music and diegetic actions, as in *Once Upon a Time in the West*. After the second explosion, the first tone of Sean's music after the introductory drum beats coincides with his removing his goggles; when he straightens his coat, his hand movement coincides with a Mickey Mousing guitar chord that binds the music to his person.

Max is always seeking new alliances and opportunities, while Noodles wants them to stay small and independent. To save his friends from Max's megalomaniacal plan to rob the Federal Reserve Bank, Noodles turns his friends in to the police over a minor smuggling job, hoping that a short jail term might restore Max to sanity. But after a shoot-out with the police, Noodles sees the corpses of Cockeye, Patsy and a horribly burned Max lying in the street. He flees to an opium den, his refuge from unbearable situations (e.g. the break-up with Deborah, sealed by Noodles raping her after she tells him that she is going to Hollywood), then flees from New York – without the collective funds of the gang, whose hiding place in a locker at the train station Noodles finds empty. 35 years later he is called back to New York and realizes that Max his still alive. The shoot-out was a set-up in which Patsy and Cockeye died while Max got away as planned, took the gang's money and went on to a career in politics and a marriage to Deborah, with whom he has a son. But due to his criminal activities, Max's career is in tatters, and to atone for his betrayal, Max asks Noodles to kill him before others do. But Noodles refuses to shoot Max, and refuses to accept the real story of his life and to destroy the memories of his love to Deborah and his friendship with Max.

The 1968 epilogue transforms the straightforward story of the rise and fall of a gangster into the tale of longing and loss, memory and regret, into the 'most melancholic of films' (Martin 1998: 54), and carries it beyond the purportedly autobiographical novel on which it is based, Harry Grey's *The Hoods* ([1952] 1997), which ends in the 1930s. But what makes this expansion of the story come to life is the film's syuzhet: those dizzying jumps across decades of the protagonists' lives that producer Arnon Milchan and the Ladd Company did not trust a US audience to comprehend or accept (while the film had its premiere in Cannes as cut by Leone, and was shown in Europe in that or a similar version; see Frayling 2000: 461 & 541; and Carlson 2001: 74).

The story takes place on three temporal levels: the mid-1920s, when the gang are in their teens; the early 1930s, when they have become successful criminals; and 1968, when Noodles is asked to reconstrue the story of his life. Apart from conventional compressions of story time into screen time, there are eight major temporal shifts.[145]

- The first 20 minutes show a jumble of images: men killing Noodles' girlfriend Eve and torturing Moe to learn where Noodles is hiding; Noodles in the opium den; Noodles' dead friends; the speakeasy; Noodles with Moe and at the empty locker. In the train station, Noodles walks through a door and returns 35 years later.
- In the second jump, we see old Noodles in Moe's bar revisit one of the key locations of his youth – the bathroom from which he used to observe Deborah practicing her ballet

---

145 Stuart M. Kaminsky, one of the film's scriptwriters, clarified the temporal structure of the script in an article published before the release of the film (see Kaminsky 1983). The temporal structure of the finished film itself (in its 'international' version) is as follows, simplified by leaving out jumps within temporal levels (chapter numbers refer to the DVD Regency Entertainment 2003): chapters 1–7: 1933; chs. 8–10: 1968; chs. 10–25: 1923–25; chs. 26–27: 1968; chs. 28–51: 1931–33; chs. 52–56: 1968; ch. 56: 1923–25; chs. 56–57: 1968; chs. 58–59: 1933.

routines, watching her through a hole in the wall. Once again he looks through the hole, we see his old face from the other side, but when the film cuts back into the storeroom, it cuts back to the teenage Deborah dancing.

- After an almost hour-long sequence showing us the gang's teenage years, the next jump comes when Noodles is brought to the penitentiary, after he stabbed rival gangster Bugsy for having shot young gang member Dominic. Max looks up to the inscription above the portal: 'Your youngest and strongest will fall by the sword.' After the cut we see the old Noodles in front of a mausoleum with the graves of his three friends that bears the same inscription.

- The old Noodles nervously walks along a street, in his hands a suitcase with the payment for the mysterious job he has been called to New York for. A frisbee flies through the air, a hand clutches at the suitcase, which becomes Max's hand clutching the suitcase with Noodles' possessions when he comes out of jail in 1931.

- During a tense exchange with Max on the night of Noodles' betrayal of his friends, he calls Max 'crazy', who starts to hit Noodles in rage. After the cut, Carol, Max's former lover, who in 1968 is living in a nursing home, explains to the old Noodles that Max had been afraid of going mad like his father, and that the shoot-out with the police may have been set up by him as his suicide.

- In the most generic flashback, during his final meeting with Max Noodles remembers how their friendship began, and dreams up images from their teenage years, images clearly implied to be in Noodles' mind. Far more straightforward than the other time jumps, this flashback leads back to the scene in which it originated.[146]

- After his refusal to shoot Max, and after Max may or may not have killed himself by throwing himself into a garbage truck, Noodles sees a cavalcade of 1930s cars with revellers in 1930s clothes, singing Irving Berlin's 'God Bless America', the song that opened the film (as diegetic music). It is not clear if he is seeing people on their way to a fancy-dress party, or if the walls between reality and fantasy (or compartments of Noodles' fantasy) are breaking down. After a cut we are back with him in the opium den in 1933, and the film ends with Noodles turning over on his bed, looking up at the ceiling and smiling blissfully at something only he can see.

It was Stuart Kaminsky who, even before the premiere of the film, pointed out that its structure entailed the possibility to understand large parts of it as a covert metadiegetic

---

146 This flashback appears (in different versions) in the shooting script (see Kaminsky 1983; Frayling 2000: 419), on the DVD used for this chapter, and in a version shown on European television, but not in other cuts (see Martin 1998: 65–66). One may deplore this 'montage of memories' and agree with Martin that 'there is no other temporal jump in the film which is as utterly conventional' (1998: 65–66). One may even quote Leone, who long before *Once Upon a Time in America*, advocated less conventional use of flashbacks. With an eye on Indio in *For a Few Dollars More* (1965), he said that 'the Americans had been using flashbacks in a very closed way [...]. This was a mistake; you have to let them wander like the imagination or like a dream' (quoted in Frayling 2000: 197). But though the montage adds a note of sentimentality to the final exchange of Noodles and Max, Leone did not make his name by prudently observing tenets of cinematic good taste, and *Once Upon a Time in America* is hardly a film afraid of sentimentality.

fantasy. In this reading Noodles, guilt-wrecked after having betrayed his friends and inadvertently caused their deaths, flees to the opium den to forget, and in his opium haze he not only remembers the gang's past, but also invents the future of an even greater betrayal by Max to dampen his own remorse (Kaminsky 1983: 62).

> This was an interpretation which apparently pleased Leone immensely. He even suggested that the time-jumping structure of the film could itself be understood as the agitated, backwards and forwards motion of Noodles' mind in the throes of his 'opium dream'. But it is important to note that, whenever he raised these matters, Leone would add a phrase that he was fond of using in relation to many topics, a phrase that translates roughly as: 'I say it here, and I deny it here.' For him the double reading, this oscillation between literal and subjective levels of representation, had to remain open. (Martin 1998: 74–75; see also Frayling 2000: 423–24, and Cumbow 2008: 109)

In the end, Kaminsky is sceptical of this 'fantasy hypothesis' because it is unclear how Noodles could have dreamt not just the outline of his and Max's future, but a panorama of life in 1968 correct in every detail (Kaminsky 1983: 72). But such literalness may miss the allure of the problem; that was certainly the case from Leone's perspective.

But whatever one thinks about this 'solution' to the form of the film, that form turns *Once Upon a Time in America* into a film about memory, and the flashback is its formal core.[147] Leone himself was quite clear about this; in the controversy about the Ladd Company's butchering of the film he stated: 'Because my film is about memory, when they take away my flashbacks, it is no longer my film' (Knee 1985: 4). Memory as psychological motive and filmic motif, and the flashback as its structural expression, run through *For a Few Dollars More*, *Once Upon a Time in the West* and *Duck, You Sucker!*, all of them built around memories invoked in flashback scenes. But the way in which music is part and parcel of the flashback structure is more complex and ambiguous in *Once Upon a Time in America* than in any of the earlier films.

e. *Once Upon a Time in America* – Three musical themes

The film provides yet another recombination of elements from Morricone's toolbox. Quitting the western setting changes the sounds Morricone can employ to anchor the music in the diegesis; but there is still the voice of Edda Dell'Orso, there is Morricone's preference for

---

147 Hardly less than a film about memory, *Once Upon a Time in America* is a film about betrayal: 'Films in which a central character is duped have, generally speaking, strikingly convoluted or baroque narrative forms. This is because every safe, classical assumption that the hero […] is on a straight line heading towards the truth […] is thrown completely out of kilter. […] In place of such certainties, we are plunged instead into a universe of […] appearances that always lie, of vertiginous traumas and hallucinations born of all-pervasive paranoia – which, cinematically, is rendered in perpetual shifts, inversions and clashes of narrative points-of-view' (Martin 1998: 41).

instruments approximating the human voice (this time the pan flute[148]), and there is the system of a small number of simple, easily recognizable themes.

As befits the sprawling tale, the music is less strictly organized than in *Once Upon a Time in the West*. There are historically fitting songs: 'God Bless America', 'Yesterday', 'Summertime', 'Night and Day'; there is Rossini's *La gazza ladra* overture as droll accompaniment to one of the gang's exploits; there is 'Amapola' as diegetic signature tune for Deborah; there is Chinese music in the opium den; there is jazz. The attachment of Morricone's themes to diegetic elements is systematic as in *Once Upon a Time in the West* (though one of them is, again a diegetic musical object), and the themes are not as sharply differentiated against each other and are varied more substantially over the course of the film.[149] My focus is on how three of the themes cross (or do not cross) borderlines between levels of narration, and how this relates to the structure of the film – a film in which the flashback ceases to be a localized element and takes over. The three themes are (as called on the soundtrack album) 'Deborah's Theme', 'Once Upon a Time in America', and the principal pan flute motif, 'Cockeye's Song'.

'Deborah's Theme'

Both 'Deborah's Theme' and 'Once Upon a Time in America' show conventional movements from one level of narration to another, and they serve – in my analysis and, I would argue, in the film as well – as a foil for 'Cockeye's Song'.

The point of 'Deborah's Theme' is its connection with 'Amapola', the music young Deborah uses for her dance practice. At first, the theme seems to represent less Deborah herself then Noodles' perception of her, nondiegetic music as focalization of his fascination. We first hear it when Noodles returns to the haunts of his youth and inspects the bathroom in Moe's bar whence he used to observe Deborah. With tender irony, Edda Dell'Orso's voice begins just when he opens the door and we see the humble location.

In the two scenes that show us (and Noodles) Deborah dance in the backroom, 'Deborah's Theme' and 'Amapola' are clearly differentiated. 'Deborah's Theme' captures Noodles' idea(l) of Deborah; 'Amapola' is part of the world he delves into when he looks through the hole in the wall.[150] The difference is reinforced by their treatment. Twice, Deborah interrupts 'Amapola' by taking the needle off the record. For her, this is functional music to practice her dancing. 'Deborah's Theme', in contrast, is handled with care. It is played all the way through even when Max interrupts Deborah's and Noodles' *tête à tête* by calling for Noodles.

---

148 In *The Hoods*, Cockeye plays harmonica (see Grey 1997: 13–14), but after *Once Upon a Time in the West*, the harmonica was not an option anymore, so Leone and Morricone chose the pan flute, according to Leone 'the most haunting of instruments – like a human voice *and* like a whistle' (quoted in Frayling 2000: 427).

149 Martin points out that Morricone seems to have designed several themes 'so that they can blur together [...]. All three are in the key of E (major and/or minor). [...] And all come to rest, at roughly the same key moment, on the 'hanging' note of D sharp' (Martin 1998: 44–45).

150 The differentiation is blurred, though, to ease the narration across 45 fabula years: 'Amapola' starts on the soundtrack while we still see the eyes of the old Noodles, indicating that what we are about to see are his memories of the scene (see also Miceli 2000: 303).

Its climactic phrase poignantly crowns Deborah's devastation of Noodles' hopes (she applies similes from the 'Song of Songs' to him, interspersed with sarcastic criticism, and finally states that her beloved is 'altogether lovable. But he'll always be a two-bit punk, so he'll never be my beloved. What a shame'), and it prepares their kiss. The long-held leading note Adrian Martin has remarked upon as common to themes in *Once Upon a Time in America* (Martin 1998: 44–45) underlies Noodles' wavering between Deborah and Max; only when he decides to go outside to meet Max do we get the tonic – he has sealed his fate with regard to Deborah, and the music confirms it.

But later the strict distinction begins to break down. When Noodles comes out of prison and visits the speakeasy for the first time, he meets Deborah again, and in their honour Moe conducts the band in 'Amapola'. Now the music is no longer at Deborah's mercy and is consequently played through, even though Deborah leaves the room before it ends, again severing her connection with it wilfully, and again making clear that this music means more for Noodles than for herself. But now the music is coordinated with the action in an unlikely way, implying careful arrangement of story facts. The dialogue between Deborah and Noodles ends just before the end of the melody. During the bridging chords before the repeat of the melody, we see Max stand impatiently in the door, and precisely with the start of the repeat he calls 'Noodles!' and once more cuts the connection between Noodles and Deborah. The narration has taken over diegetic music that so far had been under Deborah's control and makes it do its bidding.

The next scene goes further and interweaves both tunes while superficially respecting their distinction. When Noodles picks up Deborah at the theatre to take her to a restaurant, we appropriately hear 'Deborah's Theme', which also bridges the spatio-temporal leap from theatre to restaurant. But after its first two phrases, the melody is transformed into an introduction to 'Amapola', which – despite the musical connection – once again appears as diegetic music, played by a string orchestra hired by Noodles for the occasion. The pieces are separated by different levels of narration, and separated by the leap from theatre to restaurant (almost: the slight overlap of 'Deborah's Theme' into the restaurant scene is musical continuity editing, but also makes the pieces connect more easily). But the emotional charge of the situation allows the narration to join them up musically without making the audience wonder about the narrative 'category mistake'.

The final stage in merging the pieces occurs when Noodles visits Carol in the nursing home in 1968, and then Deborah at the theatre. When Noodles asks Carol about the woman on the photo in the home's entrance hall (it is Deborah, a benefactress of the institution), Carol denies knowing her; but the music answers for her with 'Deborah's Theme', guiding us to the theatre. But now the theme is interspersed with 'Amapola', which is part of the nondiegetic cue, played on a harpsichord. Ironically, the merging of the musics does not signify the coming together of the lovers, but the loss of Noodles' illusions: 'Amapola' has changed from a real-world object into another memory.

Figure 29: Cockeye playing his wooden pan flute in *Once upon a Time in America* (1984).

'Once Upon a Time'

'Once Upon a Time' (or 'Childhood Memories', a variant of the same material) is attached to the friendship of the gang. Even though we have heard it a few times by then, the scene that fixes this ascription follows their first criminal success. They have developed a method for recovering contraband alcohol that smugglers have to throw overboard when the harbour police threaten to catch them. We see the gang after the successful demonstration, newly and smartly dressed, bringing their earnings to the locker in the station, accompanied by 'Once Upon a Time' in a jaunty jazz arrangement, though one bizarrely including a pan flute, which we can see Cockeye play (Figure 29).

The music combines diegetic instrument and nondiegetic jazz band in an alloy that does not quite constitute the supradiegetic fusion of a number in a musical, but accompanies a moment of similar climactic function: narration and diegesis are in accord, and all is well with the world.

This double layering – of pan flute and jazz band, of diegetic and nondiegetic music – works as smoothly as it does because we have encountered the ingredients before, in a seemingly 'natural' progression from diegetic to nondiegetic. We first hear the tune when Cockeye plays it before the gang try to rob a drunk; the others take the melody up and whistle it: it will become their signature tune. Not long after Max is accepted into the circle, the tune, now nondiegetic and in a jazz arrangement, is played after he and Noodles have become friends. The march with the money only has to put together the diegetic and nondiegetic sides of the theme we have already seen (and heard). The narration 'takes up' music seems to originate in an autonomous, pro-filmic space, uses it to comment on the story because of the connotations attached to it; then the narration aligns itself with the diegesis and marches in step with it.

'Cockeye's Song'

Less straightforward is 'Cockeye's Song', which is not songlike at all, but just a reiterated arpeggio, mostly played not on a little toy flute like Cockeye's, but on a proper reed flute. We hear it for the first time before Noodles goes through the door that will bring him to Buffalo and through which he will return a few syuzhet seconds, but 35 fabula years later to the Beatles' 'Yesterday'. Like the bells in *For a Few Dollars More* for Indio's liberation from prison, it radiates meaningfulness without hinting at its meaning.

That is made up for by its next appearances. The first accompanies Max and Noodles being beaten to a pulp by competitor Bugsy and his men. The second follows the gang's return from their locker, once more underscored by the upbeat 'Once Upon a Time'. But when Dominic spots Bugsy and turns to run away before being shot, Cockeye's little wooden flute is replaced by the big, nondiegetic pan flute of fate. The connection with tragedy befalling the gang makes retrospective sense of the theme's first appearance in the wake of Max's, Patsy's and Cockeye's death and Noodles' flight from New York.

But then things become more confusing. The third time-jump brings us from the teenage Noodles being driven through the prison gates to Noodles in 1968 standing in front of the mausoleum allegedly containing his former friends' graves (and, according to a commemorative plate, having been built by himself). We are not surprised that as soon as Noodles opens the door 'Cockeye's Song' starts – that just confirms its conection with tragedy for the gang. The music ends when the door has closed. While it is open and the music lasts, Noodles looks around; when the music has ended, he opens the door once more, and, surprisingly, the music starts again (this time in mid-phrase). It even starts for a third time while Noodles is inspecting the graves.

Whereas the first coincidence of door mechanism and 'Cockeye's Song' fulfils the expectation of musical coordination one has for a Leone film, the second and third seem excessive and mechanical. But mechanical is just what the music is meant to be. At the third theme entry, Noodles looks up, as if irritated. When he initially inspects the mausoleum, we see dark patches on the pillar capitals; and the mechanical coordination of music and door makes these identifiable as loudspeakers: 'Cockeye's Song' is indeed diegetic music, technically coordinated with the door (and coordinated so precisely that it takes the door exactly as long to fully open as the first phrase of the tune) (Figure 30).

The mausoleum sene plays with the relationship of style, syuzhet and fabula. When we first hear 'Cockeye's Song', we hear it as nondiegetic music that carries the tragedy it is associated with into the scene. When we realize that it is diegetic, its relationship to the syuzhet changes: it is not part of the telling, but part of the tale. But that does not explain its place in the fabula. Instead, it raises a series of questions:

- The questions Noodles asks himself depend on his knowledge of the music. Either he knows it and wonders what it is doing in this place – in that case, he probably also knows the source of the theme's tragic connotations. If he does not know it, he wonders together with the audience what it means.

Figure 30: The loudspeakers in the mausoleum.

- For the audience, the question is where the music comes from. Up to this point, we have heard it only as nondiegetic music. Where would Noodles know it from? And might a diegetic origin of the music also explain its tragic connotations?
- The question the audience asks with regard to Noodles is whether *he* knows where the music comes from, and whether he wonders (or knows) who the sender of the musical message might be – that is, whether he knows more than we do, and whether we will learn the answers through him. If he does *not* know the music, he would know less than we do and miss its connotations; if that is the case, we hope that we will learn about the diegetic origin of the theme not *through*, but *with* him.

Our and Noodles' questions may differ, but result in a degree of psychological parallelism (see pp. 180–81). Someone in the diegesis is playing a game with Noodles, and the narration is playing a game with us – a double game, concerning both the diegetic origin of the theme and the construction and plot function of the mausoleum scene.

Eventually, the film provides a diegetic anchoring point for 'Cockeye's Song', one that in fabula terms precedes the mausoleum scene. After his timeout in the opium den after raping Deborah, Noodles returns to the speakeasy, where Max, increasingly volatile and power-mad, starts to quarrel with him. During the scene, we see Cockeye once again play on a little pan flute, though he has progressed to a silver one by now (Figure 31).

The scene also explains the repetitive simplicity of the theme. Cockeye is just doodling on his flute while the struggle between Max and Noodles unfolds (a diegetic sibling to Cheyenne's whistling theme in *Once upon a Time in the West*). But the diegetic 'explanation' of the theme's origin is incomplete. The problem is not that it appears earlier in the syuzhet. The later revelation of a diegetic source of music is not uncommon in film (see ch. V.iii for examples). Stranger is that 'Cockeye's Song' appears before this scene also with regard to fabula chronology – when Max and Noodles are beaten up by Bugsy's men, and when Bugsy shoots Dominic.

- We could account for that by assuming a diegetic origin for the theme that (as in *Once Upon a Time in the West*) lies even further in the past, but remains unacknowledged. In that case, Cockeye would, during the quarrel between Max and Noodles, only replay

Figure 31: Cockeye doodling on his silver pan flute and the origin of 'Cockeye's Song'.

something he already knows – an unconvincing explanation because it requires the double assumption of an earlier diegetic source for the music and of its suppression.

- Alternatively, we can use the 'opium-dream hypothesis' for a simpler construction of the syuzhet/fabula relationship. In the opium-dream explanation, everything we see and hear after Noodles' escape from the opium den would be his (re)visions, including the mausoleum scene, and we could imagine that he injects 'Cockeye's Song', which he had heard Cockeye play during his quarrel with Max, into that scene.

But the opium-dream hypothesis comes at the price of suspending narrative logic wholesale – anything goes. To make this interpretation convincing, one would have to claim that the quarrel in the speakeasy is a milestone of the gang's decline, which Noodles in his opium haze projects back upon the gang's history. Giovanna Jackson argued for such a reading: 'It is at this point, however [...] that the demise of Noodles begins: though never uttered the audience senses that Max has made the decision to dump Noodles' (Jackson 1989: 27). If this is the beginning of the end of their friendship, one could indeed imagine that Cockeye's doodling, even if it is entirely incidental, subconsciously registers with Noodles and retroactively throws its shadow over his recollections of the gang's story.

A further argument in favour of the opium-dream hypothesis involves the theme 'Poverty', connected to the life of the gang in their youth. It is the first nondiegetic music in the film, right after Noodles' escape from the opium den. The only music before that was 'God Bless America', Chinese music in the den and jazz for the end-of-prohibition party. With the first strains of 'Poverty' accompanying Noodles on his way to Fat Moe to get the key to the locker, we have entered the story proper after the initial jumble of images. But perhaps this narrative 'stabilization' also signifies the step from reality into Noodles' imaginings. This interpretation would be supported by the fact that 'Poverty' returns at the end of the film, when Noodles sees the 1930s revellers and we hear 'God Bless America' again – when, in the opium-dream explanation, Noodles' dream is beginning to break down.

- In an inversion of this argument one could hypothesize that it is the presence of the theme in the quarrel scene that marks the scene as crucial – that the semantic and affective load of the music, at this point purely derived from its previous nondiegetic use, is carried *into* the diegesis, even if only in the off-hand manner of Cockeye's doodling. In favour of this interpretation one could also point out that the quarrel scene is the last time we hear 'Cockeye's Theme' in the film.[151]

f. 'I say it here and I deny it here': Conclusions

The tangle of perspectives on 'Cockeye's Song' is only one of the musical games in *Once Upon a Time in America*. There is no central musical object as in *For a Few Dollars More*, no strict set of internal norms as in *Once Upon a Time in the West*. The labyrinth of *Once Upon a Time in America* is underpinned by a more diffuse musical structure, in which no element dominates, even though 'Cockeye's Song' may be the most intriguing one because its narrative equation cannot be solved without remainder. 'I say it here and I deny it here': Leone's way out of the conundrum of the film extends to its music.

Leone's films employ a limited range of musical means and of techniques of attaching music to images: recurring and rarely substantially changed themes and motifs with clear diegetic referents; precise coordination of music and diegetic events; sensory sounds, often related to the storyworld; diegetic musical objects, sometimes with crucial plot functions; the role of music in flashbacks; riddles attached to musical objects or other music. It is a trademark style (from which Morricone has profited as much as the films from his music). But it is not just a trademark style of composition; it is as much a style of weaving music into the narrative structure of a film.

ii. Life's troubled bubble broken: Musical metalepses in *The Truman Show*[152]

a. True life or false

The Truman Show (1998) offers any number of themes and readings. One can see it as a critique of reality TV, or of 'American parochialism' (Rayner 2003: 244), or of social control in our everyday lives; one can see it as an allegory of the relationship between god and creation (see Vittrup 2010), or of the father-son relationships so important in US fiction; one can see it as a reflection of the relationship between author and fictional figure (see

---

151 Sergio Miceli has suggested that to look for a logical account of the sequence of musical events may be pointless, and that 'we might say that this is only Cockeye's music because Leone has assigned it to him, after he had chosen it; consequently it is used in different ways in the film, according to [Leone's] wishes' (Miceli 2000: 304; my translation).

152 This case study is based on an article written in 2009 in German (Heldt 2010), which has been amended for this book.

Tieber 2010).[153] But it is also a film about the joy of playing with the structures of film, including levels of narration, and themes and form are bound up with each other.

The Truman Show tells the story of Truman Burbank (Jim Carrey), the first human being who has been born and grown up inside a fiction – in the television series *The Truman Show*, which has been constructed around him. When we meet him, he has a house and a wife (Laura Linney) in the pretty little seaside town of Seahaven. For him this is the world, but in reality it is a giant set built inside a giant dome, which – how not? – can be seen from space. Everyone around him, including his wife and his best friend, are actors; everyone is part of a big machine kept running to preserve the illusion of its reality in Truman's mind and to give the trajectory of Truman's life a shape satisfying for TV audiences around the world. The story begins when cracks appear in the façade: a studio light that falls from the 'sky' in front of Truman's feet; a car radio that lets Truman hear for a moment messages from the TV control centre. Truman begins to suspect that not all may be as it seems in his world, before he understands the truth and tries to break out of the prison of the fiction he is living in.

The double irony of his name is obvious. He is the only one in his world who is authentic, who is true. But he is also the only one who does not see the truth about his world, which is a great lie – a lie that uses Truman's blind authenticity as its USP, as a quality that sells itself to TV audiences, but also helps to sell products (via ads or product placement). That Truman is true only throws the inauthenticity around him into relief: 'There is no true life in the false one' [my translation], as Theodor Adorno stated 1951 in his *Minima moralia* (1980: 419).[154] (A minor irony concerns his surname Burbank, which alludes to the city in Los Angeles County that is home to media companies such as NBC, Warner, Disney and Viacom, the mother company of Paramount, which was the lead production company of *The Truman Show*.)

Different levels of fictionality and authorial or narrational control are central for the structure of the film. But *The Truman Show* is no classic case of embedded narration, of the orderly nesting of narrative levels (see Figures 32 & 33). In *Bride of Frankenstein* (1935), the Shelleys and Lord Byron sit by the fire, and Mary continues her story of Dr Frankenstein and his monster, the embedded story that forms the main part of the film.

In *The Truman Show*, the relationship of levels is more complex, because Truman attempts to break out of the fiction he finds himself stuck in. Apart from Truman, all protagonists of the embedded fiction (the TV series) know of its fictionality, and are in that sense located on the surrounding level of the diegesis of film, the level on which we also find its creator, Christof (Ed Harris), and the production personnel, and the film points out everyone's awareness of the fictionality of the fiction time and again. Seen from another angle, however, Truman is not located on a different level than the actors around him, because he is no fictional character, not the product of authorial invention, but authentically himself. The

---

153 For more wide-ranging readings of the film than this music-centred case study can provide see for example Bliss 2000: 169–82, or Rayner 2003: 227–58.

154 The German original of the phrase is 'Es gibt kein richtiges Leben im falschen.'

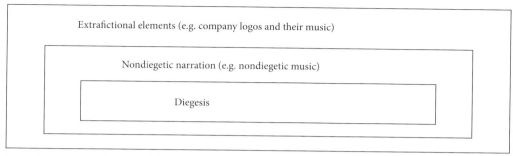

Figure 32: Structure of a standard fictional narrative film.

film shows the learning process of Christof, who has to realize that he is not the god of his little TV world and that Truman is not his creature, even if he fights this insight almost to the bitter end; the film also shows the learning process of Truman, who has to realize that what for him was the world is only a fiction, and that he has not even seen the real world (Figure 34).

The film makes this messy nesting of levels of fictionality and narrative control clear in different ways, even in its title: *The Truman Show* is both the title of the series the film is about, and the title of the film we see in the cinema; and the audience for Truman's life is both the audience of the series and us in the cinema. Just in case we might miss this trick, it is foregrounded in the title sequence: what we expect are the credits for the film *The Truman Show*, but what we get are the credits for the TV series *The Truman Show*, 'created by Christof', and here even the least attentive viewer should have understood that we are not watching the credits for the film. A title sequence has to effect the transition from extrafilmic reality into the fiction and its diegesis, and normally this process begins with the acknowledgement of the fictionality of the enterprise in the form of company logos

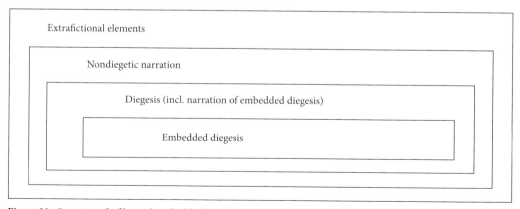

Figure 33: Structure of a film with embedded narration.

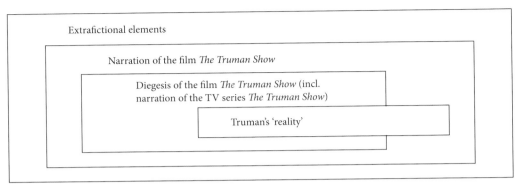

Figure 34: Structure of narration in *The Truman Show* (1998).

(see ch. II.ii). *The Truman Show*, too, has a title sequence, but it does not guide the viewer into the film, but throws us right into the middle of the fiction: into the narration of the TV series *The Truman Show*, and therefore into the diegesis of the film *The Truman Show*. If we add a timeline to the nesting of levels, it rather looks like this (Figure 35):

The acknowledgement of the made-ness of a film that is normally the task of a title sequence is avoided, but, dialectically, this only directs our attention more strongly towards the fictionality of the events on the screen. An authorial agency that veils its presence must have an agenda. There does not seem to be a space outside of the film's diegesis, and that makes us suspicious. And indeed this refusal of the film to admit its own fictionality is a crucial part of its strategy of narrative ambiguity.

The music we hear with this 'wrong' title sequence (Burkhard Dallwitz's 'It's a Life') fits the bill. A generic, repetitive cue with piano, synthesizer and percussion: fast-food music, fitting for a TV series, but hardly for a big-budget film. This impression is reinforced when we later see the music for the series being made in the studio. In the real world, the theme

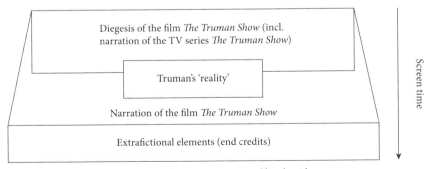

Figure 35: Structure of *The Truman Show* as it presents itself in the title sequence.

music of a TV series successful around the globe might allow more musical luxury; with its clichéd TV music the film underlines the trick of its opening.

Nota bene

Music in *The Truman Show* comes from different sources: Mozart's 'Rondo alla turca'; the slow movement from Chopin's second piano concerto; muzak and pop; original music by Burkhard Dallwitz; a piece by Polish composer Wojciech Kilar; music by Philip Glass (both original and from previous film scores). The origin of cues is mentioned only if relevant for the use of music in a scene or on a particular level of narration (cue titles refer to the CD *The Truman Show*, Milan/WEA 7313835850-2 [1999]). The question of origins is legitimate, but not central to this study, which looks at the film as a text, and at its music as a function of that text. The genesis of that text would be a different topic.[155]

*

That the narrative levels of *The Truman Show* are not cleanly nested inside each other does not mean that such nesting would not be an aspect of the film. When Truman meets his 'father', the film demonstrates how that works. The first indication is given when the image cuts away from the dialogue between Truman and his friend Marlon (Noah Emmerich) to the TV studio, while the music underscoring the conversation continues. We do not know if only we can hear it or the audience of the TV show too; the continuation of the music could just be continuity editing. The music continues further across the cut to Truman meeting his father,[156] and yet further for images of a bar where people watch the programme. Still we cannot be sure if the music is part of the TV series or nondiegetic on the level of the

---

155   However, in her study of minimal music in film scores, Rebecca Eaton points out that pieces with minimalist features are used in scenes that have to do with Truman's (thwarted) attempts to escape from Seahaven, and surmises that 'perhaps Weir did not intend for minimalism to signify escape, but rather Truman's impotence to escape' (Eaton 2008: 205). She even extends this interpretation to music that can be allocated to the TV series, and wonders if the choice of a minimalist idiom for such cues could be read as 'perhaps not a direct representation of what Truman feels, but what Christof wants him to feel, what he wants the viewer to feel too' (Eaton 2008: 207). This may be supported by Peter Weir's statement that for the TV series he was 'determining the music that the show's creator, Christof, would have chosen' (in his booklet text for the soundtrack CD, Milan/WEA 7313835850-2 [1999]).
      Sources of pre-existing music may be relevant in yet another sense, that of (ironic) intertextual references. Just one example: the cue that accompanies Truman's decision to leave his life as a fictional figure for the real world towards the end of the film is from Glass's music for *Mishima* (1985), a film about the eponymous Japanese writer. Mishima is famous for having committed ritual suicide in 1970, after a failed *coup d'état*, and so a piece that opened a film about the end of Mishima's life now ends a film about the beginning of a new life for Truman. (My thanks for this observation go to Sung-A Joy Chang.)
156   The music continues with regard to the narrative logic of the film, not with regard to its real-world origin. When Truman gets up to meet his 'father', music from Philip Glass' music for *Anima mundi* (1992) is replaced by a cue by Burkhard Dallwitz. But the change does not affect how we understand the music in the narrative structure, and stylistically cues are sufficiently similar not to jar.

221

Figure 36: Image from a 'diegetic camera' in *The Truman Show*.

film. But when we return to the studio, Christof demands 'Fade up music!', and we see studio musician and technicians play on their audiences' heartstrings. Finally, the music is clearly located as nondiegetic music for the TV series, and the ostentatious reveal of the diegetic reality of the music (diegetic on the level of the film[157]) makes that over-clear, so much so, in fact, that one wonders whether things can really be that simple (as indeed they are not).

Even without such drastic deconstruction of the potency of cheap music, other scenes also locate music on the level of the TV series. A more subtle example is the scene in which Truman 'remembers' the 'death' of his 'father' on a sailing boat when he was a kid. Truman remembers the event in the oval, slightly pixellated images that imply images filmed by a special camera of the TV series (normally in a secret location) (Figure 36).

These images tell us that what we see is not what's in Truman's mind, but images placed on the screen by the TV production, images the audience in front of the TV can see (as well as we). That lets us suspect that the music for these images (Burkhard Dallwitz's 'Flashback') is also audible to the TV audience. Truman may be thinking of something completely different while he is sitting on the beach than what the series wants its viewers to believe (that he would like to get away from Seahaven, for example). The disillusioning calculatedness of the scene, including slow-motion pictures of the father drowning, complete with drippy minor-mode piano, makes it very unlikely that we are to understand the music as nondiegetic

---

157 Rebecca Eaton calls this music 'meta-diegetic because it employs a secondary narrator – not the narrator of the film, but the narrator of the TV show' (Eaton 2008: 192–93), though that changes the meaning of Genette's term: in his system, 'meta-diegetic' is what happens in the embedded narrative (in this case, music that is diegetic on the level of the TV show). Music that is nondiegetic for the audience of the film *The Truman Show* she calls 'meta-nondiegetic' (2008: 192–93).

on the level of the film: it is staged as nondiegetic music of the TV series, as just another example of its strategy of manipulation.

So far, so straightforward. But in other scenes the attempt to assign the music to a level of narration produces questions and ambiguities.[158] The rest of this case study shows such ambiguities in three sets of increasingly equivocal examples. Taken together, they could be understood as a strategy that is part and parcel of the media critique that is one of the film's agendas.

b. Pre-existing music and the world of Seahaven

The first example concerns music we understand as part of the 'reality' of Seahaven – the innermost box of the nested levels of narration. Truman drives to work, and the voice of a radio announcer lets us conclude that he is listening to his car radio. The announcer starts during an overhead shot of Truman's car; then we are inside his car, looking at Truman from the perspective of the radio(!), while the announcer seems to pre-empt Truman's answer to one of his questions. When Mozart's 'Rondo alla turca' (from the piano sonata K331) starts, we see another long shot of the car.

The music can be understood as diegetic on the level of the TV series, though its point of audition is not Truman's. When the 'Rondo' also underscores Truman's way on foot through town, his conversation with a newspaper seller, etc., we realize that there are visual ellipses, while the music continues. The music has become displaced from its putative source in the radio and surrounds Truman's entire morning routine (and we have to assume that what we are hearing is not what is coming out of Seahaven's car radios anymore, because that routine takes too long for the piece). Again, shots in an oval frame indicate that the images can be seen by the TV audience, and we assume that they can hear the music as well, and that the shift of the music from a diegetic to a nondiegetic position in the syuzhet of the TV series (the images of Seahaven) is part of its narrative strategy, which the film once more shows us at its smooth work.

It is an 'intradiegetic variant' of the implied author. The makers of the TV series *The Truman Show* choose both the series' diegetic music (i.e. the music Truman and the actors in Seahaven can hear) and its nondiegetic music (i.e. the music only the TV audience can hear – and we in the cinema). In the 'Rondo alla turca', they have chosen a piece that does diegetic *and* nondiegetic duty, blurring the line between levels, the better to bamboozle its enthralled audience. And of course the makers of the film *The Truman Show* have chosen for

---

158 That applies not just to music. Images identified as coming from the 'TV cameras' are often combined with shots whose status is unclear (see Rayner, who points out that the inconsistency' in the camera identification 'implies [...] an observation beyond Christof's production' [2003: 248; see also Kuhn 2011: 345–47]). That even applies to the image introducing the sailing boat 'flashback', which is not unambiguously assigned to the TV series (Rayner 2003: 249).

this purpose a piece so trite, so exceedingly well-known, that it underlines the deconstruction of media manipulation in the starkest terms – so stark indeed that it acquires its own triteness by association. The taint of triviality spreads even via the attempt to unmask it, another one of the film's dialectic ironies.

A scene ten minutes later brings the matter to a head. Again, Truman is on his way to work, and again we hear is the 'Rondo alla turca'. But are we still to imagine that it is coming from Truman's car radio? Even Truman, used to the repetitiveness of his existence, would have become suspicious. In any case, now the music does not even begin in his car, but with an aerial long shot of Seahaven, and continues when we see Truman leave his car and arrive at the newspaper kiosk. Now we have to assume that the 'Rondo' is the usual (nondiegetic) morning music of the series, and that the first scene using the piece was either an exception (once in a blue moon the series may be able to use the piece as diegetic music in Seahaven as well), or that the 'Rondo' we heard in the earlier scene overlaid whatever was actually coming out of Truman's radio – as with the images of the 'death' of Truman's 'father', the series might just suggest things to their audience that bear no relation to what actually goes on in Seahaven.

Taken together, both scenes produce mild ambiguity. The simplest explanation is that the makers of the TV series control diegetic *and* nondiegetic music, and that in the first 'Rondo alla turca' scene they use the same music for both. But this requires a further assumption when the 'Rondo' is used once more as morning music: (1) Either we are witnesses to an unlikely coincidence of diegetic and nondiegetic series music; (2) or we have to assume that what the series suggests to be diegetic music in Seahaven to satisfy the expectations of its viewers is not what really comes out of the radios in Seahaven. Whichever explanation we prefer, both help to make the 'reality' of Seahaven appear as treacherous as it is, not just for Truman, but also for us, who have to make sense of the levels of narration. (However, it may be pointless to search for a reading that makes sense with regard to the film's narrative construction. A symbolic reading may be more straightforward: the 'Rondo' mirrors the repetitiveness of Truman's life, both generically, as a form based on a recurring refrain, and in this instance, which restricts itself to repetitions of the first 24 bars of Mozart's piece.[159])

c. Nondiegetic music and levels of narration

Several scenes uses music that broadly fits the stylistic model set by the title sequence, but in situations that make it unlikely that the narration of the TV series would use it in that way. In these scenes, music reacts to Truman's doubts or insights. He realizes that something is amiss, and it seems, at least at first, implausible that the TV team would let the music react to those moments as emphatically as it does. The question is how plausible we find the assumption that this music has been chosen by the makers of the series to react to Truman's

---

159 The observation has been made by Marie Bennett in a current Ph.D. project (Keele University) on Mozart's music in film.

behaviour, and from what point we assign it to the narration of the film, underlining Truman's growing understanding of his situation.[160]

- Truman has grown doubtful of the honesty of his wife, and secretly follows her on his bike on her way to work as a nurse. The energetically repetitive music for his pursuit ('The Beginning' from Glass' music for *Anima mundi* [1992]) fits the situation perfectly. But where is it coming from? Is it reasonable to assume that Christof's team would take up Truman's doubts and make them part of the show, when generally they do all they can to quell Truman's concerns? The film shows through oval special-camera images that on the image track the series pursues Truman's pursuit (that is the series' *raison d'être*, so it does not have much of a choice). But the music reinforces the idea that we are witnessing a development in the relationship between Truman and his wife, and Christof's best hope may be that viewers assume that Truman doubts his wife's fidelity, not her reality.

- After the already mentioned mistake involving the mix-up of radio programme and staff signals which allows Truman to listen to TV production staff, we hear soothing pseudo-classical music that cuts out when he switches off his car radio, locating it in the diegesis of the series: an attempt to calm down Truman. The music immediately after that accompanies questions triggered in Truman's mind because of the mistake. The repetitive texture (from Glass' music for *Powaqqatsi* [1988]) fits the stylistic bill of the TV series, but underlines that something is fermenting inside Truman. To assume that the series would assuage Truman's doubts by feeding soothing music into his radio, but then use nondiegetic music to point out to the TV audience that something upsetting has happened, would be implausible. We would have to assume a calculated attempt to make Truman's growing doubts into a feature of the series, but given the risk that Truman's doubts mean for its very foundations, that would be a stretch.

  It would be simpler to locate the *Powaqqatsi* music on the level of the film, because there makes eminently good sense to stress Truman's growing realization of his situation. But this raises the question what sense it would make for the film to use music that fits the stylistic template of the series it deconstructs. This becomes even more obvious when, after a brief break, the music starts again, but now precisely coordinated with Truman's movements as he tries out his theory that he might be the one controlling what happens in Seahaven (the music stops when he stops a truck with a hand gesture). If this is TV series music, then the musician is able to react to (and indeed pre-empt) Truman's actions with alarming agility.

---

160 Rebecca Eaton accounts for the uniformity of much of the musical material in the film by arguing that the narration of the film and Christof both use a minimalist idiom to stress Truman's entrapment, albeit for different reasons (see Eaton 2008: 206–08). But whether one finds this plausible or not, it does not answer the question to what level of narrative control we assign which bits of the music, and for what reasons and with what degree of certainty.

- The same question already comes up earlier when Truman recognizes the actor who used to play his father (i.e. the man who for him *is* his father, the father who was supposed to have died 20 years before) and who seems to have sneaked back into the series as an extra. The authorities are quick to spot the problem and remove the 'father' from the scene, while everyone around tries to prevent Truman from following his father and his attackers. The production team, in short, does all it can to head off a threat, but the music underlines the moment with a dramatic percussive cue unlikely to have been chosen by the makers of the series. But again the cue fits the template of music unambiguously locatable on the series level.
- The same applies to the scene showing Truman's attempt to escape from Seahaven in his car, an attempt in which he is impeded at every corner, because he cannot go anywhere without coming to the ends of his world, and the production of the series has to prevent his reaching those ends under any circumstances. One of the actors at a roadblock by the nuclear power station that supposedly has had an accident makes a mistake and addresses Truman by name, although he has never met him in the fictional world of the series. Again the music (Burkhard Dallwitz's 'Underground') forcefully underlines Truman's surprise and subsequent attempt to break through the roadblock. The music makes sense if we locate it on the level of the film, not if we assign it to that of the series, which again it fits stylistically.

d. Music on the level of the film (or not?)

There are more examples that make most sense if we assign them to the film, not the TV series, but involve music heard before, with different consequences for their localization:

- Truman has managed to escape from the all-seeing cameras, and Christof decides for the first time ever to interrupt the broadcast to have time to search for Truman. For the search of the entire TV crew we hear a variant of the music heard in the scene showing Truman's doubts and omnipotence fantasy after the car radio mistake (see above). In that scene, the scales seemed to tip towards locating the music on the level of the film. To hear it again in a scene in which the TV series is not broadcast reinforces that interpretation – the film seems to be unambiguous in this case.
- Christof and his team are staring into their screens in the studio for a glimpse of the fugitive Truman. Finally, Christof spots him in a boat and gives the order to resume broadcast – he has finally decided to make Truman's attempt to escape a part of the show (fittingly when Truman is recaptured by the camera: the invisible Truman is useless for TV, and visibility is more important than the question whether his belief in the reality of his world remains intact or not). But the music starts when we see

the studio monitor showing the sailing boat: a moment *before* Christof says 'Resume transmission!' That would mean that the music is there for *our* benefit, and is not part of the series. But it is based on the cue used for Truman's reunification with his 'father', where its identity as TV series music was made blatantly clear by the reveal of the music-making in the studio. Has the film now taken over the music of the series for its own purposes – in this case music from the culmination of the father-and-son story for the culmination of the (quasi-)father-and-son story of the film? But what does it say about the film that it would reuse music the series used for its most shamelessly manipulative moment; or rather for the moment the film showed most strongly to be shamelessly manipulative?

- The music that accompanies Truman's flight (Burkhard Dallwitz's 'Raising the Sail') ends mid-phrase when the boat collides with the wall of the dome, but we cannot be sure how to read the moment. Is the music nondiegetic on the level of a series that has made its peace with the escape of its title character, and is trying to milk it for the last drop of drama? Or is it nondiegetic on the level of the film, which underlines the shock of the crash for us in the cinema? And does the distinction matter any more?

While these scenes rather tip towards the level of the film, which has replaced the series as the locus of dramatic interest (while the series is falling apart before our eyes), at the very end things take yet another turn, and we are back with the musical tricks of Christof and his team. When Truman finally touches the wall of the dome, Wojciech Kilar's 'Father Kolbe Preaching' is heard. With its accompaniment of repeated block chords and its simple, tonal melody, it is close enough to the musical tone of the series (and the film), yet different in its naïve simplicity and its conventional piano-and-strings instrumentation – a fitting balance for Truman's terrible epiphany (and fitting music for the piling-up of religious imagery in this scene; see Eaton 2008: 212–13). But Kilar's music is only an interlude, and ends when Christof barks at Truman to say something since he is on live television. For the moment of Truman's decision to leave his gilded cage, and for the subsequent jubilation of TV viewers around the world, we are back with the synthesizer music of the series, in the shape of a jubilant cue from Philip Glass' music for *Mishima* (1985). It is not immediately clear how we are to read the music, but then one of the TV managers gives the order to cease transmission, and on the push of a button the music ends, which locates it firmly on the level of the series.

This is more than just another example for the meandering of the music between levels of narration, because it may make us reconsider some of those earlier moments – moments that suggested that we locate music on the level of the film, because it seemed implausible that the TV team would direct our attention at Truman's growing doubts. But more or less any music in the film could have been chosen by the makers of the series if they are prepared to celebrate even Truman's escape and the series' downfall with jubilant music – a downfall that is also their greatest triumph as makers of reality TV. Truman's breakthrough to reality is as much part of the nexus of total entertainment as everything else in the series, and the reactions of the viewers in front of the TV screens the film shows us demonstrate that they at least are taken in by this totality.[161]

*

Throughout the film, the music weaves inconsistently in and out of levels of fictionality and narrative agency, does not only not achieve a consistent distinction between levels, but not even a consistent movement from the level of the series to that of the film. We could argue with David Bordwell that films tend not to be narrationally consistent and use whatever is at their disposal to tell their stories effectively (see Bordwell 2008: 126). But the set-up of *The Truman Show* means that it hardly matters whether the inconsistency is strategic or pragmatic. The zig-zag course of the music blends the musical strategies of the fictional TV series and the film into each other. It is a film *about* media manipulation and exploitation, but it is also a film that fails to clarify how much its means differ from that of the series – a lack of clarity that is the point of the film.[162] The TV audiences we see on-screen are one of its key elements. They hold a mirror up to our own media reception. Once again: 'There is no true life in the false one.' Do we too fall for the false one, like the viewers of *The Truman Show* we have seen in *The Truman Show*?

iii. *Far from Heaven, Breakfast at Tiffany's,* Hollywood melodrama and the retrospective prolepsis[163]

a. Present film

In what tense do films tell their stories? The question is rarely central for the way we think about films – different from, say, a novel, which firmly engraves the tense into its narrative voice(s), into the verb forms used by its narrator(s). The novelistic default setting is the past tense. Events have taken place, and the telling happens in the knowledge of their order, causality and outcome, a knowledge used to let the reader know what is necessary to understand the story, but also to follow it with curiosity. That events lie in the past does not mean that a story could not arouse suspense or surprise; that is just a question of what information the narration has access to and what it dispenses when.[164] Other solutions are possible. Not a few (and indeed an increasing number of) novels are told in the present tense, and some even use the future tense (see Chatman 1978: 79–84).

---

161 See also Rayner (2003: 251–52), who points out that Truman's espace uses no less clichéd story tropes than his entrapment in Seahaven.

162 This fuzziness of levels is also crucial for Michael Bliss's reading of the film (2000: 169–70).

163 This case study is based on an article written in 2007 in German (Heldt 2008), which has been amended for this book.

164 In David Bordwell's terms the 'knowledge' and 'communicativeness' of the narration (1985: 57–61).

Even a 'presentist' narration, however, does not have to follow events with breathless simultaneousness: most show in their storytelling strategies that the narration knows of the eventual outcome of things and dispenses information accordingly – what is called 'historical present'.

But what about film? Deictic means as obvious as the tense of a verb in a written text film does not have at its disposal; a cinematographic picture seems to show nothing but its own presence, and by extension its present-ness:

> It is commonplace to say that the cinema can only occur in the present time. Unlike the verbal medium, film in its pure, unedited state is absolutely tied to real time. To read 'John got up, dressed, and took a taxi to the airport' takes only a fraction of a second; to watch it could theoretically take as long as to do it. (Chatman 1978: 84)

Of course Chatman compares narratological apples and oranges. In an important sense, the literary equivalent of his unedited film scene would not be the narrator telling us about John's actions, but a dialogue passage uninterrupted by a narrator: equivalent not with regard to informational content, but with regard to the implicit source of information, with regard to the fact that such a dialogue would be understood by the reader as a part of the 'mimetic stratum', part of the 'real world of the fictional universe' (Stam, Burgoyne and Flitterman-Lewis 1992: 114). To read such a passage – or, rather, to read it aloud as the spoken language it pretends to be – would take roughly as long as it would take 'in reality'.

What in the average film is radically different from the average novel is, in André Gaudreault's terms, the relationship of 'monstration' and 'narration', of showing and telling (see Gaudreault 1987 & 2009). In most novels, narration dominates, and the narrator calls up only little bits of 'monstration': direct speech, letters, etc. – anything speaking in a voice other than that of the primary narrator. In a film, these mimetic bits expand and may make us forget what betrays a narrating agency: the framing of images, camera movements, cuts, nondiegetic music, etc. Fittingly, Chatman continues thus:

> But, of course, almost all films are elliptically edited (Andy Warhol's and Michael Snow's experiments are rare exceptions). Like the author the filmmaker routinely counts on the viewer's capacity to reconstruct or supply deleted material that he feels is too obvious to show. (Chatman 1978: 84)

Elliptical narration, i.e. the selection of relevant information and the resulting sequence of shots, can in itself be seen as a marker of temporal perspective. The narration knows what is going to happen and chooses the bits of the 'mimetic stratum' that need to be shown: 'the "editing" activity of the film narrator makes it possible to inscribe a true narrative past tense on the story' (Gaudreault 2009: 86). But film as a sequence of shots separated by cuts, dissolves, etc. (as unrealistic as such a way of experiencing the world is compared to our uncut perception of reality) is so much the standard technique of filmic narration for us that we are rarely aware of its consequence for the temporal perspective of a film. In the absence of other temporal markers, we are likely to experience a film as a running present rather than the narration of a closed series of events. Such temporal markers can be introduced into a film with varying obviousness. Typical examples are:

- A voice-over in the past or future tense (visualized or not). A past-tense voice-over locates its tale in the past, while one in the future tense indicates that the main story is told in the knowledge of its progression, pre-empted by the voice-over (at least if we assume that it relates actual future events, not just hypothetical ones, which would produce a quasi-prolepsis [Ireland 2005: 591]).
- A full audiovisual flashback or flashforward, with the same temporal implications. Flashforwards are far rarer in film than flashbacks, probably because they so clearly shatter the illusion of a 'cinema […] in the present time' (Chatman 1978: 84), and foreground the way the narration steers our understanding of the story.

A flashforward belongs to a broader category of temporal ordering in narrative Genette calls a prolepsis (with analepsis as its past-facing complement): 'any narrative manoeuver that consist of narrating or evoking in advance an event that will take place later' (Genette 1980: 40). A fleeting anticipation of future events within the primary narrative Chatman calls 'foreshadowing': the production of premonitions either through the 'semination of anticipatory satellites', i.e. little hints, or through 'inferences drawn from existents', i.e. assumptions regarding the probable continuation of events on the basis of those already witnessed (Chatman 1978: 59–62).

Nondiegetic music is often used for such advance evocation. In *The Sea Hawk* (1940), Geoffrey Thorpe meets Doña Maria on the ship that brings her to England with her father, the new Spanish ambassador. The lyrical version of Thorpe's theme begins when he enters the cabin, but before he has noticed Maria: the narration tells us love is in the air long before the lovers themselves know it (see also p. 128). Not that we would not suspect this anyway, because we know how such stories go: 'inferences drawn from existents' and musical anticipation work hand in hand to leave no doubt. Typical to the point of cliché is such musical anticipation in thrillers and horror films, where they are part of the 'implicit contract' between film and audience, which wants to be artfully scared and expects hints and red herrings as part of the game (see ch. IV.i). When in *The Descent* (2005) the women set out on their caving expedition, the ominous soundscape leaves no doubt that things are unlikely to end well. (More precisely, we know that we are watching a horror film and expect that at least some of the women will come to a sticky end. What the music confirms is that the film will keep the horror contract, and on that meta-level the scary music is rather reassuring.)

But this chapter is about a kind of anticipation that shows itself for what it is (and therefore its past-tense implication) only in retrospect: a retrospective prolepsis.[165] The starting point of my argument is once again the question where the music comes from, or more precisely, what consequences for our understanding of a film might arise from a particular way of changing where the music comes from during a film. Narratologically, the least remarkable change is that from diegetic to nondiegetic music (see also ch. II.iv.f). Music originates in the diegesis, whence it derives significance and its capacity to nondiegetically comment upon or connect later scenes (later in fabula terms). Important is that in such cases, the film leaves the fiction of an autonomous pre-filmic reality intact. The transition from diegetic to nondiegetic music implies that a narrating agency observes what happens in the storyworld, and reacts to it by selecting music suitable for its purposes. Of course most films are imbued with temporal perspective simply because the narration does not 'follow' diegetic developments in 'real time', but selects what we need to know (see above). But crucially, this does not affect the integrity of the implied autonomous pre-filmic reality. Things get more interesting, though, if the music moves in the opposite direction, as it does in the following example.

b. Dancing to the music of time: *Far from Heaven*

Retrospection is inscribed into *Far from Heaven* (2002) in any case, a necessary feature of a film whose stylistic self-awareness is no mannerism, but the core of its attempt to invoke Douglas Sirk's by then canonic 1950s melodramas in a way that echoes the models and shows their historical distance at the same time, with critical awareness, perhaps even subversion, but without overt irony (see e.g. Willis 2003: 134–37; Richardson 2006; and Gill 2011: 12–14). The hyperprecision with which the film resurrects its 1950s (film) world can be seen as a distancing gesture in itself: so perfect did things look neither in reality nor in Sirk's films – a 'better-than-the-original copy' (Gill 2011: 24), a simulacrum in Umberto Eco's sense.

---

165 A retrospective prolepsis differs from a flashforward whose place in the causal chain of the fabula is understandable only in retrospect (see Bordwell 1985: 79 or Branigan 1992: 42 for examples). I am interested in cases that do not involve re-ordering of fabula events in the syuzhet, but musical discourse – initially unmarked as a temporally relevant manoeuvre – that turns into (i.e. retrospectively turns out to be) story fact. Such cases work also slightly differently than foreshadowing that does not show itself as such when it occurs, but is later 'cashed in' by the story. Such foreshadowing typically involves bits of diegesis that anticipate diegetic development (a phrase of dialogue that turns out to be prophetic, a diegetic object that will become important etc.), while (most of) my examples involve the crossing of levels of narration.

A 'retrospective prolepsis' is also different from layering of analepsis and prolepsis: a character remembering plans she once had for her future, or a character anticipating being told about something that has happened (in the past of that future) (see Genette 1980: 48–85, especially 79–85).

Plot-wise, the link to Sirk and the acknowledgement of historical distance are provided by overabundance. The conflicts that drive Sirk's films would not have worked for a modern audience, not even in an exercise in retrospection. Haynes' script raises the bar and layers the conflicts. In *Far from Heaven*, we have not just the class conflict between middle-class housewife and gardener from *All That Heaven Allows* (1955), not just the racial conflict from *Imitation of Life* (1959), but both rolled into one and further into the 'drama of heterosexual discontent' (Willis 2003: 132) of Sirk's *Written on the Wind* (1956). The latter is recast in *Far from Heaven* as a conflict between conventional marriage and homosexuality; a topic that in the Hays Code Hollywood of the 1950s could at best have been broached indirectly. Model housewife-and-mother Cathy Whittaker (Julianne Moore) finds out that her husband Frank (Dennis Quaid) is gay. All attempts to 'cure' him naturally fail, while Cathy, due to the increasing tension in her relationship with Frank, falls in love with her black gardener, Raymond Deagan (Dennis Haysbert), a relationship that breaks under the strain of the racism endemic in the small-town idyll of Hartford. It is an unlikely piling-up of conflicts, but that may have been necessary to give a modern audience at least a glimpse of the slightly feverish atmosphere of a Sirk film.

To get the 80-year-old Elmer Bernstein for the film was part of the retrospective programme. A composer who had earned his spurs when Sirk made his best-known films (even if Bernstein was anything but a living fossil in 2002), Bernstein wrote his first film score in 1951 for the sports movie *Saturday's Hero*. With *The Man with the Golden Arm* (1955) or *Walk on the Wild Side* (1962), he was one of the composers who introduced jazz into Hollywood scoring. But like most of his colleagues he worked for a range of films: thrillers such as *Sudden Fear* (1952), war movies such as *The Great Escape* (1963), epics such as *The Ten Commandments* (1956), western such as *The Magnificent Seven* (1960), dramas such as *Sweet Smell of Success* (1957) or *To Kill a Mockingbird* (1962), used by Haynes as a temp track for *Far from Heaven* (see Jeffries 2003). Bernstein did not work with Sirk, and is not known as a composer for melodramas. He did score films with melodramatic elements, e.g. *Desire under the Elms* (1958), *God's Little Acre* (1958) or *Some Came Running* (1958), but nothing in the Sirkian mould: 'We called them weepies, and they weren't our kind of thing at all. We were into dark, cutting-edge movies, not pictures for women with Rock Hudson in them' (Bernstein in Jeffries 2003). For *Far from Heaven*, he delivered an Oscar-nominated score that fits snugly into Haynes' retro exercise.

But style is only one of the music's contributions to the look back the film takes, and how music is built into its narrative structure has its own role to play. Relationships are crucial for the plot, and given the leitmotivic traditions of 1950s Hollywood scoring, it makes sense that the music assigns both of them a theme. The one linked to Cathy and Frank is also the theme music for the film (and it is 'their' theme not least because their story is central to the film): a tentative piano melody, which after a brief woodwind passage re-enters in orchestral splendour, as can be expected from a retro Hollywood film. Here the historical model shines through: the autumnal trees, the establishing shots of the small town of Hartford, even the little blue car, all reach back to the title sequence of *All That Heaven Allows* (albeit with slight displacements; see Willis 2003: 131). A piano also features in the title sequence of *All That Heaven Allows*, though not at the start, but as an interjection (more about which later) – another displacement announcing that shows its knowingness in the echoes of its models as well as the deviations.

When the theme accompanies the credits, it is – beyond generic appropriateness – still fairly unspecific. It could be linked to the setting or to Cathy, who towards the end of the title sequence is picking up her daughter from ballet class. The link to Cathy and Frank develops over time. We hear the theme when Cathy is bringing Frank – who in shamelessly clichéd manner has to 'stay longer in the office' one evening – something to eat and catches him kissing another man. Significantly, the theme does not underscore the *in flagranti* moment: it peters out when Cathy enters the office building, and is replaced by unspecific suspense music when she wanders through the corridors – the theme itself begins to attach itself to Cathy and Frank's relationship, not to its breakdown. That is reinforced when the theme is used for the dinner party the two give to show their social world that everything is fine and dandy. Here, the theme accompanies the arrival of the guests and could be linked not just to Cathy and Frank, but also to the public performance of their relationship.

The theme for Cathy and Raymond we first hear as a sweetly pastoral melody when he takes her for a walk in the autumnal woods, providing their first opportunity to escape the watchful eyes of the neighbours. It is another allusion to *All That Heaven Allows*, to the scene that shows gardener Ron Kirby (Rock Hudson) give a goldenrain twig to Cary Scott (Jane Wyman), while Raymond in *Far from Heaven* gives Cathy a witch hazel twig. The music bridges the cut to the next scene, which shows Raymond invite Cathy to dinner in Deagan's Restaurant. (The scene echoes another film referencing *All That Heaven Allows*, Rainer Werner Fassbinder's *Fear Eats the Soul/Angst essen Seele auf* [1974]; for Fassbinder and Haynes, see Richardson 2006; see also Gill 2011: 91–94.) In the restaurant, a tense situation develops that is in a way the mirror image of the critical looks Cathy and Raymond drew at an art exhibition earlier in the film. Cathy is the only white person there, and the looks of other customers and the behaviour of the waitress, Esther, make clear that she is not welcome. In the background of Cathy's and Raymond's conversation we hear implicitly diegetic lounge jazz. Then a new piece begins, one vaguely familiar and further in the acoustic foreground. Cathy and Raymond look at the band, she thanks him 'for a lovely afternoon', and the music turns out to be the theme that had nondiegetically underscored their tryst in the woods. Cathy asks Raymond to ask her to dance, they are slowly spinning on the dancefloor to 'their theme', and our narratological consciousness may be slightly irritated by the fact that the music – which so far has been 'their theme' only for us – has somehow managed to enter the diegesis.

Leitmotifs or themes that blithely ignore the diegetic/nondiegetic distinction are common enough in film music, especially in the Hollywood tradition. Doña Maria's leitmotivic song to her beloved Geoffrey Thorpe in *The Sea Hawk* has been mentioned (see pp. 56–57), and not a few film scores are more or less monothematic or at least develop many different

Figure 37: Cathy & Raymond (left) and Cathy & Frank (right) dancing to their respective themes in *Far from Heaven* (2002).

cues from a core theme (e.g. *Laura* [1944]; *Out of the Past* [1947]; *Twisted Nerve* [1968]; *The Long Goodbye* [1973]). While the chameleon nature of such music can prompt interpretation, it does not have to. Nothing suggests a further-reaching reading of Maria's song in *The Sea Hawk*; the scene is not particularly relevant for the plot, and such motivic relationships were a normal musical procedure for Korngold, part of a musical layer legitimately working at least partly according to its own rules.

But in *Far from Heaven*, music seems to be used with more specific narrative intent. The transition from nondiegetic to diegetic music that happens to Cathy and Raymond's theme also happens to that of Cathy and Frank. To shore up their crumbling marriage, Cathy gives Frank a New Year holiday for Christmas. They go to Miami and on New Year's Eve dance to their theme, transformed into diegetic music from the band on the hotel roof terrace. At the end of the dance, Frank spots a pretty blonde boy, with whom he will have sex during their holiday – the last straw for the marriage.

Twice in the film a theme introduced as nondiegetic music becomes diegetic and, more precisely, becomes dance music in scenes crucial for the development of Cathy's relationships. In Deagan's Restaurant, she gives in to her fascination for Raymond, and in Miami the fate of her marriage is sealed (Figure 37). This structure, carefully developed across the film, with the Cathy/Raymond theme being bracketed by the Cathy/Frank theme, is too noticeable to be dismissed as accidental or marginal, the more so in a film in which every detail is not just made to measure, but meant to be seen to have been made to measure.

Here, the narratological 'explanation' is not as straightforward as for a transition from diegetic to nondiegetic music. In *Far from Heaven*, the narration cannot be thought of as 'reacting', as taking up and later using what happens in the (fictitious) pre-filmic reality. Three ways of understanding the structure suggest themselves:

1. With regard to film style, the music can be understood to be organized by a leitmotif system whose musical integrity and referential function are more important than the observance of the diegetic/nondiegetic boundary. The use of a leitmotif system fits the

retrospective programme of the film, but such a historical reading of the musical strategy does not explain its effect on the narrative structure of the film.

2. We could also see it as the foregrounding of implied authorial agency (see ch. II.iv.d). Music that had been used to tell the story is placed *in* the storyworld, pointing both towards the diegetic/nondiegetic distinction and to the constructedness of story facts. Traditionally, music could engage in such self-consciousness more easily than other elements of film style (as shown by leitmotivic or even monothematic scores). This is common enough to pass over the moments without making much of them (see Gill 2011: 72 with regard to the second of the scenes).

3. But one could also understand the musical strategy in a way that leaves the integrity of an imagined pre-filmic reality intact (and also fits the kind of story *Far from Heaven* tells). The 'implied author' reading constructs an agency that *acts* in the story. Yet we can also imagine the narration as *prefiguring* story events. It knows what will happen and in that knowledge uses music nondiegetically before its diegetic entry. This reading construes the narration as one in the past tense. What we see and hear has already happened and is shown to us in the knowledge of the sequence of events.

On that basis alone, there is no good reason to prefer one 'explanation' over the others. But in *Far from Heaven*, two further reasons may give the past-tense version the edge:

- If retrospection is the name of the game, the third reading 'narrativizes' it. As the film looks back at film history, its narration looks back at the story, and the emotional intensity that generically defines melodrama is effortlessly explicable as the result of the narration knowing to what end things will come.
- The melodramatic identity of *Far from Heaven* intersects with that of the 'woman's film' as a label for films foregrounding 'woman's themes' and aimed mainly at a female audience, and the third of the reading above fits that label quite neatly. Cathy is the only one who is present at both dances, the only one for whom both pieces of music have emotional import[166]: She is the 'switch point [...] the central fulcrum through which the film constructs its parallel worlds' (Willis 2003: 159). A narration we imagine as retrospective would also be centred on Cathy's perspective. The story is not just told in retrospect, but in her retrospect. It is her story anyway, but the music does its bit to ram home the point. That does not mean that everything is told from Cathy's perspective. We witness scenes she is not present at and could at best imagine in a retrospective telling. But consistency is not the point; the point is that the retrospectively proleptic

---

166 While the application of the 'woman's film' label to Cathy seems straightforward, it has been argued that the true 'Sirkian heroine' of *Far from Heaven* is not Cathy, but Frank, part of a queer reorientation of the Sirkian model the film ostensibly follows (see Richardson 2006).

use of the two musical themes moves Cathy even more firmly into the centre of the film than she is anyway.

Every prolepsis shows that the narration knows about the continuation of the story. That it can be understood to set the story in the past tense is not the defining feature of the musical trick in *Far from Heaven*. Its narrative peculiarity lies in something else. A common musical foreshadowing – a close-up on a pistol in a drawer, accompanied by string *tremoli* – is recognizable as foreshadowing, even though one may not yet know what exactly is being foreshadowed (or if it is a red herring). A retrospective prolepsis does not show itself for what it is when it happens. Only when the two themes turn up in the diegesis of *Far from Heaven* – and really only when we have grasped the relevance of the scenes – do we retrospectively realize that their nondiegetic forms were proleptic. Through this, another level of retrospection comes into play: the diegetic entry of the music invites us to look back over the film and to become aware of the hidden anticipation.

c. Urban pastoral: *Breakfast at Tiffany's*

At first glance, *Breakfast at Tiffany's* (1961) seems to pursue the same musical strategy as *Far from Heaven*, perhaps even more intriguingly, because here the retrospective prolepsis is not completely unnoticeable. The title sequence shows Holly Golightly (Audrey Hepburn) come home in the morning hours in a taxi – from a party? from one of her men friends? – and alight outside Tiffany's. It is an iconic scene of what is urban and urbane: Holly's elegant figure, in a long black dress with piled-up hair, many-splendoured pearls and, given the hour, slightly absurd sunglasses; the empty streets of Manhattan, the display in the shop windows; even her croissant and coffee-to-go (where else could one get a coffee-to-go in 1961?). With all of this, we hear Henry Mancini's 'Moon River', whose elegiac elegance fits the scene perfectly – or rather, almost perfectly. The first time the melody is played by a harmonica, accompanied by the simple strumming of a guitar and mandolin: none of them particularly urban instruments (at least not if played as here). They rather evoke – and were meant to evoke – a pastoral scene of which the images show no hint (see Caps 2012: 62–65; also Smith 1998: 89). The harmonica and simple accompaniment match Holly's lonely figure amidst towering skyscrapers, and do not strike us as inappropriate. Without a context that would make sense of this tiny chink in the armour of an otherwise consistent scene, we are unlikely to wonder too much about the choice of instruments, and in any case they are quickly replaced by strings and a wordless choir, whose opulence covers up the chink.

But the film systematically develops the initial idea. The next time we hear 'Moon River', Holly has surprised Paul Varjak (George Peppard) in his bedroom and begins to dismantle his writerly façade. She tells him that he has not written anything in a long time, and she knows that he is the toy boy of a rich woman. But her own façade starts to crumble as well.

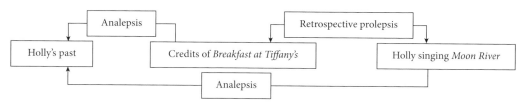

Figure 38: Temporal perspectives around 'Moon River' in *Breakfast at Tiffany's* (1961).

She tells him that she ran away from home at 14, and talks about her brother Fred, with whom something is not right. And the music follows suit. When Paul asks her if her men really give her $50 whenever she goes to the 'powder room', we hear a few jazzy piano chords that quickly change to a string texture which transits into 'Moon River' when she begins to tell him about her brother and her past. Again the melody is played by a harmonica, and when Holly muses that her brother's size may have to do with all that peanut butter, we are suddenly in a world very different from the one on-screen: rural and southern, and the harmonica begins to make a different kind of sense.

The strategy reaches its goal when it becomes clear that 'Moon River' is not just a nondiegetic pointer to Holly's past, but part of it – when Holly, sitting on the windowsill, sings the song. As in *Far from Heaven*, we are at a critical point of the plot. She starts to sing just when Paul starts to write again, starts to write Holly's story, and just before we see for the first time the strange man loitering in front of the house, who will soon turn out to be 'Doc' (Buddy Ebsen), Holly's common-law husband. The discovery completes her backstory: the New York good-time girl used to be Loula Mae Barnes from the South, and her New York life was her attempt to reinvent herself after having run away from a past that now has caught up with her. If we look back, we realize that the narration has not only 'known' Holly's secret, but told us about it in the retrospective prolepsis of the harmonica and guitar in the title sequence. *Breakfast at Tiffany's* is a film for which retrospection is crucial, and the web of temporal perspectives around 'Moon River' goes beyond the retrospective prolepsis and involves external analepses[167] to Holly's past (Figure 38).

If that were all *Breakfast at Tiffany's* would be an exact match (or even model?) for *Far from Heaven*. But the musical reality is less tidy, and 'Moon River' does not fit fully into the corset of the retrospective prolepsis. The song appears in the diegesis already, before Holly sings it during a party she gives. Here, 'Moon River' is arranged as a Latin dance number playing in the background. Its diegetic status is never made manifest, but as 'Moon River' is followed by another piece of dance music, we interpret it as random dance music from a record. This crossing of the diegetic/nondiegetic borderline cannot be integrated into the

---

167 The analepses are 'external' because they reach back beyond the first fabula event enacted in the syuzhet (see Genette 1980: 49, and Bordwell 1985: 78, who adds the syuzhet/fabula distinction to Genette's differentiation between external and internal analepses).

interpretative framework of a retrospective prolepsis. The party scene has no part in the deconstruction of Holly's façade – is in fact part of that façade – and the moment does not invite a (re)interpretation of the film's narrative structure.

That does not mean that the use of 'Moon River' at this point would not have interesting semiotic and pragmatic aspects (see Smith 1998: 82–99). An explanation for the use of the song in different guises, though, may rather be found in marketing. With 'Moon River', the film had a designated hit, and different versions of the song in the film – instrumental or vocal, pastoral or jazzy – is the intrafilmic complement to the recorded versions the Famous Music Corp., which marketed the music for Paramount, threw on the market (see Smith 1998: 77). The aim was to anchor the song in the audience's minds, and perhaps to foreground Mancini as a composer of pop hits. This does not mean that the retrospective prolepsis would be a 'wrong' way of reading the use of the song. Music can be used in different ways and for different reasons in a film; as in other filmic matters, consistency is the exception rather than the rule.

An interpretation of 'Moon River' in the party scene that aims for dramaturgy rather than marketing could perhaps argue that even here it prefigures the uncovering of her backstory. The song is omnipresent in her life, even here, where she seems completely at one with her party-girl façade. For such a reading, however, the assumption of an autonomous pre-filmic reality has to be suspended, and we have to assume a narration that occasionally switches to implied authorial mode and momentarily takes responsibility for the 'facts' of the fiction by smuggling 'Moon River' into the diegesis.

d. The language of melodrama: Antecedents in *All That Heaven Allows* and *Imitation of Life*

As pointed out above, transitions from nondiegetic to diegetic music may not be as common as those in the opposite direction, but especially in the context of leitmotivic scores they are common enough not to require specific narratological interpretations. But it may be no accident that two of the films that informed *Far from Heaven* also let music introduced nondiegetically enter the diegesis later on. But they do it in a throwaway fashion that does not suggest interpretive surplus value – the films seem to toy with an idea without doing much with it.

In *All That Heaven Allows*, this concerns a passage from Franz Liszt's 'Consolation' no. 3 for piano, a strangely extraterritorial interjection in the orchestral music of the title sequence with its establishing shots of model small-town America. The music is used nondiegetically in scenes that are important for the development of the relationship between Cary (Jane Wyman) and Ron (Rock Hudson): after their first encounter; when Cary's daughter kisses her lover and her mother observes her and then looks at the China tree twig Ron had given her earlier; and when Ron proposes to Cary (though now the Liszt quotation is woven into the underscore). In the title sequence, the music is noticeable because it is not integrated into the orchestral texture, but stands out as what it is: a pre-existing piece of music. The use of the piano has – as in *Far from Heaven* – its point in the domestic drama that is about to unfold. But the piano as an instrument of domestic music-making is not enough for the film, which 'diegeticizes' the allusion when Cary herself plays a bit of the 'Consolation' on the piano in her home. It is not a crucial scene in itself, but it comes right after her first kiss with Ron – after a spatial and temporal ellipsis in the fabula, but consecutive in the syuzhet. The film does not develop the idea; but the little splinter of a retrospective prolepsis may do its bit to affectively charge the film in a way appropriate for the genre.

In *Imitation of Life*, it is the eponymous theme song that reappears in the diegesis after the nondiegetic music has alluded to it numerous times. When Lora Meredith (Lana Turner), at a party after a successful premiere, waves at Steve Archer (John Gavin) and asks him to come into the kitchen to her and Annie (Juanita Moore), 'Imitation of Life' is played on a piano. We cannot see the instrument, but it is played with an improvisatory irregularity that makes us wonder if it might not be played in the next room. Only after a delay do we actually see, in passing, the pianist in that room play the piece.

This is a significant plot point. In the next scene, Lora and her daughter Susie (Sandra Dee) are in the garden, where Susie sees a falling star and seems to be making a wish, while Lora gets a wistful expression. Susie lets on that her wish has to do with 'all of us [being] together', to which Lora replies, 'I'm going to do something about it. I will not do another play for a long, long time.' She promises her daughter to sacrifice her career as an actress for her family – an echo of the lyrics of the song that ask 'what is love without the giving' and assert that 'without love you're only living an imitation, an imitation of life'. But again there is no context for the musical idea: 'Imitation of Life' occurs only casually, played by a nameless pianist as party background, rather like 'Moon River' as dance music in *Breakfast at Tiffany's*. Like *All That Heaven Allows*, *Imitation of Life* is content to flirt with the metalepsis without going anywhere with it.

It makes sense that *Far from Heaven* develops these moments into a strategy: a film that is not a classic melodrama but 'a "deconstruction" of the language of melodrama', a film that sets itself the 'task of investigating forms of melodramatic narration' (Landy 2007: 21–22). How it does that with regard to music is a question film scholarship has so far missed, par for the course of its lack of interest in matters musical. Whether the retrospective prolepsis is tyical for the melodrama or also occurs in other generic contexts, and whether it is common enough to deserve a place in the history of film scoring, remains to be seen.

e. Singing the king: A retrospective prolepsis in *The Adventures of Robin Hood*

While the transition from nondiegetic to diegetic music was a key component of the retrospective prolepses discussed so far, a weaker version of such retrospective musical anticipation can work with nondiegetic music alone. In *The Adventures of Robin Hood* (1938),

Figure 39: Part of the opening text in *The Adventures of Robin Hood* (1938).

Richard Lionheart (Ian Hunter) is absent from the screen for almost the entire film and only turns up ten minutes before the end. But Richard's absence is what motivates the story around Prince John's (Claude Rains) attempt to usurp the throne, and Richard's return to England is required to give the story closure. But how can the film imply Richard's significance without being able to show him? How can it demonstrate his importance for events the country in his absence, and demonstrate what he stands for, and what is missing while he is not there?

The solution is to let an idea of what Richard stands for build up through the film, and Korngold's music is crucial to that strategy. Key is the time-honoured leitmotif, but in this case a leitmotif that has no clear referent in the diegesis when we first hear it, and only gradually becomes identifiable as 'Richard's theme', as which it is revealed alongside its bearer when he returns at the end.

- We first hear the theme as the 'lyrical' section of the music for the title sequence. After the merry march opening the titles, the theme in question starts with the text that explains the situation (Figure 39).

   The theme with its incessant repetition of the tonic, its diatonic suspensions and passing notes, and emphatic leaps of sixths is a model of diatonic stability and nobly restrained richness.[168] But while Richard is mentioned in the text displayed, it is not clear what, if anything, the theme may be associated with. It could be the king, but it could also be more generally the 'romance of history' the film capitalizes upon.

- The next time we hear the theme more than 20 minutes into the film, when Robin (Errol Flynn) asks his men to swear an oath to steal only from the rich, give to the poor, protect the helpless and fight for a free England until Richard's return, and it is when 'a free England' is mentioned by Robin that the theme sets in.
- We hear the theme not much later, again among the Merry Men in Sherwood Forest, when they confirm to Maid Marian (Olivia de Havilland) that the treasure they have stolen is for the ransom of the king, who is kept hostage in Austria.
- Next we hear the theme during a conversation between Robin and Marian. She wonders why he helps even the occasional Norman, and he replies 'Norman or Saxon – what's that matter? It's injustice I hate, not the Normans.' Neither Richard nor England are mentioned, but the theme makes sense: Robin is talking about the idea of national unity and justice, both embodied by the king. Do we attach the idea to the theme, or is it the theme that tells us to understand Robin's words in the light of this idea?
- The penultimate time we hear the motif comes closer to revealing its referent. We see black-hooded men ride through the forest whose faces we cannot see. They could be potential victims of the Merry Men's raids, but they are accompanied by the theme, which tells us that they are probably not.
- At the end of that scene, Richard reveals himself to Robin and his men, and the theme sounds again, at stately speed and not at all in full orchestral regalia, but with the restraint that is part of Richard's kingly persona, both revealing its meaning and investing Richard with the meaning it had collected throughout the film.

We are so used to leitmotifs in Hollywood scores that we may overlook how ingeniously this one is used. It accrues meaning over the course of the film, but it also dispenses meaning, intertwining the idea of the king and the deeds and words of those loyal to him during his absence, allowing him to symbolically affect the fate of his country from afar. Until he reveals himself, Richard is a variant of Michel Chion's *acousmêtre*. Chion's *acousmêtre* is present through voice alone, not in the sense of a 'clearly detached narrator', but 'implicated in the action, constantly about to be part of it' (Chion 1994: 129). Richard is certainly implicated in the action, and about to be part of it indirectly through those for whom he is a symbol of values and a hope for the future, and eventually directly, as the one to bring closure to the personal and national stories. Yet it is not his voice that is the source of his interaction with the storyworld, but the nondiegetic theme. What this leaves to be desired in terms of the mysterious power Chion sees as characteristic of *acousmêtres*, it may gain in capacity to be invested with symbolic meanings that can spread to other people, deeds, words and ideas underscored by the theme.

---

168 See Winters (2007: 117) for a music example of the theme in its initial version, and Winters (2007: 115–18) for an account of the development of the theme throughout the film.

The nexus of meaning is fully revealed when Richard throws off his hood and we can look back over the film to the journey of 'his' theme and its contexts. The music's proleptic effect is, however, less clearly retrospective than the others discussed, because the piling up of meaning through the repeated use of the theme edges it closer and closer to its goal, so that the final appearance is not so much a reveal but a confirmation of something long suspected. Instead of the stepwise accrual of meaning in *The Adventures of Robin Hood*, *Far from Heaven* makes the crossing of the nondiegetic/diegetic borderline into marked events: musical metalepses that make the two themes meaningful not just symbolically, but also in the storyworld.

Chapter VI

The Future's Not Ours to See: Outlook

The surge of interest in narratological questions in film musicology of the last decade may be a late flowering of an established, but hardly fashionable approach to film in a peripheral discipline (in)famous for often being a bit behind the times of other arts and humanities. On the other hand, it may eventually feed back into film studies and contribute to a more sustained engagement with music, something that has been a desideratum for a long time. What it will be remains to be seen (and may in part depend on the ability of film musicologists to show that narratological analyses of film music can contribute to our understanding of films). If a productive development is to take place, film musicology needs to get beyond the diegetic/nondiegetic borderline (important as it is) and explore the wider landscape and some of the more remote corners of narratology. Not all that is out there will be fruitful for the discussion of music in film, but one has to try to find out.

The other expansion of the range of film music narratology concerns not its concepts, but its material. This study, like so many others, has focused on western, live-action fiction films, the kind of films that for most of us represent the core of the repertoire, but also the Platonic idea, the core of our understanding of what film is. But other genres and traditions may offer other options and problems: non-western films based on different narrative traditions (the narratology of Bollywood musicals would just be the most obvious example); different forms of animation film; different kinds of experimental film; documentaries; television series and other narrative television forms, etc. On a lower level, a widening of the repertoire may simply mean a closer look at narrative features of music in specific genres; comedies (romantic or otherwise) would provide rich pickings, as would musician biopics or other films about musicians.

Film music narratology will only work, though, if the development of theory and its application go hand in hand: if the theory provides ideas of what to look (and listen) for, and how to describe and understand it, and the study of films and their creative musical solutions provides the theory with problems that need solving. Mieke Bal, one of the most inquisitive of narratologists, has argued in favour of a narratology that finds its rationale not in categorization, but 'implicates text and reading, subject and object, production and analysis, in the act of understanding' (Bal 2009: 227):

Delimitation, classification, typology, it is all very nice as a remedy to chaos-anxiety, but what insights does it yield? [...] [T]he pervasive taxonomical end of narratology is epistemologically flawed; it entails skipping a step or two. Between a general conception of narrative and an actual narrative text – or object – lies more than classification. The distribution of actual objects over a restricted number of categories is only meaningful – if at all – after insight into a text has been gained. […] There is no direct logical connection between classifying and understanding texts. And understanding – if taken in a broad sense that encompasses cognitive as well as affective acts, precisely, not distinguished – is the point. (Bal 2009: 226)

Bal's 'if at all' is not very encouraging for a sub-discipline of film (music) studies that is still very much engaged in defining and refining the concepts and categories to distribute its objects of study over. But her exhortation that insights into texts are the justification for any kind of narratological enquiry should be heeded, especially at a time when film music narratology has to show that, beyond conceptual games in the theory sandbox, it can actually contribute to our understanding of music in films, and by implication, of films as a narrative form crucially involved with music. Understanding is the point: the proof of the pudding is in the eating, and that of film theory in what it makes us see and hear when we watch and listen to films.

Bibliography

Abbott, H. Porter (2008), *The Cambridge Introduction to Narrative*, 2nd edition, Cambridge: Cambridge University Press.

Adorno, Theodor W. (1980), 'Gesammelte Schriften', in Rolf Tiedemann (ed.), *Minima moralia. Reflexionen aus dem beschädigten Leben*, vol. 4, Frankfurt: Suhrkamp.

Adorno, Theodor W. and Eisler, Hanns (1994), *Composing for the Films*, 2nd edition, London & Atlantic Highlands: Athlone Press. First published 1947.

Aizenberg, Edna (1999), '*I Walked with a Zombie*: The Pleasures and Perils of Postcolonial Hybridity', *World Literature Today*, 73: 3, pp. 461–66.

Allison, Deborah (2001), 'Promises in the Dark: Opening Title Sequences in American Feature Films of the Sound Period', Ph.D. dissertation, Norwich: University of East Anglia.

––––––– (2006), 'Novelty title sequences and self-reflexivity in classical Hollywood cinema', *Screening the Past*, 20, http://tlweb.latrobe.edu.au/humanities/screeningthepast/20/novelty-title-sequences.html. Accessed 2 June 2013.

Altman, Rick (1987), *The American Film Musical*, Bloomington & Indianapolis: Indiana University Press.

––––––– (1999), *Film/Genre*, London: British Film Institute.

Arroyo, José (2000), 'How do You Solve a Problem Like Von Trier?', *Sight & Sound*, 10: 9, pp. 14–16.

Atkins, Irene Kahn (1983), *Source Music in Motion Pictures*, East Brunswick, London, Toronto: Associated University Presses.

Bailey, Peter J. (2001), *The Reluctant Film Art of Woody Allen*, Lexington: The University Press of Kentucky.

Baird, Robert (2000), 'The Startle Effect: Implications for Spectator Cognition and Media Theory', *Film Quarterly*, 53: 3, pp. 12–24.

Bal, Mieke (2009), *Narratology: Introduction to the Theory of Narrative*, 3rd edition, Toronto: University of Toronto Press.

Barham, Jeremy (2009), 'Incorporating Monsters: Music as Context, Character and Construction in Kubrick's *The Shining*', in Philip Hayward (ed.), *Terror Tracks: Music, Sound and Horror Cinema*, London & Oakville: Equinox, pp. 137–70.

Barron, Lee and Inglis, Ian (2009), 'Scary Movies Scary Music: Uses and Unities of Heavey Metal in the Contemporary Horror Film', in Philip Hayward (ed.), *Terror Tracks: Music, Sound and Horror Film*, London & Oakville: Equinox, pp. 186–97.

Bass, Saul (1993), 'Man kettet den Zuschauer an seinen Sitz', in Lars-Olav Beier and Gerhard Midding (eds), *Teamwork in der Traumfabrik. Werkstattgespräche*, Berlin: Henschel, pp. 409–24.

Belletto, Steven (2008), '*Cabaret* and Antifascist Aesthetics', *Criticism*, 50: 4, pp. 609–30.

Biancorosso, Giorgio (2001), 'Beginning Credits and Beyond: Music and the Cinematic Imagination', *ECHO: a music-centered journal*, 3: 1, http://www.echo.ucla.edu/Volume3-Issue1/biancorosso/index.html. Accessed 2 June 2013.

—— (2009), 'The Harpist in the Closet: Film Music as Epistemological Joke', *Music and the Moving Image*, 2: 3, pp. 11–33.

Binns, Alexander (2008), 'Desiring the Diegesis: Music and Self-Seduction in the Films of Wong Kar-Wai', in David Cooper, Christopher Fox and Ian Sapiro (eds), *CineMusic? Constructing the Film Score*, Newcastle: Cambridge Scholars, pp. 127–40.

Björkman, Stig (ed.) (2003), *Trier on von Trier*, London: Faber and Faber.

Black, David Alan (1986), 'Genette and Film: Narrative Level in Fiction Cinema', *Wide Angle*, 8: 3–4, pp. 19–26.

Bliss, Michael (2000), *Dreams within a Dream. The Films of Peter Weir*, Carbondale & Edwardsville: Southern Illinois University Press.

Böhnke, Alexander (2007a), *Paratexte des Films. Über die Grenzen des filmischen Universums*, Bielefeld: transcript.

—— (2007b), 'Die Zeit der Diegese', *montage/av*, 16: 2 (special issue *Diegese*), pp. 93–104.

Booth, Wayne C. (1961), *The Rhetoric of Fiction*, Chicago & London: University of Chicago Press.

—— (1977), '*The Rhetoric of Fiction* and the Poetics of Fiction' (1968), in Mark Spilka (ed.), *Towards a Poetics of Fiction*, Bloomington & London: Indiana University Press, pp. 77–89.

—— (2002), 'Is There an "Implied" Author in Every Film', *College Literature*, 29: 2, pp. 124–31.

Bordwell, David (1985), *Narration in the Fiction Film*, Madison: University of Wisconsin Press.

—— (1996), 'Contemporary Film Studies and the Vicissitudes of Grand Theory', in David Bordwell and Noël Carroll (eds), *Post-Theory: Reconstructing Film Studies*, Madison & London: University of Wisconsin Press, pp. 3–36.

—— (2008), *Poetics of Cinema*, New York & London: Routledge.

Bordwell, David and Thompson, Kristin (2010), *Film Art: An Introduction*, 9th edition, New York: McGraw-Hill.

Bordwell, David and Carroll, Noël (eds) (1996), *Post-Theory: Reconstructing Film Studies*, Madison & London: University of Wisconsin Press.

Bordwell, David, Staiger, Janet and Thompson, Kristin (1985), *The Classical Hollywood Cinema: Film Style and Mode of Production to 1960*, London: Routledge & Kegan Paul.

Bortolussi, Marisa and Dixon, Peter (2002), *Psychonarratology: Foundations for the Empirical Study of Literary Response*, Cambridge: Cambridge University Press.

Branigan, Edward (1986), 'Diegesis and Authorship', *Iris*, 7 (special issue *Cinema & Narration 1*), pp. 37–54.

—— (1992), *Narrative Comprehension and Film*, London & New York: Routledge.

Brinckmann, Christine N. (2007), 'Diegetisches und nondiegetisches Licht', *montage/av*, 16: 2 (special issue *Diegese*), pp. 71–91.

Brophy, Philip (2004), *100 Modern Soundtracks*, London: BFI.

Brown, Julie (2010), '*Carnival of Souls* and the Organs of Horror', in Neil Lerner (ed.), *Music in the Horror Film*, New York & London: Routledge, pp. 1–20.

Brown, Royal S. (1994), *Overtones and Undertones: Reading Film Music*, Berkeley, Los Angeles & London: University of California Press.

Brustellin, Alf (2003), 'Das Singen im Regen. Über die seltsamen Wirklichkeiten im amerikanischen Filmmusical', in Andrea Pollach, Isabella Reicher and Tanja Widmann (eds), *Singen und Tanzen im Film*, Vienna: Paul Zsolnay Verlag, pp. 13–39.

Buhler, James (2001), 'Analytical and Interpretive Approaches to Film Music (II): Analysing Interactions of Music and Film', in Kevin Donnelly (ed.), *Film Music: Critical Approaches*, New York: Continuum, pp. 39–61.

——— (2010), 'Music and the Adult Ideal in *Nightmare on Elm Street*', in Neil Lerner (ed.), *Music in the Horror Film*, New York & London: Routledge, pp. 168–86.

Buhler, James, Flinn, Caryl and Neumeyer, David (eds) (2000), *Music and Cinema*, Hanover & London: Wesleyan University Press.

Buhler, James, Neumeyer, David and Deemer, Rob (2010), *Hearing the Movies: Music and Sound in Film History*, New York & Oxford: Oxford University Press.

Bullerjahn, Claudia (2007), *Grundlagen der Wirkung von Filmmusik*, Augsburg: Wißner.

Burch, Noël (1990), *Life to Those Shadows* (trans. Ben Brewster), London: BFI.

Burlingame, Jon (2000), *Sound and Vision: Sixty Years of Motion Picture Soundtracks*, New York: Billboard Books.

Caps, John (2012), *Henry Mancini… Reinventing Film Music*, Urbana, Chicago & Springfield: University of Illinois Press.

Carlson, Michael (2001), *Sergio Leone*, Harpenden: Pocket Essentials.

Carroll, Noël (1990), *The Philosophy of Horror; or, Paradoxes of the Heart*, New York & London: Routledge.

——— (1996), 'Prospects for Film Theory: A Personal Assessment', in David Bordwell and Noël Carroll (eds), *Post-Theory: Reconstructing Film Studies*, Madison & London: University of Wisconsin Press, pp. 37–70.

Cecchi, Alessandro (2010), 'Diegetic versus nondiegetic: a reconsideration of the conceptual opposition as a contribution to the theory of audiovision', *Worlds of Audiovision*, http://www-5.unipv.it/wav/. Accessed 2 June 2013.

Chatman, Seymour (1978), *Story and Discourse: Narrative Struture in Fiction and Film*, Ithaca & London: Cornell University Press.

——— (1990), *Coming to Terms: The Rhetoric of Narrative in Fiction and Film*, Ithaca & London: Cornell University Press.

Chattah, Juan (2006), 'Semiotics, Pragmatics and Metaphor in Film Music Analysis', DPhil dissertation, Florida: Florida State University.

——— (2007), 'Non-traditional sound design: a model for analysis', conference paper at *Sound, Music and the Moving Image*, 10–12 September, Institute of Musical Research: London.

Chion, Michel (1994), *Audio-Vision: Sound on Screen* (trans. C. Gorbman), New York: Columbia University Press.

——— (2009), *Film, a Sound Art* (trans. C. Gorbman), New York: Columbia University Press.

Code, David J. (2010), 'Rehearing *The Shining*: Musical Undercurrents in the Overlook Hotel', in Neil Lerner (ed.), *Music in the Horror Film*, New York & London: Routledge, pp. 133–51.

Cohan, Steve (ed.) (2010), *The Sound of Musicals*, Basingstoke: Palgrave Macmillan for the BFI.

Collins, Karen (2009), '"Like razors through flesh": *Hellraiser*'s Sound Design and Music', in Philip Hayward (ed.), *Terror Tracks: Music, Sound and Horror Cinema*, London & Oakville: Equinox, pp. 198–212.

Cooke, Mervyn (2008), *A History of Film Music*, Cambridge: Cambridge University Press.

Cooper, David, Fox, Christopher and Sapiro, Ian (eds) (2008), *Cinemusic? Constructing the Film Score*, Newcastle: Cambridge Scholars.

Copland, Aaron (1949), 'Tip to Moviegoers: Take Off Those Ear-Muffs', *New York Times*, 6 November, section 6, p. 28.

Coyle, Rebecca (2009), 'Spooked by Sound: *The Blair Witch Project*', in Philip Hayward (ed.), *Terror Tracks: Music, Sound and Horror Cinema*, London & Oakville: Equinox, pp. 213–28.

Coyle, Rebecca and Hayward, Philip (2009), 'Texas Chainsaws: Audio Effect and Iconicity', in Philip Hayward (ed.), *Terror Tracks: Music, Sound and Horror Cinema*, London & Oakville: Equinox, pp. 125–36.

Csikszentmihalyi, Mihaly (1975), *Beyond Boredom and Anxiety: Experiencing Flow in Work and Play*, San Francisco: Jossey-Bass.

Cumbow, Robert C. (2008), *The Films of Sergio Leone*, Lanham & Plymouth: Scarecrow.

Darby, William and DuBois, Jack (1990), *American Film Music: Major Composers, Techniques, Trends, 1915–1990*, Jefferson & London: McFarland.

Davis, Nick (2012), 'Inside/Outside the Klein Bottle: Music in Narrative Film, Intrusive and Integral', *Music, Sound and the Moving Image*, 6: 1, pp. 9–19.

Davison, Annette (2004), *Hollywood Theory, Non-Hollywood Practice. Cinema Soundtracks in the 1980s and 1990s*, Aldershot: Ashgate.

Delapa, Thomas (2000), 'Review of *Dancer in the Dark*', *Boulder Weekly*, 22 December, section 'Reel to Reel', http://archive.boulderweekly.com/101900/reeltoreel.html. Accessed 13 July 2012.

Donnelly, Kevin J. (ed.) (2001), *Film Music: Critical Approaches*, New York: Continuum.

—— (2005), *The Spectre of Sound: Music in Film and Television*, London: BFI.

—— (2010), 'Hearing Deep Seated Fears: John Carpenter's *The Fog* (1980)', in Neil Lerner (ed.), *Music in the Horror Film*, New York & London: Routledge, pp. 152–67.

Dyer, Richard (2002), *Only Entertainment*, 2nd edition, London & New York: Routledge.

—— (2010), *Nino Rota: Music, Film and Feeling*, Basingstoke: Palgrave Macmillan for the BFI.

Eaton, Rebecca (2008), 'Unheard Minimalisms: The Function of the Minimalist Technique in Film Scores', Ph.D. thesis, Austin: University of Textas at Austin.

Elsaesser, Thomas and Hagener, Malte (2010), *Film Theory: An Introduction through the Senses*, New York: Routledge.

Evans, Mark (2009), 'Rhythms of Evil: Exorcizing Sound from *The Exorcist*', in Philip Hayward (ed.), *Terror Tracks: Music, Sound and Horror Cinema*, London & Oakville: Equinox, pp. 112–24.

Feuer, Jane (1993), *The Hollywood Musical*, 2nd edition, Bloomington & Indianapolis: Indiana University Press.

—— (2010), 'The International Art Musical: Defining and Periodising Post-1980s Musicals', in Steven Cohan (ed.), *The Sound of Musicals*, Basingstoke: Palgrave Macmillan for the BFI, pp. 54–63.

Fitzgerald, John and Hayward, Philip (2009), 'Inflamed: Synthetic Folk Music and Paganism in the Island World of *The Wicker Man*', in Philip Hayward (ed.), *Terror Tracks: Music, Sound and Horror Cinema*, London & Oakville: Equinox, pp. 101–11.

Fletcher, Jonathan (2008), '"Anything can happen": Narrative Ambiguity and Musical Intertextuality in *The Holiday*', *Kieler Beiträge zur Filmmusikforschung*, 2, pp. 135–41, http://www.filmmusik. uni-kiel.de/artikel/KB2-Fletcherarc.pdf. Accessed 2 June 2013.

Flückiger, Barbara (2001), *Sound Design. Die virtuelle Klangwelt des Films*, Marburg: Schüren.

Fludernik, Monika (2009), *An Introduction to Narratology* (trans. P. Häusler-Greenfield and M. Fludernik), London & New York: Routledge.

Fordin, Hugh (1996), *MGM's Greatest Musicals: The Arthur Freed Unit*, New York: Da Capo. [Originally published as *The World of Entertainment!* (1975), New York: Doubleday.]

Frayling, Christopher (1981), *Spaghetti Westerns: Cowboys and Europeans from Karl May to Sergio Leone*, London: Routledge and Kegan Paul.

——— (2000), *Sergio Leone: Something To Do with Death*, London & New York: Faber and Faber.

Fuxjäger, Anton (2007), 'Diegese, Diegesis, diegetisch. Versuch einer Begriffsentwirrung', *montage/av*, 16:2 (special issue *Diegese*), pp. 17–38.

Gabriel, Gilbert (2011), 'Altered States, Altered Sounds: An investigation of how "subjective states" are signified by the soundtrack in narrative fiction cinema', Ph.D. thesis, Cardiff: Cardiff University.

Gardies, André (2006), 'Am Anfang war der Vorspann', in Alexander Böhnke, Rembert Hüser and Georg Stanitzek (eds), *Das Buch zum Vorspann*, Berlin: Vorwerk 8, pp. 21–33.

Gaudreault, André (1987), 'Narration and Monstration in Cinema', *Journal of Film and Video*, 39, pp. 29–36.

——— (2009), *From Plato to Lumière: Narration and Monstration in Literature and Cinema/ Du littérarie au filmique* (trans. T. Barnard), Toronto: University of Toronto Press. First published 1988.

Genette, Gérard (1980), *Narrative Discourse* (trans. J.E. Lewin), Oxford: Blackwell.

——— (1988), *Narrative Discourse Revisited* (trans. J.E. Lewin), Ithaca & London: Cornell University Press.

——— (1997), *Paratexts: Thresholds of Interpretation* (trans. J.E. Lewin), Cambridge: Cambridge University Press.

Gill, John (2011), *Far from Heaven*, London: Palgrave Macmillan on behalf of the BFI (BFI Film Classics).

Godsall, Jonathan (forthcoming), 'Pre-existing Music in Fiction Sound Film', Ph.D. thesis, Bristol: University of Bristol.

Goldmark, Daniel, Kramer, Lawrence and Leppert, Richard (eds) (2007), *Beyond the Soundtrack: Representing Music in Cinema*, Berkeley, Los Angeles & London: University of California Press.

Gorbman, Claudia (1987), *Unheard Melodies: Narrative Film Music*, Bloomington & London: Indiana University Press & BFI Publishing.

——— (1991), 'Hanns Eisler in Hollywood', *Screen*, 32, pp. 272–85.

——— (2006), 'Ears Wide Open: Kubrick's Music', in Phil Powrie and Robynn Stilwell (eds), *Changing Tunes: The Use of Pre-existing Music in Film*, Aldershot: Ashgate, pp. 3–18.

——— (2011), 'Artless Singing', *Music, Sound and the Moving Image*, 5: 2 (Autumn), pp. 157–71.

Gottfried, Martin (2003), *All His Jazz. The Life and Death of Bob Fosse*, Cambridge: Da Capo. (Originally published in 1990.)

Grant, Barry Keith (2003), 'Experience and Meaning in Genre Films', in Barry Keith Grant (ed.), *Film Genre Reader III*, Austin: University of Texas Press, pp. 115–129.

Grey, Harry (1997), *Once Upon a Time in America*, London: Bloomsbury. [Originally published as *The Hoods* (1952), New York: Crown].

Hagen, Earle (1971), *Scoring for Films: A Complete Text*, New York: E.D.J. Music.

Halfyard, Janet K. (2009), 'Music of the Night: Scoring the Vampire in Contemporary Film', in Philip Hayward (ed.), *Terror Tracks: Music, Sound and Horror Cinema*, London & Oakville: Equinox, pp. 171–85.

Hanich, Julian (2010), *Cinematic Emotion in Horror Films and Thrillers: The Aesthetic Paradox of Pleasurable Fear*, London: Routledge.

Hannan, Michael (2009), 'Sound and Music in Hammer Horror Films', in Philip Hayward (ed.), *Terror Tracks: Music, Sound and Horror Cinema*, London & Oakville: Equinox, pp. 60–74.

Hardy, Thomas (1985), *The Return of the Native*, London: Penguin. First published 1878.

Hartmann, Britta (2003), '"Gestatten Sie, daß ich mich vorstelle?" Zuschaueradressierung und Reflexivität am Filmanfang', *montage/av*, 12: 2, pp. 19–38.

——— (2007), 'Diegetisieren, Diegese, Diskursuniversum', *montage/av*, 16: 2 (special issue *Diegese*), pp. 53–69.

Hartmann, Britta and Wulff, Hans J. (2007), 'Alice in the Spiegeln: Vom Begehen und Konstruieren diegetischer Welten', *montage/av*, 16: 2 (special issue *Diegese*), pp. 4–7.

Hausberger, Florian (2006), 'Main Titles – Titelsequenzen im Film. Eine analytische Kategorisierung', diploma thesis, Hagenberg: Fachhochschule Hagenberg.

Hayward, Philip (ed.) (2009a), *Terror Tracks: Music, Sound and Horror Cinema*, London & Oakville: Equinox.

——— (2009b), 'Introduction: Scoring the Edge', in Philip Hayward (ed.), *Terror Tracks: Music, Sound and Horror Cinema*, London, Oakville: Equinox, pp. 1–13.

Heimerdinger, Julia (2007), *Neue Musik im Spielfilm*, Saarbrücken: Pfau.

Heldt, Guido (2001), 'Klangfiguren.Zur Musik in *C'era una volta il West*', *Plurale. Zeitschrift für Denkversionen* 0, issue *Oberflächen*, pp. 31–48.

——— (2004), 'Auf Schritt und Tritt. Musik und Bewegung bei Sergio Leone und Ennio Morricone', in Christa Brüstle and Albrecht Riethmüller (eds), *Klang und Bewegung. Beiträge zu einer Grundkonstellation*, Aachen: Shaker, pp. 267–83.

——— (2005), 'Das vorletzte Lied. Musik, narrative Struktur und Genre in Lars von Triers *Dancer in the Dark*', in Andreas Dorschel (ed.), *Tonspuren. Musik im Film: Fallstudien 1994–2001*, Wien: Universal Edition (Studien zur Wertungsforschung 46), pp. 125–48.

——— (2008a), 'Die Lieder von gestern. Filmmusik und das implizite Imperfekt', *Kieler Beiträge zur Filmmusikforschung*, 1, pp. 10–25, http://www.filmmusik.uni-kiel.de/kielerbeitraege/liedervongestern-heldt.pdf. Accessed 2 June 2013.

——— (2008b), 'Grenzgänge – Filmisches Erzählen und Eislers Musik', in Peter Schweinhardt (ed.), *Kompositionen für den Film. Zu Theorie und Praxis von Hanns Eislers Filmmusik* (Eisler-Studien 3), Wiesbaden: Breitkopf & Härtel, pp. 43–62.

——— (2009), 'Playing Mozart: Biopics and the Musical (Re)Invention of a Composer', *Music, Sound and the Moving Image*, 3: 1 (special issue *Invention/Re-Invention*, ed. by Miguel Mera), pp. 21–46.

—— (2010), 'His master's voice: Musik und Fiktionalitätsebenen in *The Truman Show*', *Kieler Beiträge zur Filmmusikforschung*, 4, pp. 104–15, http://www.filmmusik.uni-kiel.de/kielerbeitraege4/KB4-Truman.pdf. Accessed 2 June 2013.

—— (2012), '"... there's no music playing, and it's not snowing": Songs and Self-reflexivity in Curtisland', *Music, Sound and the Moving Image*, 6: 1 (special issue *Music and Narrative in Film*, ed. by Ben Winters), pp. 73–91.

Hentschel, Frank (2011), *Töne der Angst. Die Musik im Horrorfilm*, Berlin: Bertz + Fischer.

Herman, David (2005), 'Storyworld', in David Herman, Manfred Jahn and Marie-Laure Ryan (eds), *Routledge Encyclopedia of Narrative Theory*, New York & Abingdon: Routledge, pp. 569–70.

Herman, David, Jahn, Manfred and Ryan, Marie-Laure (eds) (2005), *Routledge Encyclopedia of Narrative Theory*, New York & Abingdon: Routledge.

Hills, Matt (2005), *The Pleasures of Horror*, New York & London: Continuum.

Holbrook, Morris B. (2005a), 'Ambi-diegetic Music in the Movies: The Crosby Duets in *High Society*', *Consumption, Markets and Culture*, 8: 2, pp. 153–82.

—— (2005b), 'The Ambi-Diegesis of *My Funny Valentine*', in Steve Lannin and Matthew Caley (eds), *Pop Fiction: The Song in Cinema*, Bristol & Portland, OR: Intellect, pp. 47–62.

Howard, Luke (2007), 'The Popular Reception of Samuel Barber's *Adagio for Strings*', *American Music*, 25: 1, pp. 50–80.

Hubbert, Julie (ed.) (2011), *Celluloid Symphonies: Texts and Contexts in Film Music History*, Berkeley, Los Angeles & London: Berkeley University Press.

Ireland, Ken (2005), 'Temporal Ordering', in David Herman, Manfred Jahn and Marie-Laure Ryan (eds), *Routledge Encyclopedia of Narrative Theory*, New York & Abingdon: Routledge, pp. 591–92.

Jackson, Giovanna (1989), 'The Myth and the Mythmaker: Sergio Leone's *Once Upon a Time in America*', in Douglas Radcliff-Umstead (ed.), *Varieties of Filmic Expression*, Kent: Kent State University, pp. 24–30.

Jahn, Manfred (2005a), 'Cognitive Narratology', in David Herman, Manfred Jahn and Marie-Laure Ryan (eds), *Routledge Encyclopedia of Narrative Theory*, New York & Abingdon: Routledge, pp. 67–71.

—— (2005b), 'Focalization', in David Herman, Manfred Jahn and Marie-Laure Ryan (eds), *Routledge Encyclopedia of Narrative Theory*, New York & Abingdon: Routledge, pp. 173–77.

Jameson, Richard T. (1973), 'Something To Do With Death: A Fistful of Sergio Leone', *Film Comment*, 9: 2, pp. 8–16.

Jeffries, Stuart (2003), 'Some you win' [interview with Elmer Bernstein], *The Guardian*, 6 January, http://www.guardian.co.uk/film/2003/jan/06/classicalmusicandopera.artsfeatures?INTCMP=SRCH. Accessed 2 June 2013.

Jordan, Randolph (2007), 'Does Anybody Hear?', *Offscreen*, 11: 8–9 (Forum 2: *Discourses on Diegesis – On the Relevance of Terminology*), http://www.offscreen.com/biblio/pages/essays/soundforum_2. Accessed 2 June 2013.

Kalinak, Kathryn (1992), *Settling the Score: Music and the Classical Hollywood Film*, Madison & London: University of Wisconsin Press.

Kallberg, Jeffrey (1996), *Chopin at the Boundaries. Sex, History, and Musical Genre*, Cambridge, MA & London: Harvard University Press.

Kaminsky, Stuart M. (1983), 'Narrative Time in Sergio Leone's *Once Upon a Time in America*', *Studies in the Literary Imagination*, 16, pp. 59–74.

Karlin, Fred and Wright, Rayburn (1990), *On the Track: A Guide to Contemporary Film Scoring*, New York: Schirmer.

Kassabian, Anahid (2001), *Hearing Film: Tracking Identifications in Contemporary Hollywood Film Music*, New York & London: Routledge.

Kerins, Mark (2007), 'Constructing the Diegesis in a Multi-channel World', *Offscreen*, 11: 8–9 (Forum 2: *Discourses on Diegesis – On the Relevance of Terminology*), http://www.offscreen.com/biblio/pages/essays/soundforum_2. Accessed 2 June 2013.

Kessler, Frank (1997), 'Etienne Souriau und das Vokabular der filmologischen Schule', *montage/av*, 6: 2 (special issue *Stars [I]*), pp. 132–39.

——— (2007), 'Von der Filmologie zur Narratologie. Anmerkungen zum Begriff der Diegese', *montage/av*, 16: 2 (special issue *Diegese*), pp. 9–16.

Kindt, Tom and Müller, Hans-Harald (2006), *The Implied Author: Concept and Controversy*, Berlin & New York: Walter de Gruyter.

King, Claire Sisco (2010), 'Ramblin' Men and Piano Men: Crises of Music and Masculinity in *The Exorcist*', in Neil Lerner (ed.), *Music in the Horror Film*, New York & London: Routledge, pp. 114–32.

King, Emily (1993), 'Taking Credit: Film title sequences, 1955–1965', MA thesis, London: Royal College of Art and Victoria & Albert Museum, https://www.typotheque.com/articles/taking_credit_film_title_sequences_1955-1965_1_contents. Accessed 2 June 2013.

Knee, Adam (1985), 'Notions of Authorship and the Reception of *Once Upon a Time in America*', *Film Criticism*, 10, pp. 3–17.

Koizumi, Kyoko (2009), 'Creative Soundtrack Expression: Tôru Takemitsu's Score for *Kwaidan*', in Philip Hayward (ed.), *Terror Tracks: Music, Sound and Horror Cinema*, London & Oakville: Equinox, pp. 75–87.

Kramer, Lawrence (1995), *Classical Music and Postmodern Knowledge*, Berkeley: University of California Press.

Kuhn, Markus (2011), *Film-Narratologie. Erin erzähltheoretisches Analysemodell*, Berlin & New York: Walter de Gruyter.

Laing, Heather (2000), 'Emotion by Numbers: Music, Song and the Musical', in Bill Marshall and Robynn Stilwell (eds), *Musicals: Hollywood and Beyond*, Exeter & Portland: Intellect, pp. 5–13.

——— (2005), *The Gendered Score: Music in 1940s Melodrama and the Woman's Film*, Aldershot: Ashgate.

Landy, Marcia (2007), 'Storytelling and Information in Todd Haynes' Films', in James Morrison (ed.), *The Cinema of Todd Haynes: All That Heaven Allows*, New York: Wallflower, pp. 7–24.

Larsen, Peter (2005), *Film Music*, London: Reaktion Books.

Larson, Randall D. (1996), *Music from the House of Hammer: Music in the Hammer Horror Film, 1950–1980*, Metuchen: Scarecrow.

Lee, Michael (2012), 'Sound and Uncertainty in the Horror Films of the Lewton Unit', in James Wierzbicki (ed.), *Music, Sound and Filmmakers. Sonic Style in Cinema*, New York & London: Routledge.

Leinberger, Charles (2004), 'The Good, the Bad and the Ugly': A Film Score Guide, Lanham, Toronto & Oxford: Scarecrow.

Lerner, Neil (ed.) (2010a), Music in the Horror Film, New York & London: Routledge.

―――― (2010b), 'The Strange Case of Rouben Mamoulian's Sound Stew: The Uncanny Soundtrack in Dr. Jekyll and Mr. Hyde (1931)', in Neil Lerner (ed.), Music in the Horror Film, New York & London: Routledge, pp. 55–79.

Levinson, Jerrold (1996), 'Film Music and Narrative Agency', in David Bordwell and Noël Carroll (eds), Post-Theory: Reconstructing Film Studies, Madison: University of Wisconsin Press, pp. 248–82.

Link, Stan (2010), 'The Monster and the Music Box: Children and the Soundtrack of Horror', in Neil Lerner (ed.), Music in the Horror Film, New York & London: Routledge, pp. 38–54.

Lionnet, Leonard (2003), 'Point Counter Point: Interactions between Pre-Existing Music and Film Structure in Stanley Kubrick's "The Shining"', DMA dissertation, New York: City University.

Lissa, Zofia (1965), Ästhetik der Filmmusik, Berlin: Henschel.

Lovecraft, H.P. (2007), 'The Night Ocean', in The Loved Dead: Collected Stories vol. 2, Ware, Hertfordshire: Wordsworth Editions, pp. 363–383.

MacKinnon, Kenneth (2000), '"I Keep Wishing I Were Somewhere Else": Space and Fantasies of Freedom in the Hollywood Musical', in Bill Marshall and Robynn Stilwell (eds), Musicals: Hollywood and Beyond, Exeter & Portland: Intellect, pp. 40–46.

McMillan, Brian (2004), 'Complicitous Critique: Dancer in the Dark as Postmodern Musical', Discourses in Music, 5: 2 (Autumn), http://library.music.utoronto.ca/discourses-in-music/v5n2a1.html. Accessed 2 June 2013.

Manvell, Roger and Huntley, John (1957), The Technique of Film Music, London & New York: Focal Press.

Marshall, Bill and Stilwell, Robynn (eds) (2000), Musicals: Hollywood and Beyond, Exeter & Portland: Intellect.

Martin, Adrian (1998), Once Upon a Time in America, London: BFI.

Merlin, Didi (2010), 'Diegetic Sound. Zur Konstitution figureninterner- und externer Realitäten im Spielfilm', Kieler Beiträge zur Filmmusikforschung, 6, pp. 66–100, http://www.filmmusik.uni-kiel.de/KB6/KB6-Merlinarc.pdf. Accessed 2 June 2013.

Metz, Christian (1965), 'Apropos de l'impression de réalité au cinéma', Cahiers du cinema, 166–67, pp. 75–82.

―――― (1971), Langage et cinema, Paris: Larousse.

―――― (1974), Film Language: A Semiotics of Cinema (trans. M. Taylor), New York: Oxford University Press.

―――― (1980), 'Sur un profil d'Etienne Souriau', Revue d'Esthetique, 3–4, pp. 143–60.

Miceli, Sergio (2000), Morricone – die Musik, das Kino (trans. C. Imig-Robrecht), Mülheim: edition filmwerkstatt.

Mitchell, Tony (2009), 'Prog Rock, the Horror Film and Sonic Excess: Dario Argento, Morricone and Goblin', in Philip Hayward (ed.), Terror Tracks: Music, Sound and Horror Cinema, London & Oakville: Equinox, pp. 88–100.

Moormann, Peter (ed.) (2009), Klassiker der Filmmusik, Stuttgart: Reclam.

Mulvey, Laura (2006), Death 24x Times a Second: Stillness and the Moving Image, London: Reaktion.

Neumeyer, David (1997), 'Source Music, Background Music, Fantasy and Reality in Early Sound Film', *College Music Symposium*, 37, pp. 13–20.

—— (2000), 'Performances in Early Hollywood Sound Film: Source Music, Background Music, and the Integrated Sound Track', *Contemporary Music Review*, 19: 1, pp. 37–62.

—— (2009), 'Diegetic/Nondiegetic: A Theoretical Model', *Music and the Moving Image*, 2: 1, http://www.jstor.org/stable/10.5406/musimoviimag.2.1.0026. Accessed 2 June 2013.

—— (with Flinn, Caryl and Buhler, James) (2000), 'Introduction', in James Buhler, Caryl Flinn and David Neumeyer (eds), *Music and Cinema*, Hannover & London: Wesleyan University Press, pp. 1–29.

Neupert, Richard (1995), *The End: Narration and Closure in the Cinema*, Detroit: Wayne State University Press.

Niederhoff, Burkhard (2011), 'Focalization', in Peter Hühn et al. (eds), *The Living Handbook of Narratology*, Hamburg: Hamburg University Press, http://www.lhn.uni-hamburg.de/article/focalization. Accessed 2 June 2013.

Nijdam, Elizabeth (2010), 'Rock statt Marx: Rock and Roll Narratives in Leander Haußmann's *Sonnenallee*', *gfl-journal*, 3, pp. 116–36.

Norden, Martin F. (2007), 'Diegetic Commentaries', *Offscreen*, 11: 8–9 (Forum 2: *Discourses on Diegesis – On the Relevance of Terminology*), http://www.offscreen.com/biblio/pages/essays/soundforum_2. Accessed 2 June 2013.

Odin, Roger (2000), *De la fiction*, Brussels: De Boeck Supérieur.

Ohler, Peter (1994), *Kognitive Filmpsychologie*, Münster: MAkS.

Peranson, Mark (2000), 'Dancer in the Dark: Music is the Doctor', *indieWIRE*, 19 May, http://www.indiewire.com/article/cannes_review_dancer_in_the_dark_music_is_the_doctor. Accessed 12 July 2012.

Pier, John (2005), 'Metalepsis', in David Herman, Mafred Jahn and Marie-Laure Ryan (eds), *Routledge Encyclopedia of Narrative Theory*, New York & Abingdon: Routledge, pp. 303–04.

Powrie, Phil (2006), 'The Fabulous Destiny of the Accordion in French Cinema', in Phil Powrie and Robynn Stilwell (eds), *Changing Tunes: The Use of Pre-existing Music in Film*, Aldershot: Ashgate, pp. 137–51.

Prendergast, Roy M. (1992), *Film Music: A Neglected Art: A Critical Study of Music in Films*, 2nd edition, New York & London: W.W. Norton.

Rabinowitz, Peter (1987), *Before Reading: Narrative Conventions and the Politics of Interpretation*, Ithaca & London: Cornell University Press.

Rayner, Jonathan (2003), *The Films of Peter Weir*, New York: Continuum.

Richardson, Niall (2006), '*Poison* in the Sirkian System: The Political Agenda of Todd Haynes's *Far From Heaven*', *Scope,* 6 (October), http://www.scope.nottingham.ac.uk/article.php?issue=6&id=183. Accessed 2 June 2013.

Schaeffer, Pierre (1966), *Traité des objets musicaux*, Paris: Seuil.

Schepelern, Peter (2003), 'Kill Your Darlings: Lars von Trier and the Origin of Dogma 95', in Mette Hjort and Scott MacKenzie (eds), *Purity and Provocation: Dogma 95*, London: BFI, pp. 58–69.

Scheurer, Timothy E. (2008), *Music and Mythmaking in Film: Genre and the Role of the Composer*, Jefferson & London: McFarland.

Scruton, Roger (1997), *The Aesthetics of Music*, Oxford: Oxford University Press.

Seidman, Steve (1981), *Comedian Comedy: A Tradition in Hollywood Film*, Ann Arbor: UMI Research Press. [Ph.D. dissertation (1979), University of California].

Shen, Dan (2005), 'Diegesis', in David Herman, Manfred Jahn, and Marie-Laure Ryan (eds), *Routledge Encyclopedia of Narrative Theory*, New York & Abingdon: Routledge, pp. 107–08.

Simons, Jan (2007), *Playing the Waves. Lars von Trier's Game Cinema*, Amsterdam: Amsterdam University Press.

Smith, Jeff (1998): *The Sounds of Commerce: Marketing Popular Film Music*, New York: Columbia University Press.

——— (2009), 'Bridging the Gap: Reconsidering the Border between Diegetic and Nondiegetic Music', *Music and the Moving Image*, 2: 1, http://www.jstor.org/stable/10.5406/musimoviimag.2.1.0001. Accessed 2 June 2013.

Souriau, Etienne (1951), 'La structure de l'univers filmique et la vocabulaire de la filmologie', *Revue international de filmologie*, 2: 7–8, pp. 231–40.

——— (1990), *Vocabulaire d'esthétique*, Paris: Presses universitaires de France.

Stam, Robert, Burgoyne, Robert and Flitterman-Lewis, Sandy (1992), *New Vocabularies in Film Semiotics: Structuralism, Post-Structuralism and Beyond*, London & New York: Routledge.

Stanitzek, Georg (2009), 'Reading the Title Sequence (Vorspann, Générique)' (transl. Noelle Aplevich), *Cinema Journal*, 48: 4, pp. 44–58.

Stilwell, Robynn J. (2007), 'The Fantastical Gap between Diegetic and Nondiegetic', in Daniel Goldmark, Lawrence Kramer and Richard Leppert (eds), *Beyond the Soundtrack: Representing Music in Cinema*, Berkeley, Los Angeles & London: University of California Press, pp. 184–202.

Straw, Will (1999), 'Ornament, Entrance and the Theme Song', in Philip Brophy (ed.), *Cinesonic: The World of Sound in Film*, North Ride, Australia: Australian Film Television and Radio School, pp. 213–28.

Taylor, Henry M. (2007), 'The Success Story of a Misnomer', *Offscreen*, 11: 8–9 (Forum 2: *Discourses on Diegesis – On the Relevance of Terminology*), http://www.offscreen.com/biblio/pages/essays/soundforum_2. Accessed 2 June 2013.

Taylor, Laura Wiebe (2009), 'Popular Songs and Ordinary Violence: Exposing Basic Human Brutality in the Films of Rob Zombie', in Philip Hayward (ed.), *Terror Tracks: Music, Sound and Horror Cinema*, London & Oakville, pp. 229–37.

Thom, Randy (2007), 'Acoustics of the Soul', *Offscreen*, 11: 8–9 (Forum 2: *Discourses on Diegesis – On the Relevance of Terminology*), http://www.offscreen.com/biblio/pages/essays/soundforum_2. Accessed 2 June 2013.

Thompson, Kristin (1981), *Eisenstein's Ivan the Terrible: A Neoformalist Analysis*, Princeton: Princeton University Press.

Tieber, Claus (2009), 'Zur filmischen Inszenierung musikalischer Innovation. Die obligatorische Szene in musikalischen Biopics', *Kieler Beiträge zur Filmmusikforschung*, 3, pp. 11–21, http://www.filmmusik.uni-kiel.de/artikel/KB3-Tieberarc.pdf. Accessed 3 July 2012.

——— (2010), 'Informationsgehalt und Dramaturgie der Musik in *The Truman Show*', *Kieler Beiträge zur Filmmusikforschung*, 4, pp. 83–94.

Todorov, Tzvetan (1966), 'Les catégories du récit littérarire', *Communications*, 8, pp. 125–51.

——— (1975), *The Fantastic: A Structural Approach to a Literary Genre*, Ithaca: Cornell University Press.

Tompkins, Joe (2010), 'Pop Goes the Horror Score: Left Alone in *The Last House on the Left*', in Neil Lerner (ed.), *Music in the Horror Film*, New York & London: Routledge, pp. 98–113.

Türschmann, Jörg (2007), 'Die Metalepse', *montage/av*, 16: 2 (special issue *Diegese*), pp. 105–12.

Varma, Devendra (1966), *The Gothic Flame: Being a history of the Gothic novel in England: its origins, efflorescence, disintegration, and residuary influences*, New York: Russell & Russell.

Verstraten, Peter (2009), *Film Narratology* (trans. S. van der Lecq), Toronto, Buffalo, London: University of Toronto Press.

Vittrup, Christian (2010), 'Wo spielt die Musik in Peter Weirs *The Truman Show*? Der Erlöser zieht aus', *Kieler Beiträge zur Filmmusikforschung*, 4, pp. 95–103.

Walton, Kendall (1982), *Mimesis as Make-Believe: On the Foundations of the Representational Arts*, Cambridge, MA: Harvard University Press.

Wierzbicki, James (2009), '*Psycho*-Analysis: Form and Function of Bernard Herrmann's Music for Hitchcock's Masterpiece', in Philip Hayward (ed.), *Terror Tracks: Music, Sound and Horror Cinema*, London & Oakville: Equinox, pp. 14–46.

Winters, Ben (2007), *Erich Wolfgang Korngold's 'The Adventures of Robin Hood'. A Film Score Guide*, Lanham, Toronto & Plymouth: Scarecrow.

——— (2010), 'The Non-Diegetic Fallacy: Film, Music, and Narrative Space', *Music & Letters*, 91: 2, pp. 224–44.

——— (2012), 'Musical Wallpaper? Towards an Appreciation of Non-narrating Music in Film', *Music, Sound & the Moving Image*, 6: 1, pp. 39–54.

Wollen, Peter (1972), 'Godard and Counter Cinema: *Vent d'est*', *Afterimage*, 4, pp. 6–17.

——— (1992), *Singin' in the Rain*, London: BFI (BFI Film Classics).

Woodgate, Ken (2007): '"Gotta Dance" (in the Dark): Lars von Trier's Critique of the Musical Genre', in Gerhard Fischer and Bernard Greiner (eds), *The Play within the Play. The Performance of Meta-Theatre and Self-Reflection*, Amsterdam: Rodopi, pp. 393–402.

Wulff, Hans J. (1991), 'Das Wisconsin-Projekt. David Bordwells Entwurf einer kognitiven Theorie des Films', *Rundfunk & Fernsehen*, 39: 3, pp. 393–405, http://www.derwulff.de/2-28. Accessed 2 June 2013.

——— (2007), 'Schichtenbau und Prozesshaftigkeit des Diegetischen: Zwei Anmerkungen', *montage/av*, 16: 2 (special issue *Diegese*), pp. 39–51.

——— (2010), 'Das Bild, das Hörbare, die Musik: zur Analyse der Ertaubungsszene in Abel Gance, *Un grand amour de Beethoven* (Frankreich 1936)', in Christoph Henzel (ed.), *Geschichte – Musik – Film*, Würzburg: Königshausen und Neumann, pp. 139–60.

Wuss, Peter (1999), *Filmanalyse und Psychologie. Strukturen des Films im Wahrnehmungsprozeß*, 2nd edition, Berlin: Edition Sigma. First published 1993.

Yacavone, Dan (2012), 'Spaces, Gaps, and Levels: From the Diegetic to the Aesthetic in Film Theory', *Music, Sound & the Moving Image*, 6: 1, pp. 21–37.

Young, Gwenda (1998), 'The Cinema of Difference: Jacques Tourneur, Race and *I Walked with a Zombie*', *Irish Journal of American Studies*, 7, pp. 101–19.

Filmography and Index of Films

With regard to music, the filmography normally lists only composers of original music; only for musical films, composers and lyricists of the (main) songs are listed as well.

Abbreviations: Comp. = Company; Corp. = Corporation; d. = director; Ent. = Entertainment; Feat. = Features; fn. = footnote; Int. = International; l. = lyrics; m. = (original) music; Pict. = Picture(s); Prod. = Production(s)

8½ (Italy, France: Cinerix, Francinex, 1963; d. Federico Fellini; m. Nino Rota): 118

42ⁿᵈ Street (USA: Warner, 1933; d. Lloyd Bacon, Busby Berkeley [musical numbers]; m. Harry Warren, l. Al Dubin): 139–40, 163

Adventures of Robin Hood, The (USA: Warner, 1938; d. Michael Curtiz, William Keighley; m. Erich Wolfgang Korngold): 10, 239–42

Alien (USA, UK: Brandywine Prod., Twentieth Century Fox, 1979; d. Ridley Scott; m. Jerry Goldsmith): 85, 173/fn. 114, 190–91

All That Heaven Allows (USA: Universal, 1955; d. Douglas Sirk; m. Frank Skinner): 10, 232–33, 238–39

All That Jazz (USA: Twentieth Century Fox, Columbia, 1969; d. Bob Fosse; m. Ralph Burns): 159, 164

Almost Famous (USA: Vinyl Films, DreamWorks, Columbia, 2000; d. Cameron Crowe, m. Nancy Wilson): 114–16

Amadeus (USA: The Saul Zaentz Comp., 1984; d. Milos Forman): 117

American Graffiti (USA: American Zoetrope, Lucasfilm, 1973; d. George Lucas): 116–18

American in Paris, An (USA: MGM, 1951; d. Vincente Minelli; m. Conrad Salinger; songs: m. George Gershwin, l. Ira Gershwin): 123, 139, 146–50, 152

Angst essen Seele auf: see *Fear Eats the Soul*

Anima mundi (USA: Studio Equatore, Bulgari, 1992; d. Godfrey Reggio, m. Philip Glass): 221/fn. 156, 225

Badlands (USA: Warner, Pressman Williams, Jill Jakes Production, Badlands Comp.; 1973; d. Terence Malick; m. George Tipton): 77–78

Bananas (USA: Jack Rollins & Charles H. Joffe Prod.; 1971; d. Woody Allen; m. Marvin Hamlisch): 4, 91

Band Wagon, The (USA: MGM, 1953; d. Vincente Minelli; m. Alexander Courage, Adolph Deutsch, Conrad Salinger; songs: m. Arthur Schwartz, l. Howard Dietz): 163

Battaglia di Algeri, La: see *Battle of Algiers, The*

Battle of Algiers, The/La Battaglia di Algeri (Italy, Algeria: Igor Film, Casbah Film, 1966; d. Gillo Pontecorvo; m. Ennio Morricone, Gillo Pontecorvo): 53–54/fn. 36

Planet of the Apes (USA: 20th Century Fox, APJAC Prod., 1968; d. Franklin J. Schaffner; m. Jerry Goldsmith): 113

Platoon (UK, USA: Hemdale Film, Cinema 86, 1986; d. Oliver Stone; m. Georges Delerue): 61, 64–65

Playtime (France, Italy: Jolly Film, Specta Films, 1967; d. Jacques Tati; m. Francis Lemarque): 95/fn. 72

Pointe-Courte, La (France: Ciné Tamaris, 1955; d. Agnès Varda; m. Pierre Barbaud): 93

Powaqqatsi (USA: Golan Globus Prod., North South, Santa Fe Institute for Regional Education, 1988; d. Godfrey Reggio; m. Philip Glass): 225

Prodigal Son, The/Der verlorene Sohn (Germany, USA: Deutsche Universal-Film, 1934; d. Luis Trenker; m. Giuseppe Becce): 94, 110

Ran (Japan, France: Greenwich Film Prod., Herald Ace, Nippon Herald Films, 1985; d. Akira Kurosawa; m. Tôru Takemitsu): 65

Rashomon (Japan: Daiei Motion Picture Comp., 1950; d. Akira Kurosawa; m. Fumio Hayasaka): 122

Red River (USA: Charles K. Feldman Group, Monterey Prod., 1948; d. Howard Hawks, Arthur Rosson; m. Dimitri Tiomkin): 69

Règle du jeu, La: see *Rules of the Game, The*

Reverie/Träumerei (Germany: UFA, 1944; d. Harald Braun; m. Robert Schumann, Werner Eisbrenner): 130

Rien que les heures: see *Nothing But Time*

Rose-Marie (USA: MGM, 1936; d. W.S. van Dyke; m. Herbert Stothart, Rudolf Friml; l. Oscar Hammerstein II, Otto A. Harbach, Gus Kahn): 130

Rosemary's Baby (USA: William Castle Prod., 1968; d. Roman Polanski; m. Krzysztof Komeda): 174

Rules of the Game, The/Règle du jeu, La (France: Nouvelles Éditions de Films, 1939; d. Jean Renoir; m. Joseph Cosma): 5/fn. 3, 92/fn. 70

Saturday's Hero (USA: Columbia, 1951; d. David Miller; m. Elmer Bernstein): 232

Sauve qui peu (La vie): see *Slow Motion*

Slow Motion/Sauve qui peu (La vie) (France, Austria, Germany [FRG]. Switzerland: Sara Films, MK2, Saga-Prod., Sonimage et.al., 1980; d. Jean-Luc Godard; m. Gabriel Yared): 5/fn. 3, 92/fn. 70

Sea Hawk, The (USA: Warner, 1940; d. Michael Curtiz; m. Erich Wolfgang Korngold): 56, 69, 118–19, 128, 230, 233–34

Seven Year Itch, The (USA: Charles K. Feldman Group, 20th Century Fox, 1955; d. Billy Wilder; m. Alfred Newman): 129–30/fn. 92

Shall We Dance?/Shall we dansu? (Japan: Altamira Pict., Daiei Studios et.al., 1996; d. Masayuki Suo; m. Yoshikazu Suo): 159–60/fn. 106

Shall we dansu?: see Shall We Dance?

Shining, The (UK, USA: Warner, Hawk Films, Peregrine, Producers' Circle, 1980; d. Stanley Kubrick; m. Wendy Carlos, Rachel Elkind): 174/fn. 116, 179

Show Boat (USA: Universal, 1936; d. James Whale; m. Jerome Kern, l. Oscar Hammerstein II): 139

Sibelius (Finland: Artista Filmi Oy, 2003; d. Timo Koivusalo; m. Jean Sibelius, Osmo Vänskä): 103

Sing As We Go! (UK: Associated Talking Pict., 1934; d. Basil Dean; m. Ernest Irving): 69

Singin' in the Rain (USA: Loew's, MGM, RKO-Pathe, 1952; d. Stanley Donen, Gene Kelly; m. Lennie Hayton; songs: m. Nacio Herb Brown, l. Arthur Freed): 119–20, 123, 139, 146–55

Sixteen Candles (USA: Channel Prod., Universal Pict., 1984; d. John Hughes; m. Ira Newborn): 65

Sonnenallee: see *Sun Alley*

Sound of Music, The (USA: Robert Wise Prod., Argyle Enterprises, 1965; d. Robert Wise; m. Irwin Kostal; songs: m. Richard Rodgers, l. Oscar Hammerstein II): 43/fn. 26, 155, 160, 162–67

Sous les toits de Paris: see *Under the Roofs of Paris*

Spider's Stratagem, The/Strategia del ragno (Italy: RAI, Red Film, 1970; d. Bernardo Bertolucci): 95/fn. 72

Stand by Me (USA: Columbia, Act III, The Bocy; 1986; d. Rob Reiner; m. Jack Nitzsche): 95–97

Star Wars/Star Wars – Episode IV: A New Hope (USA: Lucasfilm, 20th Century Fox, 1977; d. George Lucas; m. John Williams): 28, 59/fn. 41

Steamboat Willie (USA: Disney Brothers, 1928; d. Walt Disney, Ub Iwerks; m. Wilfred Jackson, Bert Lewis): 95

Step across the Border (Germany, Switzerland: Cinomades Prod., Balzli & Cie Prod., Pro Helvetia, 1990; d. Nicholas Humbert, Werner Penzel; m. Fred Frith): 58, 105–06

Strictly Ballroom (Australia: M & A, Australian Film Finance Corp., Beyond Films, The Rank Organization, 1992; d. Baz Luhrmann; m. David Hirschfelder): 159–60/fn. 106

Sudden Fear (USA: Joseph Kaufmann Prod., 1952; d. David Miller; m. Elmer Bernstein): 232

Sun Alley/Sonnenallee (Germany: Boje Buck Prod., Ö-Film, SAT.1, 1999; d. Leander Haußmann; m. Stephen Keusch, Paul Lemp): 85, 107–09

Sweet Charity (USA: Universal, 1969; d. Bob Fosse; m. Cy Coleman, l. Dorothy Fields): 159

Ten Commandments, The (USA: Paramount, Motion Pict. Associates, 1956; d. Cecil B. DeMille; m. Elmer Bernstein): 232

Thelma & Louise (USA, France: Pathé Ent., Percy Main, Star Partners III, MGM, 1991; d. Ridley Scott; m. Hans Zimmer): 115

There's Something About Mary (USA: 20th Century Fox, 1998; d. Bobby Farrelly, Peter Farrelly; m. Jonathan Richman): 40, 89, 91/fn. 69

Third Man, The (UK: Carol Reed's Prod., London Film Prod., 1949; d. Carol Reed; m. Anton Karas): 60–61

Three Colours: Blue/Trois couleurs: Bleu (France, Poland, Switzerland: MK2 Prod., CED Prod., France 3 Cinéma, CAB Prod., Torr Prod. et.al., 1993; d. Krzysztof Kieslowski; m. Zbigniew Preisner): 186/fn. 130

Till the Clouds Roll By (USA: MGM, 1946; d. Richard Whorf; m. Conrad Salinger; songs: Jerome Kern): 138

To Kill a Mockingbird (USA: Universal, Pakula-Mulligan, Brentwood Prod., 1962; d. Robert Mulligan; m. Elmer Bernstein): 232

Top Hat (USA: RKO, 1935; d. Mark Sandrich; m. Max Steiner; songs: Irving Berlin): 137–39, 141–47

Trainspotting (UK: Channel Four Films, Figment Films, The Noel Gay Motion Pict. Comp., 1996; d. Danny Boyle): 100–02, 117

Trapp-Familie, Die: see *Trapp Family, The*

Trapp-Familie in Amerika, Die: see *Trapp Family in America, The*

Series (television and cartoons)

Am laufenden Band (German [FRG]: ARD, 1974–1979): 85

Dragnet (USA: TBA, 1951–1959, 1967–1970, 1990–91, 2003–04): 65

Frasier (USA: NBC, 1993–2004): 35

Generation Game, The (UK: BBC, 1971–1980, 1990–2002): 85

Looney Tunes (USA: Warner, 1930–1969): 86/fn. 65, 94

    Episode 'Baton Bunny' (1959; d. Chuck Jones, Abe Levitow; m. Milt Franklyn): 86/fn. 65

    Episode 'Fast and Furry-ous' (1949; d. Chuck Jones; m. Carl Stalling): 94

Peter Gunn (USA: NBC, ABC, 1958–1961): 65

Raumpatrouille. Die phantastischen Abenteuer des Raumschiffes Orion: see *Space Patrol. The Phantastical Adventures of the Spaceship Orion*

Screen Songs (USA: Fleischer Studios, 1929–1938): 95

Song Car-Tunes/Ko-Ko Song Car-Tunes (USA: Max Fleischer, Dwve Fleischer, 1924–1926): 95

Space Patrol (USA: ABC, 1950–1955): 44/fn. 28

Space Patrol. The Phantastical Adventures of the Spaceship Orion/Raumpatrouille. Die phantastischen Abenteuer des Raumschiffes Orion (Germany [FRG]: ARD, 1966): 44/fn. 28

Star Trek (USA: NBC, 1966–69): 44/fn. 28

Tom and Jerry (USA: MGM, 1940–1957): 94

    Episode 'The Yankee Doodle Mouse' (1943; d. William Hanna, Joseph Barbera; m. Scott Bradley): 94

Twilight Zone, The (USA: CBS, 1959–1964): 43–44, 65

    Episode 'Where Is Everybody?' (1959; d. Robert Stevens; m. Bernard Herrmann): 43–44

Index of Names

NB:

- Names are only indexed if they are mentioned in the main or footnote text, not if they are only mentioned in a bibliographical reference.
- Names of actors and actresses are not indexed if the text only gives them in brackets after the names of their characters.

Mekas, Jonas 58
Merlin, Didi 53–4
Metz, Christian 6, 8, 9, 41, 53
Miceli, Sergio 217
Milchan, Arnon 208
Mondrian, Piet 13
Mörike, Eduard 111
Morricone, Ennio 197–217
Mozart, Constanze, née Weber 104, 111–2
Mozart, Wolfgang Amadeus 85, 97, 104,
    116–7, 127, 140, 221, 223, 224
Mussorgsky, Modest 86

N

Neumeyer, David 7, 26, 63, 71–2, 123
Newman, Alfred 26, 28
Niederhoff, Manfred 122
Norman, Monty 81
Nowell-Smith, Geoffrey 41
Nünning, Ansgar 6

O

O'Connor, Donald 154–5
Odin, Roger 24
Orff, Carl 77

P

Peerce, Jan 39
Penderecki, Krzysztof 174
Penzel, Werner 58, 105–6
Piatigorsky, Gregor 39
Plato 50
Pons, Lily 39
Porter, Cole 112, 147
Presley, Reg 33
Prévost, Antoine François 119
Propp, Vladimir 8
Puccini, Giacomo 97, 119, 130

R

Rabinowitz, Peter 175
Rachmaninoff, Sergej 130
Raksin, David 6, 86

Randall, Tony 42
Rayner, Jonathan 223, 228
Reiner, Fritz 39
Reyland, Nicholas 186
Rimmon-Kenan, Shlomith 6, 122
Rodgers, Richard 80, 163
Rogers, Ginger 139, 142, 158
Roosevelt, Franklin Delano 64–5
Rossini, Gioachino 86, 211
Rota, Nino 58
Russell, Ken 103
Ruttmann, Walter 140–1

S

Sagan, Françoise 132
Salieri, Antonio 117
Schaeffer, Pierre 180
Schlickers, Sabine 130
Schumann, Clara, née Wieck 130
Schumann, Robert 130
Scruton, Roger 13
Seidman, Steve 41
Serling, Rod 43
Shelley, Mary 131, 218
Shelley, Percy Bysshe 131, 218
Shostakovich, Dmitri 33, 92
Sibelius, Jean 103
Simon, Paul 114
Sinatra, Frank 93
Siodmak, Curt 192
Sirk, Douglas 162, 197, 231–2, 235
Sleeper (band) 100
Smith, Jeff 55, 56, 59–60, 89, 90, 93, 95,
    99–102, 201
Souriau, Etienne 19, 20, 50, 52–4
Souriau, Anne 19
Spielberg, Steven 6
Stanitzek, Georg 26, 34
Stilwell, Robynn S. 11, 12, 54, 57, 59, 90, 93,
    99–100
Stokowski, Leopold 39
Stoller, Mike 88
Stone, Oliver 64, 65

Index of Terms

NB:

- Index entries refer to terms in footnotes as well as the main text.
- Index entries are also made for sections of the text that are about the concept in question, even if the term itself does not occur on that page.
- Terms originating in the work of a particular scholar are given with the name of the scholar.
- *Passim* indicates that a term occurs frequently (though not necessarily on every page) in a section.
- Key passages defining/discussing important terms are indicated by bold entries.

comedy, comedic 33–4, 40–3, 59, 65, 82,
    85–6, 89, 91–2, 173–4, 176, 245
  comedian comedy 41
  romantic comedy 30–1, 56
communication model (of narration) 22,
    75–6, 79
communicativeness (D. Bordwell) 89, 91–2,
    100, 228
company logo (or company credits) 21,
    25–31, 33, 35–6, 42–3, 219
continuity 46, 64, 98, 112, 156–7, 212, 221
costume drama 59
credits 25, 82
  end credits 23–4, 26, 33, 35, 107, 168
  opening credits 23–4, 27, 33–8, 41–2,
    44–5, 82, 141, 149, 189, 219, 232
  See also: title sequence

D
de-diegetization (*see under:* diegesis)
diegesis (or storyworld), diegetic 3–5, 7, 9,
    11–2, 19–27, 30, 31, 32, 33–8, 40–47,
    48–119 *passim* (esp. **48–64**), 120–9,
    133, 137, 139, 140–1, 143–7, 149–50,
    152–8, 160–1, 164, 168, 174, 177,
    179–87, 189–90, 198–207, 211–27,
    231, 233–5, 237–42, 245
  de-diegetization 95, 113–5, 127, 140–3
  diegetic commentary 49, 72, 79, **84–5**, 87,
    89, 132, 156, 157–8, 190
  diegetic reveal (or reversal) 3, 4, 30–4, 49,
    56, 59–60, 83, **89–92**, 103, 105–6,
    189, 221–2
  displaced diegetic music/sound 21, 59–60,
    81, 89, 93, **97–106** *passim*, 114–5,
    155–9, 192, 200, 223
diegetize, diegetization 12, 52, 55–6, 94,
    115, 239
discourse 27, 48–50, 54, 55, 57, 61, 153, 231
  See also: narration
displaced diegetic music/sound (*see under:*
    diegesis)
documentary 10, 19, 58, 97, 176, 245

E
emanation (music as) **64–6**, 68, 127, 182,
    204, 207
embedded narration or diegesis 30–1, 119,
    123, 131–3, 149–51, 218–28 *passim*
  See also: metadiegetic
enunciation, enunciatory 41
epitext (*see under:* paratext)
excess 14, 63
extradiegetic (*see:* nondiegetic)
  extra-diegetic (B. Winters) 61, 64
extrafictional, extrafictionality 9, 11, 21–24,
    23–39 *passim* (esp. 23–7), 40, 42–6,
    63, 75, 83, 89, 181, 219–20
  extrafictional narration 39–48 *passim*

F
fabula **50–1**, 54, 61, 63, 79, 83, 88, 90, 105,
    113, 115, 143, 156, 180, 214–6, 231,
    237, 239
  See also: style; syuzhet
fantasy film 51
fiction, (intra)fictional, fictionality 5, 9, 19,
    22–4, 26, 27, 28, 31, 33, 36, 38–44, 47,
    51, 54–5, 61, 72–7, 79–81, 83, 86, 91,
    151–2, 177–8, 197, 218–20, 228, 238
film musicology 8–9, 11, 19–21, 23, 48, 52,
    56, 77, 79
film music narratology 9–11, 19, 21, 23,
    48–9, 173, 245–6
film narratology 6, 8, 12, 19, 72–3, 82, 121, 245
filmology, filmological 19
film studies (or film scholarship) 6, 8–9, 20,
    25, 245–6
  See also: filmology
filter (S. Chatman) 122
  See also: slant
flashback 99, 114, 123, 126, 132, 199–201,
    205–6, 209–11, 217, 223, 230
flashforward 230–1
focalization 9, 14, 22–3, 78, **119–33** *passim*
  auricularization 130
  external focalization 22, 70, 121–4, 128–30